POWER
AND
INFLUENCE

D1712774

POWER AND INFLUENCE

AN INTRODUCTION TO INTERNATIONAL RELATIONS

D. G. Kousoulas

Howard University
Washington, D.C.

Brooks/Cole Publishing Company
Monterey, California

Brooks/Cole Publishing Company
A Division of Wadsworth, Inc.

Printed in the United States of America

10 9 8 7 6 5 4 3 2 1

Library of Congress Cataloging in Publication Data
Kousoulas, D. George (Dimitrios George), 1923–
    Power and influence

    Bibliography: p.
    Includes index.
    1. International relations. I. Title.
JX1391.K68 1985   327   84-23290
ISBN 0-534-04704-1

Sponsoring Editor: *Marie Kent*
Editorial Assistant: *Amy Mayfield*
Production: *Ex Libris □ Sara B. Hunsaker*
Permissions Editor: *Carline Haga*
Interior Design: *John Edeen*
Cover Design: *Debbie Wunsch*
Interior Illustration: *Douglas Luna*
Typesetting: *Kachina Typesetting, Inc., Tempe, Arizona*
Printing and Binding: *Malloy Lithographing, Inc.*

Photo Credits:

Chapter 1 UPI/Bettmann; **Chapter 2**
Magnum Photos; **Chapter 3** Courtesy
Shell International; **Chapter 4** UPI/
Bettmann; **Chapter 5** Magnum
Photos; **Chapter 6** Courtesy United
Nations; **Chapter 7** Magnum Photos;
Chapter 8 Courtesy United Nations;
Chapter 9 UPI/Bettmann; **Chapter
10** UPI/Bettmann

"The nation which indulges towards another an habitual hatred or an habitual fondness is in some degree a slave. It is a slave to its animosity or to its affection. . ."

George Washington in his
Farewell Address

Preface

International relations is a fascinating subject. On every given day, events involving international actors command front-page coverage in our newspapers and top billing in the broadcasts on radio and television. What happens in the international arena affects our lives in a variety of ways.

Before we can deal with major international issues or events of our time, we need to gain a clearer understanding of the basic concepts, processes, and relationships—the "nuts and bolts"—that make the discussion of these issues more meaningful and exciting. This approach has been the guiding principle in writing *Power and Influence*.

A textbook draws on the scholarship of those who have contributed to the development of the discipline. To be useful, it must be firmly grounded in the established knowledge. At the same time, it must not turn a blind eye to the future and refrain from fresh explorations, especially in political analysis. There are signs that the international environment has undergone major changes in the last 40 years and that these structural transformations will expand, accelerate, and deepen as we move into the twenty-first century. There has been a reluctant and uneven shift from the power approach that has traditionally dominated international relations to a transactional approach, which relies primarily on bargaining and persuasion. This shift has been caused by:

- The growing economic interdependence

- The growth of worldwide network of instant communication

- The uneven relevance of force to the solution of the enormous economic social problems facing humanity

- The emergence of new entities such as the multinational corporations

- The proliferation of international organizations dealing with political, economic, technical, and social problems

Age-old traditions, of course, are not easily discarded. The attachment of policy makers to the power approach remains a fact of international life. Yet, even a giant such as the United States with all its tremendous resources and power potential finds it increasingly difficult to impose its will on others or to resolve vexing international problems by fiat or force.

A clear understanding of the difference between the power approach and the transactional approach will help our discussion of the larger international issues that are likely to dominate international relations. A mere listing of these issues reveals the changes that have occurred and the diminishing relevance of the power approach in addressing them:

- Control of the weapons of mass destruction

- Trade and economic relations among the developed countries

- Trade and economic relations between developed countries and the less developed countries

- The increase in food production and distribution to meet the needs of a rapidly increasing world population

- Control of violent revolutionary movements, which feed on poverty, frustration, injustice, and oppression

- Protection of the physical environment on an international scale

- Development of seabed resources

- Exploration of space

- Flow of information

- Activities of multinational corporations

- Management of international monetary relations

Few, if any, of these problems can be solved by force or by fiat; this does not mean the the resolution of international issues is no longer sought by the application of force. With so many military confrontations currently underway, reliance on the power approach is still very much a fact of international life. Nonetheless, it is also a fact that current problems have become so complex that force—even when "victorious"—seldom leads to genuine solutions.

Whether international actors resort to the power or the transactional approach (or a combination of both) the outcome of any interaction depends on their assets and their ability to use these resources effectively. In a way, we may view international relations as business transactions. In business, the outcome of a "business deal" depends largely on the *economic* assets each side can bring to the bargaining table. The side with more economic assets has an advantage that no rhetoric can dissipate. Although effective negotiating skills can improve the chances of the weaker side, the content of the final agreement is bound to reflect the relative bargaining position of the participants—namely, which side is in greater need of reaching an agreement, which has alternative courses of action, and which possesses greater economic resources.

In international relations, the resolution of any conflict, confrontation, or transaction also depends on the relative assets. However, in international relations the relevant assets are much more varied: military force, economic resources, geographic location, population, industrial capacity, political leadership, ideology, alliances, political influence in other countries, and imaginative diplomacy, which can maximize the effect of all other assets.

The study of international relations requires some knowledge and understanding of what has happened in the past. Too often we tend to take an episodic view of foreign issues, devoid of history. Few current issues are unrelated to the past. For this reason I have included historical references to current disputes and developments and to the origins of existing institutions.

Part One answers questions about the international environment:

- Why do international actors behave as they do?

- Who are the international actors?

- What are the tangible and intangible assets that determine their power and influence potential?

Part Two focuses on the instrumentalities of international relations:

- The making of foreign policy decisions

- Diplomacy and the transactional mode of interaction

- The use of force

- International economic relations

- The significance of international law and international organization

Part Three moves on to a discussion of the great issues of today:

- The East–West rivalry

- The North–South dialogue

Parts One and Two will give the student sufficient background and familiarity with the "basics" to make the discussion in Part Three more meaningful.

One special feature which students and instructors may find particularly welcome, is the "Digest" at the end of the book—an easy reference compilation of concise discussions of basic terms, background on international organizations or treaties of particular interest, and key historical events or developments that could not be covered adequately without digressing from the subject matter.

I am grateful to the following people who reviewed the manuscript: Luther Allen, University of Massachusetts, Amherst; Francis Hoole, Indiana University; Ronald Meltzer, State University of New York, Buffalo; Joseph Nogee, University of Houston; Suzanne Ogden, Northeastern University; Thomas Palmer, College of Charleston; Gholam Razi, University of Houston; Neil Richardson, University of Wisconsin; Michael Schechter, Michigan State University; Richard Sears, Wake Forest University; Kurt Tweraser, University of Arkansas.

D. G. Kousoulas

Contents

PART THREE
THE GREAT ISSUES   219

....POWER
AND
INFLUENCE

THE
INTERNATIONAL
ENVIRONMENT

1

Patterns of Interaction

Churchill, Roosevelt, and Stalin at Yalta

Understanding the forces that affect the relations among international actors is not merely an academic exercise, nor is it of concern only to diplomats and politicians. It is a practical matter of vital significance to all of us. Consider these selected illustrations:

- Government officials decide that it is in the interest of the United States to prevent North Vietnam from taking over South Vietnam, and tens of thousands of United States soldiers lose their lives in a distant land.

- The U.S. government decides to send a "peace-keeping force" to Lebanon. A few months later, a young Arab opposing the move, because it conflicts with his perception of the problem, drives a truck full of explosives into the compound housing the U.S. marines and blows up the building, himself, and 246 U.S. soldiers.

- In 1973, the Organization of Petroleum Exporting Countries (OPEC) decides to raise the price of oil and impose an embargo on shipments to the United States, causing long lines of cars at gasoline stations and sending inflation to unprecedented heights.

- The external debt of countries such as Mexico or Brazil reaches such a magnitude that the possibility that they may be unable to repay what they owe causes tremors in the Western banking establishment, which has lent most of the money.

- Japanese cars are sold in large numbers in the United States, and automobile workers in Detroit find themselves on the unemployment line.

What Is "International Relations"?...................................

Our illustrations give a glimpse into the subject matter of international relations. As an academic discipline, international relations can be defined as *a branch of the social sciences dealing with those policies, developments, and interactions the effects of which*

Figure 1-1
Three types of international interaction.

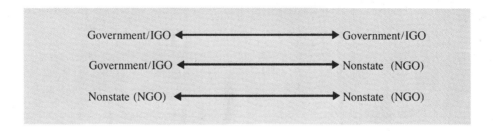

cross national boundaries and affect the lives of people in different countries and in several parts of the world. This definition is intended to be broad enough to encompass the tremendous variety of actions that can be regarded as falling within the scope of international relations, and yet be precise enough to draw the boundaries of this branch of political science. Policies or activities that have no repercussions beyond a country's borders are regarded as *domestic affairs*. We should not be too rigid about this division, however; the dividing line is not as clear-cut as we might wish, and the linkage between domestic affairs and international relations often is quite close. However, it is possible to differentiate between policies or actions that have primarily or exclusively domestic significance and other interactions whose effects are not confined to within a country's borders.

International interactions may be divided into three major categories (see figure 1-1):

1. Those between sovereign governments or intergovernmental organizations (IGOs)

2. Those between sovereign governments or IGOs and nongovernmental organizations (NGOs)

3. Those between nonstate entities

....Type 1 Interactions

• The foreign and defense ministers of the North American Treaty Organization (NATO) countries meet in Brussels

• The premier of Italy visits the U.S. president at the White House

• Japanese officials discuss trade relations between their country and the United States with their Washington counterparts

- A South African delegation meets with representatives of the Angolan government to discuss a cease-fire agreement

- Zaire officials discuss a loan with the World Bank

- The government of the Republic of Cyprus appeals to the UN Security Council for a resolution condemning the Turkish invasion of Cyprus

- The British government signs an agreement with the International Civil Aviation Organization (ICAO) regarding commercial flights

Type 2 Interactions

- The government of Nigeria negotiates an agreement with a multinational corporation for the construction of a plastics factory or for the exploration and marketing of oil resources

- King Hussein of Jordan meets with Yasser Arafat, the leader of the Palestinian Liberation Organization (PLO), to discuss the parameters of potential cooperation

- The government of Italy negotiates with a terrorist group for the release of airline passengers held hostage

- The government of Bangladesh signs an agreement with the International Red Cross for assistance on health matters

- A candidate for the presidential nomination in the United States visits China and talks with government officials there

Type 3 Interactions

- Irish Revolutionary Army (IRA) terrorists blow up a department store in London

- Scientists from various countries meet in Switzerland for an international conference on environmental issues

- Shiite Moslems engage in combat with Christian Phalangists in Lebanon

- The Japanese automobile company Toyota signs an agreement for a joint venture with the U.S. company General Motors

Obviously, these three categories of interactions do not have equal significance. Type 2 and especially type 3 interactions are normally less important than those involving governments or IGOs.

Why Participants Act as They Do ....

Identifying the *what* of international relations is only the beginning of our exploration. The next question is *why* these entities, especially the governments of sovereign states, behave as they do in their relations with each other. Since ancient times, philosophers and political thinkers have sought answers to this question, and the search for a theory of international relations continues. A few years ago, Quincy Wright suggested that:

> A general theory of international relations means a comprehensive, comprehensible, coherent, and self-correcting body of knowledge contributing to the understanding, the prediction, the evaluation, and the control of relations among states and of the conditions of the world.[1]

Such a definition of an international theory may be too strict, although it can provide an ideal for which theorists should strive.

A more modest definition was offered by James E. Dougherty and Robert L. Pfaltzgraff, Jr.: "Theory is a way of organizing our knowledge so that we ask questions worth answering, and guide our research toward valid answers."[2] A theory of international relations should provide a plausible explanation for and a way to interpret and understand international interactions, events, and long-range developments that will enable the theorist (and the practitioner) to predict future outcomes—at least within the limits imposed by the volatility of human reactions and choices.

Although we can trace the search for a theory of international relations to ancient China (Mencius), India (Kautilya), and Greece (Thucydides), modern theories reflect the influence of two Italian renaissance thinkers: Niccolo Machiavelli (1469–1527) and Dante Alighieri (1265–1321). In *The Prince,* Machiavelli set the stage for a *realist* view of the relations among governments. Governments, he argued, are not motivated by noble values and good intentions—they pursue their interests by any effective means at their disposal. A prince should act in keeping with this reality.[3] Machiavelli's writings can be viewed as the antecedents of the modern analysis of power as the principal moving force in international relations.

Dante was one of the earliest advocates of an international organization capable of enforcing peace.[4] In effect, Dante attributed the conflicts that often led to costly wars to the anarchic international system that gave free rein to people's basest instincts. The way to safeguard peace was to change the rules of the game, allowing people's noble nature to assert itself. In the following centuries, many other thinkers supported similar views.[*]

....Idealist Approach

Dante's *idealist approach* received fresh impetus during and after World War I, which brought such appalling destruction and loss of life. The idealists argued forcefully—and with considerable justification—that the war was the result of *power politics* and of the

---

[*]Pierre Dubois, Émeric Crucè, the Duc de Sully, William Penn, Abbé de Saint Pierre, Jean-Jacques Rousseau, Jeremy Bentham, and Immanuel Kant.[5]

unrestrained pursuit of national interest. A powerful drive was launched by influential elites, in the United States in particular, seeking to restructure the international system. The idealists spoke of the ways states *ought* to behave in their relations with each other, and they rejected the notion of a balance of power, the use of force in pursuing the national interest, and the methods of unrestrained conflict. They argued that with the proper restructuring of the international system, states would shift from conflict to cooperation.

The idealists focused on the legal elements in international relations, such as international law and international organization. International treaties signed before the war to promote cooperation had been helpful, but were not sufficient to prevent the devastating conflict. With President Woodrow Wilson as their most influential advocate, the idealists pressed for an international organization to regulate relations among sovereign states and to safeguard peace. The League of Nations emerged as the most impressive accomplishment of this idealist approach.

The optimistic expectations of the idealists were not borne out. In the 1930s, the governments of Japan, Italy, Germany, and the Soviet Union ignored the League as they pursued their objectives through use of threat or by force. The reemergence of power politics in a most virulent form raised grave doubts about the intellectual validity of the idealist approach. The belief that nations shared "a harmony of interests" had proved to be a utopian illusion.[6]

However, World War II did not destroy altogether the belief that a proper restructuring of the international system could alter human behavior and strengthen the preservation of peace. The United Nations was established in 1945 to replace the League.

.... Realist Approach

With the onset of the Cold War, the proponents of the *realist approach* saw their views vindicated once again. It was clear, they argued, that the basic nature of the international system had not changed. Governments still pursued their national interests by whatever means they could muster. In such an anarchic system, officials acting in the name of their country have but one obligation: to achieve their foreign policy objectives without being constrained by ethical considerations. Echoing Machiavelli, the realists said that state representatives are free to maximize the gains of their country by any means, as long as they do not endanger that country's existence. To fulfill their mission, the realists added, officials must increase the *power* of their state. Power, according to the realists, is the key concept in international relations.

As early as 1948, Hans Morgenthau, who had a pivotal influence on the postwar development of the realist theory, presented several propositions as the foundation of a realist approach.[7]

1. Human nature follows certain norms that are "impervious to our preferences." More specifically, those who act in the name of sovereign states "think and act in terms of *interest defined as power*" (italics added).

2. Diplomats and heads of state cannot apply universal moral principles. Such principles must be "filtered through the concrete circumstances of time and place."

3. Each policy must be judged by political criteria and on the basis of its political consequences. The political realist must ask: "How does this policy affect the power of the nation?"

According to Morgenthau, states satisfied with the existing distribution of power (the status quo) will seek to *keep power* to prevent change. Those dissatisfied with the status quo will try to force changes, *expand their power*, and reverse the power relations between two or more nations. Dissatisfied countries will engage in *imperialist policies* designed to achieve local preponderance, continental empire, or world domination. States, Morgenthau argued, engage in power struggles to preserve the status quo, to achieve imperialist expansion, or to gain prestige: "A political policy seeks either to keep power, to increase power, or to demonstrate power." Most important, he identified *power* with *interest:* repeatedly, he used the expression "interest defined as power."

.... Radical Approach

The idealist approach held that governments would behave differently if only the international system did not condone and even encourage conflict and power politics. The realist approach, by contrast, claimed that the reliance on power is inherent in the nature of the international system and even more so in the "impervious" traits of human nature. Both of these approaches were charged with missing the point by a third school of thought based on Marxist theory. The *Marxist* or *radical approach* claimed that conflict in international politics was the product of capitalism. This economic system, in the radical view, breeds conflict because, to survive, it needs to:

1. Expand into new markets

2. Place under its control the sources of raw materials

3. Exploit the weak to maximize its profits

The capitalist countries fight each other to grab a larger slice of the pie. Since the emergence of the "socialist commonwealth," the capitalist powers try to prevent, even by force, the transfer of power from the capitalist elite in a given country to the people. Peace, therefore, will remain in jeopardy as long as the capitalist and imperialist forces continue to dominate the international system. If the working class were to assume power everywhere, the conditions that foment conflict would disappear.[8]

As shown, this optimistic expectation has not been borne out by the relations between China and the Soviet Union, China and Vietnam, the Soviet Union and Yugoslavia, or Yugoslavia and Albania.

Bureaucratic Approach

A different interpretation of international relations, with echoes of both the realist and the radical approaches, is the *bureaucratic approach*. It argues that foreign policy decisions reflect a desire not so much to promote *national* interests as to pursue the selfish interests of government officials and other influential individuals concerned with their careers, their own business interests, or the objectives of their own organizational structure.[9] The proponents of this approach shift the emphasis from the power of the state and the national interest (of the realist approach) to the pursuit of personal power, advancement, and gratification. Not infrequently, government officials tend to identify the "national interest" with their own personal aspirations and objectives. The proponents of the radical view may find this interpretation somewhat congenial, for much mischief thus can be attributed to the so-called military–industrial complex, whose members presumably have a personal interest in power politics, continuing conflict, and armament buildup. On the other hand, the logical implications of the bureaucratic approach could not be very acceptable to the radicals, because the interests of Soviet bureaucrats (military officers, heavy industry managers, scientists working on weapons development) may affect Soviet policies in the same way.

Systems Approach

Several political scientists have focused on the concept of the "system" and have tried to explain the functioning of the international system by using concepts and methodologies developed by other disciplines, such as physics, biology, psychology, sociology, communications science, or mathematics and statistics.[10] Anatol Rapoport has suggested that a system is "a whole which functions as a whole by virtue of the interdependence of its parts."[11] The international system is viewed as an aggregate of components (international actors) that interact along certain patterns. Like other systems, it involves "inputs" and "outputs"; it is subject to disturbances, decay, and adjustment; it has certain regulating mechanisms to restore and maintain its equilibrium and essential characteristics. The adherents of systems theories are concerned with the role of elites, resources, and environment as factors that "enhance or detract from stability in the system."[12] They focus on the role of communication, they construct models to make certain processes or configurations more understandable, and they analyze the functions performed by the various structures within the system.

Systems theories of international relations have been popular and influential because they have broadened the field by drawing on several disciplines and by providing interesting and illuminating insights. On the other hand, they have been criticized because each seems to focus too narrowly on one aspect to the exclusion of others, and because they "do not capture the stuff of politics."[13]

Neorealist Approach

Recent developments on the international stage have raised doubts about the validity and reliability of the theoretical approaches outlined. The United Nations has not fulfilled the expectations of the idealists. The realists' obsession with power seems overdrawn in a world of more than 155 sovereign states, in which even the superpowers seldom can impose their will. The radical view is undermined by the policies of the very states that should be the prime examples of its validity. The bureaucratic approach does not fully explain why policy orientations continue even though individuals come and go. The systems theories appear to be too mechanistic, although their contributions can be used fruitfully in a selective manner to broaden and deepen our understanding of international relations.

The international system is complex enough and does not need to be made even more so through complex theories. In this text, we shall certainly draw on those aspects of the various theoretical approaches that can help us understand the workings of the international system; however, our focus will be on a flexible and pragmatic approach.

Our pragmatic, *neorealist approach* does not reject the role of power in international relations; but it focuses on its limitations and takes a more balanced view of the role played by *influence*. Experience shows that governments do not necessarily try to "keep power, increase power, or demonstrate power." In the complex and interdependent international system of today, they try *to protect and promote their interests*. Seldom can they do so by imposing their will on others. Most of the time, they have to bargain, engage in persuasion, and accept compromise solutions to problems that cannot be resolved by fiat.

This theoretical approach, which will guide our steps through this text, applies the following seven propositions to explain why international actors behave as they do.

1. The primary moving force in international relations is *interest*, understood as a beneficial outcome for the entity engaged in a transaction or confrontation.

2. Government officials, in their relations with other international actors, pursue what they consider to be the *national interest* of their country.

3. Officials' definition of what constitutes the national interest at a given time is determined by (a) certain basic imperatives such as the survival, security, prestige, and well-being of their country; (b) their perception of what is beneficial for their country in a specific transaction or confrontation, and (c) their own view of their personal or political interests as these may be affected by the outcome of their policies or actions.

4. The natural tendency of international actors is to try to accomplish their objectives to the fullest possible extent.

5. State representatives can reach the highest degree of satisfaction by imposing their will on others and thus shaping the outcome of a transaction or confrontation at will.

6. Because they are not always able to impose their will on others, officials and other actors find it necessary to resort to bargaining and persuasion and to accept compromise solutions.

7. When faced with insurmountable obstacles or pressures, government officials may capitulate, in effect accepting the maximum demands of the other side; however, this is avoided when possible and is rare.

Propositions 5 and 6 imply that, depending on the actual circumstances, international actors will employ either the power approach (trying to impose their will) or the transactional approach (trying to influence the decisions of others through bargaining and persuasion).

Power and Influence

In everyday life, there are two ways to make people comply with our wishes. Either we *tell* them what to do or we try to *persuade* them to act along the lines we favor. We are able to accomplish the former if and when the other person has no alternative but to comply with our wishes or if and when our relationship requires such compliance. In such cases, noncompliance almost always can lead to unpleasant consequences for the person who disobeys. We use persuasion, on the other hand, when we are unable to impose our will because the other person can ignore our wishes with impunity or has no obligation to comply.

We use two familiar terms to identify these interactions: *power* and *influence*. Generally speaking, *power is the ability to* make *another person act in a given way, regardless of his or her personal preferences or inclinations.*[14] Power should not be equated with *force,* although force is certainly one of the sources of power.

Power differs from influence. The key element in a relationship involving influence is that neither side can *impose* its will on the other. As a result, *one person tries to affect the thinking and actions of another through persuasion or bargaining.* In a business transaction, as a rule, neither side can exercise power over the other. The outcome is determined instead by the relative ability of each side to influence the decisions of the other. The parties are involved not in a *power relationship* but in a *transactional relationship,* which relies chiefly on bargaining and persuasion.

These patterns of interaction apply as much to international relations as they do to everyday life.

Power in International Relations

Power long has been considered to be the key concept in the study of international relations.[15] Hans Morgenthau held that governments, in their relations with each other, try "either to keep power, increase power, or demonstrate power." He also equated interest with power. Another scholar, Georg Schwarzenberger, argued that, in the absence of a superior authority, governments are likely to do whatever they are capable of doing to gain their ends. Power, in his view, is the prime factor in international politics—a "combination of persuasive influence and coercive force."[16] More recently, two other scholars have defined power as "the ability of an actor on the international stage to use tangible and intangible resources and assets in such a way as to influence the outcome of international events to its own satisfaction."[17]

A definition of power broad enough to stretch from "persuasive influence to coercive force," however, may bring under the single label "power" situations and relationships that are not identical. The distinction between power and influence was pointed out by Arnold Wolfers, who wrote that he deemed it important "to distinguish between power and influence, the first to mean the ability to move others by the threat or infliction of deprivations, the latter to mean the ability to do so through promises or grants of benefits."[18]

We live in a world composed primarily of *sovereign states:* entities that are not subject to any superior authority and whose governments have exclusive jurisdiction within the territory of their state. *Legally,* no government or other entity has the right to impose its will on the government of a sovereign state, and no government of a sovereign state has the legal obligation to obey another's commands. To impose its will on another, a government must resort to force, economic pressures, or the threat of painful consequences in the event of noncompliance. John Spanier identifies three factors that must be present in a power relationship:

> First there must be a conflict of values or interests. . . . Second, for the power relationship to exist, B must accede, however unwillingly, to A's demands. . . . Third, in a power relationship one of the parties invokes sanctions that the other regards as likely to inflict "severe deprivations" or pain upon itself. The cost of noncompliance for B must be greater than the cost of compliance.[19]

In the absence of any legal obligation to comply, a government facing such pressures or threats must assess the situation and decide whether, under the circumstances, it has sufficient leverage to reject the demands. If it determines that compliance is neither desirable nor inescapable, it may proceed to reject them, or to propose different arrangements. On its part, the government seeking to impose its will has three options: to persist in its power approach, increasing the pressure and even employing force; to shift to the transactional approach, engage in bargaining, and eventually accept a compromise; or to postpone the confrontation or transaction, or give up altogether the effort to resolve the issue.

It thus would be inaccurate to say that a government is exercising power when bargaining or persuasion is the principal mode of interaction. This is more than semantic hairsplitting. The term *power* tends to convey an impression of strength, superiority, and the ability "to get what you want," to have your orders obeyed or your demands accepted regardless of what the other side may think of them or what its own preferences may be.

On the other hand, if one government has to use *inducements, arguments, pressures, or even threats,* whereas the other has enough leverage to *counter the arguments, ignore the pressures or the inducements, or even use some threats of its own,* then we have a different situation—a transactional interaction. The following illustration may dramatize the difference between the two relationships.

Between 1945 and 1951, "the Supreme Commander for the Allied Powers, General Douglas MacArthur, *ran Japan*"(italics added), to quote a recent text on United States foreign policy.[20] During those years, the relationship between Japan and the

United States was a power interaction, with the United States exercising the power. Contrast this to the current relationship between the two countries: disagreements on key issues between Washington and Tokyo cannot be resolved by fiat, but must be settled through bargaining. Power has given way to influence and transactional interactions.

The emphasis given traditionally to the concept of power in international relations is understandable. For many centuries, power was indeed central to the conduct of international relations. Not long ago, the major European powers either controlled directly large sections of the planet in the form of colonies or possessions or had such overwhelming superiority that weaker (legally sovereign) states were unable to resist, ignore, or counter effectively any attempts by the great powers to impose their will. The history of the past three centuries is full of illustrations. If the government of a small or weak state was foolhardy or unwise enough to ignore or oppose the demands of a great power, economic pressures, diplomatic representations, or a small dose of *gunboat* (coercive) diplomacy usually were sufficient to bring compliance. For almost a century, the United States treated most Latin American countries as client states expected to comply with the dictates of Washington. In Europe, the great powers controlled most of Asia and Africa either directly as colonial possessions or indirectly through military and economic superiority, which made it virtually impossible for many sovereign countries, such as Greece, Ethiopia, Iran, Thailand, or China, to ignore or oppose effectively the wishes of the Europeans.

....The Decline of Power

U.S. officials as well as ordinary citizens are increasingly frustrated by contemporary international relations. The power of the United States, we are told, has eroded. The assertion is valid, but it is not only the power of the United States that has diminished. If our understanding of what power means in international relations is sound, then we have to acknowledge that the circumstances that allowed certain governments to impose their will on others are not as widely present now as they were a few decades ago.

Consider, for example, these recent developments. In June 1972, Anwar Sadat, then president of Egypt, decided to end his government's close ties with the Soviet Union and ordered several thousand Soviet advisers to leave Egypt. Sadat's decision was unquestionably a serious setback for the Soviet Union, but Moscow could not prevent or reverse it by sending units of the Soviet fleet to blockade the port of Alexandria (as Britain might have done in years past), by threatening Egypt with a shower of missiles, or by using economic pressures, because Egypt could turn to other countries for supplies or financial assistance. Nor could the Soviet Union, in 1977, prevent Somalia from ending its alignment with Moscow when the Soviet leadership decided to side with Ethiopia—Somalia's rival—over the disputed region of the Ogaden. In both cases, the Soviet Union certainly possessed the military capability to impose its will, but today's international environment and the possibility of a confrontation with the United States made such an attempt to exercise power very hazardous and politically counterproductive.

In November 1979—to shift to the other side of the fence—Iranian "students," with the tacit approval of the Iranian regime of Ayatollah Rudollah Khomeini, seized the U.S. embassy in Tehran and captured most of the diplomatic personnel. The U.S.

government, despite the tremendous capabilities at its disposal, could not exercise power to free the hostages. The freezing of Iranian assets located in the United States had no effect. The ill-fated rescue attempt in the spring of 1980 revealed how limited were the United States' options for the use of military force. In the end, the hostages were freed through a negotiated settlement.

It appears that power is not as relevant or effective in dealing with international problems as it was in the not-too-distant past. We can identify four developments that account for this.

Large Number of Sovereign States. The emergence of almost one-hundred sovereign states in Asia, Africa, the Middle East, and the Caribbean, in territories previously controlled by European or other states (Britain, France, Belgium, the Netherlands, Portugal, Italy, the United States, Japan), has drastically reduced the ability of former colonial masters to exercise power over them. Whereas previously the colonial powers were able to impose their will with hardly a ripple, now they have to resort to bargaining and persuasion.

Soviet Power. The rise of the Soviet Union as a superpower has introduced a new factor that governments can use to increase their leverage. This is particularly true in the case of the Third World countries, which constitute the numerical majority of today's sovereign states. Should the Western governments try to impose their will through threats or pressures, the governments of the new states may turn to the Soviet Union; or large segments of their citizenry may react emotionally to the foreign pressures and turn a receptive ear to Soviet propaganda. Such reorientations of public opinion cannot be prevented through the exercise of power.

Nuclear Weaponry. The development of nuclear weapons has introduced a fundamentally different content into the realities of war, at least among the superpowers and their allies. In the past, war—as the ultimate step in the power approach—was a rational alternative; potential costs were not unacceptable to a rational decision maker. The advent of the nuclear weapons has changed all this. Now threats and reprisals that may escalate to a nuclear exchange must be avoided as a matter of common sense and self-preservation. Nonnuclear countries not closely related to the superpowers may and often do engage in the use of force in dealing with their neighbors, and nuclear powers also sometimes use conventional military forces.

Governmental Interdependence. The increasing interdependence among the various governments has made the resolution of conflicts and the realization of objectives through bargaining and diplomatic efforts a more practical process than the traditional power approach permits. For example, we often hear about the interdependence between the Western industrial states and the less-developed countries (LDCs). The industrial states need the resources and the potential markets of the LDCs. On their part, the LDCs need the assistance of the advanced countries to develop their economies and improve the living standards of their people. This interdependence manifested itself in a rather dramatic fashion in the early 1980s. At that time, LDCs owed over $500 billion to banking institutions in the Western world. Some of these LDCs were unable to meet their obligations because of a worldwide economic recession and their own low growth rate. A default certainly would have caused a severe crisis in the Western banking system. Could this problem have been solved by applying the familiar instrumentalities of the power approach? Hardly. The solution was sought in policies designed to reduce the pressure on the debtor countries and make it easier for them to meet their obligations.

The Power Approach ....

Although the growing relevance and utility of the transactional approach is evident, the traditional reliance on the instruments and methods associated with the exercise of power has not disappeared. Far from it.

Governments, as a rule, wish to accomplish the objectives of their foreign policy to the fullest extent possible. Total or near-total satisfaction, however, depends on a government's ability to impose its will on the other side by threatening, either openly or implicitly, some form of "punishment" that the other government finds virtually impossible to ignore, counter, or avoid. In the most extreme circumstances, such pressures relate to the use of physical (military) force. Mao's dictum that power flows from the barrel of a gun was merely an apt restatement of a long-established axiom. More frequently, such pressures or threats may involve the denial of economic or other benefits.

...............Use of Force

To be effective, a threat to use force must be credible; credibility depends on the circumstances. For example, neither the Soviet Union nor the United States can impose its will on other governments by threatening to use nuclear weapons. The nuclear weapons of the two superpowers are more relevant as instruments of policy in pursuing the vital objective of keeping one another within the confines of the transactional approach in their relations *with each other*.

In many instances, the superpowers may find that a threat to use even conventional forces is not an effective or practical gesture because of the realities of the international environment. In several countries, the United States recently has faced developments that its policy makers would have liked to have prevented. The events in Cuba, Syria, Libya, South Yemen, Angola, Iran, Afghanistan, and Nicaragua serve as illustrations. In each case, many U.S. citizens were frustrated by their country's inability to use its military might to prevent what they perceived as undesirable changes.

Ironically, the governments of smaller states appear to be more capable of using force in dealing with their neighbors and are more inclined to do so. Since the end of World War II, military force has been used in dozens of cases to settle disputes among rival states. Table 1-1 identifies some of the more serious military encounters. The two superpowers were involved in six (but not directly against each other): the United States in Korea (1950–1953), Vietnam (1965–1972), and Grenada (1983); the Soviet Union in Hungary (1956), Czechoslovakia (1968), and Afghanistan (1979–   ). The two super-

Table 1-1
Serious Military Conflicts

Conventional Military Conflicts

- Arab–Israeli war (1948–1949)
- Suez campaign (1956)
- India's takeover of Goa (1961)
- India–China border clashes (1961–1962)
- India–Pakistan war (1965)
- Israeli–Arab six-day war (June 1967)
- Arab–Israeli war (1973)
- Turkish invasion of Cyprus (1974)

- Somali–Ethiopian conflict over Ogaden (1977–1978)
- Chinese operation in Vietnam (1979)
- Vietnamese invasion of Cambodia (1979–)
- Iran–Iraq war (1980–)
- British–Argentine war over the Falklands (1982)
- Israeli invasion of Lebanon (1982)

Superpower Involvement

- United States in Korea (1950–1953)
- Soviet Union in Hungary (1956)
- United States in Vietnam (1965–1972)

- Soviet Union in Czechoslovakia (1968) and in Afghanistan (1979–)
- U.S. military action in Grenada (1983)

Subconventional Operations

- Uprising in Iran (1945–1946)
- Revolt in Indonesia (1945–1949)
- Guerrilla campaign in Greece (1946–1949)
- Revolt in Paraguay (1947)
- Uprising in Madagascar (1947–1948)
- War in French Indochina (1947–1954)
- Guerrilla war in Malaya (1948–1958)
- Civil war in Burma (1948–1962)
- Civil war in Bolivia (1949)
- Guerrilla war in the Philippines (1949–1955)
- Guerrilla war in Colombia (1950–1958)
- Mau Mau uprising in Kenya (1953–1956)
- Algerian war (1954–1962)

- Guerrilla war in Cyprus (1955–1959)
- Warfare in Yemen and Aden (1956–1960)
- Guerrilla war in Cuba (1957–1959)
- Civil warfare in Lebanon (1958)
- Guerrilla war in Laos (1960–1962)
- Civil war in the Congo (1960–1963)
- Guerrilla war in Angola (1961–62)
- Kurdish rebellion in Iraq (1961–1962)
- Civil war in Yemen (1962–1966)
- Civil war (Biafra) in Nigeria (1966–1969)
- Angola conflict (1975–1976)
- Tanzanian action in Uganda (1978)
- Civil conflict in Chad (1983–)
- Civil warfare in Lebanon (1980–1984)

---

powers had several—mostly verbal—clashes over West Berlin, and once they confronted each other in a showdown—during the Cuban missile crisis in October 1962.[21]

Force also has been used by or against nonstate entities such as guerrilla groups. For obvious reasons, revolutionary organizations are more likely to embrace the power approach. Their adversaries seldom are inclined to enter into negotiations to reach a compromise. The revolutionary leaders have no alternative but to rely on force in the hope that they will either win and take over the government—as the Sandinistas did in Nicaragua—or make a negotiated settlement unavoidable—as in Algeria, where the French, after years of savage warfare with the National Liberation Front, negotiated Algerian independence.

.... Use of Economic Pressure

Military force is not the only source of power in international relations. A government may employ severe economic pressures in an effort to impose its will on another government. The historical record indicates that the effectiveness of such pressures is limited. Economic sanctions, embargos, or boycotts (see chapter 7) do not often bring compliance, given the diversity of today's international economic relationships.

A government facing such economic pressures usually will find other countries ready to move in to buy its products, sell to it the commodities it needs, and provide loans and other assistance in the hope of gaining new markets, political influence, or other advantages. For example, in 1972, the Nixon administration cut off all U.S. short-term bank credits for Chile in an effort to pressure the government of Salvador Allende, whose radical Marxist views it saw as a threat to U.S. interests in Latin America. This action had no decisive effect on Allende's policies, because he was able to obtain even more credits from several other countries, including many non-Marxist ones such as France, West Germany, the Netherlands, Spain, Sweden, Japan, Argentina, and Brazil.

Whatever the actual forms of pressure, a government usually resorts to the power approach only when it is convinced that its crucial interests are at stake and that its objectives cannot possibly be accomplished through bargaining or persuasion.

The Transactional Approach ....

Although efforts to exercise power often are dramatic and attract a great deal of attention, most international interactions rely on the transactional approach. In emphasizing this approach, we hope to balance the current preoccupation of our discipline with power—a preoccupation that tends to distort our understanding of international relations.

The transactional approach is *the reliance on bargaining and persuasion to influence the outcome of international exchanges, disputes, or confrontations*. The approach is not new; diplomats, diplomatic exchanges, and the methods of diplomacy have been used for many years. The transactional approach, however, goes beyond the technicalities of diplomacy. It requires a different intellectual attitude and a pragmatic appreciation of the international system as it functions now.

Bargaining in international relations becomes necessary when two or more international actors have *conflicting objectives* and neither side can impose its will on the other. The parameters of bargaining apply as much to international relations as they do to business. Government officials may not always deal with specific monetary values as businesspeople are likely to do, but they, too, are concerned with the benefits they can obtain for their country in an international transaction and with the costs or disadvantages incurred in the final agreement. The gains may be political, strategic, economic, territorial, ideological, social, or emotional, but in the last analysis the dynamics are the same. In both business and international transactions, the idea is to *gain the most at the least possible cost*.

Those who approach an international transaction, dispute, or even confrontation with a practical, businesslike attitude have a better chance of increasing their gains and minimizing their ultimate costs or losses. However, this attitude is not always evident in international relations, especially when illusions of grandeur, power superiority, self-righteousness, or nationalistic fervor becloud the judgment of government leaders.

Although business transactions can be complex affairs, they seldom approach the complexity of international transactions affecting the national interests of states. The latter exchanges require many imaginative decisions, the assessment of national capabilities or international reactions, the weighing of alternatives, a great deal of realism and flexibility, and above all a recognition that in a transactional interaction the outcome can take the form only of a compromise. We can see this complexity, for example, in the efforts that eventually led to the Camp David agreements (see box 1-1) or to the establishment of the European Economic Community (see box 1-2).

Box 1-1
Camp David

"Camp David" is a shorthand label for the agreements signed in March 1979 between Egypt and Israel. Since the creation of Israel in 1948, these two countries had relied on the power approach to gain their ends. A shift to the transactional approach became an acceptable alternative to unabating hostility and intermittent warfare only after the October 1973 Arab–Israeli war. During the combat, the Egyptian army scored a few victories, which presumably restored Egyptian national pride. At long last, Egypt and Israel came to realize that they could obtain through bargaining what they could not gain by force. By concluding a separate peace with Egypt, Israel could remove Egypt from the Arab military equation. Without the Egyptian army, the other Arab states would no longer pose a valid threat to Israel's survival. On its side, the Egyptian government expected to regain the territories lost to Israel since 1967.

Although different in content, the objectives of the two sides were compatible—except on one issue: the Palestinian question. Egypt, to satisfy Arab demands, advocated self-determination for the Palestinians—meaning in effect an independent and sovereign Palestinian state, preferably in the West Bank and the Gaza Strip, two Arab-inhabited areas under Israeli occupation since 1967. By contrast, Israel was adamantly opposed to a Palestinian state.

In the protracted negotiations that were actively assisted by the U.S. government and by President Carter personally, the divergent objectives of the sides on the fate of the Palestinians proved a difficult point of contention. The idea of "autonomy" was eventually embraced by both sides as a compromise.[22]

Box 1-2
The Schuman Plan

Following World War II, a few farsighted European leaders—among them Robert Schuman and Jean Monnet in France, Konrad Adenauer in West Germany, and Alcide de Gasperi in Italy—came to realize that the power approach that had brought so much misery in the past should be replaced by a more pragmatic form of cooperation based on mutual interest and common advantage. On May 9, 1950, Robert Schuman, then French foreign minister, proposed a plan "to place the whole Franco–German coal and steel output under a common High Authority, in an organization open to participation of the other countries of Europe."[23]

Geology has thrown into a small area—the Ruhr, Lorraine, parts of northern France, the Saar, Luxemburg, most of Belgium, and part of the Netherlands—the biggest concentration of coal and iron ore in Europe, the basis for armaments and heavy industry. This geologically integrated area was, however, divided politically among several sovereign states.

The response to the Schuman plan was immediate and positive. Belgium, West Germany, Italy, Luxemburg, and the Netherlands joined France in an international conference. The treaty establishing the European Coal and Steel Community was signed less than one year later, on April 18, 1951, and was ratified by all participants before the end of the summer of 1952. The process did not end there. After protracted and complicated efforts, on March 25, 1957, the six countries signed the Treaty of Rome, "a negotiated document, containing concessions and counter-concessions, careful wording, ingenious compromises, and special protocols which [settled] residual details."[24] This treaty set the foundation for the European Economic Community (EEC), the familiar Common Market.

As the practical significance of the transactional approach has increased since World War II, the instrumentalities for the resolution of conflicts also have become more numerous. The United Nations, the various specialized agencies, regional organizations, and special forums for the discussion of crucial issues are currently available, although, admittedly, they are not always effective.

The National Interest ....

Each sovereign state has to deal with changes in the international environment, and with the objectives of other states. The objective of each sovereign state, as it engages in international transactions or confrontations, is to improve the possibility of beneficial outcomes and to hold down its losses. This is the theoretical foundation of the *national interest*.[25] The term is widely and frequently used, yet on close examination we find that it cannot be employed as an analytical tool to explain or evaluate foreign policy decisions because it lacks precision and an objectively defined content.[26] Only when policy choices are posed in terms of national survival can the national interest be defined with minimal ambiguity. Such clear-cut choices are rare in a nation's history. Policy makers must deal every day with issues that are subject to varied evaluations and interpretations. The problem is: How can a government tell with certainty what is in the national interest under the circumstances? For example, was it in the national interest of the United States to commit troops in Vietnam? Three presidents—Eisenhower, Kennedy, and Johnson— believed that an extension of communist control into the southern half of Vietnam would be detrimental to the national interest of the United States. President Nixon accepted disengagement reluctantly. Now, in retrospect, we may question whether a noncommunist South Vietnam was vital or even important to the survival, the independence, prosperity, or prestige of the United States. On the other hand, we could argue that once the United States had become involved directly and extensively, its *prestige* was at stake, and in that sense a successful outcome was in the national interest. From yet another perspective, we might ask whether it was in the national interest to continue a war that was causing tremendous dissension at home and tarnishing the image of the United States abroad.

....Determining Factors

The subjective elements that help to define the national interest have long occupied the attention of scholars and practitioners of international politics.[27] The following are among the factors that have been identified as determining the perception of national interest under specific circumstances.

Nationalism. Nationalism appears to have considerable relevance to the way governments define their country's national interest.[28] In a general sense, any policy that safeguards the survival and independence of the nation, promotes its prestige and wellbeing, expands its material resources, or increases its power and influence potential is in the national interest. Those who act in the name of the nation tend to identify intellectually and emotionally with their nation in every international transaction or confrontation involving their country. Their perception of what is good for the nation may be faulty, but in most cases the final judgment belongs to the historian. At the time a decision is reached, the decision makers invariably claim—and perhaps sincerely believe—that their policy is serving the nation.

Ideology. A government may define the national interest on the basis of its own ideological preferences or prejudices. Although ideology may be only a contributing factor, its effect on a government's perception of the national interest should not be ignored. Certainly the perception of Cuba's national interest was different under Fulgencio Batista from what it is now under Fidel Castro. The same can be said of Iran's foreign policy under the Shah compared to that under the Islamic Republic.

Politics. Government leaders have their own political objectives: to win the next election, keep the support of influential constituencies, neutralize opposition, vindicate past policies, and improve their national and international standing in the eyes of history. These objectives tend to affect their perception of their country's national interest. For example, in February 1984, when President Reagan decided to withdraw from Lebanese soil the U.S. military contingent of the multinational peacekeeping force, several observers suggested that he did so because he was concerned that their continuing presence—and exposure to terrorist action—could prove a serious liability in the upcoming election.

Subordinates' Biases. To decide what the national interest is in a specific situation, government leaders rely on information, analyses, data interpretation, and policy recommendations supplied by subordinate officials and bureaucratic personnel. Career considerations and other personal interests and objectives may tint those persons' view of the national interest. For example, members of the U.S. military establishment usually argue that greater defense outlays are in the national interest. Even within this group we find different subdivisions espousing their own priorities. Those associated with strategic (nuclear) weapons argue that the national interest requires more such weapons; those associated with the Navy advocate more carriers; and so on. Although the motives of many of those officials may be aboveboard, one cannot ignore the fact that an expansion of forces means greater advancement opportunities and other personal benefits for these people.

Morality and Legality. In determining the national interest, a government may take into account moral and legal considerations, but only if other factors do not take precedence. Morality in the political arena usually is relative and subjective.[29] Nevertheless, attempts to justify a policy in ethical or legal terms are not uncommon; moreover, such rationales should not be regarded always as a cynical effort to deceive the citizenry. Quite often, the invocation of moral precepts may be a necessary refinement. Citizens are not easily moved by unemotional, pragmatic policies, however sound they may be. They need to be convinced that they are supporting a noble and patriotic cause, and that the policy pursued by their government is not only sound but also *just* and morally unassailable.

Special Interest Groups. Pressure groups invoke the national interest to justify the policies they advocate. Some Catholics argued that it was in the national interest of the United States to come to the aid of South Vietnam (where the Catholic Church had a large religious following). Jewish-American organizations have successfully promoted pro-Israel policies on the grounds that Israel is a valuable ally for the defense of U.S. interests in the Middle East. Virtually every such group justifies its advocacy in terms of the national interest. Depending on the extent of their political influence, their perception of the national interest may in the end affect that of the decision makers themselves.

Other Governments. Decision makers, especially in smaller and weaker countries, may find that their perception of their country's national interest is affected by the views of foreign governments. Certainly the governments of Poland, Hungary, and Bulgaria tend to identify their national interest with the policies espoused by the Soviet Union. In fact, those who speak of "penetrated" or "dependent" political systems actually refer to governments that for political or economic reasons have come under the strong influence of a major power and find it necessary or profitable to equate their national interest with the views of their patron.

The "national interest," despite its familiarity, remains an elusive and imprecise concept. The actual content in each specific case depends on subjective assessments and motives and on the effects of conflicting and complex influences. Out of a veritable maze of factors, considerations, pressures, and priorities, a government is expected to forge its conception of the national interest and then proceed to formulate policies designed to serve and promote that interest. Only rarely are the options so clearly defined and the ultimate effect of specific policies so evident that the national interest can be identified with minimal subjectivity.

The Moving Force in International Relations

We have presented the view that government officials in charge of their country's foreign policies neither try compulsively to impose their will on other international actors nor act as though their major concern and fundamental interest is the pursuit of power. What they actually do is to define and then try to achieve what they consider good or necessary for their country (or their entity): what is in the interest of the entity they represent, at least as they see it. A policy meets this requirement if it is likely to result in gains and benefits or to minimize losses and costs. This pursuit of *interest*—actually the pursuit of advantageous and beneficial outcomes—is the moving force in international relations.

Summary

- International relations is a branch of political science dealing with policies, developments, and interactions that have consequences across national borders and affect the lives of people in different countries.

- Basic theories explaining why international actors behave as they do include the idealist, realist, radical, bureaucratic, and systems approaches. The idealist approach holds that power politics and conflict can be replaced by cooperation through the appropriate restructuring of the international system and through legal and organizational arrangements. The realist approach asserts that governments pursue power and that no structural changes in the international system (such as the founding of the UN) can change human behavior, which follows norms "impervious to our preferences." The radical approach claims that the source of international conflict is the economic system of capitalism and the imperialist policies it spawns. The bureaucratic approach attributes conflict and power politics to the selfish interests of bureaucratic elites. The systems approach focuses on the concept of a *system* and uses analytical concepts from other disciplines.

- The neorealist approach holds that governments and other international actors pursue what they believe to be in their interest (understood as a beneficial outcome for them) in an international confrontation or transaction. If circumstances permit, they try to impose their will on other actors by using power. Most of the time, however, in the contemporary complex and interdependent international environment, they pursue their interests through bargaining and persuasion (by exercising influence) in transactional interactions.
- The opportunities for applying the power approach have diminished in recent decades for a number of reasons (the end of the colonial empires, the rise of the Soviet Union, the advent of nuclear weapons, the increasing interdependence). At the same time, reliance on the transactional approach (bargaining, persuasion, compromise) is expanding.
- Governments pursue their "national interest," whose content is affected by a variety of factors (nationalism, ideology, biases, the interests of bureaucratic elites, moral or legal considerations, the objectives of pressure groups, or other governments).
- The pursuit of interest understood as a beneficial outcome is the moving force in international relations.

Notes

1. Wright, Quincy. "Development of a General Theory of International Relations." In *The Role of Theory in International Relations,* ed. Horace V. Harrison. Princeton: Van Nostrand Reinhold, 1964.
2. Dougherty, James E., and Pfaltzgraff, Robert L., Jr. *Contending Theories of International Relations*. Philadelphia: Lippincott, 1971, p. 25.
3. Machiavelli, Niccolo. *The Prince* and *The Discourses*. New York: Random House, 1940.
4. Dante Alighieri. *On World Government*. 2nd ed., trans. Herbert W. Schneider. New York: Liberal Arts Press, 1957.
5. Dougherty and Pfaltzgraff, *Contending Theories*, p. 2.
6. Carr, Edward Hallett. *The Twenty-Years' Crisis; 1919–1939: An Introduction to the Study of International Relations*. London: Macmillan, 1939, p. 62.
7. Morgenthau, Hans. *Politics among Nations*. 5th ed. New York: Knopf, 1978, p. 6.
8. For a good example of such a radical interpretation, see Kolko, Gabriel and Joyce. *The Limits of Power*. New York: Harper & Row, 1972.
9. The effect of "bureaucratic politics" on foreign policy is discussed in Allison, Graham T. *Essence of Decision: Explaining the Cuban Missile Crisis*. Boston: Little, Brown, 1971.
10. Best known in this group are Gabriel Almond, Kenneth E. Boulding, Karl W. Deutsch, David Easton, Morton A. Kaplan, Charles A. McClelland, Robert K. Merton, George Modelski, Anatol Rapoport, Richard N. Rosencrance, J. David Singer, and Kenneth N. Waltz.
11. Rapoport, Anatol. "Foreword." In *Modern Systems Research for the Behavioral Scientists*. ed. Walter Buckley. Chicago: Aldine-Atherton, 1968, p. xvii.
12. Dougherty and Pfaltzgraff, *Contending Theories*, p. 117.
13. Hoffmann, Stanley. "International Relations: The Long Road to Theory." In *International Politics and Foreign Policy*, ed. James N. Rosenau. New York: Free Press of Glencoe, 1961, p. 426.

14. Dahl, Robert A. "The Concept of Power." *Behavioral Science* (July 1957): 203.

15. Bertrand Russell, in his treatise on power, argued that "the fundamental concept in social science is Power, in the same sense in which Energy is the fundamental concept in physics." Russell, Bertrand. *Power*. New York: Barnes and Noble, 1962, p. 9.

16. Schwarzenberger, Georg. *Power Politics: A Study of World Society*. 3rd ed. New York: Praeger, 1964, pp. 13–14.

17. Rosen, Steven J., and Jones, Walter S. *The Logic of International Relations*. 3rd ed. Cambridge, Mass.: Winthrop, 1980, p. 203.

18. Wolfers, Arnold. *Discord and Collaboration*. Baltimore: Johns Hopkins University Press, 1962, p. 103. We find several definitions of *power,* some of them quite broad, equating "power" with "influence." See Walter, E. V. "Power, Civilization, and the Psychology of Conscience." *American Political Science Review* 53 (1959): 641–642; Roseman, Cyril. et al. *Dimensions of Political Analysis*. Englewood Cliffs, N.J.: Prentice-Hall, 1963, pp. 196–203. In other cases, the term *influence* is used to describe situations that unquestionably involve the exercise of power. See, for example, Froman, Louis A., Jr. "Politics in Everyday Life." In *Readings in Modern Political Analysis,* ed. Robert A. Dahl. Englewood Cliffs, N.J.: Prentice-Hall, 1963, pp. 36–38. For a detailed discussion of the concepts of "power," "influence," and "authority," see Kousoulas, D. G. *On Government and Politics*. 5th ed. Monterey, Calif.: Brooks/Cole, 1983, pp. 23–31.

19. Spanier, John. *Games Nations Play*. 4th ed. New York: Holt, Rinehart & Winston, 1981, p. 135.

20. Paterson, Thomas G., et al. *American Foreign Policy: A History*. Lexington, Mass.: Heath, 1977, p. 457.

21. Kennedy, Robert F. *Thirteen Days*. New York: Norton, 1967.

22. For more details see Carter, Jimmy. *Keeping Faith: Memoirs of a President*. New York: Bantam Books, 1982, pp. 376–379.

23. Mayne, Richard. *The Community of Europe*. New York: Norton, 1963, p. 85.

24. Mayne, *Community,* p. 117.

25. Beard, Charles Austin. *The Idea of National Interest*. Westport, Conn.: Greenwood Press, 1977, pp. 15–17.

26. Sonderman, Fred A. *The Theory and Practice of International Relations*. Englewood Cliffs, N.J.: Prentice-Hall, 1979, pp. 121–138.

27. Frankel, Joseph. *National Interest*. New York: Praeger, 1970, p. 74.

28. Kohn, Hans. *The Idea of Nationalism*. New York: Macmillan, 1944.

29. Osgood, Robert. *Ideals and Self-Interest in America's Foreign Relations*. Chicago: University of Chicago Press, 1953, p. 4.

2

The Actors in the International System

Yasser Arafat at the UN

Every day we can identify myriad interactions among diverse entities and private individuals whose actions have an effect across national borders or affect the functioning of the international system. These are the *actors* on the world stage, and their actions and interactions form the substance of what we call *international relations*. In practical terms, the most important actors are the sovereign states and state-related entities, which operate through individuals acting in their name. What these persons say or do—or fail to say or do—determines to a very large extent the content and the direction of international relations.

The diversity of these interactions is enormous. Consider these random illustrations:

- A decision by the U.S. government to propose a peace plan for resolving the Arab–Israeli conflict

- An escalation of guerrilla activity in El Salvador

- An easing of import restrictions by the Japanese government

- The approval of a loan to Mexico by the International Monetary Fund

- The deployment of United States, Italian, and French peacekeeping troops in Lebanon

- A decision by OPEC to lower the price of crude oil

- The assassination of a Turkish diplomat by Armenian terrorists

- An application by a U.S. firm wishing to establish a subsidiary in France

- Antinuclear demonstrations in Britain and West Germany

- The signing of a new "Convention" dealing with the "Law of the Sea"

- A meeting of the Nonaligned group in New Delhi

- A decision of the Soviet government to withdraw from the arms limitation talks

- Regulations issued by the International Civil Aviation Organization (ICAO) concerning overflights by commercial jets

- Expulsion of Soviet diplomatic personnel from Norway on spying charges

- A Council of Ministers meeting of the European Economic Community

- An appeal by the government of Nicaragua to the UN Security Council, prompted by the incursion of guerrillas from Honduran territory

- The personal initiative of 1984 presidential candidate Jesse Jackson, who went to Syria and negotiated successfully the release of a captured American pilot

All these events—which were actually culled from the daily press—resulted from decisions made by individuals acting either on their own or, much more frequently, in the name of a sovereign state, an international organization, or another entity such as a revolutionary group.

A grasp of the identity of these international actors, their varied features, their assets, and their functions and objectives is fundamental to an understanding of current international problems. This chapter is designed to provide that foundation.

Despite their diversity, the principal international actors can be placed in three major groups:

- Sovereign states

- Intergovernmental organizations (IGOs)

- Nongovernmental entities (NGOs)

Sovereign States..

Practically every human being in the world today is legally associated with one of the entities known as *sovereign states* or *nation-states*. Although these entities vary in size, resources, assets, and population, they all share certain characteristics that set them apart from other organized groups or from other actors in the international system. What are their essential features? They are sovereignty, land, population, and government.

....Sovereignty: A Legal Concept

We must emphasize one point at the outset: sovereignty is a *legal concept*. In no way should we assume that a sovereign state is immune to political pressures or interference by other states. Legally, however, (1) a sovereign state is not subject to any superior authority, and (2) its government has exclusive jurisdiction over the state's territory and the people who live within its borders. There is no entity in the world that has the legal authority to order the government of a sovereign state to act in a given way. In other words, there is no entity that can exercise *power with authority*[1] over a sovereign state.

The origin of sovereign states can be traced to the Treaty of Westphalia (1648), which ended the Thirty Years War. The term *sovereignty* itself was originated by the French philosopher Jean Bodin (1530–1596), who, in an effort to provide a philosophical justification for the growing power of the French monarchy, defined sovereignty as "the supreme power over citizens and subjects, unrestrained by law."[2] Bodin was not inventing a new political concept; he was simply offering a brief description of a reality that had existed since the dawn of history. Certainly the pharaohs of Egypt, the kings of Persia, or the emperors of Rome would have found the essential elements of sovereignty quite familiar.

Sovereignty provides a *legal* shield against unwanted interference by other governments or other international actors. Although not always effective, this legal shield nevertheless has performed such valuable service so often that no known government in the world today seriously advocates the abolition of its own sovereignty or of the concept itself.

At times, the government of a state may barricade itself behind the legal shield of sovereignty and commit acts of violence or inhumane treatment against its own people. Other governments or the international community as a whole can do little more than issue denunciations or at best try to induce more humane policies by using whatever influence they can bring to bear. In 1966, the UN General Assembly adopted an International Covenant on Civil and Political Rights and an International Covenant on Economic, Social and Cultural Rights. Both documents reaffirm the sanctity of sovereignty, and neither contains any provisions for effective enforcement. Violations have not disappeared; the international community can do little to prevent them.

Territory

Even the smallest sovereign state is associated with a piece of land. Although the actual boundaries may be disputed occasionally by other states, the possession and effective control of a more or less clearly defined territory is a prerequisite for the existence of a state.

When a state disappears as a legal entity, or when a state gives up control over territory it legally owns, the land passes on to another state—either to an existing state or to a new state established on the land. For example, when the colonial powers terminated their rule over their possessions in Africa, the former colonies were turned into new sovereign states that became known as Ghana, Nigeria, Zaire, Kenya, Zambia, and Uganda, to name a few.

A new state also may result from the revolutionary action of a dissident group, often supported from the outside. Panama emerged as a separate sovereign state in 1903, when a group of revolutionaries, encouraged and aided by the United States, detached a piece of territory from Colombia and established a government claiming control over a new state called Panama.

In every case, the land passed under the authority of a sovereign government.

The governments of sovereign states are extremely conscious of the importance of territory and consider their state's *territorial integrity* to be a sacred trust worth defending at all costs. We often use the term *country* when referring to a sovereign state, which may reflect our subconscious identification of the state with its land. Not surprisingly, during the past 300 years most of the major conflicts that occurred in Europe and elsewhere involved disputes over the possession of territory.

Until the end of the nineteenth century, the conquest of territories by force was an acceptable mode of behavior, especially when practiced by the major powers of the time. Even during the period between World Wars I and II, conquest was practiced with no effective opposition, although Article 10 of the Covenant of the League of Nations appeared to imply an obligation on the part of the League members to deny acceptance or recognition of "unlawful acts of conquest." For example, Japan seized Manchuria in 1931–1932; Italy invaded Ethiopia in 1935 and Albania in 1939; Hitler's Germany annexed the territories of Austria and Czechoslovakia in 1938. These territorial changes were overturned after the end of World War II.

Today the conquest of territory belonging to another state generally is regarded as a violation of the rules of international law. The United Nations Charter (especially Article 2, Paragraph 4) establishes beyond doubt that the use of force for the acquisition of territory is prohibited. Because of this rule, the takeover of a sizeable portion of the territory of Cyprus by Turkish forces in 1974 and the occupation of the West Bank, the Gaza Strip, and the Golan Heights by Israel are not recognized as legitimate. It must be noted that because the UN has no effective means to enforce the ban on conquest, such action can be attempted with impunity unless the victim is capable of resisting with its own military forces or the assistance of friendly nations. Still, *conquest by force does not confer legal title* on the conquered land to the aggressor.

·· Population

No state can exist without a population. Although there is no specific number of people that must inhabit a territory to justify the existence of a sovereign state, the presence of a viable community with some economic resources, some fairly effective governmental structure, and the ability to have relations with other members of the international system is indispensable.

The size of population varies widely. The present roster of the United Nations (1982) includes states with very small populations, such as Dominica (85,000), Seychelles (65,000), and Vanuatu (110,000), and giants such as China (estimated 1 billion), India (estimated 665 million), the Soviet Union (265.75 million), and the United States (226.235 million).

During the last three centuries, we have witnessed the emergence of the *nation-state*. In the period of feudalism, people's allegiances attached mostly to their immediate community or to their manorial lord. When royal power in Europe expanded over the fragmented entities of the feudal fiefs, large portions of territory came under the control of a single central government. Because of improved communications, people who previously had been aware of only their immediate vicinity gained a wider perception of the world around them. The royal authority became a connecting link, giving rise to new loyalties. In most cases, a common language served as the unifying catalyst. Through a process of indoctrination (political socialization)—using history, legend, and myth; nurtured by poets and writers, community leaders and high officials; and passed from generation to generation—new emotional attachments and traditions slowly took hold and eventually turned the small, fragmented communities into the building blocks of the *nation*. The king remained the visible personification of the nation until the American revolution and, to an even greater extent, the French revolution showed that a nation could exist as a viable entity in itself without royal authority.

The development of a national culture with an overriding loyalty to the nation generally is recognized as a critical element for the survival and vitality of a sovereign state. The significance of this national culture has been most recently recognized by the new African states, which were established on the former colonial territories. The colonies had been delineated initially to accommodate the interests and objectives of the colonial powers, splitting the local ethnic (tribal) groups in the process. To overcome this handicap, the new states have now embarked on a conscious effort of "nation building."

In every sovereign state, the people are connected to the state through a legal relationship: they are *citizens* of the state. Today, only in very rare instances can we find individuals who are not citizens of any state (stateless persons). The legal status of citizenship (or nationality) is common to practically all people on this planet. Stateless-ness is a rather unpleasant condition resulting from some major political upheaval. At the end of World War II, many people in Europe had lost their papers or other documents of identification and for a period of time were classified as stateless. Sooner or later, however, they were placed under the legal mantle of an existing state by becoming its citizens.

....Government

A sovereign state interacts with other international actors primarily through representatives vested with the authority to speak for the state and make commitments in its name. The decisions of these state officials are binding on the members of their political community—on the population of the state. Moreover, the government officials who are empowered to formulate and execute foreign policy decisions are accepted by their counterparts in other states as the authoritative spokespersons and decision makers for their sovereign states. There also is an assumption that commitments made by these officials obligate the state itself, whether a particular government came to office through free elections or as a result of a military coup.

Even in the most democratically organized countries, foreign policy decisions are made by a small number of government officials at the top of the political structure. For example, the decision to commit U.S. troops in 1965 to the ongoing civil war in Vietnam was reached by a small number of high-ranking officials in the Department of Defense, the State Department, and the White House.[3]

Whereas we should not underestimate the ability of public officials to reach and implement foreign policy decisions, neither should we ignore the effect of popular views and pressures on those who forge foreign policy. Especially in countries with pluralistic political systems, groups with important political or economic assets may affect the content of important decisions, even against the best judgment or preferences of public officials.

....The Goals of Sovereign States

Long experience indicates that almost all sovereign governments, regardless of differences in their political systems, share certain basic goals that shape their perception of their country's national interest. Those goals can be expressed in terms of what each seeks to preserve.

The State. Virtually without exception, all governments regard the preservation of their state as the central goal of their foreign policy. A government will make every effort and take any measures possible to resist a threat to its country's existence. Very seldom in history can we find sovereign governments that voluntarily consented to the extinction of their state as an independent and sovereign entity. One such rare illustration is the agreement of the thirteen states that in 1788 signed a federal constitution creating the United States of America. As a rule, the extinction of a sovereign state follows a catastrophic defeat in war. For example, the Austro–Hungarian empire was abolished in 1919 following its defeat in World War I. Its territory was taken mostly by new sovereign states such as Austria, Hungary, Czechoslovakia, and Poland.

Only in extreme cases will a threat be directed against the existence of a sovereign state. Although for several years most Arab states refused to acknowledge Israel's right to exist, much more frequently, a threat is made against a country's territorial integrity.

Territory. As we noted earlier, every sovereign state is associated with territory; preserving every inch of that territory is another basic goal of every government.

The reasons for this universal attachment of people to their country's territory vary. In most cases, possession of any asset itself creates the perception that one has a "right" to continue to own it. Like individuals, nations also say, "This land is mine." Often the territory is inhabited by people who are considered to be part of the nation. For example, the islands in the Aegean sea are inhabited by ethnically Greek populations. For this reason, Greece will resist vigorously any attempt to detach those islands from its sovereignty. In other cases, the territory may be important because it contains vital resources. A large part of Libya is uninhabited desert, but the oil deposits found beneath the desert are crucial to Libya's prosperity. A particular piece of territory may be important for reasons of security. Israel, for example, regards the control of the Golan Heights—seized from Syria in 1967—as essential to its defense. However, Syria considers those barren hills an inalienable part of its domain. Even when a piece of territory is not particularly important for its material assets, its possession is likely to be defended for reasons of prestige.

Although a country's territorial integrity is now protected under the rules of international law, violations are neither impossible nor uncommon. Several international conflicts have resulted from territorial disputes—even after the UN Charter clearly established the sanctity of a country's territorial integrity. The defense of territory remains a basic goal of a country's foreign policy.

Independence. Another goal of a country's foreign policy is the preservation of its independence against the possible interference or domination by others. The legal concept of sovereignty provides a barrier against outright interference or domination; however, this barrier can be pierced. Whenever a country faces such a threat, it will resist the attempt to the extent possible.

Prestige. A fourth goal of foreign policy is to preserve a country's prestige. This should not be viewed as a childish game of pride. A country's influence is affected by its international prestige. The individuals who are in charge of a country's foreign policy remain in office for a relatively limited period of time; however, their actions usually have lasting effects. What they do while in office adds to (or detracts from) the country's image. If they are perceived as being impotent, incompetent, irresponsible, or unreliable, this is bound to have an effect on the way other governments are likely to deal with their country. An impression of weakness may even whet the appetite of potential aggressors.

Prestige may be a primary issue in a variety of circumstances, even when its centrality is not evident. We know now, for instance, that the late President Anwar Sadat of Egypt decided to risk a war against Israel in 1973 mainly to restore his country's prestige; once its military honor was freed of the stigma of humiliation from previous defeats, Egypt could move to a peaceful solution through bargaining.

Prosperity. A fifth goal is to preserve and advance the nation's prosperity and wealth. Sovereign entities in the past often tried to increase their material wealth and possessions simply by seizing those that belonged to their neighbors. In more recent times, the possession of colonies was not merely a matter of prestige; it also was a means for the acquisition of material resources. Nazi Germany embarked on an expansionist policy in search of *Lebensraum* (living space) in Europe and European Russia to improve the lot of the German people. In Asia, Japan followed a similar policy with its *co-prosperity* campaign.

One of the major changes in the realm of international relations since the end of World War II has been the shift from forcible acquisition of resources to acquisition through bargaining and exchange. Trade, borrowing, aid, and investment are among the techniques governments use to improve the material conditions of their people. Although less glamorous than the more dramatic confrontations that seize the headlines, economic transactions play a much more extensive and central role in today's international relations.

These five general goals usually are combined with political, ideological, and even personal considerations by the decision makers to determine the national interest in each specific transaction or confrontation, as we mentioned in our discussion of national interest (chapter 1).

Intergovernmental Organizations (IGOs)..

One of the striking developments of the twentieth century, and particularly of the period since the end of World War II, is the emergence and proliferation of intergovernmental organizations (IGOs) formed by sovereign governments. Whenever governments are convinced that their national interests can be best served through some form of structured cooperation with other governments, an IGO is likely to emerge. Two other considerations usually affect a government's decision to join: the belief that the problem involved is such that it cannot be solved by unilateral action, and the conviction that a decision to join does not pose a political threat to its domestic standing or to the future prospects and interests of the political group it represents.

The emergence of IGOs reflects the current trend toward *international regionalism*.[4] Integration may involve countries located within a specific geographic area, such as in the case of the European Economic Community (EEC). This is *regional integration*. Integration, however, may involve countries that share certain fundamental interests although they may be located in different parts of the globe. The Group of 77 and the Organization of Economic Cooperation and Development (OECD) are illustrations of such *functional integration*.

Governments participating in an IGO do not give up their country's sovereignty; nonetheless, they accept voluntarily some limitations to the exercise of their sovereign rights. They consider those limitations a necessary price for the benefits they expect to derive through their participation. This is a key point because it implies that:

1. The extent and form of cooperation is determined by the participating governments.

2. Participation cannot be seen as a permanent abridgment of sovereignty.

3. Cooperation and participation may be terminated or modified at the discretion of each sovereign member-state either unilaterally or in agreement with other members. For example, the French government decided in 1967 to withdraw from the military wing of NATO because De Gaulle wished to have the French military forces under exclusively French control. The decision to withdraw was greeted with expressions of regret by the other members—but it could not be prohibited by them. France remained active in NATO's political structure. The NATO IGO continued to function.

In other cases, IGOs disappeared altogether when the participating governments believed that the organization no longer served their interests. For example, in 1967, Kenya, Uganda, and Tanzania agreed to establish an East African Community to reduce trading barriers among themselves and promote their economic development. Ten years later, Tanzania closed its border with Kenya because of a dispute over the operations of East African Airways, leaving the East African Posts and Telecommunications Corporation as the only joint agency still functioning. A year later, in November 1978, Ugandan troops invaded Tanzania; however, within weeks Tanzanian troops, assisted by 3,000 exiles opposed to Uganda's President Idi Amin, launched a counteroffensive and in April 1979 captured the Ugandan capital, Kampala. One of the casualties of the conflict was the East African Community, which disappeared altogether.

A new IGO may be created to replace another. The League of Nations, for example, disintegrated in the storm of World War II, but in 1945 the United Nations emerged to take its place.

On occasion, governments participating in one organization decide to take more ambitious steps. The European Steel and Coal Community proved so successful that the participating European nations eventually decided to construct a more comprehensive and far-reaching organization, the European Economic Community (EEC).

An IGO may die quietly through prolonged inactivity. The Southeast Asia Treaty Organization (SEATO), one of the international organizations created in the 1950s to "contain" communist expansion, lapsed into limbo during the years of the Vietnam conflict and was never revived.

Although all IGOs share one common feature—they are voluntary associations of sovereign governments—they may be classified into several categories determined by the primary objective of each organization. Currently we have political, political–military, economic, technical, cultural, and service organizations. A few illustrations will give some idea of their diversity in structure, functioning, and objectives.

.... Political IGOs

The United Nations Organization

The most universal political IGO ever established is the United Nations Organization, founded in 1945. The effectiveness of the United Nations as a *political* IGO depends almost entirely on the willingness of its sovereign members to use its facilities and instrumentalities to settle their conflicts. We shall deal with the United Nations in more detail in chapter 8. Other political IGOs have a regional scope.

The Organization of American States

The Organization of American States (OAS), established in 1951, is designed to help settle inter-American disputes and promote regional cooperation in the Western hemisphere. A major weakness of this organization is the tremendous disparity in wealth and military might between one of its members, the United States, and other participants. This inequality has caused resentment, especially because Washington has repeatedly used the organization to clothe its policies with the appearance of hemispheric support. Another cause of weakness is the worldwide role of the United States. During the British–Argentinean dispute over the Falklands (Malvinas) Islands, Washington in the end sided with Britain, its NATO partner, rather than with Argentina, an OAS member.[5]

Be that as it may, the OAS has proved a useful forum for the discussion of issues that might otherwise have become overly divisive, and can be credited with moderating the traditional domination the United States has often sought to exert over other countries in the hemisphere. The OAS also has been useful in promoting economic, technical, and cultural cooperation among its members. One example was the "Alliance for Progress" launched by the Kennedy administration in 1961 at the Punta del Este meeting of OAS. Twenty years later, in February 1982, President Reagan announced to the OAS Permanent Council in Washington a $350 million program, known as the Caribbean Basin Initiative, designed to promote the economic development of Central American and Caribbean states. (In 1984, President Reagan proposed a more ambitious $8.6 billion economic and military aid program for Central America.)

The Organization of African Unity

Another organization designed to help settle disputes among its members and promote regional cooperation is the Organization of African Unity (OAU), founded in May 1963 by 32 African countries. Since that time, the organization has expanded its membership to include practically all African states—with the exception of South Africa, which is specifically excluded because of its apartheid policies.

The Charter of the OAU identifies certain basic principles supported by all its members. Among these principles, the organization includes the respect for the sovereignty and independent existence of each member; noninterference in the internal affairs of member-states; peaceful settlement of disputes by negotiation, conciliation, mediation, or arbitration; total commitment to the emancipation of all African peoples still under foreign rule; reaffirmation of a nonalignment policy with regard to all blocs; condemnation of political assassination and other subversive activities engineered by one member against another.

The OAU Charter provides for four principal organs: an Assembly of Heads of State and Government; a Council of Ministers; a General Secretary and a Secretariat; and a Commission of Mediation, Conciliation, and Arbitration.

Although the organization has not lived up to the ambitious expectations of some of its founders, and on occasion it has appeared on the verge of disintegration, it has been useful as a forum for the discussion of issues and the sketching of policies the members could pursue by joint action in other forums such as the United Nations, the United Nations Conference on Trade and Development (UNCTAD), the United Nations Conference on the Law of the Sea (UNCLOS), and elsewhere.

As does the OAS, the OAU to some extent deals with economic and technical matters, especially in the area of communications; nonetheless, its primary function is to provide a forum for political exchanges among its sovereign member-states. For this reason we include it among the political IGOs.

The Arab League

Another political organization that merits mention is the Arab League, which was originally formed in 1945 to coordinate the political activities of its members and to encourage their cooperation in economic, social, and cultural matters. The membership now includes all Arab states and the Palestinian Liberation Organization.[6] The supreme decision-making organ is the Council, which is composed of one representative from each member. Binding decisions require a unanimous vote. The most important political issue, of course, is the Palestinian question and the confrontation with Israel. Although the League meetings often are marked by dissension, the organization has survived, its membership has expanded, and its influence has increased.

Other Regional IGOs

The Association of Southeast Asian Nations (ASEAN) was established in 1967 to promote Asian solutions to Asian problems through cooperative arrangements. The group includes Indonesia, Malaysia, the Philippines, Singapore, and Thailand. Other less-familiar organizations include the Nordic Council, a Scandinavian regional organization with representatives from Denmark, Finland, Norway, Sweden, and Iceland; established in 1952, it has served as a forum for the discussion of social, cultural, legal, and economic matters of interest to the region. The Organization of Central American States (ODECA) was established in 1951 to promote cooperation among Costa Rica, El Salvador, Guatemala, Honduras, and Nicaragua. With the current turmoil in the region, this organization remains in limbo.

....Political–Military IGOs

The organizations in this category are in effect *alliances* designed to increase either each member's security against potential foes or its potential to exercise power in an aggressive fashion and realize gains it could not obtain by itself. We use the term *political–military* instead of *alliances* because in today's complex world some of the more important of these IGOs deal as much with political as they do with military matters.

In a way, alignments of this type have been in evidence longer than any other type of intergovernmental association. Although their organizational sophistication or complexity may have been limited, the basic elements were always present: sovereign governments agreed to work together—and fight together—to safeguard or advance their national interest. Usually, alliances were short-lived, and it was not uncommon for allies to turn against one another once the reasons that brought them together had disappeared.

The Inter-American Defense System

Since the end of World War II, several political–military IGOs have been founded. One of the earliest among them was the Inter-American Defense System (IADS), commonly known as the Rio Pact. This IGO was set up in 1948, with the participation of the United States and the Latin American republics. Canada did not become a member but was supportive of the objectives of the organization. The IADS was designed to provide a system of collective security for the members. The Pact stipulated that an act of aggression committed within the Western hemisphere would be faced jointly by all signatories.[7]

IGOs Founded to Counter
Communist Expansion

In the early 1950s, in the wake of the Korean War, Washington promoted the establish-
ment of several political–military IGOs in the context of its "policy of containment,"
designed to hold back Communist expansion. Among them, the Australia/New Zealand/
United States Pact (ANZUS) was signed in 1952, followed two years later by the
Southeast Asia Treaty Organization (SEATO), signed in Manila by representatives of
Australia, France, New Zealand, the Philippines, Thailand, Britain, and the United
States. Significantly, several important and strategically located countries in the region,
such as India, Ceylon, Indonesia, Burma, Cambodia, and Laos, stayed away. In 1955,
the Baghdad Pact brought together Turkey, Iraq, Iran, Pakistan, and Britain in a defense
structure designed to form a shield against Communist expansion in the Middle East.
The 1958 revolution in Iraq and the overthrow of its pro-Western monarchy removed
Iraq from the organization. The headquarters were moved out of Baghdad to Ankara,
and the organization was renamed Central Treaty Organization (CENTO). In the
following years, this organization lost much of its vitality in the cauldron of Middle
Eastern disputes and upheavals, and it eventually was dissolved in 1979. SEATO also
passed out of existence in the middle 1970s. ANZUS, on the other hand, composed of
three states with strong political, cultural, ideological, and economic ties, remains
active.

The North Atlantic
Treaty Organization

Currently, the two most important political–military IGOs are, of course, the North
Atlantic Treaty Organization (NATO) and its opposite number, the Warsaw Treaty
Organization (WTO). NATO evolved from the Brussels Pact, which was signed in
March 1948 by Britain, France, Belgium, the Netherlands, and Luxemburg. The
primary objective of the Brussels Pact was to prevent a resurgence of German militarism. The advent of the Cold War, however, soon shifted the emphasis toward European
defense against Soviet expansion. Lacking resources for such a task, the Pact members
invited the United States and Canada to participate. The two countries came in initially
as observers. Before long, in view of the increasing truculence of the Soviet Union in
Eastern Europe and in divided Germany, a new, wider arrangement gained support
among all the participants. In April 1949, the North Atlantic Treaty was signed, initially
by the five signatories of the Brussels Pact, and by Canada, the United States, Denmark,
Iceland, Italy, Norway, and Portugal. In 1952, Greece and Turkey were admitted, and in
1955 the Federal Republic of Germany became the fifteenth member. Spain joined in
1982, bringing the membership to sixteen.

Over the years, quite elaborate structures and procedures have been developed to
coordinate strategy, force requirements, weapons development, and detailed tactical
plans, which are constantly updated. These arrangements provide the means for coordinating the defense efforts of the individual members, identifying weaknesses, and
facilitating a continuous exchange of information and views among officers from
different (national) military establishments. All this is unique in the annals of history;
never before have partners in a military alliance agreed willingly to exchange detailed

military information and submit their own national military policies to the scrutiny of others.

The principal objective of NATO is to convince the Soviet Union that any attempt to change the status quo in Western Europe by military action will result in a military confrontation with the United States. NATO, of course, is not free of internal disagreements. American and European views on arms development, arms-control agreements, relations with the Soviet Union, or basic questions of strategy and tactics do not always coincide. Repeatedly, political analysts have predicted impending disintegration.[8] Thus far, however, the organization retains its vitality.

Although U.S. officials play a highly influential role in both the political and the military wings of NATO, it is inaccurate to say that NATO is merely an instrument of American foreign policy. Cooperation and policy coordination depend on extensive bargaining, give-and-take, and persuasion. In this regard, NATO differs from its eastern counterpart, the WPO, which is clearly dominated by the Soviet Union.

The Warsaw Pact Organization

In the early post–World War II years following the installation of pro-Soviet governments in the Eastern European countries (Poland, Czechoslovakia, Hungary, Romania, Bulgaria, Albania, and East Germany), the Soviet Union signed bilateral mutual defense pacts with each of its satellites. The Eastern European countries also signed similar agreements with each other. The treaties basically stated that if one of the signatories faced an attack, the other would come to the threatened country's aid. This mutual defense network was placed under one roof in May 1955, when a Collective Security Pact was signed in Warsaw by the Soviet Union and the seven East European satellites. This pact, justified by the Soviet government as a countermeasure to the rearming of West Germany within the NATO system, included six key provisions. The Warsaw Pact Organization (WPO) members agreed to:

(a) Settle international disputes peacefully and refrain from acts or threats of violence

(b) Consult with the other treaty members on all significant international problems, especially in the event of a threat of armed attack to one or more members

(c) Provide immediate assistance in case of armed aggression in Europe against any of the parties, such assistance to end when the Security Council of the United Nations has adopted measures designed to bring peace

(d) Establish a joint command of their armed forces and strengthen their defenses

(e) Create a political committee for consultative purposes

(f) Advance economic and cultural links between the parties without interference in the internal affairs of any member

The WPO does not have as elaborate a structure as does NATO. For all practical purposes, the Soviet Union provides an effective link with its military presence, political influence over the governments of the other member-states, and almost exclusive supply of armaments. The WPO military structure is under the command of a senior Soviet general.

The pledge of noninterference in the internal affairs of the member-states has been violated by the Soviet Union on at least three dramatic occasions: in Hungary (1956) and Czechoslovakia (1968) with open military intervention, and in Poland (1981–82) with political pressure. Moreover, under the so-called Brezhnev Doctrine, the Soviet Union claims the right to come to the rescue of the Marxist–Leninist regimes of the member-states if and when those regimes are in danger of being overthrown by *internal* political forces.

NATO and WPO thus far have kept the peace in Europe by confronting one another with unacceptable alternatives. WPO is superior in conventional military forces, but a Soviet attack on Europe could trigger a U.S. retaliation with nuclear weapons. Under the circumstances, the use of military force to alter the status quo is fraught with such risks that, thus far, war has been averted.

....Economic IGOs

Technological advances in communication, transportation, and the use of resources have undercut parochial views of self-sufficiency and economic ethnocentrism. Economic giants like the United States, Japan, and West Germany depend heavily on raw materials and fuels from areas that are outside their borders and controlled by other sovereign governments. The Soviet Union needs to import wheat and other grains from the United States and other countries. The developing countries in Africa, Asia, and Latin America need the cooperation and assistance of the industrialized countries of the Northern hemisphere, and primarily of the West, to improve the lot of their people and to promote their economic development. OPEC members cannot take advantage of their oil revenues except by buying goods and services from their oil customers or by investing their petrodollars mostly in the industrial nations.

Since the end of World War II, this multifaceted interdependence has led to a proliferation of organizations, agencies, and treaty arrangements designed to facilitate and promote trade, investment, and other economic exchanges on both a worldwide and a regional basis.

Worldwide ("Universal") Economic IGOs

One of the most important and active agencies that has a virtually worldwide scope is the International Bank for Reconstruction and Development (IBRD), popularly known as the World Bank. A product of the Bretton Woods Conference, which met in 1944 to create a new international monetary order, the IBRD has developed in ways its founders never imagined. Not only has its membership grown to over 145 member-states, but it also has become an important conduit for channeling financial resources from the rich, industrialized Northern hemisphere states to the Third World countries in the Southern hemisphere.

The World Bank, of course, is not a charitable organization. Prior to granting a loan, the World Bank must make certain that the prospective borrower cannot obtain the necessary capital through ordinary private capital markets, that the project is sound, and that the borrower will be able to repay the loan. Because of its conservative and restrictive lending practices, pressures from the less-developed countries (LDCs) led to the establishment of the International Finance Corporation (IFC) in 1956, designed to provide loans for private investment in LDCs without the governmental guarantees required by the IBRD. Another offshoot of the Bank, authorized to make "soft" loans at low interest rates and for long repayment terms to developing countries, is the International Development Association (IDA), established in 1960.

An initial component of the system introduced by the Bretton Woods agreements was the International Monetary Fund (IMF). This agency was designed to prevent a recurrence of the anarchic financial conditions of the 1930s, with their wildly fluctuating exchange rates and uncontrolled currency depreciations. The task of the IMF, also known as the Fund, was to promote exchange rate stability, establish a worldwide payments system, and create a pool of monetary reserves to help member states overcome destabilizing deficits in their balance of payments.

The experience with protectionist trade laws, especially before World War II, led U.S. and allied policy makers to focus on instrumentalities that would lead to freer trade arrangements. The General Agreement on Tariffs and Trade (GATT) initially was drawn up in 1947 to provide guiding principles to the delegates who held negotiations in Geneva. Eventually, GATT established an elaborate system for the mutual reduction of trade barriers, and from a temporary agreement it evolved into an international organization with a secretariat and a director general, authorized to oversee the implementation of GATT rules, follow changes in world trading patterns, and do the preparatory work for the international trade conferences that are called periodically to resolve problems or take additional measures. (More details on the World Bank, IMF, and GATT are given in chapter 7.)

IBRD, IFC, IDA, IMF, and GATT, despite the near-universality of their membership, have been dominated by the industrialized countries of the West, especially the United States. The LDCs have been able to exert only limited influence on the decision-making bodies of these IGOs. They believe, with good reason, that their bargaining ability, especially in trade negotiations, is weak and that the free trade policies of GATT in fact work against them. In 1961, the Third World countries in the United Nations, despite opposition from the Western industrial countries, succeeded in passing a resolution that called for an international conference on trade. In 1962, the Western powers abandoned their opposition and agreed to convene the first United Nations Conference on Trade and Development (UNCTAD). To strengthen their bargaining position, seventy-seven developing countries joined in sponsoring a Joint Declaration. This was the origin of the Group of 77 (although its membership has increased to 121 by the admission of more LDCs, it is still called by that name).

UNCTAD gained practical significance in 1964, when it became a permanent organization with a secretariat and a secretary-general. In this structured form,

UNCTAD has provided a valuable forum for the Third World countries, allowing them to present their views, especially their demand for greater participation in decisions affecting their economies.

An early achievement of UNCTAD was the modifications to GATT accepted by the industrial states under the terms of the so-called Part IV, which came into operation in 1965. The fifth UNCTAD meeting—UNCTAD V, held in 1979—affirmed the growing influence and cohesion of the LDCs. However, the industrialized countries of the West still show a marked reluctance to accept some of the more far-reaching reforms being sought by the Group of 77. The LDCs are pressing for a New International Economic Order (NIEO) and for "global negotiations" to devise arrangements that will help close the widening gap between the industrialized North and the underdeveloped South. The increasing reliance of the industrial powers on raw materials and energy resources located in and controlled by governments in the Group of 77 is gradually changing the bargaining realities between North and South.

Regional–Functional Economic IGOs

The most successful, and unquestionably the most important, regional IGO having primarily economic functions is the European Economic Community (EEC), popularly known as the European Common Market. In fact, the EEC is one of the three entities that make up the European Communities (EC), the other two being the European Coal and Steel Community (ECSC) and the European Atomic Energy Commission (Euratom). Currently, the full members of the EEC are France, West Germany, Italy, Britain, Belgium, Greece, the Netherlands, Denmark, Ireland, and Luxemburg. Early expectations that the EEC would pave the way to a "United States of Europe" are not near fulfillment. Despite occasional disagreements, however, the EEC has been quite successful in promoting economic cooperation and growth in Western Europe. It has virtually eliminated trade barriers among its members, established a common agricultural policy, eased labor and capital mobility, and created an economic entity that, in population, equals the United States and the Soviet Union and, in gross national product (GNP), is just behind the United States and far ahead of the Soviet Union. Most important, it continues to demonstrate how much can be gained through cooperation—after centuries of power politics, fighting, bloodshed, and destruction.

Relations among the members are not without friction. The December 1983 meeting in Athens, for example, ended in stalemate over the issue of member contributions to the common fund. Disagreements, however, are thrashed out within the various organs of the EEC and compromise solutions usually are found. Despite occasional reports that the EEC is in trouble, its prospects for the future are good. An indirect indication of the EEC's success is the desire of more countries either to become members or to forge some kind of special association with the EEC. Currently, Spain and Portugal are actively seeking membership. In addition, the EEC has established special economic arrangements with several African states and has accorded associate membership status to Turkey, Cyprus, Malta, Morocco, and Tunisia. It also has established a "special relationship" with Yugoslavia.

The trend toward economic cooperation among Europeans was initially fostered after World War II by the United States–financed Marshall Plan for European Recovery, which in 1948 led to the Organization of European Economic Cooperation (OEEC), an early regional organization with economic objectives. Initially, the Soviet Union and the East European states were invited to participate in the Marshall Plan. The Soviet government, however, declined the invitation and forced its satellites to do so as well; Czechoslovakia, which had accepted the invitation, was forced by Moscow to retract. This turned the OEEC into a Western European organization. In 1960, the membership of this organization was expanded beyond its regional scope to include non-European states. Its name was changed to Organization of Economic Cooperation and Development (OECD).[9] The OECD cannot be classified as a geographically regional organization; nor is it "universal"—its membership is restricted to developed capitalist states. It reflects rather a functional integration of advanced market economies.

In 1949, in reaction to the Marshall Plan and the OEEC, the Soviet government established the Council for Mutual Economic Assistance (CMEA or COMECON, as it is commonly known). Initially, the organization included the Soviet Union and its Eastern European satellites: Bulgaria, Czechoslovakia, East Germany, Hungary, Poland, Romania, and Albania. Albania dropped out after 1961, following its rift with the Soviet Union. Today the organization has ten full members, including Mongolia, Vietnam, and Cuba. Yugoslavia—which also has a "special relationship" with the EEC—has a "limited participation status" in the COMECON. Afghanistan, Angola, Ethiopia, Laos, Mozambique, and South Yemen have been accorded "observer status."

Other regional economic organizations of some importance include the Latin American Free Trade Association (LAFTA), whose members include Argentina, Brazil, Chile, Colombia, Ecuador, Mexico, Paraguay, Peru, Uruguay, and Venezuela. LAFTA has been only moderately successful in lowering tariffs because of the competitive nature of their trade, which consists mainly of primary commodities. In 1980, the ten LAFTA members formed with Bolivia a new Latin American Integration Association (LAIA) designed to overcome the shortcomings of LAFTA. Under the new arrangement, the more developed countries in the group were expected to grant more liberal concessions to the poorer ones. To encourage such action, LAIA divided the eleven signatories into three groups according to their level of economic development: the more advanced (Argentina, Brazil, and Mexico), the moderately developed (Chile, Colombia, Peru, Uruguay, and Venezuela), and the less developed (Bolivia, Ecuador, and Paraguay). LAIA has not been very successful in its efforts to overcome the difficulties that plagued LAFTA.

We can also include the Central American Common Market (CACM), the members of which are Costa Rica, El Salvador, Guatemala, Honduras, and Nicaragua. This organization virtually eliminated all customs duties among the members and, despite difficulties caused by underdeveloped economic conditions and nationalistic rivalries among the member-states, the CACM was fairly successful. In the 1980s, however, guerrilla warfare, revolutionary movements, governmental changes, and internal political difficulties sapped much of CACM's vitality.

Nongovernmental Organizations (NGOs)...

From multinational corporations to terrorist groups, the nongovernmental organizations (NGOs) have only one feature in common: they cannot claim sovereign authority and their membership is not composed of sovereign entities. Otherwise, they show tremendous variety in structure, objectives, operational methods, and importance. We include in this category business concerns, charitable organizations, professional associations, religious organizations, ideological and other *cause-oriented* groups, artistic associations, guerrilla bands, and terrorist groups.

....Multinational Corporations

The more important business enterprises of the NGOs are the so-called multinational corporations: business enterprises with operations in more than one country. Investments and commercial operations in foreign countries are not unique to our time. Ever since people started trading across frontiers, they have used commercial entities on foreign soil to facilitate operations. In more recent times, during the centuries of colonial expansion, large trading companies were formed to exploit the riches of far-flung possessions. The British East India Company in India, the Dutch East India Company in Java, the Hudson Bay Company in North America, and the Belgian *Fondation* in the Congo are illustrations. In the nineteenth century, subsidiaries were formed to engage not only in commerce but also in manufacturing, mining, and farming. By the end of the century, several U.S. companies had established branch operations in other countries. Neither the size of operations nor the extent of involvement, however, can compare to the dramatic expansion of international business activities since the end of World War II.

In the last thirty years, a new form of direct investment has emerged: the multinational corporation (MNC). These business entities engage in myriad activities ranging from mining and oil extraction to manufacturing of products, hotel and tourist services, banking, farming, or construction—virtually in all the familiar activities associated with business enterprises in the developed industrial states.[10]

MNCs normally start as companies operating within the boundaries and incorporated under the laws of their country of origin. As they grow, they establish subsidiaries in other countries under the host states' laws. MNCs differ in this from big corporations that merely market their products abroad. To be regarded as an MNC, a business must have direct investments in five or six foreign countries. [There is no formal requirement regarding the number of foreign locations; a company could have subsidiaries in only three. However, the overwhelming majority (80 percent) of U.S. MNCs have subsidiaries in six or more countries.]

As a rule, the subsidiaries are owned by the parent corporation either directly through sole ownership or indirectly through joint arrangements with local firms. In any event, the major advantage of an MNC is that through centralized control of world-wide operations it can achieve greater efficiency and profitability.

The size and wealth of many MNCs has become a political issue, because the possibility that they could interfere in the domestic affairs of a host country cannot be discounted.[11] Each of the 200 major MNCs realized more than $2.5 billion in gross income from sales and operations in 1981. Exxon, the largest MNC, made $103 billion in sales—having a larger income than that of 142 member-states of the United Nations, and being between those of Belgium ($107.3 billion GNP) and Sweden ($98.5 billion GNP).[12]

Because an MNC's gross income from sales and services is the rough equivalent of a sovereign state's GNP, we conclude that MNCs have a remarkable record in productivity and efficient use of resources. No MNC employs more than 600,000 people, yet the gross income of MNCs far exceeds the GNP of states with much larger populations.

MNCs often are associated with the notions of exploitation and domination. We should then expect that these giants would be attracted to the weaker, underdeveloped countries of the Third World, which are logically more exposed and vulnerable. However, more than two-thirds of all foreign direct investments by MNCs are located in the developed, industrialized countries.[13]

It would be unrealistic to expect that MNCs would not exercise influence over political and economic decisions in the countries where they operate—just as they exercise influence over decisions made in their country of origin. But there is a great deal of difference between *power* or *domination* and *influence*. Only rarely are MNCs able to impose their views on the government of their state of origin or of the host country. As a rule, the most they hope to achieve is to protect their interests through bargaining, knowing that their continuing presence in the host country depends on the willingness of the host government to allow their operations.[14] If an MNC is either nationalized or thrown out, it cannot expect that its country of origin will try to pressure the host country by using force. The most an MNC in trouble can expect is some assistance through bargaining between the government of the host country and that of the country of origin.

MNCs may have a positive effect on the preservation of peace. After all, to be profitable the MNCs need to be able to operate as freely and as safely as possible across national frontiers. This is best achieved under conditions of relative stability and order. Without overlooking the fact that there may be exceptions, one may argue that to the extent MNCs can influence international relations their thrust is likely to be on the side of the peaceful resolution of conflicts. This is not to say that MNCs are never involved in domestic or international conflicts when their interests may be served by the conflict itself or by a particular outcome. The available record, however, shows that such involvement is the exception, not the rule. (MNCs will be further discussed in chapters 7 and 10.)

Militant NGOs

Armed groups of revolutionaries have more than once played a significant role in giving a new direction to the course of world history. Since the end of World War II, the activities of *national liberation movements* have become a major source of international conflict: more than fifty serious military conflicts have been provoked by the activities of nongovernmental groups seeking to bring about changes by force. Such operations included the Communist-led guerrilla operation in Greece, which led to the Truman Doctrine; the civil war in China, which ended with a Marxist–Leninist government in

Beijing, the Mau Mau uprising in Kenya, which convinced the British that the colonial era was rapidly coming to an end, either peacefully or in a bloodbath; the Vietcong campaign in South Vietnam, which led to the involvement of the United States and the first major military failure of one of the superpowers; the guerrilla operation in Cuba, which brought Fidel Castro to power; the Sandinista campaign in Nicaragua, which brought down the Somoza regime. Dozens of similar movements are active in various parts of the world at this moment, such as the Polisario in Western Sahara, the Moslem guerrillas in Afghanistan, the Eritrean People's Liberation Front in Ethiopia, the Farabundo Marti Liberation Front in El Salvador, and the South-West African People's Organization (SWAPO) in Namibia.

Revolutionary organizations, as a rule, do not gain recognition by sovereign governments until they succeed in taking over inhabited territories. One of the few exceptions is the Palestinian Liberation Organization (PLO), which was accorded a degree of recognition and legitimacy by the United Nations, several European governments, and most countries of the Third World, as well as by the Soviet Union and its satellites.

As is true of other international actors, the ability of the national liberation organizations to exercise power or to wield influence depends on the assets they can mobilize; the support they can generate and receive, both from their own public and from other international actors; and the quality of their leadership.

....International Terrorism

Although the activists and fighters of national liberation organizations often are regarded as terrorists by their opponents, and although national liberation organizations on occasion engage in terrorist activities, the groups that we classify as *terrorist* differ in several important aspects:

1. Terrorist groups are composed of a relatively small number of individuals.

2. They do not seek wide popular support and cooperation.

3. They make their presence known through specific acts of violence, usually directed against exposed, undefended targets.

4. They are not associated, as a rule, with a territory and a national group seeking a drastic change in the status quo.

5. They are not necessarily connected with broad, popular organizations or movements, except at best in an emotional, ideological way.

Because terrorist groups cannot expect to promote their goals through bargaining and negotiation, they rely heavily on force and violence. Assassinations, kidnappings, hijackings of airliners, attacks against unarmed civilians or public officials, and bombings of buildings are their stock in trade. Terrorists may be regarded as criminals by their victims or their adversaries, but in their own eyes they are revolutionaries or patriots fighting for a "just and noble cause." Rajaie Khorassani, the Iranian delegate to the United Nations, said, "Who are the terrorists? They are individuals who when they look at the world see only the dirt and the treachery and the awful things, and they throw themselves into destroying it."[15] In the eyes of their supporters, terrorists who engage in suicide attacks are martyrs.

Defense against terrorist operations is extremely difficult because neither the time, nor the place, nor the intended victim can be predicted.

Social, Humanitarian, and Service NGOs

Numerous organizations of an ideological, occupational, artistic, social, religious, scientific, humanitarian, or economic nature exist. Although many of them receive occasionally some financial or moral support from governments, their key characteristic is their composition; their members as well as their leaders invariably are private citizens. Another important feature of these NGOs is their mode of operation. They rely exclusively on bargaining and persuasion to deal with governments. Force is not one of their operational tools. A random listing will show how widely they vary in structure, composition, and objectives: the International Red Cross; Amnesty International; the Tri-Lateral Commission; the Socialist International; the Catholic Church; the International Political Science Association; the Rotary Club; the Inter-American Press Association.

Although the influence potential of these organizations should not be exaggerated, they do provide contacts and opportunities for human interaction that in the long run may have a beneficial effect on the overall conduct of international relations.

Summary

- The principal international actors fall into three major groups: sovereign states, intergovernmental organizations (IGOs), and nongovernmental organizations (NGOs).

- Sovereign states are associated with a fairly specific piece of territory inhabited by a population under a sovereign government.

- A sovereign government is not legally subject to any superior authority and has exclusive jurisdiction over the territory of the state it governs.

- Sovereign states pursue certain goals that affect their perception of their national interest. These goals are: the preservation of the state, the defense of its territorial integrity, the preservation of its independence against outside interference, the protection of its international prestige, and the promotion of its prosperity and wellbeing.

- IGOs are formed by sovereign governments and reflect the current trend toward international regionalism, which may be based on regional or functional integration. IGOs can be classified as political, political–military (alliances), and economic (universal and regional–functional).

• NGOs are composed of private individuals, not sovereign entities. A great variety of entities is included in this group: multinational corporations, militant (revolutionary) groups, and social, humanitarian, and service organizations.

Notes

1. These concepts are used here as defined in Kousoulas, D. G. *On Government and Politics*. 5th ed. Monterey, Calif.: Brooks/Cole, 1983, p. 248.

2. Sabine, George H. *A History of Political Theory*. 3rd ed. New York: Holt, Rinehart & Winston, 1961, p. 405.

3. Johnson, Lyndon B. *The Vantage Point*. New York: Holt, Rinehart & Winston, 1971, pp. 121–132.

4. Nye, Joseph S., Jr., ed. *International Regionalism*. Boston: Little, Brown, 1968.

5. Del Carril, Bonifacio. *The Malvinas/Falklands Case*. Buenos Aires: Camara de Industriales Graficos de la Argentina, 1982.

6. Following its treaty with Israel (1979), Egypt was expelled from the League. In 1984, however, a move was underway to bring Egypt back into the organization.

7. In the spring of 1982, the United States did not interpret the British military action to retake the Falkland (Malvinas) Islands as "aggression" and did not side with Argentina; see Goebel, Julius. *The Struggle for the Falklands: A Study in Legal and Diplomatic History*. New Haven: Yale University Press, 1982.

8. See, for example, Freedman, Lawrence. "Is NATO Obsolete?" *World Politics 83/84,* pp. 70–72. Reprinted from *World Press Review,* November 1982.

9. Currently the OECD members are Australia, Austria, Belgium, Canada, Denmark, Finland, France, the Federal Republic of Germany, Greece, Iceland, Ireland, Italy, Japan, Luxemburg, the Netherlands, New Zealand, Norway, Portugal, Spain, Sweden, Switzerland, Turkey, the United Kingdom, and the United States.

10. Frank, Isaiah. *Foreign Enterprise in Developing Countries*. Baltimore: Johns Hopkins University Press, 1980.

11. Piñelo, Adalberto J. *The Multinational Corporation as a Force in Latin American Politics: A Case Study of the International Petroleum Company in Peru*. New York: Praeger, 1973; Connor, John. *The Market Power of Multinationals: A Quantitative Analysis of U.S. Corporations in Brazil and Mexico*. New York: Praeger, 1977.

12. Sales data are from *Fortune,* August 10, 1981, p. 205.

13. United Nations. *Transnational Corporations in World Development: A Reexamination*. New York: United Nations, 1978, p. 254.

14. Huntington, Samuel. "Transnational Organizations in World Politics." *World Politics,* April 1973, pp. 333–368.

15. *The Washington Post,* February 10, 1984.

3

.................The Determinants
of Capability:
Tangible and
Intangible Assets

Arab villager and oil well

The ability of international actors to exercise power or to influence the outcome of international events or transactions depends on the resources and other assets they can bring to bear. Because among all international actors the sovereign states continue to hold the center of the stage, it is appropriate to discuss in greater detail the assets their governments can use to protect or promote their country's national interests. Some of those assets are tangible, subject to measurement and quantification, such as natural resources, territory, population, industrial output, armaments, or financial and other economic resources. Others are intangible, such as the quality of leadership, the cohesion of the nation, the traditions, qualities, and social habits of its people, the determination and effectiveness of its fighting force, and the effect of ideological convictions.

Tangible Assets ....

We will discuss each tangible asset separately, beginning with those that are related to the state's territory.

.... Geography

Every sovereign state occupies territory. The location, size, climate, topography, and shape of that territory may affect seriously, for good or ill, a government's ability to exercise power or influence in its relations with other governments. The effects and significance of each of these aspects of geography deserve some discussion. A nation's fate is often determined by them.

Location

Location may be a serious handicap, an advantage, or a potential bargaining chip. Twice in this century, Belgium and the Netherlands suffered the hardships of invasion and foreign occupation because they happened to be located between two major powers, France and Germany. Israel is another country whose location is at the root of much of its insecurity. Located in a strategically critical part of the globe, surrounded by millions of Arabs, Israel is suffering the effects of its geographic location.

The United States, on the other hand, certainly has benefited from its location. Located between two great oceans, it has been virtually immune to military invasion.

Although Soviet ICBMs (intercontinental ballistic missiles) can now reach and destroy both civilian and military targets on U.S. soil, a Soviet invasion is still virtually impossible. By contrast, both the Soviet Union and the West European states are capable of invading each other's territories. In other words, whereas the United States is not exposed to a Soviet invasion, the Soviet Union is subject to an invasion by U.S. forces acting in concert with the NATO forces in Europe.

Location may contribute to a country's influence potential. For example, Turkey's control of the Straits of the Dardanelles is a strategic asset that increases Turkey's leverage and makes its foreign policy orientations a major concern for its NATO allies or for the Soviet Union.

It is difficult to quantify the effects of geographic location on a country's power or influence potential. We can, however, make certain obvious generalizations. Proximity to powerful neighbors inhibits a country's freedom of action in time of crisis and may even jeopardize its very existence. Unhindered access to the open seas is a significant advantage, whereas a land-locked territory tends to be a handicap. Control of strategic locations that may facilitate or inhibit transit, especially in times of crisis or war, enhances a country's influence potential. It may also become a cause of trouble if other, more powerful states decide to bring the strategic location under their own control to deprive access to their adversaries. For centuries, Russia fought against the Ottoman Empire to bring the Bosporus and the Dardanelles under its control, only to be frustrated by the counteractions of Britain and other European powers. On the other hand, remoteness from the major centers of international conflict and interaction can be an advantage. The countries of Latin America were completely spared the havoc wrought by World War II, primarily because of their geographic location.

Geographic location becomes a factor affecting the power or influence potential of a state for another reason: climate.

Climate

We have yet to develop effective means that can change a country's climate. Yet climate has a direct bearing on several factors that affect a country's power or influence potential. The production of food, for example, is heavily affected by climate. Inadequate rainfall, a short growing season, or extremely low or very high temperatures have an adverse effect on agriculture. Conversely, a country blessed with a benign climate and a highly productive agriculture may use its abundance of foodstuffs to exercise influence around the world. We must note, however, that in our complex world food is only one of the assets a country may use in its transactional relationships; its overall influence potential depends on a complex combination of factors. The United States, for example, accounts for approximately 40 percent of world wheat exports and over 55 percent of feed grains. This is certainly an advantage that could be used to enhance its influence potential; but when other factors enter the picture, such as U.S. policies that conflict with the objectives of other actors on the world stage, the influence of the United States may be adversely affected. In any event, although an abundance of food may not secure a country's influence, the absence of adequate supplies definitely inhibits its power potential.

Climate also may affect the ability of human beings to function effectively. In the arctic regions, living conditions are not conducive to vigorous work or the growth of a large and vigorous population. History does not record the emergence of great empires north of the 60th parallel. On the other hand, it appears that it is easier for humans to sustain relatively high temperatures, although such a climate may tend to inhibit activity. In earlier centuries, significant civilizations emerged in the general area of equatorial Africa, such as the Kushites, or in Central America, such as the Incas. However, it is an undisputed fact of history that practically all the major empires emerged and flourished in the lands located between the 20th and 60th parallel (north) in the temperate zone where they were not subject to extremes of climate.

Climate also may undercut the effect size usually has on the power or influence potential of a country. Canada's territory is larger than that of the United States (3,851,809 square miles and 3,512,406 square miles, respectively), but the cold climate renders two-thirds of Canada virtually uninhabitable. Libya covers an area of 679,536 square miles, but only a narrow strip along the Mediterranean coast is suitable for human habitation; the rest is arid desert. Libya's population is less than 3 million. Contrast this to France, which has a comparable area of 551,600 square miles, but has a population exceeding 54 million.

Terrain

Like the location or climate of a country, the morphology of its terrain is not subject to drastic changes by human action. Only minor changes are possible. Mountains cannot be leveled and turned into fertile plains, arid deserts cannot be transformed into lakes, the course of rivers can be changed only marginally. Canals may be opened to supplement navigable rivers or to connect separate bodies of water (Suez Canal, Panama Canal), or rivers may be dammed to form large lakes (Aswan), but the fact remains that the overall topography of our planet has changed little since the last ice age.

The configuration of the terrain is an important factor in determining a country's influence and power potential because it affects other critical elements. The United States possesses a total of 736 million acres of good farmland, of which only 350 million acres are currently in cultivation. These expanses of land covered with good soil form the foundation of U.S. food production.[1]

The fairly level lands that extend from the Rhine to the Ural Mountains on the western edge of Siberia have been a mixed blessing for those who inhabit them. Fertile and productive in times of peace, they become a corridor of death in time of war. Since antiquity, great armies have swept in both directions: the Huns in A.D. 360; the Mongol invasions of 1241 and 1259; Tamerlane in 1400, the Polish invasions of Russia in the fifteenth and sixteenth centuries; and, in more recent times, Napoleon's fateful campaign into Russia in 1812; Hitler's invasion of the Soviet Union in 1941; and the advance of the Red Army from the banks of the Volga to the Elbe river in the heart of Germany. All of these events attest to the role the morphology of central Europe and the European part of Russia has played through the ages.

On occasion, the morphology of a relatively small—and normally insignificant—piece of territory may acquire extraordinary importance for a given country. The Golan

Heights, rising steeply above the Israeli territory, offered Syria a vantage point for shelling the Israeli positions and rural settlements below until 1967, when the Israeli army seized the strategic heights. In 1981, the Israeli government defied international opprobrium and formally extended its political rule to the Heights in a move that amounted to annexation.

Size

Certainly it is no mere accident that the two superpowers today cover several million square miles. Size obviously is potentially an important factor in power and influence; but, as our previous discussion about climate and morphology has shown, the significance of size may be affected by other factors. Nonetheless, large size has advantages.

An expanse of territory located in the temperate zone is bound to be inhabited by a large population. It is also likely to include within its boundaries various types of terrain, rivers, mountains, valleys, lakes, and fertile plains. Chances are that such a large area also will be endowed with minerals and other underground resources. When this large territory is brought under the political control of a single sovereign entity, the potential for the exercise of power and influence is considerable.

In time of war, size may be a critical factor. A most familiar illustration is offered by Russia. As both Napoleon and Hitler discovered, the expanses of territory allowed the Russian high command to prepare for a counterattack in secure areas far away from the front. A large size further enables a country to disperse its vital production centers in time of war and thus prevent their destruction. Of course, this is relevant only in the case of conventional warfare; in a nuclear exchange, dispersal may not provide effective protection.

A large country will have long frontiers with other countries or extensive coastlines. Unless the country has managed to maintain peaceful relations with its immediate neighbors, the long frontiers may necessitate a large military force, which may prove a heavy economic burden. The Soviet Union finds it necessary to maintain large forces along its border with China, and along its western frontier to counter the NATO forces.

By contrast, the United States needs no more than immigration officials and local police to patrol the 3,000 miles of its common border with Canada or the 1,500 miles of border with Mexico.

Large size may have certain disadvantages. Administration by a central government may pose practical problems, as effective supervision and coordination calls for an efficient bureaucratic apparatus. Another disadvantage may be the need to devote considerable resources to develop an effective network of transport and communication. Technological developments in the last 200 years have made communication among various regions of a large country easier.

Whatever the drawbacks of a large size may be, the advantages are so great that history does not record many governments that deliberately and willingly opted for less territory.

Unlike location or climate, the size of a country is subject to change by human action. Most of the wars throughout history were fought over the acquisition or the defense of territory, which is indicative of the advantages of larger size.

....Natural Resources

Since the earliest days of history, governments have sought to acquire territory for several reasons ranging from an effort to gratify the instinct of acquisition and possession, to the need to provide for defense or gain greater power and influence potential. One very important motivation that deserves special attention at this point is the acquisition of economic resources.

The natural resources directly associated with a given piece of territory are found either on the surface or underground.

In the first group we include fertile soil, abundance of fresh water, forests, and animal life on land or in the sea. These resources become relevant to a country's influence or power as they are developed for energy or the production of food, fiber, or housing materials.

Important as above-ground resources are, they are overshadowed by the importance of the resources that are underground, primarily minerals and fossil fuels.[2] For the past 6,000 years, the extraction and processing of ores has contributed critically to the emergence of the great civilizations and empires. With the advent of industrialization in the last 200 years, the importance of underground resources took a quantum leap.

Natural resources may be classified as (1) energy resources and (2) raw materials. The simplest criterion for distinguishing them is that the energy resources are used primarily to provide power for the transportation and processing of the raw materials. However, the distinction is not absolute. Oil is one of today's most significant energy resources, yet oil also is the raw material for a tremendous variety of finished products. The same applies to coal. Water can be used as an energy resource (hydroelectric power), but it is also indispensable to the sustenance of human life in many other ways. Be that as it may, our discussion will be less confusing if we focus separately on those resources that primarily are needed to provide energy, and on those that primarily are used to manufacture finished products.

Energy Resources

The five principal resources used to produce energy today are: oil, coal, nuclear energy, natural gas, and water.[3] All five are used to produce some form of mechanical motion through electricity, steam, or contained and controlled combustion. Only water uses the natural force of gravity to move mechanical devices (turbines), which in turn produce electricity.

Oil. Even a large country may not be completely self-sufficient in energy resources. Currently, the United States, a country richly endowed by nature, imports approximately 42 percent of the oil it uses annually. Other industrial countries are even less fortunate. Japan relies almost totally on imported oil (over 99 percent), its domestic production being merely 0.6 million metric tons. The same is true of France and West Germany (France produces 1 million metric tons, West Germany 5.4). Britain also was heavily dependent on imported oil until the discovery of the North Sea oil deposits. The Soviet Union is currently self-sufficient in oil and other energy resources, but this may change in the future as its economy expands.[4]

Access to oil resources obviously is vital to the countries that have a deficit of this fuel. Because those resources are controlled by sovereign governments, an interruption (as happened during the 1973 oil embargo) or a serious disruption because of price increases or production cut-backs may occur. Also domestic upheavals, such as those of Iran, may disrupt supplies. Thus far, the oil-exporting countries have relied on the revenues from the sale of their oil for their own economic development and purchase of foodstuffs, industrial commodities, or arms. They have a practical incentive to continue exporting oil regardless of political or ideological considerations. For example, Angola's Marxist government amiably cooperates with Western oil companies for the extraction and marketing of its oil.

Access depends on the unhindered transportation of oil, mostly over the open seas. Freedom of navigation is a major concern for the industrialized countries of the West and for other oil-importing countries. This explains the sensitivity of many Western governments, especially that of the United States, to the increasing strength and activity of the Soviet navy, which is viewed as posing a potential threat to the vital sea lanes of the world.

Coal. A critical source of energy, coal is unevenly distributed through the globe. Forty-three countries have coal deposits (as far as is currently known). Of these, only fourteen are significant coal producers. Among the major producers, ten are industrialized countries and the other four (China, India, North Korea, and South Korea) are among the more vigorously developing LDCs. Currently, of 2,476 million metric tons worldwide annual production, 2,322 metric tons are produced by these fourteen countries, as shown in table 3-1.

Coal was a primary source of energy long before oil attained preeminence in the last eighty years. Since the iron age, access to coal and iron deposits has been a critical element in the emergence of militarily powerful empires. In the last 300 years, the industrial revolution was launched and advanced in large measure because of the fortuitous coexistence of coal and iron deposits within easy reach in Britain, Europe, and the United States. Especially with the development of effective methods for making steel (which requires the combination of anthracite with iron), coal became an indispensable resource both for industrial development and for the forging of modern military forces.

Table 3-1
Annual Coal Production (1980)

Country	Coal (metric tons)	Country	Coal (metric tons)
United States	603.1	South Africa	85.6
Soviet Union	499.8	North Korea	45.1
China	490.0	Czechoslovakia	28.4
Poland	186.1	France	23.0
United Kingdom	122.2	Japan	18.2
India	100.0	South Korea	17.2
West Germany	91.3	Spain	12.1

Nuclear Energy. Electric energy produced through controlled nuclear fission was first achieved in the United States in December 1951, at the National Reactor Testing Station in Idaho. From that early beginning, nuclear fission has become an important source of energy. Currently, seventy-one nuclear power plants are in operation in the United States. More than twenty other countries currently operate nuclear power plants, and several others are planning such installations. Although uranium deposits have been found in various parts of the world, access to uranium ores is not enough. More important is the supply of processed fissionable material; only a very few major industrial countries (the United States, Britain, France, and the Soviet Union) are currently potential suppliers.

Because the by-products of nuclear plants may be used in the production of nuclear weapons, the United Nations established the International Atomic Energy Agency, headquartered in Vienna, Austria, in 1957. The objective of this agency is not only to promote the use of nuclear energy for peaceful purposes but, more important, to exercise some supervision over the use of nuclear power plants. The control exercised by the agency inspectors is not foolproof, however, and misuse of atomic materials for military purposes can occur. A dramatic incident, resulting from this lack of confidence in the effectiveness of international control, was the Israeli air raid against the Osirik reactor near Baghdad, Iraq, on June 7, 1981; Israel charged that nuclear by-products from this reactor could be used militarily.

Natural Gas. Found often near petroleum fields, natural gas deposits are widespread throughout the planet. Significant reserves are located in the United States, Canada, Mexico, Latin America, the Soviet Union, Poland, Romania, Norway, the Netherlands, the Middle East, Libya, Algeria, Nigeria, India, Indonesia, and Australia.[5]

The natural gas is transported from the fields to the consumption centers either in liquified form or through pipelines. Extensive pipelines have been built in North America. A trans-Mediterranean gas pipeline to take gas from Algeria to Italy was completed in 1981. Another major pipeline is the projected 3,200-mile pipeline that will bring 40 billion cubic meters of gas annually from the Yamal Peninsula in Soviet Siberia to Western European countries, notably France, West Germany, Italy, Belgium, and Austria. This project became the subject of international controversy during the early 1980s.

Water. Unlike the other energy resources, water is replenishable. Oil, coal, or gas deposits will be exhausted sooner or later. The earth can produce no more than what already exists. Water, on the other hand, is recycled continuously through rainfall and evaporation. This is a significant advantage. On the other hand, hydroelectric power can be generated only within the immediate vicinity of running water. (Transportation of water to generate hydroelectric power would be totally uneconomic.) However, electricity produced by hydroelectric plants can be moved over fairly long distances by using power lines.

Water is the most widely—and evenly—distributed source of potential energy throughout the world. Hydroelectric power has the added advantage that it results in minimal environmental pollution. The harnessing of water resources for hydroelectric power often requires the cooperation of neighboring countries, thus contributing to closer relations. The Itaipu Dam (the largest in the world in megawatt production) was constructed by Brazil and Paraguay. Cooperative projects also have been undertaken by Argentina and Uruguay, Zimbabwe and Zambia, and Romania and Yugoslavia.

Raw Materials

Much of the energy produced from the resources we have discussed is used for transportation, communications, construction, food production, and myriad other applications. Over one-half of the energy, however, is used to process raw materials.

Ever since the beginning of the iron age 3,000 years ago, access to iron ore deposits and the ability to process them for the manufacturing of tools or weapons has been a principal factor for increasing productivity and military might. The development of steel less than 200 years ago opened a new chapter in the story of economic development, and in large measure made industrialization as we know it today possible.

Although iron ore remains a critical raw material, and steel production is a basic indicator of a country's industrial capacity and military potential, other raw materials gained importance during the last 100 years as the technological and scientific revolution brought about the spectacular development of new products.

Most of the raw materials that are today indispensable to industrial production are found underground and, as are most energy resources, are unevenly distributed through our planet. No country in the world has exploitable deposits of all the important minerals and other raw materials needed to supply a developed economy.[6] Only the Soviet Union has a fairly wide variety, but even it is not completely self-sufficient. The United States, Western Europe, and Japan depend heavily on imports, primarily from countries located in the Southern hemisphere—usually those in the Third World. Table 3-2 illustrates the dimensions of this dependence.

Table 3-2
Net Imports of Nonfuel Minerals*

Mineral	United States	EEC	Japan	COMECON
Manganese	98	100	99	3
Cobalt	97	100	100	68
Bauxite	91	97	100	28
Asbestos	85	90	98	1
Chromium	91	100	98	2
Nickel	70	100	100	13
Zinc	58	91	74	9
Iron Ore	48	82	98	5
Silver	36	93	71	10
Copper	13	100	97	4
Lead	13	76	78	3

*(Percent of consumption.)
Source: Department of Commerce, Bureau of the Census and Report of the Economic Dependency Panel, World Affairs Forum, June 17, 1980.

The Issue of Exhaustibility

Most raw materials—especially minerals—are exhaustible. Although new deposits may be discovered, the planet has finite quantities of most mineral or energy sources that, once used, are no longer available—except through recycling, which is not always feasible and usually affects the quality of the product. The few industrial raw materials that are replenishable include natural rubber and fibers obtained through agriculture or animal husbandry.

Because of this exhaustibility of natural resources, some scientists have suggested that the current trend toward continuing and unlimited economic growth should be revised and that a more moderate pace should be adopted. Although this "limits of growth" school of thought has had only limited influence on public policy, it has fostered greater awareness of the problem and more public support for conservation measures and less wasteful use of resources.[7]

Concern about the exhaustibility of natural resources has prompted increasing interest in the possibility of tapping the mineral resources that are scattered on the ocean floor in the form of nodules or are buried beneath the bottom of the sea. Although actual mining of these minerals on a large scale may not occur until some time in the future, the prospect has given rise to an international controversy. The LDCs, which do not have the technological capability to exploit these ocean resources, have sought to establish an international authority to supervise extraction and assure the equitable sharing of benefits by all states. Such an Authority was included in the Convention of the Law of the Sea, which was adopted on April 30, 1982, after nine years of negotiations. The United States objected to the regimentation involved in the operations of the Authority; this was one of the reasons Washington did not sign the Convention.

The Question of Access

We hardly need point out that access to the sources of fuels as well as of raw materials is a necessity for the industrial countries. During the colonial era, the European powers were assured of access through their direct control of the territories containing the coveted resources. Today, access depends for the most part on trade and on international agreements reached through bargaining. Obviously, governments having sovereign control over the sources of supply can slow down or even stop exports altogether. In times of peace, such serious interruptions are not likely for the simple reason that such exports can provide a country with the foreign exchange it needs to purchase other products from abroad. At a time of crisis, however, interruption of supplies may be used as a means of international blackmail. This concern is at the heart of Western apprehensions over the emergence of regimes that may be willing to cooperate with the Soviet Union at a time of a serious confrontation, thus adding to the latter's leverage and strengthening its bargaining or power potential.

Access requires unhindered transportation. Because most raw materials (including oil and coal) are bulky, and because great distances separate the areas of supply from the user countries, shipping across the oceans is the most effective transportation method.

Freedom of the open seas, and uninterrupted passage through narrow straits that connect one large body of water with another, is of vital importance to all countries. Soviet support, for example, for the Marxist regimes of Ethiopia and South Yemen goes beyond ideological solidarity and reflects a strategic interest in gaining control—especially at a time of crisis—over the Straits of Aden (Bab el Mandeb), which connect the Indian Ocean with the Red Sea and, through the Suez Canal, with the Mediterranean. In another part of the globe, the suspected support by Castro's Cuba (and also presumably by the Soviet Union) for Marxist-oriented "liberation movements" in Central America was regarded by Washington in the early 1980s as posing a potential threat to the freedom of navigation through the Panama Canal.

....The Human Factor

With the possible exception of fruit growing wild in a tropical forest and picked by native children, almost all natural resources require the application of human action before they are transformed into wealth.

Population is usually an important asset; under certain conditions it may also become a serious liability. In Bangladesh, a large population in an overcrowded land with inadequate resources is not a blessing. Normally, however, a large population is an essential factor for power and influence. No sovereign entity rose to imperial eminence without the large population needed for great armies, for a working force to supply the soldiers, and for the bureaucratic structure needed to transform decisions into action and to keep the population under control.

A large population does not necessarily result in great power status. If the size of population were the only or even the major determinant of power, China would be today the first-ranking superpower, and India would be second. A large population is likely to become a decisive asset for the exercise of power and influence only when combined with certain critical elements such as composition, level of education, and productivity of citizens.

Composition

A nation made up mostly of children and old people will have a problem, because children up to the age of fifteen years and older people above sixty years are not normally suited to productive work or for military service. Moreover, a large proportion of young children requires heavy expenditures for public education, whereas a large population of older people may demand sizeable outlays for their support. These expenditures for nonproductive groups have to be financed by the productive citizens, mostly those between sixteen and sixty years of age. A population analysis has to take into account not just the total population but the number of productive citizens. Also, the number of adult men as compared to that of women may be of importance, especially in connection with the buildup of military forces. Although in many modern states women actively participate in the production effort, the military still rely primarily, although not exclusively, on men.

Figure 3-1 shows the population composition by age and sex for selected countries.

Figure 3-1
Population composition in selected advanced and developing countries.

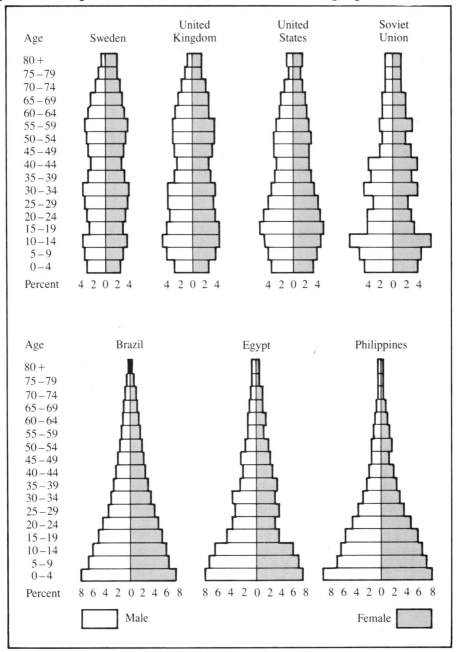

SOURCE: Based on the New International Atlas, © 1980 by Rand McNally & Co.; reprinted by permission.

Education

For a long time, both production and war relied on instruments and methods that people could master without being able to read or write. Artisans passed their trade secrets from generation to generation mostly by word of mouth and on-the-job training; soldiers learned the martial arts through practical experience, often gained on the battlefield. In the last 200 years, universal education has become a critical method for raising productivity and military effectiveness. Not only have the production techniques and military tasks become more complicated, requiring educated personnel; education itself has helped sharpen the intelligence, inventiveness, and initiative of individuals. The effects of education at times can be spectacular. In 1967, the Israeli army, although numerically inferior to that of Egypt, benefited decisively not only from the higher morale but also from the superior educational level of the average Israeli soldier. Even in 1973, the Egyptian army, despite initial successes, was unable to overpower the Israelis.

The technical sophistication of today's weapons—even conventional ones—makes their use by inadequately educated individuals problematic. After all, the most impressive weapon is no more than an ingenious assembly of metallic and other components until it is activated and put into proper use by well-trained and experienced personnel. Moreover, education is directly related to productivity.

Productivity

Every country with a large population is likely to have a sizeable gross national product (GNP; the total output of goods and services). But volume of GNP alone is not a reliable indicator of productivity. A much more relevant parameter in evaluating the effect the size of population has on a country's power or influence potential is the *per capita income* (PCI).

Bangladesh ranks eighth in population size (87.65 million) among the members of the United Nations, but its PCI is estimated at only $140 per annum. Compare this to the PCI in the United States ($12,820), France ($12,190), West Germany ($13,450), Japan ($10,080), or the Soviet Union ($5,300, estimated). Of these five countries, the United States, the Soviet Union, and Japan are among the six most populous states. The other three states that have large populations are China (over 1 billion), India (690.2 million) and Indonesia (149.5 million). Their respective PCIs are $300, $260, and $530.

The PCI is a fairly accurate reflection of productivity—that is, the ability of a working person to produce a certain amount of value within 1 hour of work. One exception is the case of those Arab states that have small populations but very large revenues from the sale of oil. For example, the per capita income in the United Arab Emirates is $24,660, in Kuwait it is $20,900, in Saudi Arabia $12,600, and in Libya $8,450.[8] In their case, the exceptionally high PCI is unrelated to the productivity of their populations, and their considerable influence potential is related directly to the fortuitous possession of a natural resource that is vital to the economic survival and wellbeing of most other countries in the world.

....Man-Made Assets

Geography, natural resources, and the size of population are factors a country's policy makers find in existence when they come to power. As a rule, they have little choice but to adjust their policies to the natural assets that happen to be under their control. Determined leaders, however, may embark on an intensive drive to transform natural assets into the two most important assets that can be developed by human effort and governmental decision: *economic wealth* and *military force*. When Adolf Hitler came to power in January 1933, he had to take into account Germany's geographic location and size, natural resources, and population. These were the assets he "inherited." To carry out his ambitious plans for territorial expansion, he had to set in motion a centrally controlled effort to mobilize Germany's economic potential and to build up a powerful military machine.

Depending on its policy objectives or its perception of the national interest, a government may give greater emphasis to improving the country's economy, standard of living, and social conditions, or it may divert a considerable part of a country's resources to build up a strong military establishment. Prior to World War II, the Japanese leadership, convinced that only through direct control could Japan ensure its unhindered supply of food, raw materials, and energy fuels, decided to mobilize a large military force. This orientation, which increased significantly Japan's power potential, eventually led to a war policy with expansionist campaigns into Manchuria, China, and Southeast Asia. Following Japan's defeat in World War II, however, a new generation of Japanese leaders shifted the emphasis to the development of a strong, competitive economy. They realized that through trade they could obtain the raw materials and other supplies their country needed. The Japanese record since the end of World War II is a textbook case of a country that deliberately chose reliance on the transactional approach while reducing to a minimum its reliance on power. Japan's orientation was made easier by Washington's firm commitment to safeguard Japan's security and independence.

The *guns or butter* option succinctly states the two policy orientations a government may follow in deciding how best to use the various assets under its control. We must keep in mind, however, that this is not normally an either–or choice; after all, a strong military force requires a strong economic foundation.

Economic Capability and Performance

Increasingly, interactions among governments involve economic matters; a country's bargaining strength is determined in large measure by its economic capability and performance. It is not difficult to see, for example, why the United States plays such a pivotal role in world affairs. In 1982, its GNP stood at a staggering $3 trillion. To grasp the magnitude of such a sum, consider that a gambler starting with this much money who lost $166,000 every hour would need 2,000 years to lose the last penny. The United States is not only the major supplier of foodstuffs for the world; it is also a major supplier of manufactured products, and a major buyer of raw materials and other products from other countries. Washington's economic policies, even when they are related to purely domestic issues or objectives, tend to have a worldwide influence.

We can see just as easily why many LDCs are at a disadvantage when dealing with the developed industrial states or the OECD group. Trade relations and other economic exchanges are primarily business transactions. In a business transaction, disparate factors such as the economic assets of each participant, its need for what the other side has to offer, the availability of alternative markets or sources of supply, the pressures to buy or sell under the circumstances, or the possibility of avoiding a disadvantageous agreement by holding out for better terms all affect the outcome of the transaction. Economic transactions between states are no different. Many LDCs have a limited range of exportable products and a limited choice of potential markets. They usually are under greater pressure to sell than their potential customers are to buy. Under such conditions, their bargaining position is weak.

It is not impossible, of course, for a country with a single export commodity to be in a favorable bargaining position provided the demand for its product is fairly inelastic. Oil is a familiar illustration of this kind of product. Nevertheless, oil-producing countries still have a degree of vulnerability because demand for oil may slacken through conservation, substitution, or an economic slowdown in the importing countries, as it happened between 1980 and 1984.

The development of a country's economic resources requires:

1. Organization of the productive effort to maximize productivity

2. Incentives that encourage individual effort

3. Capital accumulation through saving or by attracting capital from abroad

4. A constant broadening of public participation in the distribution of the increasing domestic product.

These four conditions can be promoted, thwarted, or distorted by governmental action. There is no universal agreement on the most effective method to advance a country's economic development and wellbeing. The Soviet Union claims that a centrally planned command economy, with government control of most economic resources, is the wave of the future. Many countries in the Third World have embraced one or another version of socialism, the common thread being a bias against private enterprise and a strong reliance on government-controlled economic initiatives. The United States and the other OEDC countries rely primarily on private economic activities and on a legal and social environment that provides incentives for such activities. The issue is complex; opinions vary. In fact, opposing views on this are at the core of the current ideological conflict between those who subscribe to Marxism and those who support a liberal democratic organization of society.

The Military Dimension

There is a great deal of truth in the familiar saying, "Force is the ultimate argument of kings." Since the dawn of history, military force has been used as the final arbiter in settling disputes between sovereign entities. In the absence of a superior authority, there was no recourse to an impartial judge capable of settling a dispute with finality; the alternatives were surrender or armed action.

For countless centuries, sovereign rulers with superior military forces were able to exercise power over their weaker neighbors. They could also use the presence of a strong military force to improve their influence and bargaining position when circumstances made bargaining a more realistic form of interaction. Military force remains the most important instrumentality for the exercise of power in the international arena as well as for a country's self-defense. A military force also continues to be an important element influencing the outcome of an international interaction, even when it is not used in combat.

The cost of modern weaponry makes the buildup of a strong military force expensive. A country with limited economic resources cannot sustain for long a large military force in combat readiness. The size of the population and its composition also are critical elements in the development of a strong military force. A country with a small population cannot reasonably expect to become a major military power. These obvious generalizations, however, require some further comment.

Relative Strength. The strengths and weaknesses of a country's military force cannot be assessed in the abstract; only by comparing them to those of the forces of a potential adversary can one reach a meaningful assessment. The numerical strength of the Israeli army can be evaluated only when it is compared to the military forces that can be fielded by its Arab neighbors and potential foes. As a rule, a government has a practical yardstick when it has to decide what will be a sufficient military force; the two criteria are the capabilities of potential adversaries and the highly probable, realistic challenges to the country's vital interests that have to be thwarted. Although this approach may appear practical and prudent, governments not infrequently embark on a military buildup either to beat back imaginary threats, to meet "worst case" contingencies, to bolster their sense of power and importance on the world stage, to promote internal cohesion, or to strengthen their capabilities as a prelude to aggression.

Combat Readiness and Morale. The numerical strength of any military force has to be correlated to the combat readiness, training, morale, and efficiency of its troops. After all, the most sophisticated weapons may be useless in the hands of inexperienced, inept, or demoralized operators.

Morale and the willingness to fight are important. We may assume that the Soviet military planners, in any evaluation of the Warsaw Pact Organization (WPO) forces, take into account personnel reliability. Will the East German troops fight against their West German brethren? Will the Polish army fight for a communist Poland, considering the anti-Soviet feelings of the Polish people?

In assessing troop effectiveness, military planners also must take into account, in addition to morale and combat preparedness, the specific form of conflict the troops are likely to encounter. For example, regular military forces fighting against guerrillas need to be almost ten times as large as their foes to compensate for the mobility and the hit-and-run tactics of the guerrilla bands; the regular military has to defend urban settlements and other important installations while sending out forces to pursue the guerrillas. The South Vietnamese government had approximately 600,000 uniformed troops as well as more than 450,000 U.S. soldiers; the Vietcong never exceeded 250,000.[9]

Matériel. Whereas the most sophisticated weapons may prove to be worthless without capable and determined personnel to use them, the best trained and efficient troops will turn into defenseless prey without weapons that are superior to or at least as sophisticated as those of their adversary. Moreover, because modern weapons systems depend so heavily on fuels and highly specialized forms of ammunition and spare parts, inadequate supplies may reduce drastically the combat effectiveness of the most efficient and determined military force.

Strategic planners, in determining the type of weapons that will be needed in the event of an armed confrontation, must answer two questions: (1) What are the military tasks? and (2) What type of enemy forces must be offset? Armaments are costly; choices are necessary.

Because it is difficult to predict with complete accuracy the type of military challenges a country may face, military planners tend to procure a greater quantity and variety of weapons than they expect to need. Moreover, the development of newer and presumably more effective weapons continues unabated, while weapons tend to become obsolete within a few years. As a result, most countries in the world spend billions of dollars every year on weapons.

Nuclear Weapons. Nuclear weapons have added a new and entirely different element to the military dimension and deserve special attention. In addition to the United States, the Soviet Union, the United Kingdom, France, and China, which have publicly acknowledged the possession of nuclear weapons, and India, which has tested a nuclear device, several other countries are suspected of having such weapons (Israel, South Africa), are in the process of developing them (Pakistan), or are interested in acquiring them (Libya, Taiwan, Argentina, Brazil, and Egypt). Because nuclear weapons can be developed, guarded, and launched by a small number of highly trained personnel, even a country with a very small population (such as Libya) can achieve nuclear capability. Neither is it necessary to have a vast economic base to develop or acquire such weapons now that the basic technology is no longer secret. The temptation to obtain such weapons is understandable: there is a widespread belief that a government may tremendously increase its power and influence potential in a relatively short time and at a manageable cost through the possession of such weapons.

The actual effect the possession of nuclear weapons may have on a country's power or influence potential may not be so dramatic. A government may use its nuclear capability as a bargaining chip or an instrument of power only if its threat to use such weapons is credible. Although nothing can be ruled out in this world, it is hard to see how a country such as India would use the threat of nuclear attack to force Pakistan into submission over the question of Kashmir. Even Israel is likely to invoke the use of nuclear weapons only if its very existence is severely threatened by advancing hostile forces.

In chapters 6 and 7 we will discuss in greater detail the various issues relating to military force and to the economic factors that affect a country's international relations.

Intangible Assets ....

The tangible assets we discussed in the preceding pages are no more than the "raw materials" that governments can use as they formulate and pursue their foreign policies. How effectively these assets are used determines how much influence or power a government is able to exercise. Imaginative, adroit use of the tangible assets increases a country's power or influence potential; ill-considered, shortsighted, or unrealistic policies may squander or neutralize the most fortuitous combination of tangible assets and resources.

In short, a country's power and influence potential at a given time depends ultimately on intangible assets such as the quality of political leadership, the degree of national cohesion, the image a country projects internationally, and the attractiveness of its ideology.

....Political Leadership

Under any political system, the charting of foreign policy and the final decisions in this crucial area are made by a small number of individuals who happen to occupy key positions in the governmental structure at a given time. These officials do not operate in a vacuum. Their decisions are influenced by others who control assets that are important to the decision makers. In the United States, for example, those who may take part in the making of foreign policy decisions include the president and certain officials in the White House, the Department of State, the Department of Defense, the Departments of Treasury and Commerce, the Central Intelligence Agency and other intelligence agencies. The final content of a decision may be affected by the views of congressional leaders, spokespersons of influential groups, and private individuals whose advice is valued by the final decision makers. The participants differ with the case; the issue usually determines who should have input. The decision makers at times find it necessary or advisable to take into account public opinion trends, especially when public opinion appears to be running strongly against a projected policy initiative. Be that as it may, the final authority rests with a handful of individuals at the apex of the executive structure.

In the Soviet Union, where the party leadership exercises highly centralized control over political, economic, and social matters, the major foreign policy decisions are made by the Politburo—the standing group of the Central Committee of the Communist party (CPSU), whose members constitute the highest and most powerful policy-making group in the Soviet system. They receive advice from the ministries of Foreign Affairs and Defense, the GRU (the intelligence arm of the General Staff), the KGB (Committee of State Security), appropriate bureaus of the Communist party Secretariat, and any other individuals the policy makers care to take into their confidence or whose views they solicit. Up to this point, the decision-making process in the Soviet Union has many similarities to that in the United States. The difference is found in the role played by auxiliary or secondary participants. The Soviet policy makers do not have to contend with free-wheeling pressure groups, an independent and critical press, or a vocal public opinion. On occasion, the views of influential groups may find their way into the deliberations of the Politburo, but only if one or more of its members decide to embrace those views and bring them up for discussion.

Commentators on international affairs occasionally argue that restrictive or totalitarian systems enable decision makers to take action more rapidly and with minimal interference from those who may disagree with a particular decision. By contrast, the making of foreign policy in democratic systems is subject to pressures from influential groups with narrow interests to protect or promote, and from a public opinion that may be swayed by emotional considerations. Although both arguments are largely valid, there is another aspect that should not be overlooked. Policy makers in centralized political systems may reach decisions rapidly—including wrong, even disastrous decisions. Hitler decided to attack Poland and unleash World War II with little interference from anyone who might have counseled a different course. The interplay of different viewpoints that occasionally may affect an important decision in a democracy may prevent a hasty and dangerous decision. Although interference by opposing forces may at times block a wise and necessary decision, unhindered discussion of important issues helps to clarify the various implications and has the potential to cultivate and generate public support that eventually may be needed for the action.

Whether a political system is democratically organized or tightly controlled by a dictatorial elite, the effectiveness of a country's foreign policy depends decisively on the *quality* of the political leadership at the highest levels. Foreign policy is formulated in the minds of human beings, not in the impersonal, mechanical "brain" of some electronic computer. This being the case, the personal traits, intelligence, imagination, emotional makeup, prejudices, perceptions, and personal ambitions and cherished illusions of those in charge of foreign policy play a decisive role. Moreover, their ability to cut through a confusing maze of details and reach for the heart of the matter, to remain calm and coolheaded under extreme pressure, to be decisive when necessary and moderate and flexible when conditions require, and to anticipate the potential effects of their decisions may have a critical influence on the content and effectiveness of their foreign policy.

Because foreign policy involves interactions with other individuals who represent, as a rule, other governments, those responsible for a country's foreign relations must be able to deal persuasively with their counterparts. An insensitive, inflexible, dogmatic approach may alienate others and drastically undercut a government's influence potential.

The growing importance of transactional relations in the last forty years has thrust more complex responsibilities on those who handle foreign policy. The choices are seldom clear-cut. For example, is the national interest of the United States served best by spending over $300 billion on armaments and only $4.6 billion on foreign economic aid? Or, would the development of new nuclear weapons and delivery means be a more effective way to contain Soviet expansionist policies? Nuclear weapons are relevant in the event of a vital confrontation with the Soviet Union, but how relevant are they in the United States' relations with Mexico, Nigeria, Brazil, India, or most other countries in the world? In apportioning resources, leaders must take into account the effect their policies will have on their country's influence around the world. A successful foreign policy calls for imaginative use of resources. Making the right choices is the task of political leadership, the quality of which is a most crucial element.

National Cohesion

A capable leadership not only will chart an effective foreign policy and maximize its influence potential; it will also promote a climate of national cohesion and overall public support for its policy initiatives. To pursue bold initiatives in the area of foreign policy or to resort to armed conflict, government leaders under any political system need to have fairly broad public support. Hitler might have been unable to pursue his war policies without the fanatical support he received from millions of Germans. During World War II, Stalin put the shibboleth of proletarian loyalty on the shelf temporarily and resurrected the old symbols of Mother Russia. Significantly, the war of 1941 to 1945 is called in Soviet literature *The Great Patriotic War*. The U.S. government was able to mobilize its people in a supreme effort to defeat the Japanese and the Germans in World War II only after the Japanese attack on Pearl Harbor generated a tidal wave of nationalist indignation. Millions of U.S. citizens fought heroically, with dedication and loyalty. By contrast, during the war in Vietnam, an increasingly disillusioned and unsympathetic public in the United States eventually forced the leadership to abandon the effort and, in effect, accept defeat.

A war effort cannot succeed without high national cohesion, motivation, and positive morale. National cohesion, however, is not important only in time of armed conflict. It is important at any time, because its absence impedes the formulation and implementation of an effective foreign policy. Moreover, the lack of national cohesion undermines the confidence other governments have in the ability of a country's leadership to "deliver," to carry out the commitments it has undertaken: the absence of national cohesion and popular support weakens a government's influence potential.

National cohesion and popular support depend on the absence of conflicts within the various groups and on public perceptions of the governmental policies and objectives. There is hardly any country in the world without sources of potential conflict. Economic cleavages, social inequalities, and racial, ethnic, religious, or even linguistic differences may undermine a country's national cohesion. To these, we can add political and ideological divisions, which at times may reach the boiling point. For the past thirty years, we have witnessed internal conflicts breaking out into civil wars in several countries, including Cyprus, the Philippines, Indonesia, Pakistan, Vietnam, Nigeria, Ethiopia, Nicaragua, El Salvador, and Lebanon.

Axiomatically, every government has a vested interest in eliminating or at least dampening conflicts within its country. Rarely will a government deliberately foment internal strife.[10] Conflict left unchecked may lead to a dangerous crisis that can topple the government. Even if the government manages to survive, lack of unity and popular support is likely to undermine its ability to deal effectively with other governments.

Ideological Motivations

In earlier times, religion was used by emperors and kings as a potent instrument of influence and power. Constantine the Great used Christianity to win popular support and motivate his soldiers to fight in successive confrontations with his rivals until he emerged as the sole and undisputed master of the Roman empire. Even today, religion is used occasionally by governments as an instrument of influence beyond their borders.

In the last one-hundred years, secular ideologies have taken the place once held by religion as a political force. An ideology is a cluster of beliefs, assumptions, and prescriptions relating to society's basic organization, its core values, and an individual's place in it. Three basic ideological orientations have commanded wide followings during this century. Marxism, with its several variations, fascism, also with its own variations, and liberal democracy.

The Soviet Union has certainly used (with varying degrees of success) *Marxism–Leninism,* or the less dogmatic forms of *socialism,* as an element of identification, political orientation, and emotional connection with political elites and ordinary people in other states. In many countries of the Third World, large numbers of people have been led to accept the Marxist–Leninist view of imperialism as one of the basic facts of international life. Even the non-Marxist Islamic regime in Iran accepts the Marxist view and condemns the "imperialist West."

Ideology is a particularly effective instrument of influence when political elites espousing a certain ideology engage actively in a country's political life and eventually gain power by whatever means. We must note, however, that cooperation between these elites and their ideological mentors is neither automatic nor necessarily permanent. Unless those who control the ideological center are able to impose their will physically, their ideological affiliates are likely to limit their compliance and cooperation. The countries in Eastern Europe, being vulnerable to Soviet military power, have been unable to chart domestic or international policies unacceptable to the Soviet Union. By contrast, geographically distant countries beyond the reach of Soviet military power were able to cut their close ties with the Soviet Union when those ties appeared to be in conflict with their national interests, as occurred in Guinea, Egypt, and Somalia. Mozambique also showed signs in early 1984 that it wanted to improve relations with the United States and distance itself from the Soviet orbit; *nationalism* proved stronger than Marxist ideology. In fact, the pervasiveness of nationalism is evident in the dispute between the Soviet Union and the People's Republic of China, or in the anti-Soviet attitudes of the Polish people.

The liberal–democratic ideology, espoused by the West and especially by the United States, has several attractive features: it advocates both individual freedom and material wellbeing. Human beings do not normally enjoy oppression or deprivation. The democratic freedoms that exist in the West could have exerted a magnetic attraction for ordinary people around the world. The additional fact that the OECD countries have promoted prosperity for the average person while preserving individual freedom could have been irrefutable proof that the liberal–democratic ideology and the principles of the private enterprise system hold the best promise for a better life. With its success record, this ideology should have been virtually irresistible. Yet millions of people, especially in the Third World countries, do not gather under the banner of liberal–democratic ideology. One of the reasons is that, in the past, colonialism was practiced by countries that espoused the liberal–democratic ideology. Many people in the former colonial areas tend to equate *capitalism, private enterprise,* and *Western democracy* with the exploitative and oppressive practices of colonialism, and to turn to a nebulous and idealized notion of *socialism,* which they see more as a promise for *social justice* than as a government-controlled form of economic organization. Whatever the validity of these ideological assumptions, the fact remains that they affect materially the public perceptions of a specific problem or of the foreign policy objectives of a major power.

The image of the West, and of the United States in particular, also has suffered in more recent times from association with oppressive regimes. The United States, anxious to contain communist expansion, has repeatedly associated itself with political regimes that pay little attention to the basic tenets of liberal–democratic ideology. Many of those regimes in effect embrace the basic tenets of *fascism* and rely on oppression rather than democratic freedom. Moreover, they usually impose or perpetuate a stifling concentration of wealth while they tolerate mass poverty. Close identification with such regimes tends to undermine the influence potential of the United States. To use in full their influence potential, U.S. policy makers need to have a realistic appreciation of ideology as an intangible asset.

Assets for Influence

Most of the assets discussed in the preceding pages can be used by governments trying to exercise power and impose on other actors solutions they favor. History is replete with illustrations. We have repeatedly noted in this text, however, that the outcome in most international interactions today is shaped through the exercise of influence—through bargaining and persuasion—not through the pursuit or exercise of power.

For this reason, the sound use of a state's assets and capabilities to augment its influence potential is a more pragmatic and effective way to protect and promote its interests.

Unlike power, influence can rely on a broad range of assets. As a result, even relatively small or weak countries with a relatively limited power potential may have assets they can use to enhance their influence and strengthen their bargaining position even when dealing with major powers.

Tangible Assets

A strategic location may prove a strong bargaining point. U.S. policy makers consider Turkey to be a valuable ally. With her land situated south of the Black Sea, next to the Soviet Caucasus, astride the Bosporus and the Dardanelles, and north of the volatile and oil-rich regions of the Middle East, Turkey plays an important role in U.S. strategic calculations; this provides any Turkish government with considerable leverage. In 1975, the U.S. Congress—acting against the wishes and the advice of the White House—imposed an arms embargo on Turkey as punishment for Turkey's use of United States-supplied weapons in its 1974 invasion of Cyprus. When Turkey retaliated by closing down most of the U.S. military and intelligence installations on Turkish soil, the U.S. executive redoubled its pressures on Congress until the embargo was lifted in 1978. Turkey obviously possessed an effective bargaining chip. The relationship between the United States and Turkey—despite their disparity in military and economic resources—is not a power relationship.

The effect of economic assets as a prime instrument for the exercise of influence can be seen in a variety of circumstances. For example, the influence exercised by South Africa in the West—despite its apartheid policies—is due in part to its strategic location and also to its possession of valuable mineral resources. The Western European governments have been much more flexible than that of the United States in dealing with the Palestinian question, partly because they depend much more heavily on Arab oil. A great deal of the influence exercised by the United States can be attributed more to its tremendous economic resources than to its possession of nuclear or even conventional weapons, which have so often proved of limited relevance (as they did in 1984 in Lebanon).

Technology is a vital asset in our contemporary world. Making available to others new technological advances can be an influence and bargaining instrumentality. Apparently, one of the factors that induced the Chinese Communists to improve their relations with the United States was their hope of obtaining much-needed modern technology. In another context, the United States has tried from time to time to influence Soviet policies by preventing the flow of technology. The effect has been marginal, because technological advances cannot remain secret for long. New technology tends to cross borders almost as fast as its products. Nevertheless, because most technological progress occurs in the West, technology can be used as an additional, positive element for influence and effective bargaining.

In short, economic resources, important or rare commodities, technological advances, trade advantages, technical assistance, loans, investments, and a strategic location are among the tangible assets a government may use to expand its influence and improve its bargaining position.

Intangible Assets

Image. A government's influence also may be strengthened through the imaginative and adroit use of intangible assets, or political and diplomatic techniques. A country's popular image abroad can be a valuable asset or a serious handicap. Image is subject to change. The negative image most people had of the Soviet Union during the days of Joseph Stalin and even in the earlier postwar years has gradually improved, and today millions throughout the world are favorably disposed toward the Soviet Union. Nonetheless, during the same period, Moscow's highhanded interventions in Hungary, Czechoslovakia, Poland, Afghanistan have detracted from its image.

Ideology. Another intangible asset that can be used to augment a country's influence potential is ideology. For more than half a century, the Soviet Union has tried to use the Marxist ideology as a major tool for expanding its influence throughout the world. The record is mixed. In Eastern Europe, the signs of popular discontent and disaffection are too evident to be dismissed lightly. Obviously, the people in the Eastern European countries have not embraced the Marxist–Leninist ideology with the zest the Soviet Union expected. As a result, Moscow relies much more on the power approach than on ideological kinship. In most Western European countries, the Communist parties are no longer as eager to obey Moscow's directives as they were during the Stalin years. The so-called Eurocommunism has become a new version, which above all implies an assertion of independence from Soviet tutelage. On the other hand, the Soviet Union has used ideology effectively in expanding its influence elsewhere, especially in Third World countries. The emergence of Marxist regimes in countries such as Cuba, South Yemen, Ethiopia, Mozambique, Angola, Nicaragua, Vietnam has certainly opened new opportunities for influence the Soviet Union did not have in the past.

Leadership and Policies. A most important asset for the exercise of influence is a country's leadership—the ability of its leaders and of its diplomatic representatives to use the tangible and intangible assets at their disposal to maximize the favorable response from another sovereign government. This means that policy makers and diplomats must be sensitive to the feelings, prejudices, and expectations of other people, especially other officials. Pronouncements that tend to alienate or offend other people do not add to a country's influence potential; on the other hand, well-chosen statements can be quite effective.

Without underestimating the influence of appropriate statements, we must point out that words can be of limited effectiveness unless they reflect actual policies. In fact, a government that habitually indulges in attractive statements that are soon refuted by its policies will lose credibility and its influence will plummet. A major power, of course, finds it impossible to please all those whose reactions are important, particularly if the country has global interests and objectives. The United States, for example, frequently faces this problem. At the time of the crisis over the Falkland (Malvinas) islands, Washington could not satisfy Britain as well as the Latin American countries in the OAS, which sided with Argentina.[11] In its relations with China, Washington cannot supply Taiwan with sophisticated weapons without causing a negative reaction in the People's Republic of China. In the Middle East, the United States has been unable to advocate and promote an independent and sovereign Palestinian state—a move likely to win support among Arabs—because to do so would cause a storm of protest in Israel and among Israel's supporters in the United States.

There is hardly any government in the world that can always pursue policies that will receive universal applause; the alternative is to make a deliberate effort to adopt and pursue policies that:

1. Serve the country's basic interests

2. Do not alienate unnecessarily other governments or people

3. Take into account, as much as possible, the interests and views of other countries

4. Properly evaluate the long-range effects these policies will have on the country's influence potential

Moreover, when policies are bound to create displeasure in other countries, a government should at least take the trouble to explain and justify the policy to minimize its negative effect.

Military Strength. The military capabilities of a given country may be more relevant to the exercise of power; however, they can also prove relevant to the exercise of influence. Military aid, for example, can provide effective leverage in negotiations. In 1983, the Greek government, reversing its preelection stand, signed an agreement for a five-year extension of the presence on Greek soil of several U.S. military installations. The reversal was prompted in part by the continuing Greek need for weapons supplied by the United States. The perceived threat from neighboring Turkey—also a recipient of U.S. military aid—decisively affected the outcome of the negotiations and the compromise reached. A government also may increase its influence over another government by promising military cooperation in the event of aggression or of a serious threat by an adversary. Finally, depending on the actual circumstances, the relative military prowess of the parties may become a factor in the negotiations, especially when crucial interests are at stake and resort to force is a potential—and realistic—course of action.

The Assets of Other Actors ....

We devoted a great deal of space to the tangible and intangible assets the governments of sovereign states can utilize to increase their power or influence potential. The reason, as we pointed out in earlier pages, is both simple and obvious: the sovereign state remains at the center of the stage.

Nevertheless, accumulating experience, especially during the second half of this century, indicates that other entities, other *actors,* play significant roles on the international stage and deserve our attention. In chapter 2, we grouped those entities into international governmental organizations (IGOs) and nongovernmental organizations (NGOs) whose activities have an important effect on international relations. Some of these entities rely primarily on the exercise of influence to achieve their objectives; a few rely chiefly on their power potential. To improve their influence or power potential, they too have to mobilize and put to use certain assets and resources.

....The Assets of IGOs

The tangible and intangible assets IGOs may use in dealing with other actors are more limited in their variety than those of sovereign states and are geared much more to bargaining and the exercise of influence than to the exercise of power; the use or threat of force is not normally one of their instrumentalities. From this general rule we must exclude alliances such as NATO or the WPO. Even these two organizations, however, have relied thus far more on transactional interactions (effected mostly through negotiations between the United States and the Soviet Union) than on the exercise of power. Nevertheless, the potential use of force is inherent in their makeup and ultimate mission.

By contrast, organizations such as the United Nations, the EEC (European Economic Community), the OAU (Organization of African Unity) and the various specialized agencies of the UN are geared above all to relying on the transactional approach, and the assets they may use are not suitable to the exercise of power. Their success depends on:

1. The support they receive from the participating governments

2. The assets these governments are willing to activate on behalf of the organization

3. The skills of those who manage the affairs of the organization or act in its name

The support such IGOs may receive from the participating governments may be material (tangible) or moral and political (intangible). As a rule, their budget is funded by the contributions of the member-states; the generosity or frugality of these governments determines how extensive are the operations of the IGO. The World Bank or the IMF (International Monetary Fund), for example, can assist developing countries only if major contributors such as the United States and other OECD members are willing to provide funds. The stature and effectiveness of the UN depend to a large extent on the policies of the member-states and their attitude toward the organization. Without their financial, political, and moral support (particularly that of such countries as the United States or the Soviet Union), the UN Secretary General, for example, can undertake no major initiatives to promote peace or resolve a dangerous conflict. The diplomatic skills, personalities, and connections of the top officials of IGOs can be a major intangible asset or a serious liability.

The Assets of NGOs

The assets that the nongovernmental entities may use on the international stage differ from one category of NGO to another. This is hardly surprising when we consider how varied are the entities grouped under the NGO label.

Multinational Corporations

Multinational corporations (MNCs) rely most heavily on their economic resources and the advantages their operations can offer to the host country. Because normally they cannot use force to further or protect their interests, MNCs have to use assets that are more suitable to the exercise of influence and that are likely to maximize their bargaining advantages. Contrary to popular belief, MNCs are vulnerable to the actions of sovereign governments much more than vice versa. Even the largest, United States–based MNCs can be thrown out of the host country or have their properties nationalized, and there is little likelihood the government of the United States will use force to rescue them. To operate, MNCs must gain and retain access to other countries through bargaining, influence, and behavior beneficial to the host country, at least in the eyes of that country's government. Lobbying by multinationals, especially in LDCs where an MNC may be one of the wealthiest and economically most important entities in the country, is certainly widely practiced—no less than it is by the parent company in the country of origin.

MNCs may attempt to use power tactics, but their opportunity for such action is limited. No MNC maintains its own private armies. To exercise power, an MNC may have to call on the government of its country of origin to intervene on its behalf and bring to bear its own power instrumentalities. There is no case in recent history of a sovereign government going to war to serve the interests of an MNC. One illustration of forcible support may be the involvement of the Central Intelligence Agency (CIA) in the overthrow of the Allende government in Chile in 1973, brought about by ITT's opposition to the economic measures of Allende's socialist government. Illustrations of this type remain rare. Economic pressures may be used, but their effectiveness is subject to a confluence of circumstances such as the country's heavy dependence on the activities of a given MNC, the absence of economic and trade alternatives, or the willingness of government leaders to succumb to such pressures for reasons of their own, ranging from political calculations to personal monetary benefits. In the 1970s, a congressional inquiry in the United States revealed that more than one hundred U.S. MNCs had spent over $100 million in bribes to foreign officials to gain the latter's cooperation. Bribery, of course, however morally reprehensible, is a prime example of a method of influencing someone, not pressuring him or her to submission.

Service NGOs

Service NGOs, such as the International Red Cross, missionary groups, charitable organizations, and the like as a rule rely on the financial contributions of their supporters; these funds are their principal material asset. Their effectiveness further depends on the competence and dedication of their officials and operatives. Finally, their ability to operate in various countries is directly affected by the attitude of the government officials in the host country. Unless these individuals are convinced that the service to be performed is beneficial and desirable, a service NGO will have no way of carrying out its intended tasks in the territory of a foreign country. The diplomatic skills of those in charge of the organization and its reputation and public image are two of the most important intangible assets that determine its eventual success. Service NGOs are in no way capable of exercising power in their relations with host governments, other organizations, or the people they try to serve.

Revolutionary/Terrorist NGOs

By contrast, revolutionary NGOs such as guerrilla movements or terrorist groups rely primarily on assets that are geared to the exercise of power—that is, assets suitable for bringing about radical changes through the use of force and violence. This does not rule out their use of a combination of force-oriented assets with political assets that may improve their influence and bargaining potential. For example, the PLO relied on violence in the earlier years when it wanted to attract international attention to its cause, but later it toned down such activities in a deliberate effort to gain international respectability and influence through diplomacy.

Terrorist groups rely almost exclusively on violence because their ability to foster change through bargaining is virtually nonexistent. For example, the Red Brigades in Italy may have wished to destroy NATO or to replace capitalism with their version of socialism, but they could not expect realistically to gain their ends in a bargaining interaction with the Italian government or with the NATO authorities. Violence, therefore, is the only type of activity they can use to attract attention to their aims; to embarrass and, if possible, weaken the established state authorities; to win some followers among disenchanted social or political groups; or to gain an illusion of power.

Summary

- The ability of the international actors to exercise power or to influence the outcome of international transactions or confrontations depends on their resources or assets.

- The relevant assets are either tangible or intangible. Tangible assets include geography (location, climate, terrain, size); natural resources (energy resources, raw materials); population (its composition, education, productivity, size); man-made assets (such as economic wealth and military forces). The intangible assets include a country's political leadership, national cohesion, and ideological and social motivations.

- Unlike power, influence can rely on a broader range of assets. A strategic location, deposits of valuable raw materials, technological innovations, financial assistance, attractive ideology, competent leadership, high prestige, imaginative and flexible policies, as well as strong military capabilities are among the assets a government can use to increase its influence potential.

- The assets of IGOs in dealing with other actors are geared much more toward the exercise of influence than toward the exercise of power. An exception to this is military alliances.

- NGOs can use a variety of assets, depending on their type. MNCs rely heavily on their economic resources and on the advantages their operations can offer to the host country. Militant NGOs rely primarily on force and the power approach. Service NGOs such as the International Red Cross depend on their financial resources, the competence of their officials, and the utility of their services.

Notes

1. Scheider, William. *Food, Foreign Policy and Raw Materials Cartels.* New York: Crane, Russak, 1976, p. 36.
2. Alexandersson, Gunnar, and Klevebring, Bjorn-Ivar. *World Resources: Energy, Metals, Minerals.* New York: Walter de Gruyter, 1978.
3. Wood is no longer of major significance as a fuel; solar energy is still of limited use.
4. Petroleum reserves are unevenly distributed through the planet. Of the 155 sovereign states in the United Nations, only 52 have any oil production at all. Even of these, one-half produce small quantities—less than 10 million metric tons, a pittance compared with the almost 3 billion metric tons produced annually worldwide. Of this total, a little over 50 percent (1,524 million metric tons) is produced by thirteen members of the Organization of Petroleum Exporting Countries (OPEC). Another 1 billion metric tons are produced by the two superpowers. Ten other countries produce fairly significant quantities of crude oil, approximately 250 million metric tons. These countries (Argentina, Australia, Canada, China, Egypt, Mexico, Norway, Romania, Trinidad–Tobago, and the United Kingdom) are not

members of OPEC, although they export part of their output. Over 85 percent of the world's production is consumed by the industrialized countries (approximately 2,540 million metric tons), which, however, produce only 33 percent (approximately 1,108 million metric tons; 947 million of this is produced by the United States and the Soviet Union). These figures dramatically reveal the deficit of the industrialized countries in domestic oil resources.

5. Proven world reserves were set in 1981 at 77,711 billion cubic meters (bcm), with the Soviet Union accounting for approximately 39.2 percent, the OPEC countries for 32.9, the United States for 7.3, and the rest for 20.6 percent. Many of these reserves are not being vigorously exploited at the present time. At the current annual production level of approximately 1,500 bcm worldwide, the known reserves are expected to last approximately another fifty years.

6. Wu, Yan-li. *Raw Materials in a Multipolar World.* 2nd ed. New York: Crane, Russak, 1979; also, *Metal Statistics: A Purchasing Guide of the Metal Industries.* New York: Fairchild Publications, 1980.

7. For more information on the "limits of growth" point of view, see Meadows, Donella H., et al. *The Limits of Growth: A Report for the Club of Rome's Project on the Predicament of Mankind.* New York: Universe, 1972.

8. *World Development Report 1983.*

9. Johnson, Lyndon B. *The Vantage Point.* New York: Holt, Rinehart & Winston, 1971, pp. 245–247.

10. One bizarre exception is the "Cultural Revolution" that tore China apart between 1966 and 1974. To quote a prominent scholar, "The Cultural Revolution defies full explanation, and many interpretations are possible. Some scholars have seen it as an ideologically inspired event in which those who [shared] a Maoist vision set out to destroy all who did not. Others have treated the Cultural Revolution as a power struggle over the succession to Mao's leadership. The truth no doubt is that it blended ideological and power considerations, but in what proportions and in what forms it is impossible to say." Pye, Lucian W. *China: An Introduction.* 2nd ed. Boston: Little, Brown, 1978, p. 289.

11. Baker, C. A. "Multiple Alliance Commitments: The Role of the United States in the Falklands War." Unpublished doctoral dissertation Howard University, Washington, D.C., 1984).

PART TWO
······················ MECHANISMS
AND INTERACTIONS

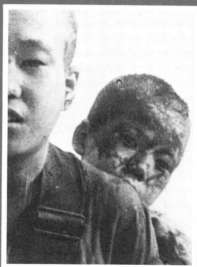

4

International Relations and Foreign Policy

President Reagan with Italian Premier Craxi at the White House

Most of the activities and interactions that are considered to be part of *international relations* result, in the last analysis, from decisions made by individuals acting in the name of an international entity. Who are these individuals whose decisions affect the international environment? What factors shape the content of their decisions? How do they reach those decisions? What problems are involved in the decision-making process? These are not merely technical questions. Time and again the world has paid a heavy price for decisions made by individuals acting in the name of major powers. We hardly need to point out that a wrong move by those who can make binding decisions in the name of the nuclear superpowers could plunge the world into a catastrophic conflagration. Such a decision will not be made by an impersonal machine or through a magical process. It will be made by human beings who happen to be vested with the authority to make such momentous decisions or who happen to be in a position that enables them to shape or affect the content of the decision. Moreover, those decisions are the product of a multifaceted interplay of conflicting values, perceptions, vested interests, individual traits, and preferences; the process is presented schematically in figure 4-1.

You may already be familiar with the term *decision-making approach* as used by Richard C. Snyder and other authors.[1] Although this chapter will draw on such writings, no attempt will be made here to discuss the conceptual framework of this approach. Our search will be somewhat wider, drawing on social–psychological, administrative, organizational, behavioral, and systemic aspects of decision making, focusing on what we believe is most relevant and illuminating.

Important decisions affecting the international environment are made not only by government officials but also by the officials of international organizations or even by private individuals. Certainly, the Iranian "students" who seized the U.S. embassy in Tehran affected the course of international relations. Yet we must emphasize that the effect of decisions made by those who act in the name of a sovereign state by far exceeds that of decisions made by others. In the following pages, our discussion will focus primarily on governmental decisions that cluster to form a country's foreign policy— that is, the policy *made by the governmental leaders of one state in dealing with other states or international entities, and aimed at achieving certain specific objectives that presumably will serve the national interest as defined by the decision makers.*

Decisions that affect the international environment, as a rule, are made in response to events and problems that have already occurred or are anticipated.[2] To promote changes they favor or prevent developments they oppose, the decision makers have to weigh alternative courses of action.[3] They may opt for nonviolent modes of interaction or they may decide that their goals can best be realized by the use of force or at least the threat of physical destruction through violence. In any international transaction or confrontation, the participants usually fall into two major categories: *domestic participants* contributing directly or indirectly to the formulation of a country's foreign policy; and *foreign participants*—namely, third entities whose decisions have a bearing on the outcome of a transaction or a confrontation.

Domestic Participants ....

Under any political system, foreign policy decisions are made by a relatively small number of individuals; however, larger numbers of people may participate or contribute directly and even more individuals or entities may influence the final outcome. The identity, the motivations, and the role of those who take part in the decision-making process are critical variables in international interactions.

Figure 4-1
Foreign policy making and implementation.

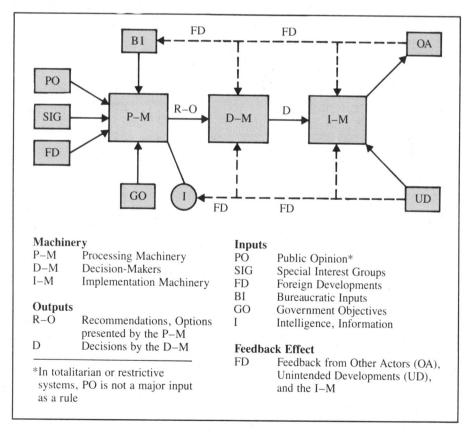

Machinery

P–M	Processing Machinery
D–M	Decision-Makers
I–M	Implementation Machinery

Outputs

R–O	Recommendations, Options presented by the P–M
D	Decisions by the D–M

Inputs

PO	Public Opinion*
SIG	Special Interest Groups
FD	Foreign Developments
BI	Bureaucratic Inputs
GO	Government Objectives
I	Intelligence, Information

Feedback Effect

FD	Feedback from Other Actors (OA), Unintended Developments (UD), and the I–M

*In totalitarian or restrictive systems, PO is not a major input as a rule

As a rule, we find two major categories of domestic participants directly involved in the decision-making process: the principal decision makers who actually pronounce a country's foreign policies, and the subordinate bureaucrats and technicians who provide the information and the recommendations that serve as the raw material for the decision-making process, and who implement the decisions.

Principal Decision Makers

Even when an international issue becomes the subject of public debate in a democratic country, the final decisions, as a rule, are made by a few individuals at the apex of the governmental pyramid. Although such final decisions may reflect recommendations or options advocated at lower levels, the decision-making power of the highest officials should not be underestimated.

President Johnson in his memoirs[4] describes in considerable detail the steps that led to some crucial foreign policy decisions during his presidency, and identifies those who played a key role. One such decision—which had fateful consequences—resulted from reports that on August 4, 1964, North Vietnamese PT boats had attacked the U.S. destroyers *Maddox* and *C. Tucker Joy* in the Gulf of Tonkin. As soon as the first reports reached the President, he called a meeting with some of his senior officials: Secretary of State Dean Rusk, Under-secretary of State George Ball, Secretary of Defense Robert McNamara, Deputy Secretary of Defense Cyrus Vance, General Curtis LeMay of the Joint Chiefs of Staff, CIA Director John McCone, USIA Director Carl T. Rowan, and Edward A. McDermont, Director of Emergency Planning.

Although the final decisions were made, of course, by President Johnson, his thinking was undoubtedly affected by the views expressed by those participating in the meeting. For all practical purposes, such high-level participants should be regarded as principal decision makers. In such small and usually cohesive groups, the tendency to concur and support what appears to emerge as the dominant line of thought results in a collectively formulated decision. This convergence of views is not necessarily a factor contributing to a sound decision. As Irving L. Janis points out, "the concurrence-seeking tendency, which fosters overoptimism, lack of vigilance, and sloganistic thinking" may be "a powerful source of defective judgment that arises in cohesive groups."[5] This tendency appears to have been present in the deliberations that led to the Gulf of Tonkin Resolution and the escalation of the Vietnam War.[6] Evidently, the personal qualities of such decision makers; their ideological prejudices, political commitments and connections, individual ambitions and calculations; their judgment, imagination, or rigidity; their breadth of perception or shortsighted obstinacy; and their knowledge and experience are critical variables that inevitably affect the final content of foreign policy decisions.

Human beings do not fall neatly into well-defined categories in terms of their personal qualities, motivations, or weaknesses; for this reason, the following observations should be taken only as useful generalizations that can help us understand some of the principal motivations and attitudes that account for the content of foreign policy decisions and, by extension, the course of international relations.

The Fear of Failure

The individuals who are eventually empowered to make foreign policy decisions usually have overcome many obstacles and won many contests to reach their powerful positions. Because most international issues involve a contest of wills between individuals who represent conflicting interests and viewpoints, "backing down" or accepting a compromise often is viewed as a sign of failure, and the idea of failure is particularly abhorrent to such individuals.[7]

"Failure" is unacceptable for another reason. The citizens of sovereign states, motivated as they normally are by nationalistic feelings, expect their leaders to defend the country's interests and emerge from the contest with a "victory" over the other side. The political personalities that formulate or implement foreign policy want to feel worthy of the trust placed in them by the nation, and also want to receive the acclaim that goes with success.

We may detect a third reason for avoidance of "failure." A conciliatory attitude may embolden the other side and lead to an outcome that may be viewed as a failure. Commentators and politicians are fond of citing the Munich Agreement of 1938, when British Prime Minister Nevill Chamberlain acquiesced to the dismemberment of Czechoslovakia to appease Hitler. As Hans Morgenthau pointed out, Chamberlain "was probably less motivated by considerations of personal power than were many other British prime ministers, and he sought to preserve peace and to assure the happiness of all concerned."[8] Hitler did take advantage of Chamberlain's conciliatory attitude and pressed on, only to provoke the outbreak of the war, which eventually ended with the destruction of his regime. Although Hitler's success in Munich proved a rather empty victory considering Nazism's eventual demise, many continue to cite the "capitulation in Munich" as a lesson decision makers should never forget.[9] To be duped by the other side is the most distasteful form of failure in international relations. Inevitably, such an attitude turns intransigence into virtue and makes conciliation and compromise a difficult and unglamorous endeavor.

The Quest for Prestige

The makers of foreign policy are not only conscious of their personal standing as successful players of the international game; they also tend to identify with their country, the prestige of which then becomes a paramount consideration. Preserving the country's prestige—its standing in the eyes of other governments and peoples—is viewed as a principal responsibility. This is hardly surprising given that a country's prestige and popular image is in itself one of the important intangible assets that a government can use to strengthen its power or influence potential.

Humiliating defeats or unflattering compromises at the negotiating table do not bolster a country's prestige. The guardians of this important national asset feel compelled to protect and augment it. This orientation tends to tilt foreign policy toward the power approach rather than the transactional approach, which by its own basic dynamics leads to the scaling down of demands, conciliation of conflicting viewpoints, and compromise solutions. John S. Stoessinger, discussing the reasons nations go to war, described in detail the events that led to World War I: "There was a pervasive tendency to place the preservation of one's ego before the preservation of peace," the author notes ruefully.[10]

A national leader also may justify her or his policies as an inescapable "duty" to uphold a country's commitments and preserve its image as a reliable friend. In the 1960s, the U.S. government set as a key objective of its foreign policy the blocking of communist expansion in Southeast Asia. National Security Action Memorandum (NSAM) 273, issued on November 26, 1963 (four days after President Kennedy's assassination), stated formally: "It remains the central objective of the United States in South Vietnam to assist the people and Government of that country to win their contest against the externally directed and supported communist conspiracy. The test of all U.S. decisions and actions in this area should be the effectiveness of their contribution to this purpose." This was not a propaganda statement for domestic or foreign consumption. It reflected "a Presidential decision in the field of national security affairs and generally requiring follow-up action by the department or agency addressed."[11] As President Lyndon Johnson stated in his memoirs, he felt "duty-bound" to continue the policy his slain predecessor had initiated. Convinced that the threat to South Vietnam could be removed only by force, President Johnson opted for a *power approach,* and committed increasingly larger military forces to achieve his objectives.

The Element of Mistrust

Many of those who have been successful in business or politics will acknowledge in moments of confessional candor that they did not reach the high plateaus of success by being overly trusting in their fellow humans.

This propensity to mistrust is particularly evident among those who chart a country's foreign policy and those who deal with the representatives of other international entities. In their international relations, governments are very reluctant to entrust the security and wellbeing of their country to the good will of other governments.

One of the principal obstacles to nuclear arms control was the difficulty in verifying compliance with any agreements that might be reached. The Soviet Union was unbending in its opposition to any verification arrangements that involved foreign observers on Soviet soil.

The breakthrough came not because of any changes in the political environment but as a result of technological developments—space satellites and other devices—that made on site verification unnecessary. Only then did the two superpowers begin to use the transactional approach in their efforts to bring the nuclear arms race under control, resulting in another novel development. Traditionally, information about a country's armaments and war potential was a most highly guarded state secret. With the new detection means and under the provisions of the SALT I and SALT II agreements, both superpowers know a great deal about each other's nuclear capabilities. Nevertheless, mutual mistrust between the two superpowers remains an important and dangerous aspect of our contemporary international relations.

This tendency among government officials to be suspicious and distrustful of their counterparts in the international arena is not confined to confrontational situations. Even in transactional interactions, government officials and diplomats tend to play their cards very close to the chest. This propensity to mistrust is a central fact of life in international relations, and one of the basic attitudes decision makers quickly embrace regardless of their personal inclinations.

Conflicting Perceptions

Students of international relations need to come to grips as early as possible with the disconcerting fact that, in international relations, reality does not have a single dimension, with the same shape and content for everyone. Reality is multidimensional; its shape and content change when viewed from different angles by different international actors. This relativity of reality is a constant element of international relations.

Quite often, outsiders can readily see the solution to an international problem, and yet those directly involved seem unable to embrace arrangements that others find logical and realistic. As we move through this book we shall find many reasons for this, but in one way or another they all seem to have their roots in varying perceptions of reality.

We live in a prismatic world, where each international actor sees the issues through a perceptual filter made up of ideological convictions, a skewed view of the historical past, vested interests, and a self-centered belief in their own "right" and superior "truth." Palestinians and Israelis do not see the same reality in the Middle East; Iranians and Iraqis underscore with bullets their conflicting views of what is right; Greeks and Turks see differently the realities in the Aegean; the South Africans and their neighboring African states have virtually irreconcilable perceptions of the racial question. We cannot ignore these conflicting perceptions of reality; they are the raw material of policy.

Although all international actors are susceptible to this type of distorted vision, we are justifiably most concerned with the conflicting perceptions held by major international actors such as the United States, the Soviet Union, China, the countries of the EEC, and those in the Third World.

Diplomats are the product of their national environment and cannot entirely escape its mental and emotional parameters. Even when they are personally persuaded that their more narrow and nation-oriented perceptions are extravagant and unjustified, they tend to uphold these views because the perceptions are also held by their national constituencies. This advocacy by the leaders has the effect of reinforcing the popularly held perceptions, and this in turn makes it even more difficult for decision makers to change course.

Nationalism is not the only source of conflicting perceptions. Ideological convictions or religious affiliations may prove a potent factor. In Lebanon, Moslems and Christians have fought each other bitterly in recent years, as have the Protestants and Catholics in Northern Ireland, and the Hindus and Moslems in India. As we shall see in chapter 10, the East–West rivalry cannot be divorced from its ideological underpinnings.

Extensive experience indicates that even when dispassionate assessment of the actual interests suggests reasonable solutions, the conflicting perceptions of the parties can be a formidable obstacle to compromise.

The Consensus Syndrome
(Groupthink)

In any political system, the principal decision makers tend to form a fairly cohesive group with similar ideological, political, and intellectual orientations; compatible experiences; and a low propensity to espouse acutely conflicting views on specific issues—particularly in the area of foreign policy and international relations.

In dealing with a specific question, the members of such a group tend to converge toward a common viewpoint, even when conflicting views initially are considered. Any member that persists in advocating a policy that is diametrically opposed to the prevailing view is likely to be either ignored or overruled. Sooner or later, a habitual dissenter is likely to be removed from the group altogether.

The tendency to concur—or *groupthink*[12] appears to be one of the key dynamics of decision making. One author, who studied in detail the U.S. decisions during the Korean War, noted the high degree of "intra-group solidarity." He quoted one of the participants as saying that "the finest spirit of harmony I have ever seen" prevailed at a meeting at which a major decision was made.[13] In fact, there is abundant evidence that the members of a decision-making group place a high value on cohesiveness and convergence of views. Many foreign policy blunders can be traced to this groupthink syndrome. The possibility of a defective decision is increased because any members having inner reservations about the wisdom of a proposed course of action tend to submerge their disagreement so that they can remain part of the team. The effort to downplay personal objections—which may not always be conscious or deliberate—does not present a major personal problem in most cases; the participants are predisposed to a common or compatible viewpoint as they enter the process, and they have fairly uniform backgrounds and political–ideological orientations. This often leads to stereotyped views of adversaries, contagious optimism or pessimism, and a mutually reinforcing reasoning that may compound a defective analysis and solidify it into an unshakable conviction and a sacrosanct guideline for future action.

.... The Subordinate Officials

The role of subordinate bureaucrats in the formulation of foreign policy is extensive and even decisive for two reasons:

1. Most day-to-day decisions originate within the appropriate bureaucracy, take shape as they move up through the bureaucratic apparatus, and are not drastically revised by the high-level decision makers who are likely to give their imprimatur to what the bureaucrats have already worked out.

2. However wise, imaginative, or experienced, the principal decision makers cannot possibly reach valid decisions through mere intuition or divine inspiration; international problems are much too complex for such haphazard handling. Those who make the final decisions need reliable and specific information that has been processed, verified, analyzed, and evaluated by individuals who can draw on long experience and accumulated knowledge.[14]

Winston Churchill, Harry Truman, Henry Kissinger, and others who have written about their experiences while in office repeatedly refer to unnamed staff employees, foreign service or military personnel, technical experts, and other bureaucrats who contributed to the decision-making process by providing the raw material from which specific decisions could be fashioned. We mentioned the memoirs of President Johnson, and in particular the August 4, 1964, meeting that he convened as soon as he was told that Vietnamese PT boats had attacked two U.S. destroyers in the Gulf of Tonkin. At the meeting, the high-ranking officials discussing alternative courses of action to deal with an alleged incident 9,000 miles away needed factual information to reach a valid decision.

During the initial stages of the crisis, the information reaching the White House was limited and uncertain. At the meeting of August 4, the secretaries of state and defense told President Johnson that their staffs were "developing a set of options for response but that the proposals were not ready for presentation." During the day, "action reports continued to arrive from our destroyers, and from the Pacific Command. A few were ambiguous. One from the destroyer *Maddox* questioned whether the many reports of enemy torpedo firings were all valid."[15]

The quotation reveals how much the principal decision makers depend on reliable and unambiguous information. It also highlights the role played by those who gather, transmit, process, and eventually bring the needed information to the officials at the top of the pyramid. President Johnson gives a further glimpse into the actual intricacies of the process:

> I instructed McNamara to investigate these reports and obtain
> clarification. He immediately got in touch with Admiral U. S. G. Sharp
> Jr., the Commander in Chief, Pacific, and the Admiral in turn made
> contact with the De Soto patrol. McNamara and his civilian and military
> specialists went over all the evidence in specific detail. We wanted to
> be absolutely certain that our ships had actually been attacked before we
> retaliated.

Neither President Johnson nor McNamara nor even Admiral Sharp had personal, eyewitness knowledge of what had actually happened. They relied on a chain of subordinates, reaching all the way down to those actually present at the scene.

President Johnson continues his valuable description: "Admiral Sharp called McNamara to report that after checking all the reports and evidence, he had no doubt whatsoever that an attack had taken place. McNamara and his associates reached the same firm conclusion." (We may view this as another illustration of groupthink.) The Admiral's report obviously had grown out of a heavy traffic of messages coming from the ships at the scene, the reports supplied by radarscope operators, and by sailors and officers who had some visual impressions of what was happening, as well as by technicians knowledgeable of the types of weapons used by the North Vietnamese. Because the U.S. ships were not hit or damaged in any way, the reports had to rely on what eyewitnesses thought they saw.

Such a situation is far from rare, especially at a time of crisis. Much of the information that eventually reaches the principal decision makers originates from obscure, low-level government employees, diplomatic representatives, intelligence agents, technical experts or other specialists, or even ordinary individuals who happen to have—or claim to have—personal knowledge of some significant piece of information.

Although lower-level officials and subordinate bureaucrats often set the building blocks of policy and may even make policy on many routine issues, their principal tasks relate to gathering, verifying, evaluating, and interpreting *information*.

Information Gathering and Verification

Primary information comes from a variety of sources. Routine reports by diplomatic representatives provide their governments with a constant stream of information. Intelligence agencies have their own operatives in the field. Certain governments spend considerable sums to monitor broadcasts, newspaper articles, magazine stories, and other items. Electronic surveillance has been elevated to an art. The superpowers have space satellites to scan the Earth's surface and send back pictures with extremely high resolution and detail. Journalists, travelers, individuals working abroad may at times provide information of practical significance. Agents with access to significant information continue to be a valuable and widely used source.

Subordinate bureaucrats involved in the gathering of information do not always have eyewitness, direct knowledge of the intelligence they pass on to their superiors. Verifying the accuracy of information often is a difficult task, especially in international relations, because the sources of primary information usually are beyond the administrative control of those who are entrusted with gathering and evaluating the information and because conditions at the point of origin may not allow foolproof verification.

The original information may be inaccurate because the primary source was misinformed. Or the primary source may be the victim of deception. The primary source may be deliberately lying. Here is a little-known incident that reveals with stark clarity this basic weakness of the information-gathering process. On July 15, 1974, the National Intelligence Bulletin (NIB), which is submitted daily to U.S. officials at the highest levels, contained the following brief statement: "Ioannides is taking a moderate line while he plays for time in his dispute with Archbishop Makarios." For several weeks, there had been reports that then Greek strongman Brigadier D. Ioannides was planning a coup against Cypriot President Archbishop Makarios, whom he regarded as a pro-Communist and an obstacle to a solution of the Cypriot problem through a joint arrangement with Turkey. The reassuring report was based on information given CIA operatives in Athens by a source who claimed that Ioannides had changed his mind and that there was not going to be a coup against Makarios after all. The information turned out to be grossly inaccurate. On the morning of July 15, 1974, at the very moment the high-level U.S. officials in Washington were reading the report in the daily NIB, the coup had already started in Nicosia, and Makarios had barely escaped alive through a back door of the presidential palace.

To be useful, information must be reliable and accurate. False information is worse than no information at all. How can the decision makers tell whether the information passed on to them is valid? One key element is the *reliability* of the source. Space satellites, which report mechanically and unemotionally on what their cameras and scanning devices see, constitute perhaps one of the most reliable sources. Statistical data compiled by foreign governments or other entities for internal, professional use may be regarded as a fairly reliable source if properly correlated and analyzed. Official documents of verifiable authenticity may be another good source. In the age of photo-copying, even highly classified documents can be easily and swiftly copied. Such verifiable information is not always available, however. Quite often the primary information has to come directly from human sources. The veracity and reliability of such sources cannot be ascertained easily. Even a seemingly reliable source may be untrust-worthy. Stories surface from time to time of strategically placed informants who are deliberately fed false information to pass on to their clients. In subsequent hearings regarding the Makarios incident, witnesses implied that the informant—whom they described as "an untested source"—might have passed deliberately misleading information; the experts call this *disinformation*.

To overcome these inevitable pitfalls of information gathering, governments use several means to improve verification, such as a multiplicity of sources for cross-checking and a constant review of a source's reliability. Today, advance technologies of data processing, storage, and retrieval and the use of computers and other technical developments have tremendously expanded our capacity to obtain, verify, and evaluate information. Nevertheless, in many ordinary—or even momentous—decisions, policy makers have to depend on much more mundane and vulnerable means of information gathering; despite technological advances, the verification of information remains an imperfect art.

Even when the authenticity of information is fully established, we still have the problem of evaluation and interpretation.

Evaluation and Interpretation

Information originating from primary sources is moved up through several layers of professional evaluation and interpretation. Even the most accurate information may be misinterpreted as it goes through this process.

Henry Kissinger has cited one such case in his book *Years of Upheaval*. According to the author, prior to the 1973 "Yom Kippur" war in the Middle East, U.S. officials had received numerous reports that Syrian and Egyptian military preparations appeared to be too extensive and realistic to be related to mere war games. Yet those who analyzed and interpreted these reports discounted the evidence and concluded that "an Egyptian attack is unlikely." Kissinger says, "Between June and September, the reporting from our various diplomatic posts converged on the proposition that war was improbable." In the opinion of those who processed the information, "Egypt and Syria were said to be suspicious of Soviet motivations and were thought to be relying increasingly on economic pressures, especially the oil weapon."[16] To the very last day, the consensus was that "Egypt does not appear to be prepared for war with Israel."[17] Interestingly, Israeli intelligence fully concurred with this assessment. Convinced of their military superiority, the Israelis were unwilling to accept the possibility that Egypt and Syria could attempt a war that in the Israeli view could lead to only another Arab defeat. As Kissinger ruefully observes, neither the Israeli government nor that of the United States "could take seriously the notion of starting an unwinnable war to restore self-respect."

The evaluation and interpretation of information also may be affected by the self-oriented concerns of subordinate bureaucrats. Those familiar with the dynamics of administrative behavior point to the tendency of subordinates to avoid the advocacy of views that may be in conflict with the views or the vested interests of superiors who can affect the subordinate's promotion or career development. Another self-oriented concern that may have a detrimental effect on the decision-making process is manifested in the tendency of subordinates to supply interpretations that vindicate their own predictions or those of their immediate superiors. These tendencies often are deliberately encouraged or at least tolerated by superior officials who want to justify their own policy decisions.

The evaluation and interpretation of information also may suffer if the principal decision makers have solidified perceptions that almost automatically preclude the acceptance of information that contradicts their views. For several years, successive U.S. administrations had accepted the viability and strength of the Shah's government in Iran almost without questioning. Reports forecasting internal troubles were given low priority and even lower credence. In the few months before the fall of the Shah, intelligence reports from Iran conveyed two different images: some reports emanating from the political section of the American Embassy expressed pessimism about the stability of the regime; other reports, primarily from the CIA operatives in Iran, stressed the loyalty and effectiveness of the Iranian military. Few reports touched on the political influence of the Moslem clergy and even fewer dealt with the personal standing of Ayatollah Khomeini, then living in Paris as a political exile.

Because evaluation and interpretation depend mostly on human judgment, not on the impersonal objectivity of electronic devices, vested interests, prejudices, individual biases, or the tendency to cling tenaciously to previously held positions may intrude and distort the outcome.

The evaluation and interpretation of essential information can be improved if greater attention is given to independent sources. Press reports can be useful. They may focus on "facts" that raise questions about the official data or interpretation. Again, the effectiveness of such independent sources should not be exaggerated. Journalists can be misled, ill-informed, or biased, no less than government officials. Even when press reports are factual and reliable, they may be ignored by government officials, especially when they seem to contradict conventional wisdom or an established policy.

Domestic Input Sources ....

In addition to the principal decision makers and subordinate bureaucrats, a variety of other domestic entities may affect the content of a country's foreign policy. These entities can be regarded as "influential outsiders"; they normally are not part of the formal decision-making machinery. Especially in democratic countries, such entities may include business groups, labor unions or other organizations, legislatures, the press, political parties, study groups, or private individuals.[18]

On occasion, influential outsiders are brought into the process by the principal decision makers themselves. In March 1983, for example, President Reagan called on the representatives of conservative religious organizations to use their influence against a nuclear freeze. This was not a unique occurrence. Governments often try to enlist the support of influential groups.

Concerned groups or individuals may introduce themselves into the process on their own. The form of the intrusion may vary. During the Vietnam war, antiwar demonstrators used confrontational and even violent methods to influence policy in the United States. A different illustration is offered by the so-called Jewish lobby, which relies on the considerable influence and extensive political connections of its members both in Congress and in the executive to promote policies favorable to Israel.[19] Its influence often has been quite dramatic. On March 1, 1980, for example, the U.S. delegate to the United Nations joined the other fourteen members of the Security Council and voted for a resolution rebuking Israel for increasing the number of Israeli settlements in Arab territories seized in the 1967 war. The following day—under pressure from pro-Israeli groups—President Carter personally disavowed the vote to the consternation of domestic and foreign observers.[20]

Business groups or labor organizations in democratic countries often act to influence foreign policies, especially when those policies affect their economic interests. In the early 1980s, for example, farm organizations in Western Europe exerted considerable pressure on their governments to preserve in the EEC the protectionist measures that favored the economic interests of European farmers by limiting the imports of American farm products.

When pressure groups or other interested parties find that their influence is not sufficient to affect a decision, they may enlist the support of others with greater clout. These may be other pressure groups, political parties, friendly legislators, influential personalities within or outside the government, or even officials of other governments.

In restrictive and totalitarian systems, governments may be indifferent to public opinion but they cannot ignore the prevailing domestic conditions without risking failure. The status of the domestic economy, the views of their own narrow but indispensable constituencies (usually in the military), the risk of opening the gates to those who oppose the regime, and the actual potential of the tangible assets at their disposal are among the domestic factors they have to assess as they formulate their policies.

Foreign policy may be affected by domestic elements that benefit directly from conditions of prolonged confrontation. In the United States, the so-called military–industrial complex mentioned by Eisenhower in his farewell address is such an element. This complex is assumed to include the professional military, whose careers depend on a protracted—albeit nonviolent—conflict justifying sizeable expenditures for defense, and the managers of corporations that depend on and benefit handsomely from military orders for equipment and weapons. These groups have their own allies in Congress as well as in the higher echelons of the executive. Many thousand workers are employed in the defense industries; the major labor unions in the United States—the AFL–CIO, the Teamsters' Union, the Longshoremen's Union—have supported defense outlays and Cold War policies.[21]

We can assume that comparable pressures are not unknown in the Soviet Union. The Soviet military establishment also has a vested interest in greater outlays for defense. The managers of heavy-industry enterprises can expect to receive greater bonuses and other benefits, as can scientific and technical institutes engaged in defense projects, during a protracted conflict. All those associated with defense can expect to receive a larger slice of the pie.

Pressures from political, economic, or other entities are not the only factors government officials must assess when they formulate foreign policy. Economic and social conditions also may act either as a constraint on or as an encouragement to the pursuit of a specific policy. A troubled economy may present a barrier to ambitious foreign policies. On the other hand, a government facing serious economic or social problems may try to shift public attention by embarking on some military adventure that can whip up the people's nationalistic feelings. This is a dangerous subterfuge that can backfire easily. Some observers have argued, for example, that in 1982 the military regime in Argentina seized the Falkland (Malvinas) islands in an effort to divert Argentine public opinion from the unsatisfactory economic conditions in the country. The apparent expectation was that success would gain tremendous prestige for the regime domestically by satisfying the nationalistic feelings of the Argentine people. When Britain resisted successfully, ousting the invading Argentine forces, the leader of the military regime, General Galtieri, had to resign.

A Multidimensional Process ....

This brief review of the effects the various domestic factors have on the formulation of a country's foreign policies shows that it is unrealistic and inadequate to view international relations as though the major actors—namely, the sovereign states—are monolithic, one-dimensional entities. The final content of their policies is a composite of many conflicting interests and viewpoints, reflecting a complex of manifest or hidden compromises necessitated by the interplay of many domestic forces and a variety of domestic conditions. Moreover, it reflects the influence of varied *foreign elements*.

Foreign Elements ....

Foreign policy is not formulated in a vacuum; it has to be correlated to the policies and capabilities of other international actors. In deciding what course to follow, a government needs to review the assets and capabilities of foreign participants, their objectives, their internal problems, their connections with other international actors, the possible reactions of secondary participants, and international developments that may affect in one way or another the bargaining position or power potential of those directly involved in an international transaction or confrontation.

The complexity of the process can be seen in the following illustration. In deciding to invade Lebanon in June 1982, the Israeli government must have taken into account the disarray of the Lebanese government and the impotence of the Lebanese army; the military capabilities of the Syrians and the PLO fighters in Lebanon; the fact that Egypt and most likely Jordan as well were not going to become involved and give military support to the PLO; the expected unwillingness of the Soviet government to go beyond mere verbal expressions of moral support for the Palestinians; the anticipated support for Israel or at least acquiescence of the United States; and the ineffectiveness of possible reactions by other entities such as the European governments, other members of the United Nations, or other Arab states. The assessment of all these diverse foreign elements apparently convinced the Israelis that they could move into Lebanon and realize their objectives—the destruction of the PLO armed contingents in Lebanon and possibly the removal of the Syrian forces from the Bekaa Valley, and the restoration of Lebanon as a state friendly to Israel or at least neutral in the Arab–Israeli conflict. At the very minimum, the operation was bound to remove the threat posed along the northern border of Israel by hostile PLO forces stationed in southern Lebanon. A review of all these factors must have convinced the Israeli policy makers that the benefits and the limited risks justified the operation.

.... Primary and Secondary Participants

In our illustration, some of the entities whose potential reactions Israel had to consider were directly involved, whereas others were of only secondary significance. In almost every international transaction or confrontation, policy makers find both primary and secondary participants. The former are governments or other actors whose policies have a direct effect on the eventual outcome. The latter are those whose views and possible reactions may have some effect and for this reason may be taken into consideration by those directly involved.

Determining the identity of the primary participants is not a mere intellectual exercise. It is of practical importance for at least three reasons:

1. If it is uncertain about the identity of the primary foreign participants, a government may waste precious resources directing its efforts against irrelevant targets or trying to deal with unrelated entities

2. Confusion on this point may unnecessarily involve countries not concerned with the issue, and may aggravate relations with them

3. A faulty identification of the primary foreign participants may lead to an erroneous strategy, because decisions on how to deal with a problem are closely linked to the identity, objectives, and assets and capabilities of the other participants

Identifying the primary participants in a given transaction or confrontation is not always easy or automatic. In fact, the identity of such participants may in itself become a controversial issue. In 1982, for example, the Reagan administration saw the Soviet Union, Cuba, and Nicaragua as countries directly involved in supporting the guerrilla campaign in El Salvador. This view was not shared by members of Congress, opinion leaders, area experts, and several Latin American governments.

Governments are primarily concerned with the policies of other sovereign governments. At times, however, other entities may be primary or secondary participants. The PLO is not a sovereign government, yet its policies cannot be ignored. SWAPO (the South-West African People's Organization) is not a sovereign entity either, but it was accepted as a participant in the discussions for an independent Namibia. Governments also are concerned with the policies of private entities such as the major multinational corporations (MNCs), especially when a government is interested in attracting such an entity into the country to foster economic development or when a government wishes to place the activities of such entities under control to curb their economic or political influence.

Governments also may be interested in the activities and policies of international organizations. Certainly the lending policies of the World Bank are of considerable interest to the governments of the LDCs. The activities of the United Nations or of regional organizations may become a subject of consideration or concern. The policies of the EEC are important not only to the member states but also to many other governments throughout the world.

Ethics and Ideology ....

Students of international relations do not agree about the actual effect of ethical or ideological considerations on the content of foreign policy decisions. To what extent and under what circumstances are such elements taken into account by those who make policy decisions? Do they play any significant role at all? These are practical questions, because the introduction of ethical or ideological inputs in the process—or the absence of such inputs—may have a profound effect on the content and the direction of foreign policy and the development of international relations. In the 1950s, for example, John Foster Dulles, secretary of state in the Eisenhower administration, viewed the Soviet Union as an "evil power" driven by the ideology of "atheistic communism" and bent on global domination.[22] This ideological perception of the Soviet Union aggravated the Cold War and left an enduring mark on American–Soviet relations. As recently as 1983, President Reagan called the Soviet Union "an evil empire."[23] There is little doubt that ideology or ethics can play a potent role.

Ethical Considerations

There seems to be a popular assumption that the makers of foreign policy are too cynical to be concerned with questions of right and wrong, good and evil. In fact, so the argument goes, officials who are overly concerned with ethics may become easy prey at the hands of opponents who prefer a hardnosed, realistic policy and leave ethical questions to the theologians and philosophers. This is a simplification. The formulation of foreign policy is too complex a process to be neatly wrapped either in a straightjacket of ethical purity or in the "evil" precepts of *realpolitik*.* To assess the effect of ethical considerations on foreign policy we need to take into account the following points.

Ethical Values Are Relative

We should keep in mind that the notions of *good* and *evil* are not the same for everyone. U.S. policy makers certainly argue that their policies are guided by their commitment to

---

*A German term implying a preference for "realistic" policies based on power and unconstrained by ethical or humanistic considerations.

individual freedom, which they regard as the epitome of good. By contrast, the Khomeini regime in Iran firmly holds to the belief that the United States is the incarnation of evil. To the Iranian leaders, the precepts of Islam as interpreted by them are the foundation of good. The leaders of many Third World countries argue with conviction that their egalitarian policies represent a genuine good, whereas the "imperialist" and "capitalist" policies of the Western industrial countries are exploitative and evil. The list of illustrations could be very long indeed.

Ethical Guidelines Are Not Self-Evident

Ethical guidelines are much less absolute and self-evident than many of us tend to believe. When President Truman authorized the use of atomic bombs on Hiroshima and Nagasaki, he appeared to be firmly convinced that his decision was ethically right because the action was likely to end the war and thereby spare the lives of "a million American soldiers." The ethical aspects of saving the lives of so many people overshadowed the questionable ethics of instantaneously exterminating the inhabitants of Hiroshima and Nagasaki. More recently, the Reagan administration was criticized for supporting undemocratic regimes in various parts of the world. The argument usually offered in rebuttal was that the alternative to such regimes was a Communist takeover, which, in the eyes of U.S. policy makers, was a greater evil.[24]

Policies Perceived as Ethically Good Are Attractive

Although ethical considerations may be adjusted to political necessity, ordinary people tend to support policies that appear to be ethical and noble. One of the tasks policy makers often face is how to convince their constituents that the policy they advocate is indeed ethical and noble. This is not always an easy task for two reasons. First, in each nation-state, traditions, history, religion, education, customs, ideology, and experiences stored in the public memory over time create certain ethical orientations, a value structure. These values become part of the emotional and intellectual "filter" that affects the views and attitudes of most people in the national community.[25] As a rule, those basic values and ethical precepts are not manufactured instantaneously by the individuals who are in charge of policy making at a given time. They find the value structure already ensconced in the firmament of the national psyche; and they have to take it into account if they are to generate wide popular support for or to avert opposition to their policies. Even Hitler had to consider the ethical values of the German people. He kept his crematoria out of the public eye, knowing that the wholesale extermination of human beings would have caused a tremendous revulsion not only abroad but among his fellow Germans as well.

Second, to gain popular support, the policy makers need to "dress up" their objectives and methods so that they will seem to be in line with the prevailing values and ethical orientations. This task requires not only a masterful use of the language but also the supporting evidence of facts and practices. During the Vietnam war, the American public accepted the official argument that the U.S. military effort was necessary to preserve the freedom of people who did not want to come under Communist control—a clearly ethical objective in the eyes of most Americans. The tide of opposition to the war began to swell only when the realities of the war came with increasing ferocity into the living rooms of American families through the visual intimacy of the television screen. The brutal actions seemed to belie the "ethical" explanations and justifications given by policy makers.

Policy Makers' and Society's Values

Because policy makers do not come from a distant planet, they too are imbued with the basic values of the society in which they live. The story is told that at Yalta, Stalin—following his custom of dropping on the conference table a politically explosive issue with a casual remark—told Churchill that one way to end forever the threat of German militarism was to execute fifty thousand German officers after the war. Churchill, knowing that Stalin had exterminated millions, took the remark seriously and rejected the idea in no uncertain terms. To Churchill, the coldblooded killing of people after the war was over clashed with a conception of ethical conduct that he certainly shared with the overwhelming majority of his fellow citizens and most other people in the democratic West.

Influence of Policy on Ethical Orientations

To strengthen their hand, policy makers try to adjust or even create new ethical orientations to serve their policy objectives. In the United States, the prevailing notion of communism as an evil system has been an indispensable underpinning for the specific policies Washington has pursued for the last forty years in dealing with the Soviet Union and a host of other countries.

Revolutionary regimes, in particular, find it necessary to twist preexisting values and create new notions of good and evil to generate popular support for their policies. The elaborate efforts of the Nazis in Germany in the 1930s to create a set of beliefs centered on the superiority of the "Aryan race" and its mission to preserve and expand the "Aryan civilization" succeeded in generating wide support. Within the short span of six years, millions of Germans were ready to march to war, sustain untold suffering on the frozen plains of Russia, commit unspeakable atrocities, and fight to a bitter and disastrous end. The Soviet government, too, has tried through the years to build an image of moral superiority for the Soviet system. Its efforts have not been wasted. The soldiers that were dispatched to Hungary in 1956, to Czechoslovakia in 1968, and to Afghanistan in 1979 were told, and appeared to be convinced, that they were serving a moral and noble purpose—the defense of socialism against the threat of Western imperialism, with all the evil connotations they were taught to attach to the latter label.

Ethical Justification of Practical Policies

Ethical considerations not only are a potential barrier to a cynical or cruel pursuit of power; they also may be used to generate popular support for a policy that has very practical, material objectives. In 1948, George Marshall, then U.S. secretary of state, presented what became known as the Marshall Plan as a noble undertaking designed to help the Europeans reconstruct their war-ravaged continent and regain their economic vitality and social stability. President Kennedy's Alliance for Progress in the 1960s and President Reagan's more modest Caribbean Economic Initiative in 1982 also were presented in ethical and moral terms that seemed to enhance the nobility of their more practical objectives.

In summing up, we may say that ethical considerations play a role in the formulation and particularly in the justification of foreign policy because ordinary citizens are more likely to support a policy they consider ethical; and, of course, policy makers, especially in democratic systems, are aware that effective implementation requires public support.

....The Impact of Ideology

Although it is unwise to assume that a country's foreign policy is shaped only by the ideological beliefs of its officials, it is equally foolish to dismiss ideology as an irrelevant element in the decision-making process.

We defined *ideology* as a cluster of beliefs relating to the basic organization of society, its core values, and an individual's place in it. Scholars may argue over definitions; policy makers are more interested in the *role* played by such ideological beliefs, because people are motivated by their beliefs and tend to view the world through ideologically tinted glasses. Ideology enters the decision-making process for three principal reasons.

Public Support. A policy that runs against the grain of popular ideological convictions may fail to win the necessary public backing. For more than twenty years, a succession of U.S. administrations found it virtually impossible to recognize the Chinese government in Beijing while holding to the political fiction that the Nationalist regime in Taiwan continued to be the government of China. They realized that those who opposed recognition of the government in Beijing could exploit the anticommunist feelings of the American people and stir up enough opposition in Congress to kill any such initiative. It took the war in Vietnam and a shift in public attitudes to allow a new President—Richard Nixon—with impeccable anticommunist credentials to reverse the U.S. policy on China and open the way to improve relations with the Chinese Communists. Even then, Nixon moved carefully and confronted the general public, the supporters of the Nationalist Chinese in the Pentagon and in Congress, as well as the so-called China lobby, with the surprise announcement on July 15, 1971, that he had accepted an invitation to visit Beijing.

Troop Morale. Ideology may be used to mobilize public support for a foreign policy favored by the government. During World War I, thousands of U.S. citizens fought in the distant battlefields of Europe "to make the world safe for democracy." Ideological opposition to fascism and nazism during World War II inspired millions of Allied soldiers and mobilized countless volunteers who fought in the Resistance, in Axis-occupied Europe.

On the other side, Hitler and his minister of propaganda Joseph Goebbels used German nationalism and the trappings of National Socialism to mobilize millions of Germans for a war of conquest. Religion has been used in the same way.

Motivation for Greater Effort.   Although ideology may not be people's only or even principal motivation (people may be moved by more selfish objectives and motives), it can add the "extra touch" that spurs human beings to greater efforts. If we are to include *nationalism* as one of the most pervasive ideologies of our time, then we can see to what extent ideology can be an indispensable input in the making of foreign policy.

Propaganda as a Tool
of Foreign Policy...

As we indicated earlier in this chapter, perceptions are central to international relations. The success of a government's foreign policy depends in large measure on what people *think* about that policy. Domestically, important constituencies must be convinced that a specific policy is advantageous, necessary, or justifiable. Abroad, it is useful to have a favorable public opinion.

Today, with the technological advances in the field of communications, messages traveling with the speed of light reach simultaneously millions of people, affecting their views and perceptions. Government officials are very conscious of the role "information" can play in international relations and try to manipulate its content to reap the benefits of its political effects both domestically and internationally.

This politically motivated dissemination of information is often called *propaganda,* especially by those who dislike the content or disagree with the originators of the communication.[26] However, the term *propaganda* may be given a more neutral connotation; the process is one of the essential and widely used tools of foreign policy. In this sense, *propaganda is the process of selectively disseminating factual as well as untrue information and arguments to create impressions and convictions politically advantageous to the originator.*[27]

Propaganda as defined is not a newly discovered political tool. Its origins can be traced to the earliest exchanges between sovereign entities.[28] In the twentieth century, technological progress and the tremendous increase of potential users of information have raised the utility of propaganda dramatically. Even illiterate people in remote hamlets in Africa, Asia, or Latin America can listen to political messages on their inexpensive transistor radios. Communication satellites bring televised images directly to our living rooms from far away countries. Governments determined to insulate their citizens from foreign influences find that their endeavors to do so are becoming increasingly difficult unless they resort to deliberate electronic interference (jamming).

The major problem facing those who try to influence the thinking and perceptions of people in other countries is not how to reach those people in a technical sense but how to make their messages acceptable and persuasive. Information from a foreign source tends to be viewed with some mistrust or suspicion unless the audience mistrusts or dislikes its own government more. During the military dictatorship in Greece (1967–

1974) antiregime reports broadcast by Deutsche Welle in West Germany found a wide and receptive audience. By contrast, Castro's radio broadcasts have made few converts to Marxism among Cuban expatriates in Miami.

Propaganda usually is more effective when carried out by nationals of the target country. In many parts of the world, particularly in developing countries, anti-Western, Marxist-oriented revolutionary groups exploit local problems and try to win converts to their ideology, hoping to bring about, by force if necessary, drastic political changes in their country. Whether they act with direct Soviet support or are more or less acting on their own, they tend to serve the foreign policy interests of the major power that claims to be the fountainhead and bastion of their common ideology. Local activists at times face the problem of being viewed by their potential audiences as agents, or even pawns, of an alien power. Such a perception tends to undermine their effectiveness.

In any event, local activists have a distinct advantage over foreign propagandists. Local activists are familiar with the problems, aspirations, and attitudes of the people they want to influence. In many cases, the activist is a member of the target population and speaks the language in both a literal and a metaphorical sense. Local revolutionaries have these critical assets.

These advantages are not associated exclusively with anti-Western political activists and revolutionaries. In the majority of countries in Africa, Asia, Latin America, and the Caribbean, we find that many influential journalists, educators, opinion leaders at the local and national level, and political, business, and even labor leaders have a non-Marxist ideological orientation. They may not always be supportive of Western objectives, or they may even oppose specific policies, but on the whole they are not willing to accept Soviet tutelage or to support a Marxist–Leninist form of political and economic organization in their countries. Their ability to communicate with their fellow citizens is a critical political advantage.

Propaganda is not necessarily related to ideology. It can be used to promote any foreign policy objective. For example, statements by U.S. and Soviet officials on the control of nuclear armaments are obviously designed to gain support for their respective proposals, quiet public fears, or generate opposition to the views of the opposite side.

To be effective, propaganda must rely on fairly simple, comprehensible, and vivid images and concepts. Prospective audiences are usually large, composed mostly of average citizens, not of sophisticated intellectuals. Their interests, attitudes, and aspirations vary. Propaganda requires a common denominator, a message that is sufficiently general to cover many differences of opinion and sufficiently dramatic to grab the imagination and the attention of the audience.

The message does not have to be true or accurate, but it must appear to be so. It must contain enough truth to make even the untrue parts believable. If the audience can easily see that the "facts" contained in the message are patently untrue, the credibility of the propagandist may be damaged beyond repair. This is not as major a problem as it appears. "Facts" are not always verifiable or known through direct, personal observation; the perception of the validity of a given "fact" often depends on the prejudices of the audience.

Propaganda is more effective when the propagandist uses some facts that are readily verifiable by the audience, and then moves on to give these facts an interpretation that serves the propaganda purposes. For example, anti-Western activists in the Third

World point to existing conditions of economic underdevelopment and poverty—which are there for all to see—and then argue that these conditions are the result of *neocolonialism* and *dependency,* code words meaning that the *capitalists* and *imperialists* are holding the developing countries to a permanent state of dependence and subservience to extract exorbitant profits from the exploitation of people and resources. Such a line of argument can be convincing unless effectively refuted by *local* leaders.

Experienced propagandists are likely to expound their theories using words that are traditionally associated in the public mind with positive images, whereas they reserve words with negative connotations for the policies or the alleged goals of their adversaries. Moreover, these words, slogans, and arguments are used time and again so that through repetition they come to appear as a true reflection of reality.

Propaganda thus is a useful tool of foreign policy, but its effectiveness depends on the manner in which it is used and on its coordination with other factors.

The Process Affects the Issue...............................

Those responsible for a country's foreign policy do not usually have a manual on their desk that describes the steps they must take to reach a decision. Does this mean that the decision-making process is a matter of improvisation and fortuitous guessing? Most practitioners agree that guessing and improvisation and a tendency to "muddle through" are not unknown.[29] Yet common sense suggests certain practical steps that must be taken to improve the chances for a favorable outcome. These steps normally include:

- Efforts to obtain reliable and relevant information

- A definition of the problem

- Clarification of the objectives to be pursued

- An assessment of the capabilities and weaknesses of both sides

- Selection of a course of action

- Provision for contingencies and "fall-back" positions

- A determination of the tactics that will be used at the various stages of bargaining or confrontation

- The overall strategy

.... Defining the Problem

Every international transaction or confrontation involves some *problem*—an obstacle or barrier standing between an objective and its realization. If the PLO wants an independent Palestinian state and Israel refuses to let such a state be established in the Israeli-occupied West Bank, a problem exists between these two international actors; to the extent that this problem threatens the peace and stability of the Middle East, it is a problem also for those governments that consider peace in the area to be in their interest. If a particular objective can be achieved without difficulty, then there is hardly any need for bargaining or confrontation. However, this is not frequently the case in international relations, in which the objectives of one actor tend to touch on the interests of another.

Identifying the problem is not always a simple matter. In fact, the *definition of the problem* may itself become a matter of dispute and controversy and may render the solution more (or less) difficult.

The 1974 Geneva conference on Cyprus is a textbook illustration of erroneous problem definition. During the conference, the Greek side defined the problem in terms of the island's illegal invasion by the Turkish army and asked for the removal of these forces. In the face of the Greek capabilities at the time, this objective was clearly unattainable. Yet the Greek side did not revise its objectives—the definition of the problem—to adjust its course of action to the actual capabilities. Turkey, on her part, defined the problem in terms of providing protection to the Turk-Cypriot community on Cyprus. Such protection, they argued, could be accomplished through some form of a federal structure, with the Turk-Cypriots having their own separate region. Had the problem been stated by both sides in terms of an equitable division of territory, reflecting the actual composition of the island population (80 percent Greek-Cypriot and 18 percent Turk-Cypriot) a solution could have been easier to find, especially given that at the time of the conference the Turkish army occupied only a very small area on the north coast of Cyprus. The Greek-Cypriots, however, insisted on their definition of the problem and rejected the concept of a federal state.[30] By so doing they were risking further military action by the Turkish army, the occupation of a much larger area, and the expulsion of tens of thousands of Greek-Cypriots from their homes in the northern part of the island. Because they had no adequate military force to prevent these consequences, their rejection of a federal structure as a compromise solution was obviously unwise. With the collapse of the conference, the Turkish army spread its occupation to almost 40 percent of the island and turned more than 180,000 Greek-Cypriots into refugees. An improper definition of the problem can lead to disaster.

If the problem is defined in terms that make its solution very difficult through a compromise, the policy makers who defined the dimensions of the problem must be prepared to consider: (1) the consequences of failing to reach a solution in keeping with their objectives, and (2) the resources that will be needed to solve the problem *as they defined it*. If, during the 1962 Cuban missile crisis, the U.S. government had stated that their country's security required not only the removal of the Soviet missiles but also the end to Castro's pro-Soviet policies or even the removal of his regime, then the solution would have been a great deal more difficult. Prudently, the U.S. government limited the problem to the presence of offensive missiles, and thus offered Moscow a compromise solution.[31]

Prudent decision makers try to avoid blowing up the dimensions and the intricacies of a particular international problem; they moderate their specific objectives to match their capabilities. After all, a problem results from the existence of barriers to the realization of a particular objective. If the objective is modest, there will be fewer obstacles to its realization and consequently more manageable problems. A clarification of the objectives goes hand in hand with the definition of the problem.

....Establishing the Objectives

Depending on the actual circumstances, policy makers may have to identify long-term, intermediate, and immediate objectives. During the negotiations that eventually led to the Camp David agreements between Egypt and Israel, the long-term objective of the Egyptian leadership was to recover the territory Egypt had lost to the Israelis in 1967. Israel, on its part, wanted a peace treaty with Egypt so that the Egyptian army no longer would be part of a military offensive by Israel's Arab neighbors. The United States was interested in the preservation of peace in the Middle East. Another military conflagration in the area carried with it the risk of a dangerous confrontation with the Soviet Union and of increased destabilization in a region whose oil resources are vital to the West.

This convergence of long-term objectives did not guarantee a speedy agreement, however. A step-by-step study of the protracted negotiations, which at times seemed to be on the verge of collapse, will show that progress toward a final agreement was impeded mostly by the vexing details, not by the broad, long-term objectives of the parties. The difficulties during the negotiations resulted from conflicting viewpoints on detailed issues such as the pace of Israeli withdrawal from the occupied areas in the Sinai, the disposition of the oil fields that were developed by Israel, the location and use of military bases, the detailed steps leading to an autonomous Palestinian entity in the West Bank and Gaza, and the status of Jerusalem. To avoid a breakdown in the negotiations, both sides had to scale down their immediate and intermediate objectives, thus rendering the related problems more manageable.[32]

Prudent policy makers do not set objectives that are bound to create problems they cannot handle with the assets and capabilities at their disposal. Confronted daily with specific issues, not abstract generalities, they need to: (1) obtain a clear and accurate understanding of the situation and of its implications, and (2) decide on what they want to accomplish under the circumstances. In fact, each decision is linked to some specific objective.

Setting the objectives is a complex process. The policy makers need to: (1) ascertain the actual circumstances and the interests that are at stake so that their objectives will be relevant; (2) weigh alternative objectives, ranging from the most ambitious to the least extravagant; and (3) evaluate the assets needed to achieve each alternative objective, in order to determine which objectives to pursue.

...................................Evaluating Assets and Capabilities

Policy makers need to have a clear and factual knowledge of the resources they can bring to bear to improve their chances for a successful outcome in a transaction or confrontation. Such a realistic assessment will help them set their objectives within manageable limits and avoid problems they cannot solve.

To evaluate properly its capabilities, a government must determine not only which assets are available but also which are suitable; on occasion, certain available assets may have no relevance to the issue or may not be of use to affect the outcome. In 1984, the U.S. government proved unable to affect the situation in Lebanon by sending a "peace-keeping" military force, which was constrained by size and mission. To avoid costly mistakes, policy makers should keep in mind the following guidelines.

Objectives and Capabilities Must Be Balanced. If the assets seem to be inadequate to solve the problem, the decision makers may find it necessary to revise and scale down or modify their objectives.

Assets Are Sufficient Only in Relation to the Assets and Capabilities of the Other Side. Colonel Quaddafi of Libya may want the demise of Israel, but his country is too distant from Israel, the Libyan forces are not large enough, and they lack necessary transport facilities to cross the eastern Mediterranean to attack Israel. Of course, the presence of the U.S. Sixth Fleet in the Mediterranean and the capabilities of the Israeli forces make the realization of Quaddafi's professed objectives even less realistic.

The Evaluation Must Be Related to Time, Place, and Potential Participants or Adversaries. An evaluation cannot stop with a mechanistic measurement of economic resources or military forces of the other side. It must include a review of the *willingness* of the other side to use its assets. It is also prudent to conduct a study of internal or international constraints that may prevent a determined use of all the relevant assets a country has at its disposal. The United States certainly has the military capability to seize Cuba and replace the Castro regime with a government friendly to it. However, such an action would provoke a serious confrontation with the Soviet Union. U.S. policy toward Cuba obviously reflects such considerations.

Policy Makers Must Remember That the Issue Determines Which Assets Are Relevant. When the issue is primarily economic, the relevant assets are likely to be economic and political, not military. Several times in the past few years, Japan and the United States had to deal with the continuing problem of large exports of Japanese products to the United States. In this case, the military superiority of the United States was not a primary consideration. Measures to raise economic barriers by imposing restrictive limitations on Japanese imports could not be used extensively or even effectively without undermining U.S. policies designed to promote free trade and without setting the stage for a wave of protectionist policies. Washington officials favored voluntary restraints and through bargaining and persuasion tried to induce the Japanese to take action on their own. The Japanese, on their part, realized that a negative response could generate an adverse political climate in the U.S. Congress and result in legislation that could hurt Japanese exports more than any voluntary curtailments. These realities led to compromise solutions.

....Reviewing the Options

Once the policy makers have determined the nature and dimensions of the problem and the objectives they wish to pursue, the stage is set for considering various courses of action and their consequences. Each alternative carries with it certain risks, creates additional problems, and requires different assets and capabilities. In fact, as the policy makers review their options, they may realize that certain alternatives are too costly, too dangerous, or too counterproductive.

To make the right choices, the officials have to ask a number of practical questions:

- How feasible is a particular course of action?

- What risks are involved?

- Which assets are relevant?

- Are the necessary assets and capabilities available?

- Will the costs exceed any potential benefits?

- What kind of reaction may be expected from the other side?

- What will be the reactions of other international participants?

- Are there any domestic elements that may block or undermine the proposed action?

- Will a particular course of action or line of argument push the other side to an uncompromising position?

- Will there be a possibility for shifting to another option in the event of rejection or failure?

- Will it be possible to change course without weakening one's bargaining or power position?

One of the possible options is to do nothing or go through certain innocuous motions designed to provide the public with emotional satisfaction while leaving the problem unresolved. Sometimes an appeal to the United Nations may serve as a substitute for a hard decision.

In choosing a particular course of action, prudent officials make allowances for possible reversals, unexpected developments, and complications, as well as for alternative courses that may be taken up when the selected option turns out to be counterproductive or unwise. This applies as much to a power confrontation as to a bargaining transaction.

Summary

- The foreign policy of a government deals with international transactions or confrontations and is designed to achieve certain specific objectives that are presumed to serve the national interest as defined by the decision makers.

- The making of foreign policy involves: (1) domestic participants (principal decision makers, subordinate officials, and influential outsiders such as pressure groups, political parties, the press, or private individuals), and (2) foreign elements (other international actors or international developments that may affect the outcome of an international transaction or confrontation).

- Foreign policy decisions are affected primarily by practical considerations such as the objectives to be achieved, the available assets, the assets and the objectives of the other side, and the input of other international actors. They are also affected by the perceptions of the decision makers and by the introduction of ethical or ideological elements into the decision-making process.

- Ethical elements become relevant because average individuals usually are moved by value systems; thus, decision makers can generate public support for their decisions by providing ethical justifications. Although ideology may not be the principal factor in the making of foreign policy, it does affect perceptions.

- Because perceptions are critical, governments engage in deliberate efforts to influence public views in their country or abroad through propaganda.

- The outcome of an international transaction or confrontation is affected by the way the decision makers define the problem. A poor definition may make the problem's solution more difficult or even impossible. To define the problem correctly, decision makers need to adjust their objectives to their assets and capabilities and to review their options on the basis of what can be achieved realistically.

Notes

1. Snyder, Richard C., Bruck, W. W., and Sapin, Burton, eds. *Foreign Policy Decision-Making*. New York: Free Press of Glencoe, 1963; Hilsman, Roger. *To Move a Nation*. Garden City, N.J.: Doubleday, 1967; Allison, Graham. *The Essence of Decision*. Boston: Little, Brown, 1971.
2. Coplin and Kegley identify three basic sets of considerations that affect the formulation of foreign policy decisions: (1) domestic politics within the state, (2) economic and military capabilities of the state, and (3) the international context. Coplin, William D., and Kegley, Charles W., Jr., eds. *A Multi-Method Introduction to International Politics: Observations, Explanations, and Prescriptions*. Chicago: Markham, 1971, pp. 9–11.
3. Lerche, Charles O., and Said, Abdul A. *Concepts of International Politics*. Englewood Cliffs, N.J.: Prentice-Hall, 1970, pp. 46–57.
4. Johnson, Lyndon B. *The Vantage Point*. New York: Holt, Rinehart and Winston, 1971, pp. 112–113; Thomson, J. G., Jr. "How Could Vietnam Happen?: An Autopsy." *The Atlantic Monthly*, April 1968.
5. Janis, Irving L. *Groupthink*. 2nd ed. Boston: Houghton Mifflin, 1982, p. 12.
6. Johnson, *op. cit.*, pp. 112–113; see also Thomson, J. G., Jr. "How Could Vietnam Happen? An Autopsy." *The Atlantic Monthly*, April 1968.
7. At the time of the withdrawal of U. S. forces from Lebanon in February 1984, the Reagan administration took particular pains to refute charges that its move signified a "failure" of its policy in the area.
8. Morgenthau, Hans. *Politics Among Nations*. 5th ed. New York: Knopf, 1978, p. 6.
9. One may argue that Munich gave Britain more time to prepare for the oncoming war, in which case Chamberlain's "capitulation" may be viewed as a prudent maneuver.
10. Stoessinger, John S. *Why Nations Go to War*. 3rd ed. New York: St. Martin's Press, 1982, p. 24.
11. Johnson, *op. cit.*, p. 45.

12. Janis, *op. cit.*, p. 9.

13. Paige, G. D. *The Korean Decision*. New York: Free Press, 1968. (Quoted in Janis, note 11, p. 49.)

14. The role of bureaucracy has attracted the attention of several writers: Allison, Graham T. *Essence of Decision: Explaining the Cuban Missile Crisis*. Boston: Little, Brown, 1971; Halperin, Morton H. *Bureaucratic Politics and Foreign Policy*. Washington, D.C.: The Brookings Institution, 1974; Halperin, Morton, and Kanter, Arnold, eds. *Readings in American Foreign Policy: A Bureaucratic Perspective*. Boston: Little, Brown, 1973: Neustadt, Richard. *Alliance Politics*. New York: Columbia University Press, 1970; Blau, Peter M. *Bureaucracy in Modern Society*. New York: Random House, 1956. The following authors hold a critical view of bureaucracy: Krasner, Stephen D. "Are Bureaucracies Important?" *Foreign Policy,* Summer, 1971; Art, Robert. "Bureaucratic Politics and American Foreign Policy: A Critique." *Policy Sciences,* Vol. 40, 1973.

15. Johnson, *op. cit.*, p. 114.

16. Kissinger, Henry. *Years of Upheaval*. Boston: Little, Brown, 1982, p. 462.

17. *Ibid.*, p. 465.

18. Ornstein, Norman J., and Elder, Shirley. *Interest Groups, Lobbying and Policymaking*. Washington, D.C.: Congressional Quarterly Press, 1978; Nathan, James A., and Oliver, James K. *Foreign Policy Making and the American Political System*. Boston: Little, Brown, 1983.

19. Isaacs, Stephen D. *Jews and American Politics*. New York: Doubleday, 1974.

20. *The New York Times,* March 2, 1980.

21. Fox, Ronald. *Arming America: How the U.S. Buys Weapons*. Boston: Division of Research, Harvard Business School, 1974.

22. Hoopes, Townsend. *The Devil and John Foster Dulles*. Boston: Little, Brown, 1973.

23. *The New York Times,* March 9, 1983.

24. Kirkpatrick, Jeanne J. *Dictatorships and Double Standards: Rationalism and Reason in Politics*. New York: Simon and Schuster, 1982.

25. Hoffman, Stanley. *Duties Beyond Borders: On the Limits and Responsibilities of Ethical International Politics*. Syracuse, N.Y.: Syracuse University Press, 1981, p. 141.

26. During a press conference in January 1983, President Reagan used the term *propaganda* in reference to the Soviet effort to explain Moscow's nuclear weapons proposals to the Europeans; he used the term *public relations* in referring to a comparable U.S. effort.

27. Lenin introduced a distinction between *propaganda* and *agitatsia* (agitation). *Propaganda* was dealing with ideological and tactical questions reserved for the party cadres; *agitatsia* was for the broad masses. In this text, we use the term *propaganda* in its conventional meaning which corresponds more closely to Lenin's *agitatsia*.

28. Communications to foreign rulers preserved in hieroglyphics speak of the superiority of Egyptian might, the wealth of the pharaohs, the justice and fairness of their laws, and the great powers of Egypt's gods.

29. Lindbloom, E. "The Science of 'Muddling Through.'" In *Readings on Modern Organizations,* A. Etzioni, ed. Englewood Cliffs, N.J.: Prentice-Hall, 1969, pp. 154–165.

30. Polyviou, Polyvios G. *Cyprus: Conflict and Negotiation, 1960–1980*. New York: Holmes and Meier, 1980, pp. 163–185.

31. Abel, Elie. *The Missile Crisis*. New York: Bantam, 1966; Kennedy, Robert F. *Thirteen Days*. New York: Norton, 1967.

32. Carter, Jimmy. *Keeping Faith: Memoirs of a President*. New York: Bantam, 1982, pp. 376–379.

5

................Transactionalism and Diplomacy

Xuan Thuy, head of North Vietnamese delegation, at Paris peace talks

Diplomacy is the principal tool of the transactional approach. In a broad sense, *diplomacy is the manner in which peaceful contacts and transactions between international actors are conducted.* With the growing importance of economic, technical, technological, scientific, social, and environmental relationships, diplomacy no longer is confined to the traditional resolution of political problems.

Diplomacy is not the exclusive province of those with the title of "diplomat." When an American president meets at the White House with the visiting prime minister of Italy to discuss matters that concern their two countries, he is engaging in diplomacy as much as any ambassador or envoy. Diplomacy calls for imagination, flexibility, toughness, perseverance, tact, guile, self-control, sensitivity, and persuasiveness. A seasoned diplomat is indeed a man or woman of many talents.

Although those engaged in diplomatic exchanges may hope to achieve their objectives with the least amount of friction, international transactions are seldom free of some element of conflict. The outcome of a particular transaction depends on the relevant assets—economic, political, military, legal, moral—the diplomat may invoke during the talks or leave standing in the background like sentinels around the negotiating table.

At times, governments may resort to a form of *coercive diplomacy:* namely, the use of threats to "persuade" an opponent to call off an offensive activity, accept a change in the status quo, or back down from an unacceptable demand.[1]

The Tasks of Diplomacy ....

The three foremost tasks of diplomacy are:

1. To resolve an international dispute without war

2. To end a military conflict by reconciling the warring parties

3. To obtain the best possible benefits and advantages in an international transaction

Whatever its origins, a dispute may be:

1. Settled peacefully through some compromise

2. Kept on the back burner for a long time

3. Allowed to lead to a violent confrontation

The task of diplomacy is either to bring about a peaceful resolution of the dispute through a mutually acceptable compromise or to postpone hostilities by keeping the lid on the dispute in the hope that with the passing of time changing conditions will remove the causes of disagreement or at least improve the chances for a solution.

A sure sign that diplomacy has failed is the decision of one or both parties to use violence. In the absence of a superior authority (a "world government"), the sovereign states continue to consider military action as a last resort or as a means of getting on the battlefield what they are unable to gain at the negotiating table.

To perform their basic tasks, diplomats engage in informal contacts and discussions or in formal negotiations.

.... Informal Contacts

A seemingly casual conversation at a dinner or a cocktail party between a diplomat and an official of the host government or the representative of another country may be a valuable way of clarifying attitudes, eliciting information, or passing on to the other side views that for whatever reason cannot be communicated formally. In today's world, in which jet flying has made travel easy, even heads of state or government, or foreign ministers and other cabinet officials, can meet routinely with their counterparts in other countries or in international gatherings to exchange ideas and review developments and problems. An almost unending stream of foreign dignitaries—kings, presidents, prime ministers, foreign ministers—passes each year through the gates of the White House. The talks of those foreign leaders with the U.S. president and other high level officials do not necessarily take the form of negotiations. Most of the time, these officials engage in general discussions touching on a number of subjects of mutual concern, designed to convey a better understanding of each other's views, clarify attitudes, and introduce a human element into the impersonal affairs of state.

In this connection, one of the significant services performed by the United Nations is to make available its headquarters in New York as a meeting place where the permanent delegates of the various member-states and their assistants see each other almost daily, talk informally about current issues, exchange views or gossip, gain information, gauge each other's attitudes on controversial or sensitive issues, and in general "touch base" without exposing themselves to unwanted publicity. This is particularly important when two governments embroiled in a dispute want to move in the direction of a settlement but wish to avoid the appearance that they are "bowing" to the other side. The secluded lounges, private meeting rooms, parties and receptions, and delegates' dining rooms are the places where the first contacts are made and where important decisions are reached and agreements hammered out prior to their public airing in the formal organs of the organization.

"Informal" written communications also may be used in the service of diplomacy. We used quotation marks around the word *informal* because any communication among high-ranking government officials of sovereign states cannot be regarded entirely as a private exchange unless it is specifically intended as such and unless it indeed deals with private matters completely unrelated to affairs of state or to their official positions. The word *informal* as used in this context simply indicates that the written exchanges are not part of a formal negotiation. The line that separates these two types of exchange is not always clear and usually it is very thin. During the Cuban missile crisis, President Kennedy and Chairman Khrushchev exchanged several letters. To a large extent these letters paved the way for the peaceful resolution of the conflict. Should they be regarded as informal exchanges or as part of ongoing negotiations? With the advent of instant communications by telephone from one part of the planet to another, high-level officials do not limit themselves to written exchanges; they can talk directly to each other.

······································Summit Meetings

As we have indicated, contacts can be undertaken directly by chiefs of state, heads of government, or cabinet officials who are not professional diplomats but are primarily political persons. This approach has not received unqualified endorsement. Summit meetings have led to disappointments, probably because they tend to generate high expectations. In 1955, for example, the meeting of President Eisenhower with the Soviet leaders in Geneva gave rise to high hopes for better relations between Washington and Moscow and for a short period there was talk of a "spirit of Geneva." The optimistic expectations disappeared with the Soviet intervention in Hungary in October 1956. Still, there is no question that when two principal decision makers meet, a great deal of ground can be covered and even seemingly intractable disagreements resolved. Certainly the meeting of President Ford with Soviet leader Leonid Brezhnev in Vladivostok in November 1974 was instrumental in paving the way for SALT II. In his memoirs, Henry Kissinger describes in considerable detail the May 1972 meeting between President Nixon and the Soviet leaders, which led to the signing of the first SALT agreement and ushered in a period of détente in East–West relations.[2]

The possibilities for resolving thorny issues are certainly appealing. However, experience shows that this type of direct diplomacy has serious shortcomings. International disputes are seldom so simple that they can be resolved through a friendly smile and a warm handshake. A long and painstaking diplomatic effort usually is necessary. For this reason, summit diplomacy has been most successful when the principal leaders come together merely to put their stamp of approval on an arrangement already negotiated by the professional diplomats. The most that can be expected from a summit meeting is the resolution of some final points in wrapping up an agreement, or the exchange of views on setting the stage for future cooperation on mutually acceptable policies. Being of relatively short duration, summit meetings cannot be used for the actual negotiation of a complex international treaty. Nevertheless, because the participants in such meetings are the principal decision makers in their countries, what they say to one another cannot be dismissed as unimportant or inconsequential.

Direct contacts of principal decision makers present another problem. Officials in top state positions tend to see things through a political prism. They often are concerned with the effect a statement or a decision will have on their political standing, their popular support, or their political ties with their constituencies. Especially in democratic countries, where electoral support is important, government leaders tend to take a more immediate, short-range view, and to consider what effect a decision will have on their own political fortunes. Professional diplomats, by contrast, are more likely to take a more objective view, and at least point out to their superiors the long-range effects a decision may have on the country's interests, regardless of its immediate political desirability.

.... Formal Negotiations

Governments have a variety of objectives when they enter into negotiations with other entities:

1. To settle a dispute peacefully or reach a mutually beneficial arrangement

2. To gain time in order to improve one's power or influence position

3. To stall in the expectation that the situation may change or that the dispute will just fade away

4. To impress third parties with one's reasonableness and good will

5. To obtain justification for the use of force when negotiations "fail"

6. To avoid or postpone a genuine solution

7. To obtain information

History is replete with illustrations.

In 1956, when Egypt's President Nasser nationalized the Suez Canal, the U.S. government initiated an international conference to negotiate a new arrangement for the Canal, which would have restored its character as an international waterway. Because such an arrangement would have taken control of the Canal away from Egypt, the American initiative could not have much of a chance. Why was it undertaken in the first place? According to Robert Murphy, a high-ranking American diplomat at the time, Secretary of State John Foster Dulles was using the conference as a means of *stalling* in the hope that some accommodation could be reached or that something would occur to solve the problem.[3] The French and British diplomats who participated in the meeting where the American proposals were discussed had no illusions. They took part to gain time, to impress other countries with their interest in a peaceful solution, and to prepare the ground psychologically and politically for the military action they were secretly planning. When their preparations were completed, they told the world that the failure of these diplomatic efforts left them no alternative but to use military force.

The 1973 Paris Peace Agreement between the United States and the Democratic Republic of Vietnam provided for the withdrawal of American military forces from South Vietnam, but made no reference to the unification of North and South—the key issue of the war and Hanoi's principal objective. During the protracted negotiations, both sides avoided the subject. Hanoi knew that Washington could not possibly sanction unification. On the other hand, such a formal agreement was irrelevant. Both sides were aware that once the American forces were withdrawn, Washington would be unable to prevent unification. The negotiators opted for an innocuous formula that bypassed the vexing issue.[4]

Time-Tested Methods ···

Whatever their actual or ultimate objectives, negotiators employ certain practical methods.

Unless the principal decision makers act directly as negotiators, diplomats need, and normally are given, specific instructions about the actual objectives of their government, the limits of concessions and compromises they can make, the assets they can bring to bear, and the basic inducements, veiled threats, pressures, or other forms of persuasion and bargaining that are appropriate or acceptable. The negotiator must be provided with as much information as possible. Only inept government officials will withhold from their negotiating team vital information. With today's instant communications, negotiators can be in an almost continuous contact with their superiors, who can revise or update their instructions or provide fresh information. Nevertheless, negotiators need some elbow room to take advantage of negotiating openings, subtle shifts in the position of the other side, or unexpected developments. They must have the latitude to develop new proposals on their own as the bargaining process unfolds (provided they do not veer too far from their basic instructions).

Negotiations always involve give-and-take. A diplomat who expects to win every point is a poor negotiator because such an approach will only lead the negotiation to a premature demise. Of course, there may be times when negotiators have instructions from their government to take an uncompromising stand to force the collapse of the negotiations. This can happen when the principal decision makers have decided either to impose their will by force or to postpone an agreement because their bargaining position at the moment is weak and a delay may be in their favor.

Because neither side can realistically expect to satisfy all its desires and aspirations, normally the end result is a compromise. Although both sides tend to open the bargaining with demands that are very close to their maximum objectives, the final outcome is bound to fall short of these goals. The area of compromise is a fairly broad band (see figure 5-1), the outer limits of which, a and b, are set by the maximum objectives of the opposing sides. The final agreement will be somewhere within this band; each side tries to gain agreement at a point that is as close as possible to its original negotiating position and maximum objective.

As the negotiations progress, both sides are likely to move by necessity away from their opening negotiating positions (a and b). Which side will have to move further away from its initial optimum position will depend on various factors that affect its bargaining position and power or influence potential.

Each negotiator needs to know how far she or he can go before the acceptable limits for a compromise are passed. These limits must be clearly set by the decision makers before negotiations begin. They may be revised during the negotiations by the principal decision makers, but only if circumstances call for such a change. How are these limits determined in each particular case? Setting the minimum acceptable limits for a compromise is not an easy task. Generally, an arrangement that would be detrimental to a country's national interest is rejected. The problem is that decision makers cannot always tell what is in the national interest. In business negotiations, the end result can be expressed in monetary terms. An agreement that results in serious monetary losses should be avoided if at all possible. In most international transactions, however, the final outcome cannot be assessed in precise monetary gains and losses.

One way to determine the acceptable limit is to place it as close to one's maximum demand as the other side is likely to accept, and as far away as possible from the point beyond which it is better not to have any agreement at all. To determine where those two points lie, a government needs above all reliable information about the weaknesses and capabilities of the other side, sound judgment to avoid unjustified optimism on its side, and a fairly realistic appreciation of what is possible under the specific circumstances.[5]

Before entering into negotiations, a government should answer three basic questions:

1. Is it more advantageous to engage in negotiations rather than to let things stand as they are?

2. Is the problem defined in terms that leave room for bargaining and accommodation?

3. Are the assets the government has at its disposal sufficient to prevent the other side from dictating the terms of a settlement?

Unless the answer to each question is clearly positive, a government should avoid entering into negotiations if it has the choice. An exception to this general rule applies to negotiations that are not intended to reach a final settlement but are undertaken merely to gain time, impress third parties, or pursue some other objective.

Figure 5-1
The maximum objective of negotiator A is a; the maximum objective of negotiator B is b; the outcome will be somewhere within the shaded area.

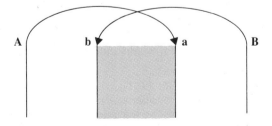

....Clarity or Ambiguity

If the negotiations aim at resolving a conflict or reaching some new arrangement or accommodation, the end product must be written in clear terms to prevent future misunderstandings or deliberate distortions. Clarity and precision are important unless the parties deliberately decide to leave certain terms vague because they want to bypass a thorny issue, to confuse third parties, or to allow flexibility to meet changing conditions in the future. It may also be necessary to leave some ambiguity because stating every point clearly and precisely may not be possible or acceptable to either or both sides. In August 1982, for example, the United States and the People's Republic of China reached an agreement with regard to the sale of sophisticated weapons to Taiwan. The wording of the agreement was deliberately vague, so that Beijing could claim a diplomatic success while President Reagan could still reassure his pro-Taiwan constituents in the United States that he had not abandoned Taiwan. As Senator S. I. Hayakawa said on that occasion, "ambiguous language reflects an ambiguous situation."[6] In the compromise, which was made public on August 17 in the form of a joint communiqué, China affirmed its "fundamental policy to strive for a peaceful solution to the Taiwan question," and Washington restated its recognition of the government in Beijing "as the sole legal Government of China," and "acknowledged the Chinese position that there is but one China and Taiwan is part of China." With regard to the weapons issue, Beijing withdrew its demand that deliveries to Taiwan be halted by a specific date. The United States, on its part, affirmed that "it intends to reduce gradually its sales of arms to Taiwan, leading over a period of time to a final solution." In addition, Washington stated that "its arms sales to Taiwan will not exceed, either in qualitative or quantitative terms the level of those supplied in recent years since the establishment of diplomatic relations between the United States and China." Clearly the two governments used ambiguous language to bypass the thorny issue of a definite cut-off of arms sales to Taiwan while giving the impression that they had made progress in reaching a solution. In fact, they used ambiguity to assure sufficient flexibility to meet changing conditions in the future.

Be that as it may, ambiguity and imprecision in the wording of an international agreement involve some risk and should be avoided unless the ambiguity is necessary or advantageous.

....Bluffing in Negotiating

Experienced negotiators do not place all their cards on the table at the outset. They know that information is itself an asset the other side can use to advantage. Particularly important is to keep from the other side any elements of weakness that, if known, would affect its bargaining position.

At times, negotiators or other officials may float misleading information to spread confusion or create impressions that may strengthen their position. To be effective, misleading or untrue information must appear valid even to officials who are usually suspicious and careful. Otherwise, it may easily backfire.

The success or failure of such a tactic depends in large measure on the dexterity of those who are using it, and also on the ability of the other side to get reliable information to evaluate what is done or said. A reputation for bluffing, of course, makes future bluffs less effective.

There is another potential drawback. In trying to impress the other side with its strength and determination, a government may resort to extravagant statements that its own people are likely to embrace at face value. If things go wrong, the letdown and consequent disappointment is that much greater.

.... Delaying Tactics

Timing is essential for success in international transactions as well as in business negotiations. It is crucial that a particular action be taken at the moment it can do the most good. It is equally important not to take a step that can be postponed without risk or cost; certainly a step must not be taken if it will help the other side. Thus, delay can be an essential aspect of timing.

Delay also may be used to gain time in the hope that changing circumstances will strengthen one's bargaining position. The question is: "Who has time on his (or her) side?" When the PLO fighters were trapped by the Israeli army in West Beirut in the summer of 1982, Yasser Arafat, the organization's leader, took advantage of the negotiations for a disengagement conducted by the American special envoy, Phillip C. Habib, to delay an agreement on the evacuation of his forces knowing full well that as time passed an all-out Israeli attack on West Beirut was becoming less and less likely.

Negotiators may use delaying tactics to wear down the other side. During the Korean War, the negotiations at Panmunjon were a classic illustration of forcing compromises through delay and intransigence.

Sending Signals ....

To influence the outcome of an international interaction, governments and other international actors often resort to *signaling*. This is a convenient way to communicate a foreign policy position, a warning, a shift in official attitudes, an inducement, or some other message they do not want to transmit through official diplomatic channels.

Signaling differs from the exchanges discussed in the previous pages:

1. The originator of the message does not address the intended recipient directly

2. Neither side is bound by the statements it makes and may easily reverse itself or drop the issue without a serious loss of prestige

3. The message may be intended as a signal but, being public, it also may be worded to generate a favorable public impression, in which case both signaling and propaganda may be involved

4. The signal may take the form of actions or omissions in addition to verbal messages

Verbal Signals

Verbal signals may be used to prepare the ground for direct negotiations, induce the other side to be more cooperative, or strengthen one's bargaining position. For example, prior to the first round of SALT negotiations, both the Johnson and the Nixon administrations gave the distinct impression that, barring an agreement with the Soviet Union, the United States was determined to deploy the antiballistic-missile (ABM) system known as Sentinel.

Public statements may be used as a warning designed to discourage certain policies or to avert a dangerous confrontation. In 1981, the American government let it be known that a Soviet military intervention in Poland to reverse the liberalizing trend initiated by the independent Solidarity trade union would lead to a serious deterioration of East–West relations. These warnings may have helped convince the Soviet leaders that a Soviet action in the pattern of the armed intervention in Hungary (1956) or Czechoslovakia (1968) might be too costly.

A verbal signal may be conveyed not only by a government official but also through nonofficial channels. A newspaper article, for example, may be used as the vehicle for a signal a government wants to convey without official sanction. This is a useful device, especially when a government wishes to test the waters before making public its views. The problem is that the intended recipient may be unable to determine how authoritative the signal is. This is less of a problem in political systems where the government controls the media. An article in *Pravda* can be reasonably expected to reflect the views of the Soviet leadership. In pluralistic systems, newspaper articles may at times convey official views, but those who evaluate the significance of such signals have to be extremely well informed about specific publications and their connections with individual leaders or political parties, or about the connections of certain commentators with the governing authorities. A nonofficial signal may be used as a "trial balloon" designed to test reactions on a certain proposal. A response to such a signal may take a variety of forms, from articles or broadcasts to statements by unnamed government officials.

As in the case of direct exchanges or diplomatic negotiations, the words used in verbal signals often are of crucial importance. In a communiqué issued at the end of a Warsaw Pact meeting in Prague in January 1983, the participants acknowledged for the first time that arms control agreements should be subject to proper verification measures including "when necessary, international procedures." The word *international* was particularly significant; it implied a shift from the traditional Soviet position that arms accords be verifiable only "by national technical means," meaning electronic devices, space satellites and the like. The communiqué was not a formal, direct proposal; but it was one more signal in the ongoing exchanges.

Action Signals

A government may send a signal without uttering a word by taking a certain action. Sometimes, instead of committing an act, it may send a signal by omitting a certain act. The action, or the omission thereof, is the message. The variety of action messages is endless. In March 1983, a seventy-seven-vessel naval exercise in the Caribbean was "intended as a 'signal' to the Soviets of U.S. concern about Moscow's activities in the region," according to Admiral James Watkins, Chief of Naval Operations, who added: "The presence is important . . . to send a signal, with our allies, to the Soviet Union that we have capabilities for the projection of power. The Soviets are watching the sophistication of weaponry, and that's a deterrent in itself."[7]

The length of a meeting between two leaders may in itself be a signal of improved relations. The postponement or cancellation of a visit may signal that relations between two governments are deteriorating. Under certain circumstances, a visit may herald a historic change, as did the dramatic visit of Egyptian President Anwar Sadat to Jerusalem in November 1977.

The meaning of a particular action or omission is not always clear, of course, and at times an action may have no intended message at all. President Carter relates in his memoirs that a meeting with the Chinese "liaison Chief" Huang Chen in Washington in February 1977 lasted longer than expected. "We learned that the Chinese considered it significant that the meeting with Huang had lasted longer than my recently concluded meeting with the Soviet Ambassador." According to Carter, the meeting had run overtime only because of "laborious translations." There was no special meaning attached to the relative lengths of the two meetings.[8]

Deciding what is the real meaning of a particular action, or whether any meaning should be attached to it at all, requires a great deal of experience, judgment, and information. Because actions or omissions may be interpreted by third parties in ways that would create problems, a government may take special steps to dispel erroneous assumptions. This becomes particularly crucial when actions such as military mobilization, deployment of weapons, increased military expenditures, and the like threaten to provoke a crisis.

The Peaceful Settlement of Disputes ....

The practical necessity and wisdom of trying to settle a dispute peacefully through negotiations before embarking on a military venture has been recognized since antiquity. With the advent of Christianity, theologians such as Augustine and Thomas Aquinas have theorized about *just* wars; an effort to reach a settlement through negotiations was regarded as a precondition to a just war. The tradition continued in the following centuries despite frequent and costly wars. Even those who were bent on aggression found negotiations useful. If they could get what they wanted through negotiations, they had no reason to embark on a military confrontation; if not, they could claim that they had tried to reach a peaceful settlement but their efforts had failed and military action was the only alternative left. The practice is still in evidence.

Today, major or minor disputes are discussed by diplomats, and hardly a month goes by without several negotiations going on or without one or more agreements being reached. Since its inception, the United Nations, as the international depository of treaties, has published many volumes containing thousands of treaties signed by member states. Needless to say, negotiations do not necessarily end with a treaty. Disputes occasionally are settled through an exchange of letters, the issuing of a joint communiqué, or unilateral actions or statements by high officials.

....The Role of Third Parties

The importance of negotiations for the settlement of disputes is underlined by the role assigned under international law to third parties. The UN Charter (Article 33) specifically calls on all its members—in fact, *any* parties to a dispute that may endanger peace and security—to "seek a solution by negotiation, enquiry, mediation, conciliation, arbitration, judicial settlement, resort to regional agencies, or arrangements, or other peaceful means of their choice." When invited, third parties may offer their services in the form of good offices, mediation, inquiry, conciliation, or arbitration. Each involves a different degree of involvement and different procedures.

Good Offices

When negotiations break down or the parties to an international dispute are unwilling to come to the negotiating table for whatever reason, a third government having good relations with both opposing parties may offer its services to see if direct negotiations can be started or if a settlement is possible. The third party acts as a go-between, meeting separately with each of the feuding governments, passing messages from one to the other, and offering discreetly some suggestions for a settlement—provided the opposing parties do not object to such informal advice.

If the good offices prove successful, the third party may be invited to take a more active and direct part in the negotiations. The United States initially offered its good offices to Egypt and Israel; eventually, however, President Carter became involved directly and acted as mediator in the Camp David talks.

Mediation

As in the case of good offices, mediation requires acceptance of the mediator by the feuding parties. The difference is that a mediator is not merely a go-between, but is a direct participant in the negotiations. Once accepted, a mediator is entitled to advance proposals, reconcile conflicting viewpoints, pass judgment on the merits of the case or on the negotiating positions of the opposing sides, ask for information necessary to perform her or his duties, and in general act as a full-fledged negotiator. There is one limitation to a mediator's role: he or she must remain impartial. The usefulness of a mediator who appears to be siding exclusively with one of the opposing parties will come to an end quickly. We should also point out that mediators cannot impose their will on the other parties. They can only try to persuade and influence.

Depending on the circumstances, a mediator may meet with each party separately. Henry Kissinger, during his "shuttle diplomacy" between Israel and Egypt in November 1973, and again in August 1975, met separately with the representatives of the two governments, which at the time were still in a state of war. Kissinger was not a mere go-between; his role was that of a mediator.

Mediation is likely to succeed when, because of special circumstances, the opposing parties favor a peaceful settlement but are unable to reach an agreement by themselves.

Commission of Inquiry

Not infrequently, international disputes result from disagreements over the facts. A border incident may lead to war, especially if the two neighbors are already at logger-heads, spoiling for a fight. The expectation that ascertaining the facts could avert a conflict has led many governments to support fact-finding entities that generally are known as commissions of inquiry. The Hague Peace Conference of 1899 initially set up a permanent panel of respected persons who could be called on by interested parties to form a commission of inquiry. The second Hague Conference of 1907 went further and prescribed detailed procedures.[9]

These ideas resurfaced in the League of Nations, which used fact-finding commissions in at least four international disputes: between Sweden and Finland (1920), Yugoslavia and Albania (1921), Great Britain and Turkey (1923), and Greece and Bulgaria (1925). These commissions were credited with averting a further deterioration of the international climate. A commission of inquiry established to investigate the facts involved in the Manchurian crisis (1931) between China and Japan was less successful; it did not prevent the outbreak of hostilities and the Japanese takeover of Manchuria.

The United Nations used a commission of inquiry in 1946 in Greece during the guerrilla campaign supported by Yugoslavia, Albania, and Bulgaria. These three countries did not allow the commission to enter their territory and by necessity its investigation was confined to witnesses found on the Greek side of the border. In 1967, the UN General Assembly passed a resolution calling on all its members to make more extensive use of the fact-finding mechanisms available. Thus far, few member-states have done so.

To function properly, a commission of inquiry must be accepted by both parties. If one party anticipates that the facts, if ascertained, will not help its case, it is not likely to accept such a commission. Refusal, however, may be viewed by many (with good reason) as an indication of which side is in the wrong.

Commissions of Conciliation

Much of what we said about commissions of inquiry applies to commissions of conciliation, which propose solutions to disputes. These commissions may be composed of representatives from third parties acceptable to the feuding governments; they also may comprise just one individual selected by mutual consent. As mediators, conciliators may meet with the opposing parties jointly or separately. The objective of a conciliator is to consider the various aspects of the dispute, the facts involved, the potential costs and disadvantages of a protracted conflict to both sides, and any related treaties, and to propose solutions that are, in the conciliator's view, equitable and practical. Neither of the opposing sides has any obligation to accept the proposed solution.

Several bilateral and multilateral treaties provide for conciliation procedures when disagreements between the signatories cannot be resolved in direct negotiations. Despite the obvious usefulness of such procedures, governments are reluctant to accept the intercession of a commission of conciliation because the conciliator's proposals are not binding and the entire effort may be wasted.

When governments are seriously prepared to accept a binding proposal for a compromise by a third party, they may opt for a different procedure known as *arbitration*.

Arbitration

The key feature of arbitration is that the opposing parties agree *in advance* to accept the decision of the arbitrator, even if the decision goes against their wishes. Arbitration has a long history in international relations as well as in the settlement of private disputes. The ancient Greek city-states had established elaborate procedures buttressed by divine sanctions. During the medieval period, many disputes involving European rulers were submitted for arbitration to the Pope or a papal representative. More recently, in the eighteenth and nineteenth centuries, several relatively minor disputes have been settled through arbitration.

In 1899, the Hague Conference established an International Court of Arbitration. The title was inappropriate, because the new institution was not a court of law. It consisted primarily of a panel to which each participating country was entitled to name four renowned jurists or legal experts. Those named on the panel were available to serve as arbitrators if called on by interested governments. If two countries embroiled in a disagreement agreed to submit their dispute to arbitration, they each chose two persons from the panel. Of the two persons chosen by each country, only one could be a national of that country. The four arbitrators chose in turn a fifth member to serve as the "umpire" and cast a deciding vote in the event the other four members were deadlocked.

Under the Hague arrangement, the opposing parties had to sign a special agreement known as *compromis*. In this document, they identified the essential elements of the dispute, the points that had to be settled, the acceptable limits of the final decision, and a formal pledge to abide by the *arbitral award,* the final verdict of the arbitrators.

The League of Nations placed particular emphasis on arbitration both in the Covenant and later (in 1928) in the so-called General Act, which dealt with arbitration in great detail. During the interwar period, several thousand arbitral awards were issued by arbitration panels in claims involving compensation to individuals for war damages. However, these arbitrators were chosen without resort to the Permanent Court of Arbitration, which was used in only four cases between 1920 and 1940.

Under the United Nations, the International Law Commission initiated in 1949 a serious effort to codify the arbitral procedures and make arbitration almost compulsory. The UN members did not go along with the Commission's ambitious proposals, and the Commission went back to the drawing board to prepare a new draft. By 1958, it had produced "a set of rules which might inspire states in the drawing up of provisions for inclusion in international treaties and special arbitration agreements."[10] Even this more modest reformulation received much criticism, and in the end the General Assembly did not give official sanction to the Commission's draft but simply recommended to the members that they take into consideration these suggestions and use them as they saw fit. Several governments have included in treaties—especially those that are nonpolitical, dealing with trade or similar transactions—special provisions for the arbitration of any disputes that may arise from the implementation of their agreements.

Coercive Diplomacy ....

There is a gray area between bargaining and persuasion and the outright use of force; this is the area of *coercive diplomacy,* which involves the *threat* of inflicting painful punishment unless the other government (or other international actor) agrees to call off an undesirable activity or to accept a change wanted by the coercing actor.[11]

Although coercive diplomacy employs primarily the threat of military force, it can also use economic measures or the denial of crucial benefits.

An actor engaged in coercive diplomacy should be aware of certain prerequisite conditions for potential success. The coercing side must be able to convince the opponent that it is more determined to obtain compliance than the opponent is to resist, that it will not hesitate to escalate the pressure if the demand is not accepted, and that the time left for compliance is short. An atmosphere of crisis and extreme urgency is indispensable for the effective use of coercive diplomacy.

The coercing side must also keep in mind that intensity of resistance is closely related to the ultimate effect the demand will have on the opponent country's national interests. The deeper the demand cuts into vital interests, the greater the motivation to resist, if resistance is at all possible. Furthermore, the coercing side must offer its opponent an opportunity to comply. During the Cuban missile crisis, President Kennedy, in a superbly orchestrated display of coercive diplomacy, threatened the Soviet Union with an escalation of the military confrontation unless Moscow removed the offensive missiles, but at the same time he carefully avoided pushing the level of pressure to a point that made compliance by Moscow impossible for reasons of national prestige. Unless circumstances are such that one government can impose complete capitulation, it is prudent to scale the demands to a level that makes compliance feasible.

Because of the extremely close relationship of coercive diplomacy to the prevailing circumstances, the actual steps must be carefully tailored to fit the situation. However, those who engage in coercive diplomacy cannot be sure that they have all the facts. Moreover, because decision makers are unable to predict the reactions of interested parties and to interpret correctly all information they receive while the crisis is in progress, they have to rely a great deal on improvisation and guesswork—a very uncertain basis for making crucial decisions. Coercive diplomacy is a risky enterprise at best.

Coercive diplomacy was used extensively for centuries by the European powers. One of its most extreme tactical devices is the *ultimatum,* a communication addressed to an opponent that usually contains specific demands of a very serious nature. The recipient of the ultimatum is given a relatively short time to reply, within a definite deadline. If the deadline passes without compliance, the coercing power threatens to take certain steps the other side will find painful—usually the advance of military forces into its territory. The menace contained in an ultimatum is critical: an excessive threat may not be believable; mild measures may be ignored. Careful calibration of the threat requires political sensitivity as well as reliable information about the opponent's resistance potential and the reactions of other international actors.

The ultimatum as a means of exerting extreme pressure poses certain risks for the coercing power. Because it is definitive in its deadline for compliance and the content of its demands, it leaves little room for flexibility. If the ultimatum is rejected, the coercing actor has virtually no alternative but to carry out the punishment it has threatened. Otherwise, it will lose face and its power and influence potential will diminish.

Unless a government is fairly certain that its pressure will bring capitulation, it should avoid issuing an ultimatum. It may instead pose a demand without a time limit for acceptance, and it may allude to consequences without excessive specificity. The coercing power needs a path for retreat as much as the subject of pressure needs room for acceptance.

Coercive diplomacy may take other, less-dramatic forms than the ultimatum. A concentration of troops at the border, a display of naval units, military "exercises," preliminary steps to impose economic restrictions, and stern warnings are among the signals that can be used in coercive diplomacy. As a rule, such signals are combined with other forms of diplomatic exchanges. This is a key aspect of coercive diplomacy. Side by side with the tactics of pressure, we usually find direct or indirect communications, some bargaining, and efforts to bring about compliance without resorting to carrying out the threat.

Crisis Management ....

The use of coercive diplomacy or the actual use of force usually provoke an international crisis. Generally speaking, *a crisis is a situation or development requiring decisions with potentially far-reaching consequences, which must be made within a short period during which conditions change rapidly and information is fragmentary.*

Derived from the Greek verb *krinein,* which means "to judge," the term *crisis* initially was used by physicians to indicate a critical point in a serious illness, usually accompanied by extremely high fever; the crisis ended either in the death or with the recovery of the patient.

A genuine international crisis must have a clearly defined focal point. An abrupt and deliberate attempt by one or several governments (or other actors) to change radically existing relationships and conditions, if strongly opposed by one or several actors, is likely to cause an international crisis. A crisis should not be confused with a protracted dispute or rivalry. The conflict between East and West is not a crisis, although it has given rise to crises several times in the last thirty years.

.... The Causes of Crises

Experience shows that an international crisis often is the unintended product of neglect and procrastination by officials who have the authority and the means to deal effectively with a simmering dispute. In other cases, one actor may decide to escalate the conflict because he or she perceives a tactical advantage. Soviet leader Nikita Khrushchev apparently thought he had such an advantage when he provoked three major crises over the fate of West Berlin between 1958 and 1961, and in 1962 when he placed intermediate-range missiles in Cuba. An international crisis may also result from an incident that is allowed—or deliberately used—to inflame passions and set the stage for a decisive confrontation in the hope that the outcome will be favorable to those who provoke or exploit the incident.

Government officials flatter themselves that they are clever enough to control events and modulate the intensity of conflict. This is not always the case. In fact, the inability of policy makers to control events may be one of the most serious weaknesses that affect the functioning of the international system.

In international relations, actions that appear promising, or have seemingly manageable objectives, can lead to counteractions and thus further escalation, which eventually gathers a momentum of its own. Control of a crisis situation is difficult because questions of prestige acquire decisive importance, and because mistrust among the protagonists tends to lead to increased escalation rather than to a carefully planned retreat from the precipice of confrontation. A classic illustration is offered by the actions of governments prior to the outbreak of World War I.[12] The crowned heads of Europe who plunged the continent into the devastation of that war could not foresee that their decisions would lead to a protracted conflagration in which millions of Europe's youth would perish and in which their thrones would be swept away. Hitler, too, never anticipated that the war he was provoking with his actions would end with Berlin being leveled under the blows of Soviet artillery shells and himself taking his own life in a dismal bunker, with only a handful of aides around him.

Although the world has witnessed several international crises in the last thirty years, it would be inaccurate to say that we live in a world where international crises are a daily occurence. Nevertheless, any international crisis is fraught with danger, especially when nuclear powers or their allies are involved. The chances for making wrong decisions, misinterpreting the intentions of an opponent, or losing control over the rapidly moving events are much greater in a crisis than during a period of relative tranquility. Because of the inherent perils, it is prudent to work out in advance some methods for the effective *management* of international crises.

Dealing with a Crisis

What is *crisis management?* Basically, it involves a decision-making machinery with a small number of principal decision makers participating, and a system of communications that expedites the transmission and verification of information while conditions change rapidly and information becomes obsolete even before it can be evaluated and used.

Assuming that such a machinery can be set up, how can it be used? Crisis-management machinery can have three objectives:

1. To enable the decision makers to follow closely the rapidly changing situation and to choose from among several proposed policies those that can best contribute to the outcome they hope to achieve

2. To prevent a crisis from escalating to confrontation

3. To monitor situations and recommend steps to prevent a crisis by resolving outstanding issues

Whatever scholars may think about the necessity of a crisis-management machine,
few governments have taken specific steps to set up such a system. Even in a highly
developed country such as the United States, we find a great deal of improvisation in
efforts to cope with crises. The number or the identity of primary participants varies. In
1962, during the Cuban missile crisis, President Kennedy called together a small group
of trusted individuals both in and out of the government, such as his brother Robert
Kennedy, who as the attorney general had no direct involvement in foreign policy
matters ordinarily, and former Secretary of State Dean Acheson, who was at the time a
private citizen. Interestingly, President Kennedy did not participate directly in the
deliberations of this team, wishing to allow its members the opportunity for uninhibited
expression of their opinions. In 1972, during the Tet Offensive in Vietnam, the crisis that
resulted was handled almost exclusively by Nixon and Kissinger, in large measure
because the President and his foreign policy advisor were preoccupied with potential
leaks.[13] Later, during the crisis caused by the 1973 Yom Kippur war between Israel and
Egypt, decisions were made largely by Henry Kissinger, then the Secretary of State, and
by Alexander Haig, the President's principal assistant in the White House. Nixon
himself was preoccupied with the Watergate affair.[14] In chapter 4, we discussed how
President Johnson handled the Gulf of Tonkin incident. In February 1984, the decision
to remove the U.S. Marines from Lebanese soil was reached in intense discussions
involving primarily President Reagan, Vice-President George Bush, Defense Secretary
Caspar Weinberger, Department of State Undersecretary for Political Affairs Lawrence
S. Eagleburger, and National Security Advisor Robert C. McFarlane; Secretary of State
George Shultz, who was touring Central America, was consulted by telephone. The
decision was reviewed and ratified by the U.S. Security Council and then communicated
to the governments of France, Italy, and Britain (participants in the multinational force),
although the exact time for the move was not indicated.[15] Technically speaking, the
formal machinery for the management of international crises by the United States is
located in the National Security Council, but in practice the president may bypass the
Council, use only a few of its members, or add other persons he or she considers useful.

Not only in the United States but in other countries as well the identities of those
who are called on to take part in the decision-making process during a crisis are
determined by the highest official, such as a president, a prime minister, or the official
who has the final say under the circumstances, regardless of any formal arrangements.
Another common feature of crisis response is that the normal channels of decision
making are bypassed.

A crisis-management machine may be provided by an international organization.
The United Nations has often served as a meeting place in this regard. Its machinery and
procedures have helped defuse gathering crises. Regional organizations, also, such as
the Organization of American States (OAS) or the Organization of African Unity
(OAU), may be used for de-escalating a crisis involving their members. A crisis-
management machine also may be organized by allied governments wishing to preserve
the cohesion of the alliance, speed up their communications, and improve their potential

for rapid and effective response. At times, the machinery may be used to defuse a crisis resulting from a dispute among the members.

Aware of the importance of reliable information, governments have taken serious steps to improve their information-gathering and communication facilities. The so-called hot line that can provide Moscow and Washington with direct communication in a moment of crisis is a dramatic illustration.

Presumably, the task of decision makers in a crisis situation can be made easier if they can turn to guidelines worked out well in advance. *Contingency planning* can be very useful, provided the planners have the imagination—even the prophetic qualities—needed to foresee all the possible circumstances that may become part of a future crisis. To some extent, several possible scenarios may be devised; the problem is that when a crisis erupts it seldom follows the course anticipated by the planners. Another difficulty with contingency planning is that conditions change with the passing of time and the best plans soon become obsolete. Generals often have been accused of fighting the last war in their plans for the future.

However appealing at first glance, a formal crisis-management machine is not necessarily the most effective way to deal with an international crisis. If it is too precisely structured, the machine may be overly bureaucratic and cumbersome. For this reason, governments faced with a crisis are more likely to set up a special task force, which can cut through the regular bureaucratic channels, get top priority for its communications, thrash out problems and complications as they come in rapid sequence, and choose among alternatives in face-to-face and informal discussions that allow maximum flexibility and speed.

Summary

- Diplomacy is the manner in which peaceful contacts and transactions among international actors are conducted. The primary tasks of diplomacy are: (1) to resolve international disputes without war, (2) to end military conflicts by reconciling the opposing parties, and (3) to obtain the best possible outcome in international transactions.

- Diplomatic exchanges consist of informal contacts, formal negotiations by diplomats, or summit meetings attended by the highest political officials in each country.

- Diplomats use time-tested methods designed to maximize potential benefits in a given transaction. Negotiations, if successful, lead to compromise solutions acceptable to all sides.

- Governments and other international actors often resort to signaling to convey messages or create impressions without resorting to direct exchanges. Signals may be verbal (public statements, newspaper articles, and the like) or action (commissions or omissions of actions with the intent of conveying a certain attitude).

- To settle international disputes peacefully, governments may conduct negotiations directly or they may use third parties (usually other governments or IGOs).The participation of third parties may take the form of good offices, mediation, inquiry, conciliation, or arbitration.

- There is a gray area between bargaining and persuasion (the transactional approach) and the use of force. This is the area of coercive diplomacy, which involves the threat of painful measures unless the other side agrees to comply with specific demands—often within a short deadline (ultimatum). The success of coercive diplomacy depends in large measure on the disparity of power potential between the parties.

- The use of coercive diplomacy or force to bring about abrupt and serious changes in the status quo usually provokes an international crisis; that is, a situation that calls for potentially far-reaching decisions within a short period and while conditions change rapidly and information is fragmentary. To deal with such situations, governments may establish crisis-management machinery, which usually involves a small number of decision makers, a minimum of bureaucratic red tape, considerable flexibility in the discussion of options, minimum interference by influential outsiders, and a system of communications that expedites the transmission and evaluation of information while the crisis is in progress.

Notes

1. Craig, Gordon A., and George, Alexander L. *Force and Statecraft: Diplomatic Problems of Our Time.* New York: Oxford University Press, 1983, p. 189.
2. Kissinger, Henry. *White House Years.* Boston: Little, Brown, 1979, pp. 1202–1257.
3. Murphy, Robert. *Diplomat Among Warriors.* New York: Doubleday, 1964, pp. 385–387.
4. Kissinger, *op. cit.,* pp. 1415–1416.
5. Lockhart, Charles. *Bargaining in International Conflicts.* New York: Columbia University Press, 1979.
6. *The New York Times,* August 18, 1982.
7. *Miami Herald,* March 16, 1983.
8. Carter, Jimmy. *Keeping Faith: Memoirs of a President.* New York: Bantam, 1982, p. 190.
9. In 1913, U.S. Secretary of State William Jennings Bryan initiated the signing of special treaties that called for the investigation of facts in disputes between signatories. The most ingenious provision was the requirement that the parties would not go to war until the commission of inquiry had turned in its report. The commission had one year to complete its work. The hope was that in the year-long cooling period, the fever of war might have passed. Paterson, Thomas G., et al., *American Foreign Policy: A History.* Lexington, Mass.: Heath, 1977, p. 457.
10. *American Journal of International Law,* 1959, Suppl., p. 234.
11. Craig and George, *op. cit.,* pp. 189–203.
12. Stoessinger, John S. *Why Nations Go to War.* 3rd ed. New York: St. Martin's Press, 1982, pp. 11–15.
13. Szulc, Tad. "Behind the Vietnam Cease-Fire Agreement." *Foreign Policy,* Summer, 1974.
14. Kissinger, Henry. *Years of Upheaval.* Boston: Little, Brown, 1982, pp. 568–666.
15. *The Washington Post,* February 17, 1984.

6

.........................The Element
of Force

Survivers of A-bomb explosion at Nagasaki

A government has three alternatives when it finds that it cannot realize its foreign policy objectives through diplomacy:

1. It can decide to let the issue simmer until conditions for settlement become more favorable

2. It can scale down its objectives to make a settlement possible

3. It can resort to force

War, to recall Clausewitz, is indeed the continuation of politics by other means, because force may be used by a government to achieve what it has been unable to accomplish through political methods and diplomacy. Normally, a government that can gain its ends through persuasion and bargaining has no rational incentive to resort to force. As Croesus, the ancient king of Lydia, said to Cyrus, the Persian: "No one is so unwise as to choose of his own free will war rather than peace, since in peace the sons bury the fathers, but in war the fathers bury the sons."

Wars have been waged for merely the vain pursuit of glory, but this has been the exception, not the rule. Most wars have practical objectives: the acquisition of territory, plunder, subjugation of other people, destruction of threatening neighbors, or defense against intruders. At times, religion or ideology are invoked to inspire fighters to uncommon exertions and sacrifices, but those who lead the war effort seldom believe in the shibboleths they hold high for the rank and file. Whatever the initial motives, the ultimate consequence of victory in war is that the victorious side can impose its will on the vanquished. Victory means greater power potential for the winner.

Since the dawn of history, war has been a rational alternative to peaceful transactions. In the twentieth century, however, global war has become potentially so destructive that its rationality has been questioned—especially in the present nuclear age. In the past, human losses in war were counted in the thousands or, at most, tens of thousands. The total number of deaths in all the wars between 1790 and 1914, including the Napoleonic Wars, the Crimean War, the American Civil War, the Franco–Prussian War, the Russo–Japanese War, and the Balkan Wars (1912–1913) cost an estimated 4 million lives. In the four years of World War I (1914–1918), losses totaled 8.6 million dead and over 21 million wounded. World War II broke all casualty records with over 15 million battle deaths and another 25 million lives lost through starvation, mass murder, attacks on civilian targets, and disease. A full-fledged nuclear war would dwarf even those appalling statistics.

Although nuclear war can hardly be viewed as a rational way to obtain benefits, localized, conventional wars between secondary powers, and the threat of using conventional forces to bring about a desirable outcome, still are considered rational and potentially profitable endeavors. Despite the dramatic transformations in the international environment in recent decades, force as a means of imposing one country's will on another remains a key element of international reality. Table 1-1 contains a summary of the most important military conflicts since World War II.

The Causes of War ....

War is an armed conflict of considerable magnitude between or among sovereign entities of somewhat comparable capabilities. If one of the combatants is so much weaker that the outcome of the confrontation is not in doubt, we speak of *military intervention*.

The history of the world is studded with the chronicles of war. Since the earliest days of civilization, hardly a year has passed without a war claiming human lives somewhere on this planet. Philosophers, theologians, moralists, and even politicians have condemned war and have sought to promote universal and lasting peace. In the Preamble of the UN Charter, the signatories boldly enshrined in the opening paragraph their solemn pledge "to save succeeding generations from the scourge of war." Yet in the four decades since this pledge was made, nations that accepted this commitment have resorted to force under one excuse or another. Why do states go to war? Explanations vary. Some are simplistic; others touch on deeper causes.

.... The Arms Merchants

One simplistic explanation attributes war to the machinations of the arms merchants who want to profit from the sale of matériel. Although the arms trade is today a multibillion dollar business, war was around long before weapons manufacturing and selling was a major industry. Moreover, in recent times, wars have been initiated by socialist states, in which (presumably) there are no private merchants to profit from the sale of weapons. The arms industry in both the capitalist and the socialist countries is doing so well only because governments and people continue to believe that their security is threatened by potential aggressors or because they think that military strength will augment their power and influence potential in their dealings with other governments. Although arms manufacturers and merchants may not welcome a totally peaceful world, they do not need to create artificial conflicts to "drum up" business. The governments of large and small states seem to have sufficient reasons of their own to purchase arms.

.... The Leninist View

Lenin, in his *Imperialism: The Ultimate Stage of Capitalism,* found the cause of war to reside in the capitalist system. Private business, he asserted, facing oversupply in their domestic markets and dwindling investment opportunities and profits at home, sought to take over the colonial areas for potential markets, sources of cheap raw materials, and high-yield investment outlets for their excess capital. He saw World War I in this light. Again, this explanation is unsatisfactory. The European powers had divided most of Africa among themselves at the conference table in the Congress of Berlin, not on the battlefield. Even if we were to agree that the quest for colonies led to military conflicts among the colonial powers, wars had been waged long before capitalism had reached the high stage of development discussed by Lenin. Military conflicts between socialist states in the last fifteen years raise further doubts about the validity of Lenin's explanation.

The Drive for Power

Another popular explanation for war is the "drive for power." The drive to dominate others is certainly part of human nature—moderate in some individuals, intense in others. In the case of governments, war is inextricably connected to the concept of power. After all, a government resorts to force either because it wants to impose its will on another government or, in self-defense, to prevent such imposition. Thus, to say that this drive for power is the main cause of war explains little. Governments seldom go to war to impose their will on others in an abstract display of superior strength. They want to achieve something of importance to them and to the nation they lead, something they consider to be a vital necessity.

The Instinct of Aggression

Closely related to the drive for power explanation is the theory that war is the product of an instinct of aggression that can be traced to man's primordial roots. If war can be attributed to an atavistic instinct, then any effort to eliminate violence in international relations is futile. Sooner or later the aggressive impulse will overpower rational thinking and war will ensue, regardless of its consequences. In the nuclear age, this is a chilling thought.

There is no question that violence has a fascinating quality, especially for those who are spectators and are not personally suffering from it. The amount of violence depicted daily on so many popular television programs certainly supports this view. The question is whether this love of violence is sufficient to lead to war in the absence of political causes. Do national leaders use international disputes as an excuse for violence? Do they use this instinct for violence and aggression to turn civilians into soldiers capable of killing to resolve a dispute to the leaders' satisfaction? Conflict research has not given us a conclusive answer to such questions, but empirical evidence suggests that when aggressive impulses are interwoven with political ambitions, ideological beliefs, conflicting interests, or perceived threats, deprivations, or affronts the possibility of war becomes greater.

The problem, in other words, is not that leaders unleash war because of an uncontrollable impulse but that they see a conflict through the distorting lens of a self-centered view of right and wrong, which transforms the use of violence into a matter of necessity and high principle.

....Distorted Communications

A distorted view of an adversary and of his or her actions and objectives may contribute to the escalation of tension and the deepening of conflict. This is often attributed to a *communications failure*. The problem is not so much that the antagonists fail to communicate with each other—that is, to *transmit* or *receive* messages directly or indirectly; rather, they tend to *interpret* the messages by passing them through their own perceptual filters. The result is often a misunderstanding of intentions, exaggeration of perceived threats, overemphasis of negative indicators, and deliberate downplay, mistrust, or rejection of conciliatory statements. This distorted perception of reality may be observed at two levels.

Worst Case Perception. At the time of a confrontational crisis, the decision makers tend to view the actions of the adversary as worst case indicators, leading to countermeasures that in turn are seen in the same light by the other side. The detailed record of the decisive four weeks in July 1914 leading to World War I is a classic illustration, as can be seen in box 6-1. Suspicion concerning the motives of potential opponents led the protagonists to give the worst possible interpretation to the steps taken by the other side, thus escalating the confrontation.

> **Box 6-1**
> Going to War
>
> ---
>
> Following the assassination of the Crown Prince of Austria at Serajevo, Austrian Foreign Minister Count Berchtold and General Conrad von Hötzendorff, the chief of the General Staff, persuaded the aging Emperor Francis Joseph to send Serbia an ultimatum so outrageous that they were certain Serbia would reject it. Their primary concern was to preserve Austria's status as a great power. Von Hötzendorff's words are illuminating: "It [is] not a question of a knightly duel with 'poor little' Serbia . . . nor of punishment for the assassination. It [is] much more the highly practical importance of the prestige of a great power. . . ."
>
> The terms of the ultimatum left very little room for compromise. Serbia was asked to arrest leading political figures, dismiss key military officers, dissolve nationalist groups. The Serbians were given forty-eight hours to comply; otherwise Austria would take the necessary steps to see that these actions were taken to her satisfaction. Although the Austrians wanted only to have a show of force to preserve Austria's prestige, the Serbians "suspected that it was a pretext to eliminate" their country as a sovereign state. The Russian minister of war, General Sukhomlinov, had no doubt that Austria was ready to take military action against Serbia as soon as the time limit for the ultimatum had expired. "One does not send such an ultimatum except when the cannons are loaded," one of his aides said. To quote Stoessinger, "The Russian perceptions of Austrian intentions produced the next logical step

for Russia: mobilization." An exchange of telegrams between Kaiser Wilhelm, the ruler of Germany, and Czar Nicholas failed to slow down the inexorable slide toward a European war. A comment written by the Kaiser on the Czar's last telegram announcing that Russia had ordered mobilization "for reasons of defense on account of Austria's preparations" shows dramatically the effects of mistrust and suspicion. The Kaiser interpreted the exchange of telegrams as a deceitful ploy on the part of the Czar and his ministers to try to gain time and get their mobilization underway. "According to this," the Kaiser wrote on the margin of the telegram, "the Czar has simply been tricking us with his appeal for assistance and has deceived us. . . . Then I must mobilize, too." A few hours later, the Kaiser received a frantic telegram from Lord Grey. The British foreign minister, in a last-ditch effort to stem the tide of war, warned that "If war breaks out, it [will] be the greatest catastrophe that the world has ever seen." Ordinarily a statement of this kind should have been accepted as wise counsel. What was Kaiser's response? This is what he scribbled on the margin of the telegram: "This means they will attack us; Aha! The common cheat."

As Stoessinger observes, "in Kaiser's view, England was combining threat with bluff 'to separate us from Austria and to prevent us from mobilizing, and to shift responsibility of the war.'" The next day, July 31, the Kaiser issued an ultimatum to Russia demanding her demobilization. When Russia refused to comply—and thus accept a terrible blow to her own prestige and standing as a major power—the Kaiser ordered full mobilization for his army. Because his generals had for years geared their plans to the possibility of war with France, the military trains started rolling toward France. The French Premier René Viviani—who had initially ordered a 10-kilometer pullback of his military units along the French–German border as a gesture of good will and a proof of France's peaceful intentions—was forced to authorize full mobilization. In Britain, the cabinet hoped to keep the country out of the war but it also realized that Britain could not let France be defeated. Lord Grey put it with typical British understatement: "If Germany dominated the continent, it would be disagreeable to us as well as to others, for we should be isolated." By the end of the day, on August 1, 1914, the European continent was at war.

SOURCE: Based on John G. Stoessinger's *Why Nations Go to War*, 3rd ed. New York: St. Martin's Press, 1982

Perceptual Stereotyping. Through a consistent, unidirectional stream of messages, the people in a particular community are imbued with a stereotyped image of a perceived adversary. However untrue or exaggerated, their perceptions become for them a reality that then acts as a political factor that affects, in turn, the actions of the decision makers and the relations between the two antagonists. The Western view of the Soviet Union as a power bent on world domination and the Soviet view of the United States as the citadel of imperialism are illustrations of such perceptual stereotyping.

At both levels this distortion of reality affects communications and contributes to the deepening of conflict. In this sense, it may be a contributing cause of war.

Social Darwinism

Somewhat related to the theory of aggression is the notion that societies are engaged in a constant struggle for the *survival of the fittest*.* Weak societies eventually succumb and expire. This may be seen as an international version of social Darwinism; it views war as inevitable and as an indispensable process for the elimination of the inferior nations and peoples and the continuous advancement of human civilization. For the proponents of this thesis, international relations are dominated by unceasing conflict, which determines the forward march of humanity. War is the instrument of progress as its outcome determines the ascendancy of the strong and the elimination of those societies that are weak and decadent.

Hitler and Mussolini subscribed to this notion, and claimed that their societies (imbued with their ideologies) represented the fittest and were destined by the most basic dynamics of human society to become dominant "for a thousand years." A consistent interpretation of this theory of international social Darwinism would have to accept that by being defeated in war those two nations proved that they were not the fittest. The absurdity of either argument is evident, yet variations of this theory continue to reappear in the form of claims of racial, ethnic, or class superiority.

Arms Races

Certain theorists have argued that the accumulation of armaments by potential antagonists tends to erupt into war regardless of the *real* causes for conflict.[1] An arms race is fueled primarily by the conviction that the other side is arming for war. Even though one side may be arming in a *defensive* reaction to the armaments of its opponent, the mere act of arming is viewed as evidence of offensive intentions. A vicious cycle is thus initiated as each side seeks to maintain a *margin of superiority,* until even a minor incident may ignite the fires of war.

Although the arming of adversaries is a prerequisite for armed conflict, there is no evidence that a relationship of cause and effect exists. The arming process begins because governments want either to defend the status quo or to push forward changes they favor. As both sides escalate their supply of arms and mobilization of military forces, they are likely to reach a point at which one or the other side may think that it can realize its objectives by using the arms it has accumulated. The war that may ensue is not *caused* by the arms race. It is the result of political conflicts, but it is made technically feasible by the presence of significant armed forces.

---

*Charles Darwin's theory of natural selection, from which social Darwinism takes its name, stated that flora and fauna evolve by natural selection to their best-adapted (most fit) form; weaker or less-fit organisms do not survive and reproduce and thus are weeded out—hence the phrase "survival of the fittest."

At the same time, considerable empirical evidence shows that an arms race is bound to aggravate the hostility between antagonists. Certainly it is not going to make them friendlier with each other. In this sense, an arms race may act as a contributing factor to the escalation of hostility.

Imbalance of Military Strength

Some who disagree with the argument that an arms race may in itself become a cause of war go to the opposite extreme and claim that an imbalance in the strength of military forces between two potential antagonists may become a cause of war. They subscribe to the Roman axiom *si vis pacem, para bellum* (if you want peace, prepare for war). Their assumption is that if the military forces of two antagonists are fairly equal, neither side will dare to initiate hostilities and peace will be preserved. (This, in effect, is the rationale that leads to an arms race.) By contrast, if one antagonist becomes decisively stronger, the temptation to go to war will become irresistible. Not necessarily so: if one side is decisively stronger, a war may be unnecessary. The stronger state will be able to realize its objectives without firing a shot. War becomes likely only if the weaker side decides to resist; the greater the disparity of strength, the *less* likely attempts at resistance.

There is no evidence that symmetry of military power will prevent war. Throughout history, wars have been fought between antagonists of comparable military capability. It appears that neither symmetry nor asymmetry of forces is a cause of war; nor are they a guarantee of peace.

The Objectives of War

The foregoing discussion indicates that the "culprits" mentioned do not provide a satisfactory answer to the question "Why do nations go to war?" Our search for the *causes* of war may be assisted by a probe into the *objectives* of war.

The Quest for Land

Since the earliest times, the acquisition or retention of land has been a major cause of conflict and war. Those who could organize a strong and effective military force were able to use their superior strength to conquer weaker neighbors and create far-flung empires. Seldom, if ever, was land given up peacefully, voluntarily, after bargaining at the conference table. Expansion of territorial possessions rarely is achieved without the use of force.

Acquisition of additional territory brings material resources, more land for farming and hunting, a more opulent life for the governing elite, and somewhat less scarcity for the common people. In earlier times, it also meant that more people in the conquered territories could be put to work—as slaves, serfs, or cheap labor—or be pressed into military service. A large population, controlled by an imperial center, provided a vast pool of people available to till the land for food, build great monuments, and form large armies for further conquest. During this century, Hitler's Germany launched a war to gain *Lebensraum* and bring under German control the European continent and its peoples from the Atlantic to the Urals. The German leadership was convinced that only through conquest could they acquire the land, resources, and labor force Germany needed to survive and prosper. Across the world, in Japan, a militarist leadership saw a large population crowded on a group of small islands poor in the vital resources modern industry needs, and sought territorial expansion through conquest as the solution to its problem. In both cases, the war had rational objectives—and given the apparent strength and the policies of the potential opponents it also appeared (before it started) as a promising enterprise with acceptable risks.

At times the conquest of territory is deemed necessary as a protective measure to put greater distance between the seat of government and a potential aggressor. To this day, we hear governments claim that certain territories are vital to their security and that they are prepared to go to war to keep those territories under their control. The Soviet Union uses the Eastern European states as a buffer between the Soviet heartland and potential aggressors from the West. The Soviet interventions in East Germany (1953), Hungary (1956), and Czechoslovakia (1968), and the effective pressure on Poland (1981–1982) leave little doubt that control of these territories is regarded by the Soviet government as a vital necessity.

Many times in history, governments have gone to war to recapture territory that they had lost and that they considered to be theirs because of long possession. In September 1980, Iraq, apparently emboldened by the disintegration of the Iranian military after the downfall of the Shah, launched an invasion designed to capture the Shatt-al-Arab waterway, which the government in Bagdad claimed to be Iraqi territory.

The realization that territorial expansion has been traditionally one of the major objectives of war led the architects of the League of Nations and later of the United Nations to outlaw conquest. Under current international law, conquest does not confer title.[2] The transfer of sovereign rights over territory can be made legally only through a treaty. Nevertheless, governments still ignore this rule on the assumption that actual possession, however illegal, is worth having.

Acquisition of territory is not the only objective of war. Although territory almost always is involved, the objectives may be varied and complex. For example, the invasion of Cyprus by the Turkish army in 1974 presumably was aimed at giving protection to the Turk-Cypriot minority and preventing a possible union of the island with Greece. The invasion of Lebanon by Israel in the summer of 1982 was designed to destroy the PLO militarily and to place under Israeli control, directly or indirectly, some territory in southern Lebanon, and thus to increase the distance between northern Israel and any potential attackers using Lebanese territory. The Iranian efforts to push into Iraq after the recapture of Iranian territories initially lost in the war in 1981 presumably had as objectives the overthrow of the regime of Hadam Hussein in Iraq and the promotion of the emergence there of an Islamic republic on the Iranian pattern.

.... The Influence of Nationalism

With the emergence of *nationalism* as a major factor in international relations, most wars could be traced to the overarching objective of protecting the nation against alien adversaries or to the expansion of a nation's domain and power. Ordinary individuals were taught through political socialization to identify with a national community that was entitled to their supreme allegiance.

Nationalism is a potent force in today's world because it provides the intellectual and emotional framework that the government of a sovereign state needs to generate popular support for its foreign policies, especially when such policies require sacrifices and involve serious risks. Almost invariably, a government embarking on a war policy will make every effort to portray its actions as necessary for the defense or advancement of the nation's most crucial interests. Standing up to an adversary becomes a matter of national honor and a sacred duty.

Under the influence of nationalism, the quest for *self-determination* became another source of conflict. The objective of self-determination is to enable an ethnic group living under foreign domination to bring itself and the territory it inhabits under its own sovereign government or the sovereignty of a country it prefers.

Self-determination gave rise to two potential causes for conflict and war: *irredentism* and *separatism*. The objective of irredentism is the liberation of ethnic "blood-brethren" still under foreign domination. For example, the nation-states that initially emerged from the gradual disintegration of the Ottoman empire engaged in successive wars to bring their still "enslaved" brethren under their own national sovereignty. The liberation of people went hand in hand with the acquisition of territory. Separatism, on the other hand, is the quest of an ethnic group living on territory controlled by a different nation to end the foreign rule and form its own separate nation-state. In a sense, all the new states that came out of the dissolution of the colonial empires in Africa and Asia were the product of separatism.

In both irredentism and separatism, the key issue is territory. The Israelis would hardly object to a Palestinian state if the Palestinians in the West Bank decided to leave the area and establish their own state somewhere in the expanses of the Arabian peninsula. In 1922, the Turks were not particularly unhappy to see the Greeks living in Asia Minor flee to Greece as refugees. The refugees were "free" and among their "blood-brethren" in Greece, but this kind of "liberation" was not what the proponents of an irredentist policy had in mind.

Nationalism has also given a new twist to a traditional objective of war. In the more distant past, kings and emperors went to war to avenge an affront to their person or to their sovereign authority. Today, nations may go to war to avenge an affront to the national honor, or because they wish to protect their country's preeminence in a certain area or even on a worldwide scale.

....Imperialism

Imperialism is a familiar term, but familiarity may conceal a certain irrelevance to the realities of today's international system. Imperialist policies have been in evidence throughout history. They were policies designed to expand the dominion of a sovereign entity, particularly through direct territorial conquest or by gaining indirect but effective control over the political and economic life of other peoples and areas. These objectives of imperialism almost inevitably led to war, not only with the intended victims but also with rival imperialist powers. Empires were created and perpetuated almost exclusively by force. As has been noted, the French, British, Belgian, and Portuguese possessions in Africa were held by a "monopoly of force."[3]

This historically valid—and ideologically neutral—understanding of imperialism has limited relevance to the current perception of imperialism. The Western colonial empires have disappeared and have been replaced by a multitude of sovereign entities whose governments are determined to defend their independence and resist even subtle attempts by outsiders to violate the sanctity of their sovereign authority. Only the control exercised by the Soviet Union over the East European states resembles the traditional patterns of an empire.

Through the centuries, empire builders were trying to either change the status quo or fill a vacuum. The Roman empire changed the status quo around the Mediterranean by subjugating existing political entities and creating a new order. By contrast, the early Spanish empire in Latin America or the British and French empires in Africa were built in areas that were vacant, sparsely populated, or inhabited by weak and primitive tribes unable to resist.

Although the material benefits of having an empire are obvious, imperialist expansion was not motivated exclusively by the pursuit of economic gains. During the nineteenth century, the possession of an empire was a precondition for *great power* status. Germany, a late-comer to the colonial scene, sought to acquire colonies in Africa, even though they were economically unprofitable, mainly because the possession of colonies was at the time a major source of prestige.

Today, references to American or Western imperialism reflect a Marxist–Leninist view of "imperialism as the final stage of capitalism"—the title of Lenin's well-known pamphlet. Marx held that the proletarian revolution would begin in the advanced industrial states, where an expanding and impoverished proletariat would rise to over-throw capitalism and the ruling class, the bourgeoisie. By the turn of the century, the realization of this prediction seemed to become increasingly remote as the standard of living of the workers in the advanced states, instead of deteriorating as Marx had predicted, improved. At this point, Lenin devised a plausible explanation. The major capitalist countries, he wrote, had found in the possession of colonial empires a way to postpone the day of their "inevitable" demise. By exploiting the resources of their colonies, they were able to amass huge profits, which they brought back to the "metropole," giving the workers at home a small portion of this largesse to keep them content and neutralized as a revolutionary force.

Because the workers in the industrial states had lost their "revolutionary con-sciousness," according to Lenin, the revolution would begin in the underdeveloped, impoverished, exploited areas. The capitalist states could only delay the end by shifting exploitation from their home workers to the people in their colonial possessions. This imperialist strategy was the last stage of capitalism. This is Lenin's contribution to the theory of imperialism and the intellectual foundation for the current conception of imperialism.

Following the breakup of the colonial empires (which did not usher in the collapse of the capitalist states), the supporters of the Leninist view of imperialism found a substitute for direct colonial control, which no longer existed, and an explanation for the continuing vigor of the advanced capitalist economies. They spoke of *neocolonialism,* a form of indirect economic control over the former colonies designed to perpetuate their dependence and exploitation. They also found a major instrument of neocolonialism in the multinational corporations, but as we indicated elsewhere in this text, the role of multinational corporations as tools of Western or American imperialism has been greatly exaggerated (see also chapter 10).

Currently, the term *American imperialism* is used, especially by Marxist-oriented commentators, with a certainty that should be reserved for facts that have long ceased to be subject to question. Yet, on closer examination, one is bound to discover that this imperialism is of a timid variety. The territorial dimension is largely missing: there is no colonial empire in the traditional pattern of direct sovereign control over foreign countries and peoples. Any indirect control over the political or economic life of other nations is rather pallid and uncertain. The U.S. government was unable to prevent successive price increases by the oil exporting countries; revolutionary changes in Cuba, Iran, Nicaragua, Ethiopia, or South Yemen; challenges to U.S. economic interests by Japan, the EEC, or other countries; rejection of its initiatives for peace in the Middle East; or occasional taunts by India or other Third World countries. *Imperialism* implies above all the ability of the imperial power to impose its will and shape developments to its own satisfaction. This kind of ability is seldom in evidence. On the other hand, the United States certainly is able to exercise a great deal of influence. It has tremendous resources to bring to bear. Its bargaining position generally is very strong and this affects the final outcome of an international transaction.

An imperialist mentality surfaces from time to time in the statements or policy proposals of U.S. or other Western politicians, journalists, or academics because past historical experiences are still embedded in the confines of conventional wisdom. However, "American imperialism," as a major factor in contemporary international relations, is not the potent force the extensive use of the term would seem to imply. In fact, the influence potential of the United States appears to increase most when its government behaves in the least imperial manner.

Noneconomic Objectives

Nations may go to war even though a dispassionate assessment shows that there is no material gain to be expected in a strictly economic sense. We mentioned earlier that nationalism has made the defense of national honor a sacred duty. National tempers are likely to flair and popular demands for revenge may force the hand of even a prudent government when action by an adversary is seen as a grave insult to the nation.

Nations may also go to war to aid other nations with similar ideological, religious, racial, or ethnic backgrounds. In 1914, the Russian czar ordered a general mobilization, thus triggering the final process that led to World War I, not because he was primarily concerned with the acquisition of territory or other material resources; his objective was to come to the aid of another Slavic nation, Serbia. The United States initially became involved in Vietnam at least in part because President Kennedy, himself a Catholic, thought it a matter of principle and moral duty to extend a helping hand to the Catholics of South Vietnam who were fighting to preserve their freedom.

A country may continue a costly and unprofitable war only because it wants to preserve its prestige and international standing. Once the United States became deeply involved in Vietnam, it could not easily disengage. Continuing the war became a matter of prestige, a question of "standing by our friends" regardless of the heavy costs, which could never have been recovered even had there been a victorious conclusion. There is no evidence that the United States went to war in Vietnam to acquire territory, subjugate the Vietnamese people, plunder their resources, or obtain any economic benefits that could conceivably justify the ensuing material expense and loss of life.

A major power may go to war to live up to a perceived mission in the international arena. To refer again to the Vietnam experience, the U.S. decision makers saw the drive from the north and the Vietcong rebellion in the south as a concerted effort to expand communist control southward as a prelude to further expansion into Southeast Asia. The *domino theory* implied that if South Vietnam were allowed to slip behind the "bamboo curtain," one after another the countries in the region would fall into the communist net. The United States, as the "leader of the free world," could not remain indifferent to such a development. (Incidentally, our references to Vietnam indicate that the decision makers may have several objectives in going to war.)

A war may start because a government wants to divert public attention away from domestic problems. History has often proved that nothing unites as strongly as a common hatred. Turning public emotions against a hated enemy can be useful; it can also be very risky. If the government that uses this device fails in its war effort, the ultimate consequence may be its own downfall. The fall of the military government in Argentina after the Falklands (Malvinas) islands defeat is a recent illustration.

Why Nations Go to War......................................

The material and emotional objectives governments have when they opt for a military venture appear to provide a clue to our initial question about the causes of war.

Government leaders go to war:

1. When they want to acquire material benefits (territory, resources) and they cannot do so at the negotiating table

2. When they believe that what they consider a vital interest is threatened and can be protected only by preemptive action or by military defense

3. When they are convinced that the prestige and the international standing of their country is at stake and can be protected or restored only by force

4. When they want to come to the aid of ethnic, religious, or ideological brethren

5. When they want to forestall changes that may adversely affect their domestic situation

6. When they want to expand the dominion of their religious or ideological beliefs

7. When they want to divert public attention from internal problems and to strengthen national cohesion and support for the government

Not infrequently, a combination of these reasons may be in evidence. In general, *nations go to war mainly to pursue or defend interests they perceive to be vital.* It is largely irrelevant how sound this perception is or what interests are considered vital by the decision makers.

The Nuclear Factor ....

Nuclear weapons that can pulverize entire cities, and delivery systems that can span the oceans in minutes instead of hours, have revolutionized warfare and have raised fundamental questions about the rationality of war itself. It is common knowledge that a full-fledged nuclear exchange between the United States and the Soviet Union would result in tens of millions of dead and incapacitated within a matter of hours in both countries, the destruction of major urban and industrial centers, the radioactive contamination of food and supplies, the breakdown of government authority and public order, and the end of both countries as functioning societies. Such a war, one may argue, cannot be regarded as "the continuation of politics by other means." No gains can possibly offset losses of such staggering magnitude. In chapter 10, we will discuss in greater detail the issues related to nuclear armaments and deterrence; our discussion here is brief.

.... Deterrence

In light of these realities, both superpowers have accepted the strategic axiom that peace can be preserved by making sure that any potential aggression in vital regions will be a suicidal venture. No rational government, according to this thinking, would deliberately embark on a confrontation and unleash nuclear war if the end result would be the annihilation of its people. This is the central reasoning of deterrence.

The concept of deterrence is not new, of course. In earlier pages, we discussed the theory that balanced military forces tend to discourage warlike ventures. The Roman dictum *si vis pacem, para bellum* implied in effect a strategy of deterrence. By being prepared for war, one could presumably preserve peace; aggression would become too costly and unattractive. In the past, this form of deterrence has not proven effective. Nuclear deterrence, however, appears to rest on more valid reasoning. Conventional deterrence was ineffective because war never posed *unacceptable* risks. Nuclear war, with its destructive potential, leaves no margin for acceptable risks.

Both superpowers have, up to this time, preserved their ability to deter each other by possessing delivery systems that cannot be eliminated in a massive *first strike*. In other words, both the United States and the Soviet Union have a *second strike* capability (the ability to survive a first strike and retaliate with devastating consequences for the opponent) so destructive that no rational decision maker would embark on a first strike.

The danger is that technological developments might increase the vulnerability of the second strike delivery systems (such as submarine-launched ballistic missiles or aircraft-launched cruise missiles) by destroying the missiles in flight, by crippling their electronic guidance systems, or by orbiting in space "killer satellites" capable of destroying the reconnaissance and guidance satellites on which detection and delivery depend—any of which could make a second strike impossible. When that happens, deterrence will no longer be a realistic strategy.

It is unlikely that one side will achieve such a technological breakthrough long before the other sides does, thereby gaining a decisive advantage. It is more realistic to expect that both sides will reach the new technological plateau at about the same time (unless special agreements are concluded to preserve the conditions of mutual deterrence). The net effect of such a breakthrough will be the removal of the conditions of deterrence, which until now have imparted an element of stability to the relations between the two superpowers.

Conventional Warfare...

Under the umbrella of nuclear deterrence, conventional warfare has been as common in the last forty years as at any other time in history. *Conventional warfare* is the use of nonnuclear military forces by governments as they try to impose their will on other governments, bring about changes they desire, prevent changes they oppose, defend their prestige, or gain some advantage at the expense of another country. A key feature is that the belligerent parties do not employ nuclear weapons of any kind. Since 1945, all wars have been conventional. Conventional warfare also differs from guerrilla attacks and from terrorist activities, which we shall discuss separately later in this chapter.

Defense against outside intruders must have been a primary preoccupation of primitive humans, second only to the necessity of finding food. Since the earliest days of recorded history, human societies organized armed forces to protect the territory they considered to be theirs. However, defense was not their only objective. Armies must have been used for defense as often as other armies were used for aggression. These two aspects of the *military imperative* (that is, the need to have forces of violence) are inseparable. Throughout the ages, rulers of every stripe have assembled mighty armies not only to defend their territories but also to bring more lands and people under their control, thereby expanding their wealth, prestige, power, and influence while pushing farther away from the heartland of their domain the potential threat of hostile neighbors. The great empires that emerged on this planet were born of violence, as superior armies under ambitious and capable commanders overpowered weaker neighbors. For those who were able to forge better weapons, devise more effective tactics in combat, and mobilize larger armies for conquest, war was an attractive and profitable enterprise. The gains far outweighed the costs. For the vanquished, the cruel aftermath of defeat was a long-remembered lesson that military weakness opens the road to disaster. Whether for conquest or for defense, the necessity of having a strong military establishment was acknowledged so widely and so consistently that the military imperative became deeply embedded in the human mind.

The advent of nuclear weapons may have transformed war from a rational enterprise to a suicidal venture, but beneath the nuclear cover conventional warfare remains a realistic possibility. Today no less than in centuries past, there is hardly any

country in the world without a defense establishment: armed forces supplied with
expensive conventional weapons, a supporting bureaucracy, and physical facilities such
as training camps, ammunition depots, military airports, and other installations. Even
countries that do not seem to face any real threat to their security and territorial integrity
spend considerable sums to maintain a costly military machine. In November 1982,
World Bank president A. W. Clausen, addressing a UN General Assembly committee
dealing with economic affairs, focused on the disparity between military expenditures
and the availability of funds for economic development. "We [at the World Bank]," he
said, "struggle for a few hundred million dollars in international development assistance, while the world is spending hundreds of billions a year in arms. . . . [This is]
global absurdity that must be reversed." There is no sign that such reversal is in the
offing.

Why Conventional Forces?

It took humanity more than ten thousand years to move from the bow and arrow to the
cannon and the firearm (invented in the fourteenth century); five more centuries to move
to the rapid-firing machine gun; and then less than fifty years to devise nuclear bombs
and intercontinental ballistic missiles.

These advances in weapons technology have not affected substantially the
rationale that through the centuries has justified the existence and use of military forces.[4]
We may cite several reasons for this.

Traditional Use. Military force is a useful factor not only in war or in coercive
diplomacy but also in improving a country's bargaining position even in a transactional
interaction. Traditionally, a strong force has been a valuable instrument of policy, used
by governments to impose changes they favored or prevent changes they opposed. Even
in nonviolent, diplomatic transactions, the implied threat of military action and the
prestige attached to a country because of its military prowess often are instrumental in
gaining a favorable resolution in a dispute. The great powers of the nineteenth century
were *great* because of their military potential.

Continued Need. The ability of the nuclear superpowers to destroy each other in a
nuclear exchange has resulted, thus far, in a precarious balance despite recent technological advances. This overall symmetry of nuclear capabilities has acted as an effective
deterrent. However, sovereign states can use their conventional forces and engage in
military conflict in the traditional manner. Israel and its Arab neighbors have clashed
five times in conventional wars (1948, 1956, 1967, 1973, and 1982); Iraq and Iran
(1980-   ), India and Pakistan (1965), China and Vietnam (1979), Tanzania and Uganda
(1978), and Britain and Argentina (1982) provide further familiar illustrations. It
appears that a conventional war remains a possibility and that in the present international
system sovereign states need to have conventional forces as insurance against a possible
challenge to their independence and territorial integrity.

Source of Prestige. An impressive conventional force continues to be a source of
prestige. Most government leaders probably feel weak and small unless they display an

impressive array of modern weapons and columns of smartly uniformed officers and soldiers marching to the sound of military bands. Governments are thus willing to divert funds sorely needed for economic development to purchase costly weapons and maintain expensive armies. Seldom is the citizenry against such a policy. Nationalist attitudes transcend all other considerations. Emotions that spring from deeply held convictions that have ancient roots work in favor of keeping a conventional military force.

Internal Control. Governments want to have a conventional military establishment not only for external reasons; many are concerned with internal threats to their authority. Because the troops for a military force do not come from another planet but from a country's population, governments uncertain of public loyalty tend to screen prospective officers and even soldiers and accept only those who happen to be reliable and loyal. In addition, massive indoctrination and special benefits are used to reinforce the fighters' reliability.

The military, however, are not always a reliable shield for the government. On occasion, the military take over the reins of power themselves, overthrowing in a coup the authorities they were expected to protect. In other cases, the armed forces may prove unable or unwilling to protect the government from an internal upheaval. The Shah of Iran, for example, spent billions of dollars to organize a formidable conventional force, which he saw not only as an instrument of his ambitious foreign policy but also as a bulwark for his regime. In diverting sizeable resources to the military while neglecting Iran's social and economic problems, he gave his enemies the opportunity to win over the people and turn them against his regime. At the critical moment, the army— particularly the ordinary soldiers, who were actually peasants and workers in uniform— proved an unreliable shield.

The Size and Mission of Conventional Forces

A country's military establishment can be assessed realistically only in relation to the forces of an adversary, a specific threat, or the government's foreign policy objectives. The Israeli military establishment is evaluated in relation to the armed forces of Israel's Arab neighbors and potential opponents. The Pakistani military establishment is assessed in relation to the Indian military. The Greeks are primarily concerned with Turkey's military strength. This localized approach to the question of adequacy is the prevailing mode. A government, in planning the strength, composition, and armaments of its military establishment, has to determine how much is enough. It must take into account three basic considerations:

1. What is the potential use of these forces?

2. What resources must be devoted to develop and maintain these forces so that they can be capable of fulfilling their mission?

3. How much can the country afford to spend without risking a serious destabilization of the political and economic system?

To answer these questions, a government has to:

1. Define its own foreign policy objectives

2. Assess as realistically and accurately as possible the objectives of the country's potential adversaries

3. Evaluate its adversary's capabilities for military action

4. Weigh the effect of third parties in the event of a military confrontation

A study of these key elements should indicate what types of forces are needed and of what size and combat capability. However, governments, and especially their military advisers, tend to overestimate the needs and the potential threats on the assumption that unforeseen contingencies may require additional forces.

Guerrilla Warfare ....

The expansion of Soviet control by brandishing (let alone using) nuclear weapons or by sending conventional forces into foreign countries does not appear to be a realistic possibility in the foreseeable future.[5] A more likely possibility is that radical changes will result from the activities of revolutionary local forces (with or without Soviet involvement) engaged in *subconventional warfare*—guerrilla warfare or "wars of liberation." The success record of this type of warfare since 1945 is uneven. It succeeded in China, Algeria, Vietnam, Cuba, Nicaragua, Mozambique, Angola, and Zimbabwe, but it failed in Greece, the Philippines, Malaya, several Latin American countries, and Thailand.

A study of these cases will show that both successes and failures were affected much more by political than military factors. A guerrilla force cannot win without wide and consistent support by the populace, especially the peasantry in the countryside. In Greece, the Communist-led guerrillas (1946–1949) were eventually defeated because a democratically elected government representing the broadest spectrum of political opinion in the country was able to isolate the Communists *politically* and win public support. In the Philippines, the Communist-led Huks were defeated in the 1950s by a politically astute leader, Ramon Magsaysay, who succeeded in isolating the Huks *politically* and gaining the support of the people, especially those in the countryside. In Malaya (1946–1960), the Communist-led guerrillas were stripped of their mantle as "liberators from colonial oppression" when the British granted independence, thus strengthening the government's political influence and prestige.

When revolutionary movements succeed, the reasons are primarily political. In China, Cuba, Nicaragua, and Zimbabwe, the revolutionaries were fighting against politically unpopular regimes; in the case of Vietnam, against a government that appeared to be a foreign puppet; in Algeria, Mozambique, and Angola, against colonial powers that had delayed their departure for too long.

Without broad popular support, a government's counterinsurgency efforts are doomed even when they appear to be doing well in a strictly military sense. The French, for example, had all but annihilated the National Liberation Forces (NLF) in Algeria by 1960, when fewer than ten thousand fighters were left of an earlier force of sixty thousand. Yet the French were forced to grant Algeria its independence because it was impossible to win politically.

To combat and eventually defeat a guerrilla operation, a government must adopt a two-pronged strategy: political and military.

Political Measures. The political side is quite obvious: it requires social, economic, and political measures designed to remove, as much as possible, the conditions that feed the popular resentments on which the guerrillas thrive. In fact, a successful fight against a Communist-led guerrilla force requires that the concepts that form the basis of guerrilla warfare be reversed. The ultimate success of the guerrillas depends on the gradual subversion of their opponent's morale and popular support (disregarding a conventional military intervention on their behalf from the outside). Conversely, strengthening the morale of the armed forces and expanding the government's popular support are the essential prerequisites to a successful antiguerrilla campaign. A parochial, narrow-minded leadership, with anti-communism as its only credential and guiding principle, cannot possibly provide the necessary foundation for a successful war against a Communist-led guerrilla offensive.

Military Measures. The military strategy and tactics of an antiguerrilla campaign cannot follow the familiar rules of conventional warfare. In fact, if generals steeped in conventional warfare are allowed to pursue the war by relying on conventional tactics, their chances of success will be minimal. *Search-and-destroy* operations and *body counts* proved completely ineffectual and misleading in Vietnam. By contrast, the strategy and tactics used in Greece deserve study. The time-limited, search-and-destroy sweeps through the countryside employed in the early stages of the fight were abandoned in favor of a systematic effort to *seize-and-hold* one area after another.

This seize-and-hold strategy involved the selection of a specific, well-defined area (a mountain range), the concentration of regular and special forces (such as commando units) to surround and seal off the target area, continuous offensive operations by saturating the area with military units, relentless pursuit of the bands even to the most remote hideouts, extermination or capture of the guerrilla forces in the area, mopping-up operations by auxiliary units, and stationing of the main force in the area for several weeks until the bulk of the guerrilla force was definitely out of commission and the villagers could be sure that the government authority was fully restored and was there to stay. The next step was to set up local units (made up of villagers) for static self-defense, install government officials, and take measures to prevent reinfiltration of the area by guerrillas. Then the process was repeated in an adjacent area.[6]

The importance of guerrilla warfare for the expansion of Communist control can be shown by a reference to countries that now have Marxist–Leninist (or strongly anti-Western) regimes. With the exception of the countries in Eastern Europe, no country has come under Communist control as a result of a conventional war launched by the Soviet Union. This indisputable historical fact indicates that a Western strategy to prevent the takeover of Third World countries by anti-Western revolutionary groups requires an understanding of guerrilla warfare and of its political and social aspects.

Terrorism..

Terrorism involves the use of violence for political ends by nongovernmental entities. In this, it resembles guerrilla warfare. It differs, however, in three aspects:

1. Terrorist activities are sporadic

2. They do not involve large numbers of people

3. They strike against targets whose high visibility guarantees wide publicity

Although the term *terrorism* has become familiar during the last two decades, no precise or generally accepted definition is available.[7] However, we can identify certain features that are peculiar to this type of violence-oriented political activity.

First of all, we should point out that terrorist activities would be ordinary crimes against life, personal freedom, or property if they were committed without political intent. Kidnappings, skyjackings, bomb explosions, torture, wounding or killing human beings, robberies, seizure of buildings and hostages, illegal incarceration, and blackmail are criminal acts in virtually every country. However, if the motives are political, they are considered to be terrorist activities.

Terrorists claim that they are committed to a certain ideology or *cause*. However, the victims are not necessarily their political or ideological adversaries. The one feature the victims have in common is that they can attract public attention and that action against them will enable the terrorists to publicize their cause. This does not mean that the individuals involved are necessarily prominent. It is enough that the action against them is likely to become a media event. More specifically, we can identify three basic aims of a terrorist act.

Achieving Name Recognition for the Terrorist Group.
Following a terrorist act, the perpetrators invariably contact the media and identify their group (ordinary criminals seldom advertise their identity). Our communications media (especially television) are essential tools in the hands of terrorist organizations. An assassination or the seizure of an airliner in flight is a dramatic event that, in this era of instant communications, guarantees a terrorist group free publicity on prime time.

Publicizing the Cause.
Having limited power or influence, a terrorist group finds a violent act the most effective way to publicize its cause. The Irish Republican Army (IRA) has committed several spectacular terrorist acts in recent years to keep its cause before the public eye. The PLO resorted to terrorist acts in its early years, until the plight of the Palestinians became widely familiar; then reliance on terrorism became unnecessary and even counterproductive, and diplomacy was given much greater prominence as the PLO's political tool. Armenian terrorist groups, sworn to avenge the massacre of their ancestors by the Turks in the early part of this century, have not been able to gain similar recognition because their basic aim is void of a specific, practical objective.

Forcing a Government to Deal with the Terrorist Group as an Equal. Negotiations with government officials to release hostages in exchange for free passage or other concessions give the terrorists a sense of power and influence as they deal with the government representatives on an equal basis.

If we judge from the publicized causes of the terrorist groups that have achieved certain prominence in the last twenty years, only a few have a strictly Marxist–Leninist ideological orientation. The Red Brigades in Italy, the Baader–Meinhof in Germany, the Red Army in Japan, the Weather Underground in the United States, and the Tupamaros in Latin America do have such an orientation; practically all of them are currently in disarray or have ceased to exist. Most of the other groups are associated with nationalist causes. In this category we include the Irish Republican Army, the PLO during the first ten years of its existence, the Armed Forces of National Liberation (FALN) of Puerto Rico, the Basque Separatists in Spain, the Armenian anti-Turkish hit squads, certain Croatian separatist groups, the Moslem fundamentalist group responsible for Sadat's assassination, the Muhajedin in Iran, and the Abu Nidal, which has operatives in Lebanon and other parts of the Middle East.[8]

Most terrorists consider themselves to be patriots serving a noble cause. That some of them give up their lives in suicidal attacks is a reflection of the strong convictions that inspire the actions of at least some groups.

For the time being, the activities of terrorist groups, however spectacular they may be at times, do not pose a serious political or strategic threat. No terrorist organization has achieved the overthrow of a government in any country. Only groups that have moved from terrorism to the guerrilla stage have become politically important. This is a critical distinction. Guerrilla movements have the potential of military and political success; terrorist groups do not.

The Balance of Power...

The *balance of power* is intrinsically related to the notion that governments seek to impose their will on other governments. As a result, the balance of power concept, in all different variations, is closely connected to military force and the potential to use violence. The effort to achieve and maintain a balance of power is justified by "the fear that, if one nation gains predominant power, it may impose its will upon other states, either by the threat of violence or the actual use of violence."[9] To counter such a threat, a state—according to the balance of power theory—needs to counterpose its own equal or superior power.

The theoretical foundation for the balance of power rests on several key assumptions:

1. States normally will try to impose their will on other states unless they are prevented from doing so

2. The interests and objectives of the various participants are not always in harmony and the potential for conflict is almost always present

3. In the absence of a superior authority, the resolution of conflicts and the settlement of disputes is the responsibility and prerogative of each sovereign state

4. Although disputes may be settled peacefully through a compromise in a transactional interaction, differences may be resolved through violence

5. To deny an adversary the advantages of superior power, a state must develop its own power resources

6. A state can best avoid submission by balancing the power of an adversary with its own or that of its allies

....Varied Configurations

In the context of the balance of power theory, the term *balance* implies equilibrium between two opposing sides in the assets that determine their comparable power. Equilibrium exists when the assets of one side are sufficient to prevent the other side from imposing its will. If one side increases its elements of power, the scale tips in its favor and the equilibrium is gone. The outcome is likely to be detrimental to the weaker side, because the stronger state may be tempted to take advantage of its power preponderance.

Obviously, this basic view of the balance of power can be applied to a number of different situations:

• Two states can balance each other's power (bipolar)

• Three states can maintain equilibrium if one of them shifts its support to the side of the weaker party (tripolar)

• Several states can maintain a balance by shifting from one to the other side to restore the equilibrium as necessary (multipolar)[10]

Bipolar Configurations

The most common situation is a "bipolar" configuration, which usually involves two neighboring states, each striving to develop its own power resources and particularly its military capabilities to balance those of the other side. One illustration of this is the insistence of Greece that military aid given to Greece and Turkey by the United States should be based on the ratio of seven to ten (seven for Greece, ten for Turkey).

Tripolar Configurations

If one state finds that its assets are inadequate to achieve and maintain equilibrium, it may try to augment its power potential by enlisting the support of other states. The pitfalls of such an association are many, as those who come to the rescue seldom do so without trying to promote their own interests or to extract a price for their aid. Defensive alliances, however, have been common throughout history because states find such drawbacks acceptable for the sake of their survival or defense of vital interests.

A balance of power system that involves three states (tripolar) is practical provided that:

1. Two of the three states are the principal adversaries

2. The third state—the balancer—is not involved in a direct conflict of its own with one or the other of the two principal adversaries

3. The third state is willing to join the weaker side when necessary to restore the equilibrium and discourage the aggressiveness of the stronger party

With the deterioration of relations between the Soviet Union and the People's Republic of China and the improvement of the latter's relations with the United States, the proposition was advanced that a tripolar balance of power was emerging, with China being the third party to be added to the side of the United States, thereby counterbalancing Soviet power and discouraging Moscow's perceived aggressiveness. We doubt, however, that China can be considered as a third pole in a tripolar system with the Soviet Union and the United States. China does not possess, as yet, the military might that would allow it to play the role of the balancer. The balancer—as played by Britain during the nineteenth century—must be as strong as the two adversaries, or at least be strong enough to tip the balance decisively and prevent the aggressive side from disturbing the status quo. For the foreseeable future, the role of China in the global power equation is much more modest. For the United States, China's independence from Soviet tutelage is a welcome and desirable condition; an unfriendly China poses a problem for Moscow and inhibits Soviet global activities.

In a more limited sense, a tripolar balance of power configuration is not uncommon, although the actual application may be less formalized than our initial description may suggest. A neighbor in a localized conflict may come to the support of the threatened party to avert a war that could harm its own interests. Such an intervention is more likely to be of a diplomatic nature than to take the form of an alliance, although the actual modalities depend on circumstances. The intervention of the third state, in whatever form, may tip the balance and induce moderation on the part of the aggressive state.

The Nineteenth-Century Multipolar Pattern

A different conception of the balance of power is associated with the balance of power system that presumably kept the peace in nineteenth-century Europe.

1. The key element in this system was the principle that no European state should be allowed to attain such preponderance of power as to become capable of imposing its will on the other participants and bringing under its control the entire continent.

2. Several states, not just two, participated.

3. The participating states were free to shift allegiance. This meant that any time one state or group of states moved to shift the balance of power in their favor, the other states would join forces to restore the equilibrium.

4. At least one strong state—the balancer—was willing to shift its support to restore equilibrium.

5. The key participants shared certain common values; states were temporarily in conflict, but they were not divided by unbridgeable chasms.

Britain, safe behind the Channel, could play the balancer role. Historical evidence shows that Britain did not do so as a service to humanity, but did so because it was in its interest to prevent any single European power from imposing its rule over the entire continent. Britain fought Napoleonic France to prevent a French hegemony and fought with France against Germany in the World Wars I and II to prevent a German hegemony.

The Balance of Power in the Nuclear Age

In 1945, one could hardly speak of a balance of power in a realistic sense. The major powers of the nineteenth and the early twentieth century—Britain, France, Germany, Italy, the Soviet Union, and Japan—were either in ruins or exhausted after five years of savage warfare. Only the United States remained unquestionably powerful. Its economy was undamaged, and its possession of the atom bomb gave it an added and awesome element of power. If power were indeed the principal motivating force, certain authors have implied, the United States should have moved to impose its will on a global scale. Even when, in 1949, the Soviet Union acquired the atom bomb and, in 1953, the hydrogen bomb, the balance remained in favor of the United States, which had superior means of bomb delivery and the advantages of geographic location. Yet for the first fifteen years after the end of World War II, successive United States administrations did not exploit their considerable advantage to impose their will on others. The major postwar policies of the United States in the international arena were either defensive or constructive. The Truman Doctrine, the Berlin airlift, the creation of NATO, and the war in Korea were *defensive* actions designed to maintain the status quo against perceived Soviet expansionism, as was the so-called containment policy, with its string of alliances from Europe to the Far East. The Bretton Woods arrangements for international monetary relations (see "The Postwar International Economy," chapter 7), the General Agreement on Tariffs and Trade, the Marshall Plan, and the support for European economic cooperation were *constructive* policies designed to restore the economies of both friends and former enemies. The U.S. policies of the early postwar years raise some doubts about the ironclad universality of the realist view that states are motivated only by the pursuit of power.

Although the United States did not utilize its preponderance of power for self-aggrandizement in a traditional, imperial fashion, its supremacy in the possession of significant assets became important in terms of *influence*. Throughout this early postwar period, Washington enjoyed tremendous influence and a strong bargaining position. In the many transactional interactions of those years, U.S. influence was a pivotal element. However, U.S. negotiators did not impose their views by fiat. Negotiations almost invariably were protracted, and the final agreements reflected many multifaceted compromises.

A balance of power eventually emerged as the Soviet Union achieved a degree of parity with the United States in strategic weapons, especially in the means of delivery. The bipolar situation that developed in the late 1950s and 1960s continues to prevail today, although in a less tight configuration.

Despite the increasing influence of Japan, Western Europe, and China, we cannot speak of a multipolar system in which the United States, the Soviet Union, China, Japan, Britain, France, and West Germany share the stage and can play a modern version of the nineteenth-century balance of power game. The nineteenth-century balance of power

Figure 6-1
NATO's civil and military structure.

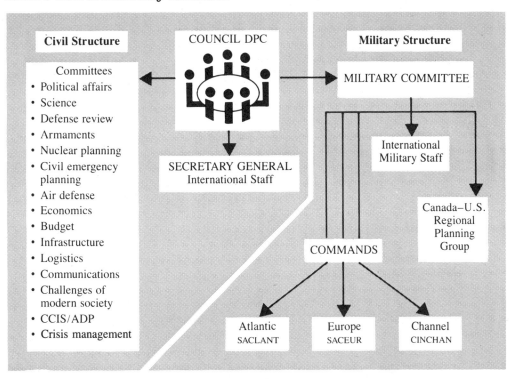

SOURCE: NATO Information Service, 1983.

system was operable because states could shift freely in their alliances. Today, Japan, Britain, France, or West Germany are not likely to join the Soviet Union, nor are Poland or Czechoslovakia likely to move to the United States camp. The lines today are more tightly drawn, in part because of fundamental ideological differences: one of the most important features of a multipolar balance of power system is missing.

A Balance of Influence?

Although an effective multipolar system has yet to emerge, there is evidence of the incipient multipolarity that President Nixon and Henry Kissinger seemed to discern in the early 1970s, but this multipolarity should not be seen in the familiar context of power, especially of military power. The current elements of multipolarity at the global level are more evident in transactional than in power situations. In the United Nations, in international organizations of global or regional scope, and in international conferences, the participants try *to balance the influence of others by maximizing their own influence potential*. They form temporary coalitions with other participants who happen to have parallel interests in a specific context. These coalitions are just as flexible and changeable as the alliances of the multipolar balance of power system in nineteenth-century Europe. In fact, they are infinitely more flexible, because they are informal and ad hoc, applying only to a given item; the same participants may today disagree on other issues with yesterday's partners. (This flexibility, however, is extremely limited when the issues relate to the strategic balance between East and West and the preservation of the status quo, especially in Europe.)

This new form of multipolarity is not confined to the major powers; the Third World countries also participate. We emphasize that this is not the traditional balance of power game. The countries in Latin America, Africa, and Asia cannot realistically expect to tip the military balance by joining one or the other superpower.

If there is a modern version of a multipolar balance of power it is more evident in the efforts of countries or groups of countries to influence decisions that affect their interests by balancing their influence against the influence of others and by improving their bargaining position through coalitions with others. This multipolar *balance of influence* is much more part of the contemporary international reality than the more familiar and more widely discussed versions of the balance of power.

Summary

- A government that cannot realize its objectives through bargaining and persuasion may resort to force. When two or more countries of comparable capabilities engage in an armed conflict of considerable magnitude, we call it *war*. If one side is so weak that the outcome is never in doubt, we speak of *military intervention*.

- Political theorists have advanced several hypotheses about the causes of war: the machinations of arms merchants, imperialist policies as viewed by Lenin, drive for power, aggressive instincts, distorted communications, survival of the fittest, arms races, and imbalance of military capabilities.

- The objectives of war help us to identify the causes of war. Governments go to war when they: (1) want to gain material resources; (2) believe that a vital interest is threatened; (3) perceive that their prestige can be protected only by force; (4) want to come to the aid of ethnic, religious, or ideological brethren; (5) want to prevent changes in the status quo; (6) want to expand the dominion of their religious or ideological beliefs; (7) want to increase their territorial possessions; (8) want to divert public attention from internal problems. In general, nations go to war to pursue or defend interests they perceive to be vital.

- Nuclear weapons have brought changes to our conception of war, which can no longer be viewed as a "continuation of politics by other means." Given the destructiveness of nuclear weapons, no gains can possibly offset the devastating losses. Both superpowers use the possession of nuclear weapons to deter each other from attempting changes in the status quo in certain critical areas such as Europe.

- Under the umbrella of nuclear deterrence, conventional (nonnuclear) warfare remains as common as in any other period.

- Military conflict may take the form of guerrilla warfare waged by revolutionary groups against the established governmental authorities. Governments faced with this type of warfare must combine effective (seize-and-hold) military tactics with political measures designed to win public support.

- Force also is used by small groups of terrorists trying to promote certain political or ideological goals.

- In the absence of a superior authority, governments try to protect their interests by maintaining a military force comparable to that of their potential adversaries. This effort to reach equilibrium in the power potential of states is related to the balance of power concept, which remains central in international relations. The realities of the contemporary international system, however, suggest that a more relevant concept is a balance of influence. Either balance system may involve two actors (bipolar), three actors (tripolar), or several actors (multipolar).

Notes

1. Richardson, Lewis. *Arms and Insecurity*. Pittsburgh: Boxwood, 1960; Huntington, Samuel P. "Arms Races: Prerequisites and Results." In *The Use of Force*, Robert J. Art and Kenneth N. Waltz, eds. Boston: Little, Brown, 1971, pp. 365–401.
2. Von Glahn, Gerhard. *Law Among Nations*. 3rd ed. New York: Macmillan, 1976, p. 281.
3. Galbraith, John Kenneth. "The Second Imperial Requiem." In *At Issue: Politics in the World Arena*. 4th ed., Steven L. Spiegel, ed. New York: St. Martin's Press, 1984, p. 18.
4. Burns, Edward McNail. *Ideas in Conflict: The Political Theories of the Contemporary World*. New York: Norton, 1960.
5. Afghanistan is a special case. It appears that the Moslem insurgency—reinforced by the emergence of the militant Moslem regime in neighboring Iran—threatened the Marxist–Leninist regime that had been installed in Kabul. The Soviet government was afraid that the success of the Afghan guerrillas might encourage dissident movements among the millions of Moslems living in Soviet Central Asia.

6. Kousoulas, D. G. *Revolution and Defeat*. London: Oxford University Press, 1965, pp. 254–270.

7. "International Terrorism." *The Annals of the American Academy of Political and Social Science,* Vol. 463, September 1982, p. 12.

8. *The Washington Post* (a series on terrorism), February 5–10, 1984.

9. Spanier, John. *Games Nations Play*. 4th ed. New York: Holt, Rinehart and Winston, 1981, p. 87.

10. Seabury, Paul, ed. *Balance of Power*. San Francisco: Chandler, 1965; Gulick, Edward V. *Europe's Classical Balance of Power*. Ithaca, N.Y.: Cornell University Press, 1955; Kaplan, Morton A., ed. *New Approaches to International Relations*. New York: St. Martin's Press, 1968.

7

International Economic Relations

Japanese cars ready for shipment to United States

Until a few years ago, those who studied international relations tended to focus their attention on the political dimensions of relations among states. Power, security, nuclear deterrence, ideological conflicts, and war were primary topics. Economic relations were treated as a secondary, even peripheral element; they were seen as "low politics" that might deserve some attention but could not compare with the exciting "high politics" of international power struggles, strategic plans, and daring confrontations.[1] High-level decision makers still prefer the traditional challenges of power politics, but they are forced by reality to devote increasing attention to economic relations with other countries.

Two major changes have been underway during the last two decades and are likely to accelerate in the years to come. The United States, which held a worldwide economic dominance and had a largely self-sufficient and self-contained economy, is now only a major star in a constellation of several economic powers. In addition, a global economic system has emerged, in which the economies of the individual sovereign states are becoming increasingly interdependent: that is, they are increasingly vulnerable to one another's economic policies and problems. Most disagreements among the industrial states of the Organization of Economic Cooperation and Development (OECD) are economic. The volume of Japanese exports to the United States, agricultural subsidy policies of the EEC, flow of investment across national borders, interest rates, currency fluctuations, inflationary or counterinflationary policies, and the removal of trade barriers are issues that cannot be resolved by mobilizing the traditional instrumentalities of military force; neither are these instrumentalities any more relevant to the economic problems of the Third World countries and the disputes that becloud their relations with the advanced industrial states.

This intrusion of economic factors into the familiar patterns of international politics continues to cause a great deal of confusion. Governments find it difficult to reconcile their traditional view of the national interest with the subtle requirements of economic interdependence. Does the security of the United States depend primarily on its military strength? Or will it be better served through economic policies that assist the Third World countries in their development efforts and make them less susceptible to revolutionary upheavals or to Soviet influence? What is the relative utility of a $300 billion military outlay compared to $20 billion in foreign economic aid (10 percent of GNP for defense versus 0.2 percent for economic aid)?

The influence of economic factors on international relations cannot be ignored or played down. The traditional issues of national security and political power, which were seen primarily in terms of military capability, now must be viewed in conjunction with the many changes taking place in the international economic environment. We shall discuss many of these issues at greater length in Part Three. This chapter will explore the basic economic instrumentalities and relationships, and the influence economic factors have on the formulation of foreign policy.

Wealth for Influence or Pressure...

Since antiquity, governments have used wealth to gain influence across their borders. In our contemporary, complex world, economic resources play an even more extensive role, whether governments engage in peaceful transactions or resort to military confrontations and war.

....Efforts to Gain Influence

We have discussed the importance of economic resources in the development of military forces. Here we shall focus on the ways governments use economic assets to improve their influence and bargaining potential.

In recent years, issues relating to international economic relations have moved from the pages of professional journals to the daily press and the newscasts. We now read stories about the economic problems facing the developing countries, heavy foreign borrowing affecting the economies of such disparate countries as Mexico or Poland, problems caused by Japanese products in the American market, agreements on monetary policy, pressures exerted by the Group of 77 (representing the LDCs) for a New International Economic Order, efforts of General Agreement on Tariffs and Trade (GATT) members to prevent policies or protectionism that could undermine free trade, OPEC's meetings to fix the price of crude oil, EEC's policies to subsidize Europe's agricultural products to the detriment of American agriculture, purchases of American wheat by the Soviet Union, commodity agreements to prevent demand and price fluctuations, and a host of other economic issues.[2]

International economic matters invariably involve conflicting interests and viewpoints. The outcome of each encounter depends on the relative influence each participant can exert. There is much bargaining, and almost always agreements reflect a compromise. How influential a government can be in such international transactions depends largely on the economic assets it can bring to bear. The use of economic resources as an instrument of foreign policy is becoming increasingly evident in today's international relations.

Reliance on economic assets is not limited to rich countries. One of today's realities is that no country is so self-sufficient that it can ignore the rest of the world: economic interdependence is a fact of international life. The Soviet Union may have ample deposits of most minerals, but it cannot feed its population adequately. The United States has a highly productive economy, but it needs raw materials to supply its industries, and markets abroad for its products. Most developing countries have valuable natural resources, but they need capital and technological expertise to develop and use these resources.

Almost every country has economic assets that can be used as leverage in pursuing its foreign policies. Nevertheless, certain countries possess extraordinary advantages and are in a stronger bargaining position. Among the LDCs, for example, the OPEC group controls a valuable commodity and its bargaining capacity is considerable; other developing countries do not have resources of comparable importance. When the latter deal with the industrial Western countries, they are at a disadvantage. Even in such cases, however, the advanced countries may follow for their own reasons more flexible economic policies to foster political stability and economic development.

To influence the policies of other governments, the industrialized countries of the First World use several instrumentalities: trade, investment, loans, and aid. We shall discuss each of these in greater detail later in this chapter.

Exerting Economic Pressure

One way to influence the decisions of another government is to use economic pressure—that is, the threat of denying economic benefits. A boycott on the purchase of another country's commodities, an embargo on the sale of certain products to an unfriendly country, tariff restrictions, indirect barriers such as delays in shipment or customs clearing of imports, and limitations to the rescheduling of foreign loans are some of the measures the wealthier countries can take when they wish to pressure another country to adopt or abandon certain policies.[3] To be effective, this variation of coercive diplomacy requires that the following three conditions be present:

1. The benefits to be denied must be of crucial importance to the country that is the target of pressure

2. The country using pressure tactics must not suffer as much as the target country

3. The target country must have no alternative outlets or sources to offset the threatened deprivations

Importance of the Denied Benefits. The significance of the first condition needs no elaboration; unless the hardships that will result from the threatened deprivations are important to the target country, the pressure will prove ineffectual.

Effect on the Pressuring Country. The second condition may not be as obvious or as easily ascertainable. The government that is trying to exert economic pressure may find that the effects of its economic policy are more harmful to its own economy than to the economy of the target country. For example, in 1982 the United States imposed certain restrictions on the export of equipment needed for the construction of the natural gas pipeline from the Soviet Union to Western Europe. The policy was rescinded a few months later because it had caused serious hardship to American firms supplying the equipment and because it had created a serious dispute with the West Europeans who were determined to proceed despite American objections. A similar situation developed with regard to the sale of U.S. grain to the Soviet Union. The embargo that had been imposed by President Carter following the Soviet invasion of

Afghanistan was lifted by President Reagan as it became increasingly evident that it hurt the American farmers more than it hurt the Soviet Union.

Availability of Alternatives.
With regard to the third condition, experience indicates that most countries find, sooner or later, alternative outlets for their products or other sources for needed supplies or resources. International trade today is so complex and variegated that a country cannot be held hostage. If one government imposes an embargo, others will purchase the goods and resell them to the embargoed country at a profit, or other suppliers will rush into the opening to take advantage of the embargo and gain a new market for their products.

For a boycott to be effective, *all* the trading partners of a given country must agree to stop buying its products. Even then, new countries may find that the commodities have a sufficiently attractive price to begin to import them.

When a particular commodity is of critical importance and the sources of supply limited, a country facing procurement problems may resort to resource substitution or conservation measures. The United States, for example, responded to the OPEC oil embargo in the 1970s and the subsequent price increases by implementing policies designed to find substitutes for oil as a fuel and to encourage lower consumption levels by reducing wasteful and inefficient uses. The attempt of the Arab countries to use economic pressure to force a radical change in Washington's Middle Eastern policy largely failed to achieve its objective.

Subtle Pressure.
Whereas highly publicized economic *sanctions,* or measures to exert pressure, usually are only marginally effective, subtle pressures may be more effective if they have modest political objectives. A delay in the delivery of spare parts, regulations requiring expensive processing of imported foodstuffs for health reasons, a requirement to have domestic components used on imported automobiles, monetary restrictions, a requirement for antipollution devices on imported items, restrictions on lending, the withdrawal of most-favored-nation status, or a subsidy for domestic products are among the limited-scope measures one government may take—or threaten to take—to influence another government to avoid undesirable actions or adopt a more cooperative posture.

The Economic Tools of Foreign Policy...

The makers of foreign policy may use economic resources to influence the outcome of both economic and political transactions. We can identify trade, lending, aid, and investment as the principal instrumentalities.

....Trade

Economists use the term *comparative advantage* to explain why it may be economically more advantageous (less costly) to import a commodity from abroad than to try to produce it domestically. This is one of the two basic reasons why nations trade with each other; the other is that a country may not be endowed with the climatic conditions or the natural resources necessary to produce a desirable commodity or satisfy important economic needs. To pay for what it imports, a country needs to export goods and services that others find desirable or necessary. Obviously, the greater the demand for a country's products the stronger its bargaining position in international trade. No amount of rhetoric can change this simple fact.

Countries with a strong trading position may use several devices to manipulate trade to achieve economic or political objectives.

Tariffs

A tariff is in effect a tax paid by the importer of foreign goods at the time the products enter the country. Obviously, if the tariff imposed on a particular commodity is high, the selling price is likely to rise commensurately. Unless demand is inelastic (unaffected by price changes), sales will go down and imports of the particular commodity will fall. This will affect the economy of the exporting country, its foreign exchange earnings (*balance of trade*), and its ability to import needed products and services. Governments impose tariffs mainly for six reasons.

Protection of Home Industry. Governments may impose tariffs to protect special industries or products that cannot compete in the domestic market with similar products imported from abroad, or that are of particular importance to defense or the economy. In such cases the comparative advantage of buying abroad versus producing domestically is overlooked to protect specialized or fledgling industries or to satisfy an important domestic group. The Common Agricultural Policy (CAP) of the EEC is a case in point. By imposing variable levies on agricultural products coming into the EEC countries, CAP limits marketing opportunities for the products of other countries, and prevents less-expensive imports. CAP, however, is important to the political cohesion of the EEC and to the European farmers; its modification, let alone abolition, would be difficult.

Reduction of Specific Imports. Tariffs may be imposed to discourage the purchase of certain products. The assumption is that the import duty will be added to the selling price and the higher cost will discourage potential customers and consequently reduce the imports of the particular commodity.

Balance of Trade Adjustment. A government may raise import duties to reduce its balance of trade deficit by discouraging imports. To combat such a deficit in 1971, the Nixon administration imposed a 10 percent *surcharge* on all imports not subject to quantitative restrictions (quotas).[4] The surcharge did not eliminate the deficit; it succeeded only in creating friction, primarily with Japan and the EEC countries.

Retaliation. A government may impose higher tariffs to retaliate against trade restrictions imposed by another country. The 1971 surcharge mentioned was expected not only to reduce the trade deficit but also to retaliate against Japanese and Western European restrictions that affected American exports.

Revenue Source. Tariffs are taxes and as such they serve as a source of revenue. Governments often use tariffs for this purpose. However, a careful economic analysis is necessary to find out whether the tariff will cut down on economic activity, thereby reducing tax revenues to a degree that exceeds the intake from the import duties.

Political Pressure. Finally, a government may use the tariff to exert political pressure or inflict punishment on an adversary, reward a friendly state, or encourage cooperation by another government. This is the strictly *political* use of tariffs as an instrument of foreign policy. In 1947, for example, the United States removed the Soviet Union from the group of states accorded most-favored-nation (MFN) status. MFN status countries do not receive special treatment; on the contrary. If the United States signs an agreement reducing the tariff on a commodity imported from West Germany, the same reduction is automatically extended to every other country that has been given MFN status by the United States. By denying the Soviet Union MFN status, the United States was free to impose trade restrictions on Soviet products regardless of what tariff regulations applied to other countries. The use of this device to induce changes in Soviet policies in Eastern Europe had practically no effect on Soviet decisions. In 1982, the same measure was used to punish Poland for the suppression of the Solidarity labor union, again with no practical effects on the decisions of the Polish authorities. By contrast, the extension of MFN status to the People's Republic of China in the 1970s was an obvious effort to reward "good behavior" and encourage friendlier relations with the United States. Yugoslavia has been accorded such status for its exports to the United States since the early 1950s to help that country maintain its independent course from the Soviet Union.

Cooperative Arrangements. One final observation on tariffs. As we shall see in later pages, the General Agreement on Tariffs and Trade (GATT) has been instrumental in wide tariff reductions by the participating countries. Under the GATT cooperative arrangements, the use of tariffs as a means of exerting political pressure has been reduced at least among the GATT members.

Quotas

Quotas are quantitative restrictions that set a limit on the number of items or the quantity of a particular product that may be imported. The objectives of quotas are not different from those of tariffs, except in one respect: quotas are not used to provide additional revenue. Quotas may cut imports more effectively than tariffs, because they limit imports even when demand for the product remains high regardless of price. As a political instrument, quotas are usually as effective (or ineffective) as are tariffs. As we shall see, GATT has virtually eliminated quotas among its members.

Embargos

An *embargo* is a ban on exports to another country, used mostly as a political measure to punish, retaliate, or induce a change in the policy of that country. Since the onset of the Cold War in 1946, the United States has imposed restrictions on the export of "strategic" items that could be used by the Soviet Union to enhance its military capabilities. Such measures have not prevented the Soviet Union from reaching military parity with the United States. In October 1973, in retaliation for U.S. support of Israel during the Yom Kippur war, the Arab oil-exporting countries imposed an embargo on the export of oil to the United States, the Netherlands, Portugal, Rhodesia, and South Africa. The Arab states threatened to continue the embargo and cut back oil production until Israel recognized the "legitimate rights of the Palestinian people" and withdrew from the occupied Arab territories, including East Jerusalem. The embargo was lifted five months later, on March 18, 1974, without any of its stated objectives having been achieved.

In 1975, the United States Congress imposed an embargo on the delivery of military equipment to Turkey as punishment for the latter's use of American-supplied weapons in its invasion of Cyprus in July 1974, and as a means of pressuring Turkey to withdraw its occupation troops from Cyprus. The embargo, which was opposed by the White House, was eased one year later and was lifted altogether in 1978. The Turkish troops were not removed from the island.

Boycotts

A *boycott* with regard to trade is a decision to prohibit imports from a given country as a retaliation for unfriendly political or economic actions or as a means of exerting pressure to induce desired behavior. In 1960, for example, when the signing of the Soviet–Cuban trade agreement signified a closer relationship between the Castro government and the Soviet Union, the Eisenhower administration suspended imports of 700,000 tons of sugar that had not been shipped yet to the United States out of the 3 million ton annual quota that guaranteed Cuba both a secure market and a selling price above that of the world market. Considering that sugar was Cuba's main export commodity and a major element in the island's total economy, the American government expected Castro to succumb to this pressure and end his relationship with the Soviets. Cuba instead shifted even closer to the Soviet Union. In 1948, Stalin cut off all trade and aid to Yugoslavia, following his rift with Tito, to force the former Soviet satellite into submission. Tito did not surrender; instead he turned to the United States and Western Europe.

A trade boycott is no more effective than a trade embargo. We may add that a boycott may take the form of a refusal to participate in a certain activity for political reasons. The 1980 boycott of the Olympic Games in Moscow by the United States and many other countries because of the Soviet invasion in Afghanistan is an illustration of such action.

Nontariff Barriers

Because the use of tariffs, quotas, embargos, or boycotts for exerting political and economic pressure is not only openly confrontational but also largely ineffective, many governments resort to more subtle and sophisticated measures. These nontariff barriers (NTBs) can take many forms. If the Japanese require that foreign products be marketed and advertised in the language of their country of origin, sales of American products may be seriously inhibited. Japan, to quote an American official, "may have a good record for adherence to international trade agreements but has not yet discarded many of its internal arrangements that inhibit imports."[5] Internal regulations imposing sanitary, safety, or environmental requirements may inhibit food or other imports, from many developing countries in particular, as effectively as tariffs or quotas, yet they fall outside international trade agreements and their effect cannot be calculated easily. Subsidizing exports or providing price supports for domestic products may keep prices artificially low, thereby making similar products from abroad too expensive to be desirable. Even complicated and time-consuming customs regulations may be used to discourage imports. The subtlety and variety of NTBs is limited only by the imagination of government officials.

Dumping

Dumping is the deliberate sale of goods in the world market at an artificially low price to saturate the market, drive prices down, and undercut the sales of other exporters. The dumping of a commodity in large quantities may cause tremendous economic hardship to a country that depends heavily on its exports of the commodity.[6]

Obviously the objectives of dumping conflict with the principle of supporting an expanding and orderly world trade. Only a country that can afford to sell a commodity in large quantities at a loss over time can engage in dumping. It is a costly device and, in the long run, not necessarily an effective one.

Exchange Rates

A country may inhibit imports and stimulate its export trade by holding the value of its currency low compared to another currency, primarily the U.S. dollar. In 1953, for example, Greece changed the official ratio of one dollar–to–fifteen drachmas to one dollar–to–thirty drachmas. This meant that the day after devaluation, one dollar could buy twice as much in Greece as it could have bought the day before. The drastic devaluation of currencies may bring a temporary upsurge of exports or tourism, but eventually domestic prices go up—or other countries follow suit—and the situation returns more or less to the levels that prevailed before the devaluation.

Because exchange rate wars can cause serious disruptions, a new institution was created in 1944 at the Bretton Woods Conference: the International Monetary Fund (IMF). One of the major objectives of this international institution is to prevent, through consultation and monetary assistance, arbitrary and disruptive changes in exchange rates. The IMF will be further discussed later in this chapter.

Lending

Credit plays a vital role in international economic relations. Trading nations need short-term credit to meet immediate obligations for imports or to cover balance of payments deficits. Developing countries find it necessary to supplement other financial resources with medium- or long-term loans. The external debt of the developing countries in Africa, Asia, Latin America, the Caribbean, and the Middle East had reached $517 billion in 1981. Almost 90 percent of this came from OECD countries, and approximately 8 percent came from the high-income oil exporters such as Saudi Arabia, Kuwait, the United Arab Emirates, and Libya. Only a small fraction came from the Soviet Union and the other COMECON countries or the People's Republic of China.

Credit tightening, insistence on prompt payments, renewal of loans at higher interest rates or under more stringent conditions, and refusal to extend additional credit or to "recycle" a loan are among the devices that a lender may use to pressure a borrower. Loans normally are made by private banking institutions. However, most governments can and do exercise control over such outflow of capital and can make lending an instrument of foreign policy. We may add that a cut-off of credit for political reasons may be counterproductive; it is likely to affect the export trade of the pressuring country, whereas the government facing such pressure is likely to find alternative sources, as Chile did in 1972.

International lending is financed primarily by private banks located mostly in the OECD and in some OPEC members.[7] However, the special needs of the LDCs for concessional loans (loans with below-market interest rates and other lenient repayment terms) have made necessary an expansion in the lending activities of the World Bank and its affiliates such as the International Finance Corporation and the International Development Association.

Additional lending is provided by regional intergovernmental banks such as the Inter-American Development Bank (IDB), the Asian Development Bank (ASDB), and the African Development Bank (AFDB). Of these three regional banks, the IDB, which has considerable financial support from the United States and Western Europe, has been most active in Latin America. The ASDB also has been fairly successful, because it has included among the participating countries the United States, Canada, Australia, New Zealand, Japan, and twelve European states in addition to its Asian LDCs. Most of the financing comes from the participating affluent states, whereas the Asian LDCs are the major beneficiaries. This expanded membership has provided the Bank with resources that otherwise would have been unavailable. By contrast, the AFDB has limited its membership to African states, which are mostly poor. With inadequate resources, its lending operations have been by necessity limited. The case of the AFDB points out the

Table 7-1
Major ODA Multilateral Institutions

Asian Development Bank   (ASDB)
Asian Development Fund   (ASDF)
African Development Bank   (AFDB)
African Development Fund   (AFDF)
Development Assistance Committee of OECD   (DAC/OECD)
United Nations Economic and Social Council   (ECOSOC)
United Nations Social Commission for Asia and the Pacific   (ESCAP)
Inter-American Foundation   (IAF)
International Development Association   (IDA)
Inter-American Development Bank   (IDB)
International Development Cooperation Agency   (IDCA)
International Fund for Agricultural Development   (IFAD)
Institute for Scientific and Technological Cooperation   (ISTC)
United Nations Capital Development Fund   (UNCDF)
United Nations Industrial Development Organization   (UNIDO)
World Food Program   (WFP)

dilemma facing the developing countries: if they try to preserve the independence and regionality of their institutions through a limited membership, they may undercut their ability to be effective.

Foreign Aid

Although regular or concessional loans from private or public banks are indispensable for the financing of economic development, many important projects are not suitable for such borrowing because the economic benefits will be delayed or are too difficult to measure in monetary terms. For example, the construction of roads, flood control or irrigation projects, communication and transportation facilities, power dams or sewage systems, schools, or hospitals can be financed best through special forms of economic assistance such as low-interest (*concessional*) loans, grants, or technical assistance. Such aid—indispensable for building the required infrastructure—can come only from governments or international institutions; private financial institutions cannot undertake this kind of financing.

The role of foreign aid is one of the international issues we will discuss in detail in chapter 10; our remarks here will be brief.

To what extent can foreign aid be used as an instrument of foreign policy? The record is not conclusive. Economic or military aid may increase the dependence of weaker countries on major donors, especially when spare parts for equipment are received from a certain country. However, there seem to be limits to the compliance a donor can obtain by suspending or threatening the cut-off of economic or military aid.

Investment

The argument often is advanced that the major capitalist countries, and especially the United States, often use investments in foreign countries as an instrument of foreign policy. Because direct investments in foreign countries—as distinct from loans or grants—are primarily made by private enterprises or individuals interested in profit, private investments abroad present peculiar problems when viewed from a foreign policy perspective. (Direct investment involves actual control, and not the mere purchase, of stock in a foreign corporation.) A discussion of certain salient features will help us understand to what extent and in what manner a government can manipulate foreign investment to influence or pressure other governments.

Nonpolitical Orientation. Corporations or individuals investing abroad seldom take into account the foreign policy objectives of their country. The questions they ask before making the decision to risk their capital in a foreign venture are:

1. Will it be a profitable enterprise under realistic projections?

2. Will it be handicapped by discriminatory practices or restrictive and punitive regulations in the host country?

3. Will the assets be exposed to potential nationalization, terrorist harassment, politically motivated or excessive labor union pressures, or a hostile political environment?

4. Is there the necessary technical infrastructure, especially in the area of transportation and communications?

5. Is a specialized or trainable workforce available?

6. Are there any special advantages in comparative labor costs or the availability of resources?

Of these illustrative questions, only the second and the third touch on "political" matters, but even they are related to the politics of the host country, not to the political objectives of the investor's government.

Limited Political Potential. Foreign investments differ in size, type of ownership, and relationship to the host country as well as to the investor's country of origin. Some investments abroad are by individuals or small entities. For example, some Greek–Americans, motivated in part by the expectation of profit and in part by their cultural and ethnic ties with Greece, invested funds in the 1960s and early 1970s in new tourist hotels, supermarkets, small industrial enterprises, and the like. This type of investment has minimal potential as a tool of foreign policy. In fact, its only "foreign" aspect is that the funds come from abroad and some of the profits can be taken out. Another possibility is that of a joint venture by foreign and local investors. Again the political potential of such an investment as a tool of foreign policy is limited. In both cases, the foreign entrepreneurs may exert (or try to exert) some influence over the government of the host country, but in this regard their influence potential is comparable to that of local enterprises of similar size or importance.

The Role of the Multinationals

The most significant and the most controversial form of foreign investment is that of the multinational corporations (MNCs) (discussed in chapters 2 and 9). These are mostly large North American, West European, or Japanese corporations with subsidiaries, associated companies, or branches on the territory of other countries. The local entities operate entirely under the laws of the host country. The parent companies do exercise control over their local offshoots, but the principal objective of such tutelage is to maximize profits, seldom to serve some foreign policy objective of the country of origin. Nevertheless, because the *economic* influence of the major MNCs is unquestionably significant, there is widespread interest in establishing a code of conduct for them. Negotiations for drafting such a code are being conducted under the auspices of the UN Commission on Transnational Corporations (as MNCs are called in United Nations' terminology). The hope is that generally agreed guidelines for both governments and enterprises can contribute to improved relations and foster a more active flow of direct investments, especially in the developing countries.

How influential are these giant entities? To what extent can they be used by the government of their country of origin to further its foreign policy objectives? As long as they confine their efforts to the protection of their business interests, they can expect to exercise as much influence as other companies of comparable size in the country of origin (or, in the case of their subsidiaries, as much as comparable local companies). If they try to influence political matters, they find that the possibilities are not as extensive. Illustrations do not often come to light, because such matters are not usually publicized. The 1982 decision of the Reagan administration regarding the ban on pipeline shipments for the Siberian natural gas pipeline to Europe provided a rare glimpse while revealing the complexities of today's international economic environment. Subsidiaries of the MNCs involved in this project had to obey the laws of the countries in which they were located, in this case primarily Britain, France, and West Germany. Their parent companies in the United States could not force them to comply with the American foreign policy on this matter. The subsidiaries, moreover, were not able to influence the decisions of the French, the British, or the West Germans any more than their parent companies could influence the American government. In fact, the dispute was raised from the corporate level to the government level, and was resolved along political lines. Although MNCs have some influence, the argument that they can be used as instruments of foreign policy must be viewed with caution.

Are these international entities, with their multibillion dollar assets, more influential in the developing countries? The record indicates that instead of being as powerful as is commonly assumed, the local subsidiaries of MNCs are vulnerable to the government decisions of the host country. On several occasions, the assets of MNCs were nationalized in Third World countries with only token compensation or no compensation at all. Even giant corporations, such as the major oil companies, found that they had no way to counter the power of sovereignty. Neither could their parent companies persuade their home governments to intervene with force on their behalf. Instead of being "domineering," MNCs are more likely to "behave" so that they can be allowed to operate in the host country.

Economic Limitations and Constraints...

Whatever the reasons behind a specific foreign policy decision, the use of economic assets and instrumentalities is limited by three practical factors:

1. A country's resources and potentials

2. The constraints imposed by domestic groups with vested interests

3. The resources and potentials of the other side and its ability to ignore inducements or pressures

....Resource Limitations

Even an economic giant like the United States has come to realize that its economic resources and potentials are not boundless. Although its highly productive system of economic organization—the capitalist system—generates tremendous amounts of goods and services that can serve human needs both domestically and internationally, its potential is not limitless. The economic limitations eventually show up in the form of budget deficits, higher interest rates, inflation, or unemployment. The Soviet Union, a continental power with a wealth of natural resources but an inefficient economic system—a socialist, command economy—also faces economic limitations, which result in shortages, long delays in the satisfaction of consumer needs, and poor quality of products and services.

Whether we focus on the major powers or on a small country, we are bound to find that a country's foreign policy is inexorably affected (1) by the natural and other material resources within its territory or under its direct control, and (2) by the efficiency of its economic organization and labor force in developing those assets.

In the past, relatively small countries such as Spain, Britain, and France became major powers because they brought under their colonial control vast territories with important resources. The loss of direct control over their former colonial possessions inevitably imposed limits on the goals of their foreign policies and affected their major power status.

The developing Third World countries are unable to embark on ambitious foreign policies because they have, *individually,* limited wealth and considerable dependence on the assistance of the industrialized countries of the First World. They have found, however, that their bargaining position can improve if they act *jointly* to pursue a moderate program of generally acceptable objectives. The Group of 77, acting in the context of UNCTAD and in other international forums, has sought to reshape international economic relations.[8] The 1980 Agreement, which established the Common Fund for Commodities, the 1982 Convention on the Law of the Sea, the continuing discussions on expanding lending and support activities by the World Bank and the International Monetary Fund, or the discussions on a New International Economic Order reflect the greater influence resulting from the joint action of the LDCs—but also the limitations of that influence. The bargaining power of the Third World countries depends on their economic assets; it also depends on the assets of the industrialized states of the First World. Any agreements are bound to reflect in large measure the relative economic strength of the two groups.

....Domestic Considerations

The makers of foreign policy cannot ignore the economic effects their policies may have domestically. An American decision to impose restrictions on trade with Poland in 1982 did not include harsh action on Poland's external debt owed to Western financial institutions because a policy pushing Poland to bankruptcy would have caused serious losses to several major banks in the United States and in Europe. Colonel Quaddafi of Libya has built a reputation as an implacable foe of "Western imperialism," but he has continued the sale of oil to the West because oil exports are critical to his country's wellbeing. The Japanese government is reluctant to lower barriers to the import of agricultural products because such imports would seriously hurt Japanese farmers. These random illustrations show some of the constraints domestic factors may impose on foreign policies that affect economic conditions.

In general, foreign economic policies can be influenced by domestic economic interests, political considerations, bureaucratic constraints, or even the personal preferences of decision makers, but above all they are shaped by the anticipated effects they may have on a country's economy.

Countermeasures
and Retaliation

In 1973, at the time of the oil embargo imposed by OPEC, certain groups in the United States advocated restrictions on food exports or a sharp price increase on foodstuffs exported to the OPEC members, to retaliate for the embargo. Considering that many of the countries in this group are heavy importers of foodstuffs, this form of retaliation could have been quite painful for their people. Such a policy was not followed because of its political repercussions on world opinion, the difficulties in structuring a food cartel, and the effect the proposed retaliatory action would have on U.S. food exports.

Ten days after the seizure of the American embassy in Tehran, on November 4, 1979, President Carter froze the Iranian assets in the United States, and later, in April 1980, Washington imposed a trade embargo in retaliation for the Iranian intransigence. These measures, however, failed to speed up the release of the hostages, because the Iranian regime under Khomeini was willing to pay the price to achieve its own political ends.

Japan, unhampered so far by heavy defense expenditures, has developed its productive capacity and export trade to an extent that other industrial countries find painful. Japanese exports of good quality, selling at attractive prices, flood the world markets. American automakers among others have tried to pressure Congress to adopt restrictive measures in retaliation for the Japanese trade policies they dislike. Both Congress and the White House have resisted such pressures, realizing that trade warfare will harm both economies while undermining the strategic relationship between Japan and the United States.

These illustrations indicate that economic coercive diplomacy must be weighed carefully. Empirical evidence suggests that economic warfare may prove more harmful than beneficial to those who initiate it.

The Postwar
International Economy

The experiences of the interwar period (1919–1939), when highly nationalistic policies resulted in the proliferation of trade barriers, exchange controls, and economic warfare, were fresh in the mind of those who met in 1944 at Bretton Woods, New Hampshire, to develop procedures and institutions that could bring some order into international economic interactions.

With Germany and Japan defeated in the war and the Soviet Union receding from the wartime alliance to self-imposed isolation, the power to shape the postwar international economic order rested with the United States in cooperation with Britain and France. Although the principal architects did not agree fully on every facet, they all shared a fundamental belief in the superiority of the market economy and of private ownership and initiative. They also favored without major reservations a world market with minimum barriers to the flow of trade and investment.[9]

The participants in the Bretton Woods conference, led by the three major allies, also agreed on the nature of the international economic structures that were needed to promote and maintain economic cooperation internationally. The representatives of the forty-four nations focused on two critical areas of international cooperation: the establishment of an effective international monetary system and the "reduction of barriers to trade and capital flows."[10] With the United States not only capable of leading this effort but also willing to do so, the conference set the stage for structured cooperation among the participating countries.

Managing Monetary Interactions

During World War II, President Roosevelt had come to the firm conclusion that the United States would have to play a pivotal role in establishing a postwar economic order as a corollary to the political order that was to be centered in the United Nations. One key element was the cooperative management of national monetary policies. Trade, investment, and all other forms of international economic transactions depend on fairly stable and generally acceptable exchange rates and on having the monetary means for the settlement of international accounts. With the cooperation of the British, the Americans drew up a new system of international monetary management, convinced that without stable exchange rates they could not promote international trade, economic growth, and political harmony.

The Origins of the IMF

The Bretton Woods planners created two public international organizations: the International Monetary Fund (IMF) and the International Bank for Reconstruction and Development (IBRD, or World Bank). Under the Bretton Woods rules, all countries agreed to establish the value (*parity*) of their currencies in relation to other currencies using gold as the standard, and to maintain exchange rates within 1 percent of this agreed value. The IMF was to be the keeper of this system. It was to be primarily concerned with short-term problems in the balance of payments of the member-states and with the stability of currencies.[11]

The IMF provided a permanent organizational machinery that members could use to coordinate their economic and financial policies. To achieve its objectives, the IMF was given both regulatory and financing functions. A country that wanted to change the parity level of its currency was required to consult the IMF and obtain approval. On the other hand, the IMF could advance credits to a country that faced balance of payments difficulties and thus avert the trade and payments restrictions that otherwise might be inevitable. To enable the IMF to carry out its stabilizing function, the members contributed gold and their own currencies to a pool, which the IMF could use to help finance temporary imbalances by lending funds on a short-term (up to eighteen months, usually) basis to members unable to meet their obligations to other countries. The recipients of such assistance were required to repay the IMF, so that the resources could be used on a revolving basis.

Each IMF member was assigned a quota based on the size of its economy and resources. Quotas ranged widely; the largest member, the United States, had a 19.64 percent contributing obligation, whereas the smallest had less than 0.1 percent. The quota determined not only a member's contribution but also its access to the IMF's resources, and of course its voting strength; the United States had 19.64 percent of the total voting power in the IMF.

The Role of the United States

The IMF system was a valid blueprint for the future. However, with the European economies in a shambles and Japan prostrate, its resources proved inadequate for the task in the early postwar years. By 1947, the United States had to assume a more direct role. The Europeans and the Japanese accepted this because they needed U.S. assistance to rebuild their domestic productive capacity, finance their international trade, and provide a setting for political cooperation and stability in the face of what was perceived as a serious Soviet challenge. With the advent of the Cold War providing a political impetus, the United States started in 1947 to perform two functions that are necessary for any monetary system, be it domestic or international: they provided a currency generally accepted as a medium of exchange (*liquidity*) and offered a system for the settlement of financial accounts (*adjustment*). A national economy has a currency accepted as legal tender that can be used for investment, trade, and payment. The international economy, however, has no central government that can issue an international currency and regulate its availability and use.

In the nineteenth and the first half of the twentieth century, gold played a key role not only in international transactions but also in buttressing the national economic systems of the various countries. Under the gold standard, gold was used to back a country's national currency, the value of which was fixed in relation to gold. Moreover, gold was used as a generally accepted medium for international payments and the settlement of accounts. During the same period, the British pound became an acceptable means of payment internationally, because of Britain's imperial power and prestige.

By 1947, it became clear that the supply of gold was not sufficient to meet the demands of growing international trade and investment. With the British economy seriously weakened because of the war, the pound could no longer serve as a primary world currency. The only nation in the world with an economy strong enough to assume the role once played by Britain was the United States. The magnitude and strength of the U.S. economy, unscathed by the war; the fixed rate of $35 per ounce of gold; and the commitment of the American government to exchange for gold any dollars held by foreigners made the dollar a natural international currency: it was *as good as gold*.

At the same time, the United States was the major supplier of goods to other countries whose economies were devastated or seriously destabilized by the war. As a result, the United States was piling up a balance of trade surplus at a time when the other countries had very little to export and limited funds to pay for what they had to import. To counter this growing "dollar gap," the United States initiated policies designed to create deliberately a balance of payments deficit. Through the European Recovery Plan—the famous Marshall Plan—and other aid programs, the United States "gave" dollars to other countries, thus creating *liquidity* for the international economy. In addition, the fear of Communist and Soviet expansionism led to the formation of military alliances that were financed primarily by the United States. These military expenditures became indirectly an additional source of dollars for international liquidity.

To promote the recovery and growth of the European and Japanese economies, the United States deliberately encouraged practices that favored exports from those economies and stimulated their growth. In the long run, Washington expected to benefit by creating expanding and vigorous markets for American exports.

With the dollar serving as an international currency, the system worked well for more than two decades. But it suffered from a built-in contradiction. Foreigners accepted the dollar with the same confidence they had once accepted gold precisely because the dollar was backed by vast reserves in gold (kept mostly in the famed Fort Knox) and because the American government was committed to converting dollars into gold in international transactions on request. As long as these gold reserves remained available, there was no problem. But the U.S. balance of payments deficits that were needed to provide the international economy with the necessary liquidity also were bound to reduce eventually the gold reserves of the United States. By 1960, the total amount of dollars held by foreigners exceeded for the first time the gold reserves of the United States.[12] Soon speculators and others were converting dollars and other currencies into gold. More serious, the price of $35 per ounce of gold was low, making speculation even more attractive. To deal with these difficulties, the United States, in conjunction with the major European countries, Canada, and Japan, embarked on serious efforts to develop new forms of international monetary management. By then, the economies of the other countries had recovered and were growing, providing their leaders with renewed confidence and increased influence.

In the 1960s, the almost unilateral management of the international monetary interactions by the United States gave way to a multilateral and cooperative endeavor.

Renewed Reliance on the IMF

The shift from United States omnipotence was dramatized by the emergence of the Group of Ten, which became the primary forum for discussion of common problems and making of decisions on necessary measures. The Group of Ten was composed of representatives from Belgium, France, West Germany, Italy, the Netherlands, Sweden, the United Kingdom, Canada, Japan, and the United States. One major outcome of these deliberations was to bring back to the foreground the IMF, which was relegated to a limited role during the years of United States preeminence. After protracted negotiations, the members of the Group of Ten agreed that liquidity was the major problem. There were neither enough dollars to finance the tremendous expansion of international trade and investment nor a sufficient supply of gold. Both of these media had to be supplemented with some kind of international currency. After five years of negotiations, the IMF was authorized in 1969 to issue an international reserve asset, the Special Drawing Rights (SDRs). This was an artificial reserve unit, soon to be dubbed by journalists as *paper gold*.

Under the SDR arrangement, IMF members are entitled to use SDRs as payment for international obligations and other members are required to accept the SDRs for payment. For the first time, something resembling an international currency had been created. Its use, however, is restricted to the settlement of balance of payments obligations between governments. This necessitates the continuing use of gold and dollars in international transactions.

The value of one SDR is set by the IMF on the basis of the market exchange rate of the currencies of those five members with the largest exports of goods and services. Currently, 42 percent is determined on the value of the U.S. dollar, 19 percent by that of the deutsche mark, and 13 percent each by that of the pound sterling, the Japanese yen, and the French franc. Exchange rates are now freely fluctuating; the exact value of one SDR is set for each business day by the IMF.

Currently, the IMF has 146 members. The membership includes not only all OECD countries but practically all LDCs. Only the Soviet Union and its COMECON partners are not members; the People's Republic of China joined the IMF in the mid-1970s.

The work of the IMF is administered by a board of governors, a managing director, and an administrative staff of approximately 1,500 from over ninety-five member-states. Each member is represented by a governor and an alternate governor on the board of governors, which is the IMF's highest authority. Between the annual meetings of the board of governors, most decisions are made by the executive board and the managing director. The twenty-two–member executive board is composed of the five directors appointed by the five members with the largest quotas (the United States, the United Kingdom, the Federal Republic of Germany, France, and Japan), the directors appointed by the IMF's two largest creditors if they are not among the five (currently, Saudi Arabia appoints one director on this basis), and the sixteen executive directors elected for two-year terms by other members or groups of members.

Continuing Problems

The SDR agreement showed that the leading capitalist countries were able not only to deal with crises but also to move toward systemic reform. At the time, the measures appeared adequate; however, within a few years new problems would rock the international economy.

Throughout the postwar era, the prevailing assumption was that governments would be able to regulate the supply and flow of their national currencies, thereby maintaining fairly stable parity to other currencies. However, in the 1960s, several developments—ironically promoted by the very growth of international economy the initial policies were designed to foster—reduced national control and increased the interdependence and mutual vulnerability of national monetary systems. By 1964, the European currencies and the Japanese yen became convertible to each other. Multinational banks brought about the internationalization of banking, facilitating the transfer of funds from one country to another, and reducing national control over such capital flows. Monetary interdependence was further increased by the growth of the multinational corporations, which controlled large amounts of liquid funds that could be transferred quickly both from one country to another and from one currency to another.

During the same period, as noted earlier, United States preeminence gave way to a sharing of influence with the other major economic powers in the OECD group. By 1971, the American gold stock had declined to $10 billion compared to outstanding foreign dollar holdings estimated at about $80 billion. Continuing balance of payments deficits, exacerbated by foreign competition and the economic costs of the Vietnam war, as well as strong inflationary pressures, growing unemployment, and structural changes in the American industrial sector led President Nixon, on August 15, 1971, to impose a 10 percent surcharge on imports subject to duty in an effort to improve the American balance of trade. More important, Nixon announced that the dollar no longer would be exchanged for gold. Soon the price of gold—relative to the dollar and eventually to the other currencies—began to rise from the original, artificially fixed price of $35 per ounce. One of the welcome consequences of this move was that the American gold reserves rose in monetary (dollar) value, but the move marked the end of the Bretton Woods system of monetary management.

Since August 1971, several efforts have been made to reintroduce an element of order into the international monetary system. An early attempt to realign the exchange rates, the Smithsonian Agreement of December 1971, provided some breathing space but nothing more. It was impossible to maintain a system of fixed exchange rates and, by 1973, all major currencies were "floating" (no longer had fixed parities).[13] In addition to the extensive capital flows we mentioned earlier, different inflation rates exacerbated the problem because they made fixed exchange rates technically impossible. Inflation, of course, was affected by national monetary policies. The United States, to finance the Vietnam War and an ambitious social program (the *War on Poverty*), triggered an inflationary spiral that spread throughout the international economy in the 1970s. This further demonstrated that in "an interdependent system, management depends on the coordination of economic policies heretofore considered strictly national prerogatives."[14]

In 1972, a Committee on Reform of the International Monetary System and Related Issues—the Committee of Twenty—was set up by the IMF to develop major reforms. While the Committee was still studying possible remedies, including an increase in the use of SDRs, the OPEC members initiated the first round of major increases in the price of crude oil. Within twelve months, the price of one barrel of oil went up from $2.50 in early 1973 to $11.65 in 1974. The effect of the oil price rise on monetary management was profound. Following 1973, vast sums were taken in by the oil-exporting countries. While they were accumulating tremendous surpluses, other countries had to borrow to pay for their oil imports; the major sources for such borrowing were countries with surpluses from oil earnings.

Normally, countries with a balance of trade surplus tend to use such resources for additional imports, foreign investments, or other international transactions, but the potential of most OPEC members to expand imports was limited. At the same time, most of them lacked the organizational means for direct investments abroad. As a result, a large percentage of the so-called petrodollars was deposited in Western banks to earn interest. These funds were loaned to oil-importing countries by the private banks, which became instrumental in this form of monetary recycling.

To deal with these multifaceted problems, the IMF members moved to revise the institution's rules as one step in the development of a multilayer (national, regional, multilateral) monetary management. The Second Amendment to the Articles of Agreement of the International Monetary Fund,[15] which came into effect in April 1978, sought to enhance the role of the SDRs by making the transfer of the SDRs easier and by eliminating the link with gold, the price of which was fluctuating widely due in part to speculation and hoarding. It also legitimized the floating exchange rates, and obligated members to collaborate with the IMF to assure orderly exchange arrangements and to promote a stable system of exchange rates.

The Second Amendment was only a limited step; it did not solve the problem of liquidity. The dollar continues to be the world's major currency with international acceptance as a medium of exchange. The other major countries continue to consider the dollar as the only "natural" reserve currency for the international monetary system. As long as other currencies are not made available widely (or are not generally accepted) the only alternatives to the dollar are gold and the SDRs. The price of gold has fluctuated widely, reaching $800 per ounce in 1980 and then falling to approximately $400 per ounce in the early 1980s. In addition, there is a political reason for reluctance to use gold. The Soviet Union is one of the two major producers of gold in the world, and can affect the price for political reasons, disrupting international economic relations by increasing or decreasing the selling of gold. These considerations limit the attractiveness of gold as a means of international liquidity. By contrast, the stability of the SDRs makes them an attractive medium as an international unit for settling accounts, but they can be used only by governments so their utility remains limited.

Efforts continue to establish a new monetary order with new rules, institutions, and procedures. Most likely negotiations will continue for a long time and reforms will be piecemeal. The international economic system is no longer dominated by the United States and a few major capitalist states: the power of making decisions is now more widely dispersed. For any new system to work, there must be a consensus not only among the members of the OECD but also support—or at least absence of unreconcilable opposition—from the OPEC and major LDCs. An expansion of the role of the IMF to the point of acting as an international "central bank" or the creation of far-reaching regulatory mechanisms will inevitably challenge national sovereignty, because such mechanisms and institutions will have to perform tasks currently considered to be the prerogative of national government. Specifically, international control of liquidity and regulation of exchange rates by some superior authority will interfere with national fiscal and monetary policies. It is doubtful that many governments will be willing to accept such controls. Yet increasing interdependence and mutual vulnerability call for a more effective monetary management. In devising such new instrumentalities, the United States still will have to play a leading role.

....................................Regulating International Trade

Monetary policies are too arcane to be fully understood by ordinary citizens. They become a popular concern only when they result in excessively high interest rates or high levels of inflation. International trade, by contrast, touches people more directly.

Farmers in Iowa, automobile workers in Detroit, cocoa growers in Ghana, electronics firm employees in Japan, wine makers in France, and textile manufacturers and workers in Taiwan or in the United States find quickly that sales, profits, and employment are sensitive to the vigor or sluggishness of international trade and the foreign demand for their products, or to the effect competition from products imported from other countries has on the domestic demand for their products. Those who find such foreign competition detrimental to their interests are likely to press for restrictive and protectionist measures. However, foreign trade restrictions in one country can be easily reciprocated by comparable policies elsewhere. The effects may be harmful all around, but by the time the adverse consequences are apparent the damage is already done.

Conscious of the importance of international trade, the planners of the postwar economic order took serious steps to establish systematic international mechanisms for the regulation of international trade. This effort was a natural corollary to the arrangements for international monetary cooperation initiated at Bretton Woods. After all, one of the major reasons for having a generally acceptable currency and stable exchange rates is that countries have to pay for their imports with "money" that others are willing to accept for their products or services. Without international trade, elaborate mechanisms for international monetary management become a superfluous luxury.

The Early Efforts

The process for establishing a new trade order started in earnest in 1945, when the United States presented a plan for drafting a commercial treaty (convention) that would reduce restrictions on international trade.[16] The proposed treaty contained rules on tariffs and quotas, subsidies, and international commodity agreements, and provided for an International Trade Organization (ITO) to be a counterpart to the IMF. Reaching agreement on a new order for international trade proved much more difficult than establishing monetary mechanisms. After long and involved negotiations, the Havana Charter was signed in 1947.[17] It was a complex instrument that reflected the efforts of the participating countries to protect their special interests and promote their particular objectives, which often were in conflict with those of other countries.

The Havana Charter never came into effect, the victim of domestic pressures in the United States. One of the objections raised was that the Charter allowed underdeveloped countries to follow protectionist policies, although under specific conditions and only to enable their economies to overcome the pressures of foreign competition during the critical years of development. Another objection raised by business groups focused on increased government involvement under the Charter in managing international trade. Finally, conservative and nationalistic groups objected to the role assigned to ITO, which they found excessive. By 1950, the Truman administration believed that it would serve no useful purpose to bring the Charter to the U.S. Senate for ratification, because it was certain to be rejected. This was the end of the Havana Charter and of the International Trade Organization.

The need for establishing an international trading system did not disappear. In fact, some of the provisions contained in the Charter had already been included in a more modest instrument, the General Agreement on Tariffs and Trade (GATT). The agreement was originally drawn up in 1947 to serve as a temporary instrument, to provide guidelines while the Havana Charter was going through the process of ratification. With the Charter dead, GATT became the principal instrumentality for managing international trade.[18]

The GATT System

Under GATT, the signatories agreed to enter into "reciprocal and mutually advantageous arrangements directed to the substantial reduction of tariffs and other barriers to trade and to elimination of discriminatory treatment in international commerce. . . ." The ban on discriminatory practices was buttressed by the stipulation that "any advantage, favor, privilege or immunity granted by any contracting party to any product originating in or destined for any other country shall be accorded immediately and unconditionally to the like product originating in or destined for the territories of all other contracting parties." This is the familiar most-favored-nation (MFN) clause. The only exceptions to this general rule applied to existing preferential systems (such as the Imperial Preference System of Britain) or future customs unions and free-trade associations (such as the EEC). GATT further provided rules on such vexing issues as subsidies and dumping. Quantitative restrictions (quotas) were allowed only for balance of payments reasons (to reduce deficits), and then only within prescribed limits. In addition, GATT contained rules and procedures for multilateral trade negotiations in the future designed to establish specific tariff reductions on the basis of reciprocity. These negotiating rules and methods became, in effect, the principal instrumentality for the management of international trade, and in large measure they remain so.

GATT was not as comprehensive as the Havana Charter. It focused mostly on the concerns of the developed market economies, leaving out those matters that were of primary interest to the developing countries in the South. Not included in the GATT were the Havana Charter provisions relating to economic development, commodity agreements, and business practices considered unfavorable to the developing countries. This is one of the reasons that GATT survived instead of following the fate of the Havana Charter and ITO.

GATT not only survived as a treaty but also was soon transformed into an international organization with a secretariat and a director general charged with overseeing the implementation of the GATT rules and carrying out most of the groundwork and coordination for international trade conferences called for under the system.[19] The growth of GATT reflected the American policy orientation toward strengthening the economies of Western Europe and Japan. Conservative groups in the United States, which in the 1950s might have destroyed GATT, were won over with arguments focusing on the need to help these countries face the perceived threat of Soviet expansionism.

The idea of opening up international trade by removing tariffs and other barriers had originated with the Roosevelt administration even before World War II, with the 1934 Reciprocal Trade Agreements Act. Under this act, tariff reductions agreed on in bilateral negotiations were based on mutual advantage (reciprocity). Agreed reductions with one country were then extended to other countries under the most-favored-nation clause, which was included in many commercial treaties the United States had with other countries. This basic approach was adopted by GATT in the postwar era, except that tariff reductions were negotiated in international conferences attended by GATT members.

During the first five multilateral trade conferences organized by GATT, the principal suppliers of specific products negotiated liberalized arrangements among themselves. The new arrangements were then extended automatically to all other GATT members under the nondiscrimination clause. In the sixth round of negotiations, initiated in 1962 (the so-called Kennedy Round), the participants changed the basic negotiating procedure. Instead of conducting item-by-item negotiations, they sought an across-the-board reduction of tariffs by a certain percentage. This approach simplified the process and made greater liberalization possible.

During the first twenty years of GATT's existence, the United States played a leading role in promoting free trade practices. Expanded trade encouraged production and led to unprecedented economic prosperity in the developed countries that had market economies. In the late 1960s, however, the same developments that undermined the monetary management system of Bretton Woods worked against the international management of trade.

The Tokyo Round

The Background. The tremendous expansion of trade during the 1950s and 1960s made the economies of the capitalist states more interdependent and more sensitive and vulnerable to external events and policies. As long as the United States had a positive balance of trade, Washington was willing to lead the process of trade liberalization and to accept arrangements that favored their trading partners in Europe and Japan. In the late 1960s, however, their traditional balance of trade surplus began to shrink in the face of Japanese and EEC competition. In 1971 and 1972, the U.S. balance of trade showed a deficit for the first time in this century. This change in the United States' trading position triggered protectionist pressures from vulnerable economic sectors such as the textile, steel, electronics, and automobile industries.[20]

With the removal of quotas and the extensive reduction of tariffs instituted during the first six rounds of GATT negotiations, protectionists had to rely on nontariff barriers (NTBs). As mentioned earlier, such barriers include cumbersome customs procedures to cause delays, health and sanitary regulations, government procurement policies favoring domestic products, antipollution regulations, and a host of other regulations designed to limit or slow imports or raise their selling price through added costs. To curb Japanese imports that could not be banned or restricted under the GATT system, the U.S. government reversed the process and pressured the Japanese government to impose voluntarily restrictions on Japanese *exports* to the United States.

The protectionist trend received indirectly additional impetus from the monetary problems of the late 1960s, mentioned earlier. To reduce the effect of deficits in their balance of payments accounts, governments resorted to exchange controls, exchange rate manipulation, controls over the flow of capital, and special duties such as the 10 percent surcharge imposed on dutiable imports by the Nixon administration in 1971.

The situation was further exacerbated by the successive oil price increases after 1973, which caused a double-digit inflation and a simultaneous serious recession. In the face of these developments, American support for a free trade system began to wane, especially in the U.S. Congress, in which pressures from special-interest groups are more keenly felt. Between 1967 and 1975, Congress refused to give the president the authority to negotiate and conclude trade agreements, as it had done in the past. The process of trade liberalization virtually ground to a halt.

Interdependence and mutual vulnerability, however, could not be wished away or overcome by a return to the trade wars and the protectionist policies of the period before World War II. By late 1972, the OECD members agreed to begin a new round of multilateral discussions in Tokyo in September 1973. In preparation for this, in March 1973 the Nixon administration submitted to Congress a trade reform bill that was to give the president the necessary authority to negotiate new trade arrangements at the forth-coming conference in Tokyo. The bill did not pass, a victim of Watergate, the shock from the oil crisis, and a controversy over the provision to grant the Soviet Union most-favored-nation status. Opponents of this last measure focused on Soviet restrictions on the emigration of Soviet Jews and made approval subject to a drastic change in Soviet emigration policies. The initial meetings in Tokyo made little progress because the United States delegation had little authority to negotiate. It was not until February 1975, one month after the approval of the 1974 Trade Act by the U.S. Congress, that the Tokyo Round trade talks could begin in earnest.

The Agreements. It took another four years (until April 1979) to complete the Tokyo Round negotiations and sign the new arrangements that further reduced tariffs on manufactured products and established codes to regulate nontariff barriers (NTBs) such as subsidies, government procurement practices, dumping, product standards, and licensing of imports. The agreements also provided the mechanism for the settlement of disputes over NTBs. Side by side with these liberalizing measures, the participants introduced certain sophisticated instrumentalities of a protectionist nature, such as the "orderly market agreements" (OMAs) designed to dampen the disruptive effects of foreign competition. The Tokyo Round negotiations were less successful in dealing with agricultural products. Liberalization of trade in this sector—advocated by the United States—foundered on the refusal of the EEC members to modify the Community's agricultural policies (CAP). (The arrangements affecting the participating LDCs will be discussed in chapter 10.)

The fight against protectionist pressures continues to be a major focus of international concern. Statements in 1983 by the IMF and the GATT officials underscored the role international trade must play and the importance of dismantling trade barriers.[21] Concern over protectionism also was expressed at the sixth UN Conference on Trade and Development (UNCTAD VI) held in June 1983 in Belgrade. Opposition to protectionism was voiced by the leaders of the seven major Western industrial countries at the Williamsburg Summit in 1983 and again at their London meeting in June 1984.

Practical measures along these lines were discussed at the November 1982 GATT ministerial meeting, which established a number of groups and committees to examine a wide range of problems. Since that time, a great deal of work has been done to prepare for a new round of multilateral trade negotiations, advocated by Japan and the United States. North–South trade issues—particularly the more effective integration of the developing countries into the GATT system—will be an important component of a new trade round. However, the developing countries will have no incentive to participate more fully in GATT and to abide by the obligations inherent in GATT membership if they are subjected to discriminatory protectionism on the part of the advanced countries.

GATT has served the interests of the developed market economies rather well up to this time. In the opinion of some experts, however, periodic international negotiations will not be able to provide effective management of international trade in the future.[22] One possible solution would be to establish a new international trade organization with the active participation of the LDCs. Politically, however, such a global institution does not now have much support in the developed countries, especially the United States. A more likely solution is the expansion of cooperation within the OECD and the GATT framework, or through frequent, ad hoc consultations among representatives from the major trading nations. One course of action that is generally recognized as counterproductive, however, is a return to rabidly nationalistic, beggar-thy-neighbor trade and economic policies.

Transactionalism and the International Economy

Our brief review of the postwar international economic environment and its problems must have made clear that solutions cannot be found through the familiar power instrumentalities. No government today can impose on the international community or on individual countries the monetary or trade arrangements it wants. The United States was able in the early postwar years to transform into international rules decisions reached by Washington officials, but this preeminence has now eroded. New arrangements require the cooperation and consent of a large number of sovereign governments that have divergent interests and viewpoints. Solutions for structural or day-to-day problems call for negotiation, bargaining, and compromise.

Throughout this text we have tried to highlight the distinction between power and influence because we believe that the long-established emphasis on the role of power in international relations is overdrawn given current conditions. This is most clearly evident in international economic relations, in which the shift away from the power approach is easily observable.

Summary

- The traditional issues of national security and political power, which once were seen in terms of military capability, must now be viewed also in the context of the international economic environment. Governments now engage extensively in economic interactions to protect their interests, promote the wellbeing of their people, expand their influence, and exert pressure.

- The economic tools of foreign policy include trade-related measures (tariffs, quotas, embargos, boycotts, nontariff barriers, dumping, and exchange-rate manipulation), lending, foreign aid, and investments. These instrumentalities are more effective in the exercise of influence than in the exercise of power. Seldom can a government impose its will on another by threatening economic deprivations. In the complex and interdependent world of today, governments facing such pressures can find alternatives.

- Even in the exercise of influence, the use of economic assets and instrumentalities is limited by (1) a country's resources, (2) constraints imposed by domestic factors, and (3) the resources and potentialities of the other side.

- In the early postwar period, the Western powers established international mechanisms and institutions for (1) the management of international monetary interactions and (2) the regulation of international trade.

- The major institution for international monetary stability is the International Monetary Fund (IMF), which was designed to prevent wide fluctuations in exchange rates and to help countries deal with short-term balance of payments deficits. Since 1969, IMF has been authorized to issue artificial reserve units known as Special Drawing Rights (SDRs), which can be used by governments to pay for international obligations (as can dollars or gold).

- To prevent excessively protectionist trade policies, the Western powers promoted the Havana Charter, which provided for liberal trade arrangements and for an International Trade Organization (ITO) as the counterpart of IMF. The Havana Charter never came into effect. It was replaced, by default, by the General Agreement on Tariffs and Trade (GATT), which since the early 1950s has become the primary instrument for the liberalization of international trade. In successive conferences, the GATT members lowered trade barriers. One of the current problems is the effect of nontariff barriers used occasionally by governments to circumvent the GATT rules against trade barriers.

- The LDCs have expressed dissatisfaction with the current arrangements and, through the UN Conference on Trade and Development (UNCTAD), have sought changes usually grouped under the label "New International Economic Order" (NIEO).

- The transactional approach is particularly relevant to, and is extensively used in, international economic relations; the power approach is either inappropriate or of limited effectiveness.

Notes

1. Kegley, Charles W., Jr., and Wittkopf, Eugene R. *World Politics*. New York: St. Martin's Press, 1981, p. 197.
2. Andrews, Stanley. *Agriculture and the Common Market*. Ames, Iowa: Iowa State University Press, 1973, p. 26.

3. Craig, Gordon A., and George, Alexander L. *Force and Statecraft: Diplomatic Problems of Our Time*. New York: Oxford University Press, 1983, p. 189.

4. Peterson, Peter G. *The United States in the Changing World Economy*. Vol. 1. Washington, D.C.: Superintendent of Documents, 1971, pp. 293–295.

5. Statement by John D. Holdridge, Assistant Secretary of State for East Asian and Pacific Affairs, before the Subcommittee on Asian and Pacific Affairs of the Committee on Foreign Affairs on March 1, 1982. U.S. Department of State Bulletin no. 374, March 1, 1982.

6. Nowzad, Bahram. *The Rise of Protectionism*. Washington, D.C.: International Monetary Fund Pamphlet, 1978.

7. Aronson, Jonathan O., ed. *Debt and the Less Developed Countries*. Boulder, Colo.: Westview Press, 1979.

8. Erb, Guy F., and Kallab, Valeriana. *Beyond Dependency: The Developing World Speaks Out*. Washington, D.C.: Overseas Development Council, 1975, p. 186.

9. Gardner, Richard N. *Sterling-Dollar Diplomacy: The Origins and Prospects of Our International Economic Order*. New York: McGraw-Hill, 1969, p. 9.

10. Spero, Joan Edelman. *The Politics of International Economic Relations*. 2nd ed. New York: St. Martin's Press, 1981, p. 25. (Our discussion on postwar economic relations has drawn extensively on the material contained in this comprehensive study.)

11. Horsefield, J. Keith, ed. *The International Monetary Fund, 1945–1965*. Washington, D.C.: International Monetary Fund, 1969, pp. 10–25.

12. Triffin, Robert. *Gold and the Dollar Crisis: The Future of Convertibility*. New Haven, Conn.: Yale University Press, 1960.

13. Artus, Jacques R., and Crockett, Andrew D. *Floating Exchange Rates and the Need for Surveillance*. Princeton, N.J.: Princeton University, International Finance Section, Pamphlet no. 127, 1978.

14. Spero, *op. cit.*, p. 55.

15. International Monetary Fund. *Proposed Second Amendment to the Articles of Agreement of the International Monetary Fund: A Report by the Executive Directors to the Board of Governors*. Washington, D.C.: International Monetary Fund, March, 1976; International Monetary Fund. *Annual Report 1979*. Washington, D.C.: International Monetary Fund, 1979.

16. Penrose, E. F. *Economic Planning for the Peace*. Princeton, N.J.: Princeton University Press, 1953; Patterson, Gardner. *Discrimination in International Trade: The Policy Issues, 1945–1965*. Princeton, N.J.: Princeton University Press, 1966.

17. Wilcox, Clair. *A Charter for World Trade*. New York: Macmillan, 1949.

18. Dam, Kenneth W. *The GATT Law and International Economic Organization*. Chicago: University of Chicago Press, 1970.

19. Jacobson, Harold K., et al. *The Anatomy of Influence: Decision Making in International Organization*. New Haven, Conn.: Yale University Press, 1973, pp. 334–340.

20. Krasner, Stephen D. "The Tokyo Round: Particularistic Interests and Prospects for Stability in the Global Trading System.:" *International Studies Quarterly,* December 1979, pp. 491–531.

21. "Prospects for International Trade." GATT Press Release 1340, August 30, 1983; and *IMF Survey*, Vol. 12, no. 9, May 9, 1983, p. 131.

22. Camps, Miriam. *The Case for a New Global Trade Organization*. New York: Council of Foreign Relations, 1980.

8

..............................In Search
of Order

The International Court of Justice building, The Hague, Netherlands

For many centuries, philosophers, diplomats, and government officials have wrestled with the anarchic character of the international system. A persistent longing for peace has inspired a continuous quest for alternatives to the unrestrained reliance on force. The search goes on, but it does not have universal support. At one end of the continuum we find those who believe that a fairly peaceful and orderly world is a utopian and impossible dream and that peace can be protected only through military force. Others argue that as long as sovereign governments are free to pursue their national objectives by any means, including military force, peace will remain a precarious and uncertain condition. Their remedy is a *world government*—a universal and *single* sovereign authority. The historical record shows that between these two extreme viewpoints three basic alternatives have been tried:

1. The imposition of order by force; that is, the order of empires

2. The order of generally accepted rules; that is, the rules of international law

3. The order of cooperative institutions; that is, the order of international organizations formed by sovereign governments as a mechanism for reducing the arbitrariness that has been the hallmark of the international system

The Order of Empires ....

Empire builders do not pursue the ideal of an orderly world. Order, nevertheless, is an inevitable byproduct as the imperial authority spreads its control over large territories, eliminating in the process existing sovereign entities. Several times in history, large sections of this planet came under the control of a strong government that, relying on its superior military force, kept order within the imperial domain.[1]

The "Roman Peace" (*Pax Romana*) imposed by the Roman legions on the Greek city-states, the kingdoms of Asia Minor and the Middle East, northern Africa, Iberia, Gaul, and the British Isles remains to this day an uncommon achievement. The Roman empire—a multinational entity that was Roman only in name—became the superior authority; even those kings and chieftains who were allowed to stay in office were no longer sovereign: they were subordinate to the Roman governor, who represented the mystical authority of Rome. King Herod was a Jewish "king," but the final authority rested with the Roman governor of Judea.

Even the Roman Peace was not immune to violence and disorder. In fact, the Roman legions were in almost constant motion, marching from one part of the empire to another trying to quell revolts, beat back incursions, restore Rome's authority over rebellious vassals—or fighting among themselves under the banners of rival aspirants to the imperial mantle.

The Chinese empire—the Middle Kingdom—is another illustration of a superior power imposing its law and order over weaker neighbors. The rulers of neighboring kingdoms were brought into the system either by conquest or through diplomacy powerfully assisted by a superior military force. The subordinate kingdoms were required to pay tribute to the Chinese as a sign of their submission and loyalty. As long as the Chinese remained strong, the empire held together, but with the first sign of weakness the tributary kingdoms reasserted their independence.[2]

The more recent colonial empires brought under the control of the metropolitan, sovereign centers a multitude of formerly independent entities. Through the centuries, this has been the essence of an *empire*—one sovereign entity bringing under its control a host of (formerly) sovereign units and ruling over them as the superior authority. Although the colonial powers were not much concerned with a more orderly international system, they suppressed local rivalries. Peace was imposed by force *within* each colonial empire.

We may even see the emergence of the European national states out of the mosaic of feudal principalities as part of a process to expand the area of central authority. For centuries, the principalities of the Italian peninsula either fought against one another or surrendered to foreign rulers, until Italy was unified into a single kingdom in 1861. The German principalities, in a process that lasted over half a century, moved from the experiment of confederation initiated at the Congress of Vienna (1815) and the *Zollverein* (Customs Union) to unification under the king of Prussia, who was proclaimed emperor on January 18, 1871, at Versailles—the unification of Germany being one of the consequences of the German victory in the Franco–Prussian War of 1870. Spain, France, Britain, and Russia went through a long process of consolidation as the strongest principality gradually eliminated its rivals through war, conquest, or dynastic marriages, eventually bringing the territory and its inhabitants under a single sovereign authority.

All these efforts to impose a higher authority over separate, sovereign, feuding entities had two central features in common. *Order* was imposed by superior force over rather reluctant beneficiaries, and the geographic area involved in each case covered only a fraction of the planet, never reaching even remotely global dimensions. Moreover, the empires did not change the fundamental workings of the international system; they only replaced, temporarily, a large number of smaller sovereign entities by a small number of larger sovereign entities, which went on feuding and fighting each other.

Obviously the quest for order is elusive. If order is imposed by force, it can be maintained only as long as force is present. Is it possible, then, for sovereign entities to bring some order to the international system while keeping their sovereign status? Can this be done on a global scale, voluntarily, without coercion, and without imposing a global authority superior to all other entities?

Two Alternatives..

In the absence of any serious drive toward world government, two other alternatives have been pursued with fairly positive results: international organization and international law. Both were known in antiquity in a rudimentary form.

International organization as a device for promoting order in the international system has gained support only during this century. First with the League of Nations and then with the United Nations, a mechanism was forged freely and voluntarily by sovereign governments that was designed to promote a cooperative arrangement as an alternative to the undisciplined pursuit of national interests. These mechanisms, however, have not eliminated the anarchic character of the international system; sovereignty remains the cardinal feature of its main components, the states.

The second alternative is *international law,* which is today an extensive system of rules regulating the conduct of sovereign states and other entities. The boundaries and complexity of the relationships and activities covered by these rules have been expanding continuously. Although the rules of international law lack enforceability, their utility should not be ignored.

Both the rules of international law and the mechanisms of international organization are expected to reduce the likelihood or the intensity of conflict and to promote peaceful and orderly interactions as much as possible.

International Organization ....

Without giving up their sovereign status, governments join in international organizations because they expect to gain benefits that are beyond reach through separate, isolated, and often conflicting efforts; at the same time, because sovereign states are the building blocks of international organizations, politics and nonviolent forms of conflict continue to be present within such organizations.

The origins of international organization can be traced to the Amphyctionic League of the ancient Greek city-states and later to the medieval and renaissance thinkers who wanted to bring together the kings of Europe into one association pledged to avoid waging war on one another.

In the nineteenth century, following the collapse of Napoleon's drive to bring all Europe under the supreme authority of a napoleonic empire by force, the European powers found it prudent and necessary to set up channels of greater consultation and cooperation. These channels and ties are remembered in history as the Concert of Europe. An outgrowth of the Congress of Vienna (1815), the Concert, however, had neither a permanent structure nor well-defined rules.

Around the turn of the nineteenth century, the Concert began to show serious signs of decay as the major European powers of the day gravitated slowly into two rival coalitions. With the outbreak of World War I in August 1914, the Concert of Europe became a page in European history.

The slaughter of Europe's youth during the war provided a macabre but powerful incentive to consider measures for the preservation of peace in the future. By the end of the war, not only private citizens but also government leaders in all the Allied nations favored some form of world organization. The United States, under the leadership of President Woodrow Wilson, played a pivotal role in forging the first such entity.

The League of Nations, which resulted from these efforts, suffered from certain congenital weaknesses. On their part, the victorious European powers—Britain and France in particular—saw the League as an instrument they could use for the preservation of the newly established international power structure that had emerged after the war. However, they had neither the military or economic strength nor the national will to prevent changes when they were later challenged by those other powers (Japan, Germany, Italy, and the Soviet Union) that were dissatisfied with the status quo and were willing to use force to change it. The absence of the United States from the League's membership compounded the problem. In the end, the League, weak and discredited, was consumed by the flames of World War II.

Although the League failed to preserve the peace, the experience gained in forging it was useful: its organization, procedures, and institutions became the prototypes for those of the United Nations. Even its shortcomings and failures offered valuable insight and guidance to the framers of the UN Charter.

The United Nations..

On April 18, 1946, the League Assembly met in Geneva and voted that on the following day "the League of Nations shall cease to exist." The delegates of fifty nations had already signed on June 26, 1945, the Charter of the United Nations Organization. Within the short span of four months, the Charter received the requisite number of ratifications and came into force. Already an elaborate machinery had been set up to prepare the ground for the first meeting of the General Assembly, and on January 10, 1946, the General Assembly of the United Nations held its first session in London.

The birth of the new organization was greeted with high—in some respects excessive—public expectations. Few focused on what the United Nations *was not*. Certainly it was not a world government, a superior authority, or a federal structure. The UN was a voluntary association of sovereign states that had signed a treaty—the Charter—pledging to cooperate under certain conditions to maintain international peace and security, resolve peacefully any disputes, and promote the general welfare. With the *sovereign equality* of the members enshrined in the Charter, the UN could be no more nor less effective than the willingness of the members to make it so. Four decades later, the inescapable assessment is that the members have not made the UN as effective as it could be. Secretary General Javier Perez de Cuellar, in his first annual report on the state of the UN in 1982, voiced disappointment and misgivings: "Certainly," he said, "we have strayed far from the UN Charter in recent years. Governments that believe they can win an international objective by force are often quite ready to do so, and domestic opinion not infrequently applauds such a course. . . . Thus the process of peaceful settlement of disputes prescribed in the Charter is often brushed aside."[3]

The Structure of
....the United Nations

The new Organization resembled in large measure the structure of the League. The United Nations system consisted of six principal organs:

1. General Assembly

2. Security Council

3. Economic and Social Council

4. Trusteeship Council

5. Secretariat

6. The International Court of Justice

Of these, five are fully functioning at present; one, the Trusteeship Council, has little left to do because virtually all trusteeships have achieved independence: the Trusteeship Council is, ironically, the victim of its success.[4] Figure 8-1 shows the basic structure of the United Nations.

The General Assembly

The General Assembly is the organ in which all member-states are represented, and in which each delegation has one vote regardless of the size, population, wealth, or military strength of the country it represents. Each member-state has a permanent delegation accredited to the United Nations, which has headquarters in New York City.

The General Assembly normally meets each year in the fall, and its annual sessions last approximately three months. During the session, the General Assembly can deal with any issue "within the scope" of the Charter and can pass resolutions designed to help resolve international disputes or other international problems. Although in the absence of an enforcement machinery such resolutions may be—and often are—ignored with impunity, many governments have through the years brought scores of specific issues before the General Assembly to bring a grievance to world attention, generate public opinion in favor of a certain course, or get a favorable resolution to strengthen their bargaining position in their dispute with another state.

With the exception of cases brought to the General Assembly under the provisions of the "Uniting for Peace" Resolution (see Digest at the end of this book), the Assembly cannot deal with an issue that is being considered by the Security Council. The primary responsibility for the preservation of peace was entrusted by the founders of the UN to the Security Council.

The Security Council

The major powers that emerged victorious in World War II and took the initiative in setting up the United Nations (the United States, the Soviet Union, Britain, France, and China) wanted to keep the crucial questions of war and peace under their control. Such questions were, therefore, entrusted primarily to the Security Council in which all five countries became permanent members. Furthermore, they included in the Charter the provision that the Council could not pass a resolution on a substantive matter if any one of them voted against that resolution. This *veto power* of the permanent members became a principal feature of the Security Council.

Initially, the Security Council had six nonpermanent members but in 1965, to accommodate the growing membership of the UN, the Charter was amended to increase the number of nonpermanent members to ten. Currently, a Council decision requires at least nine affirmative votes.

Figure 8-1
United Nations and related agencies.

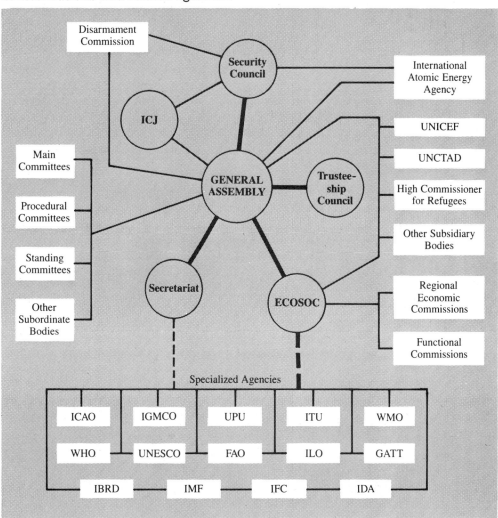

Unlike the General Assembly, the Security Council is technically in permanent session and can be summoned by its president within hours to deal with an urgent matter. The presidency of the Security Council rotates each month among the Council members in alphabetical order. The work of the Council is assisted by the secretary general, who is present at Council meetings.

The Secretariat

Unlike all other organs of the United Nations, the Secretariat is not composed of representatives from the member-states. Its staff constitutes an international bureaucracy. The officials of the Secretariat are appointed—except for the secretary general, who is elected by the General Assembly on the recommendation of the Security Council for a five-year term.

The secretary general being the chief administrative officer of the UN is in charge of the Secretariat; more important, he is normally present at meetings and assists all the major organs, and on the direction of the Security Council or the General Assembly or on his own initiative within the context of approved resolutions may undertake significant diplomatic missions to assist in the settlement of international disputes. The fairly long tenure of the individuals who have held this post has contributed to their political stature and effectiveness.

The Economic and Social Council (ECOSOC)

The belief that economic and social problems undermine international peace led the founders of the UN to establish a separate organ to deal with such matters. Initially, the Economic and Social Council had eighteen members, but the number now stands at fifty-four. Although the major powers are included in the membership (without their participation the work of the Council would not be very effective), they do not have a veto power over its decisions. The ECOSOC members are elected by the General Assembly for a three-year term, and their work, although unspectacular, has contributed significantly to economic development and social progress around the world. On more than one occasion, ECOSOC has been instrumental in promoting new institutions or programs particularly beneficial to the developing countries.

ECOSOC is responsible for coordinating the activities of the various regional agencies established by the United Nations to assist needy countries in the less developed areas of the world, as well as the activities of the specialized agencies.

The Trusteeship Council

The Trusteeship Council of the United Nations was created in the hope that because of it the need for it would disappear. The initial objective was to assign to this organ the supervision of territories that previously had been under the mandate system of the League of Nations, to prepare them for independence. Virtually all those territories have become independent and are now sovereign states, so our brief comments here have only historical relevance. Under the Charter, the membership of this Council included all member-states that had been assigned the administration of trust territories as well as all the permanent members of the Security Council. In addition, the General Assembly elected a number of other members without trusteeships to match those with trusteeships on the Council.

The International Court of Justice

The International Court of Justice (ICJ) comprises fifteen judges elected, in separate votes by the General Assembly and the Security Council, for a period of nine years. The Court decides cases by majority vote of the judges present. Its seat is at The Hague.

All member-states of the UN are entitled to bring cases before it. This, however, does not mean that all states accept automatically the jurisdiction of the ICJ over all disputes in which they may be involved. The Charter of the Court includes the *optional clause,* which member-states may decline to accept (we will discuss this clause in detail later in the chapter). Technically, only governments can bring cases before this tribunal. Individuals or other private institutions cannot do so unless their case is taken over by a government and brought to the Court. The Court, however, may issue advisory opinions at the request of an international organization.

A major weakness of the Court is the absence of an enforcement machinery. Compliance with its decisions is left to the discretion and good will of the governments involved.

The Changing Role of the United Nations

Critics of the United Nations dismiss it as a wasteful and ineffectual institution. Complaints come from different quarters and touch on different weaknesses. Some say that the UN is unable to enforce even decisions reached unanimously in the Security Council; some find fault with the veto powers of the five permanent members of the Security Council; others object to the influx of many new small countries, which has created a Third World majority in the General Assembly.

To assess the record of the UN realistically we will look at three major areas in which it was expected to play a leading role:

1. Conflict resolution

2. Collective security

3. The development of new international arrangements to promote peace, stability, and the general welfare

Conflict Resolution

Many international controversies do not even come before the UN because the parties directly involved prefer to handle their differences by other means, including force or direct negotiations. The conflicts that are considered by the Security Council or the General Assembly usually are serious and potentially dangerous to peace. A country may turn to the UN in the hope that its claim will receive international recognition and its case will be strengthened or because direct contacts with the opposing side have become difficult. When a controversy has reached a crisis point and threatens international peace, it may come before the UN on the initiative of its appropriate organs.

The resolution of conflicts depends on contacts, discussions, and negotiations. The UN has been most useful as an informal meeting ground. The permanent delegates of the member-states have the opportunity to meet unobtrusively, without embarrassing publicity, and initiate talks on issues dividing their countries. Many times considerations of prestige block direct contacts, allowing a dispute to fester and eventually explode. It is virtually impossible to document how many times a potentially dangerous conflict was nipped in the bud or how many times escalation was slowed only because the parties involved could engage in quiet diplomacy within the walls of the United Nations. Because conflicts often arise out of different perceptions and misunderstandings, the opportunity to clear the air in direct talks can be invaluable.

On numerous occasions, those who held the office of secretary general used their influence to promote solutions and assist in the settlement of disputes when all other avenues seemed closed. Dag Hammarskjold, U Thant, and Kurt Waldheim engaged in this form of quiet diplomacy during their terms in office in an effort to defuse potentially explosive conflicts or to promote interim arrangements designed to de-escalate a dispute and prepare the ground for a more comprehensive settlement. The current Secretary General Javier de Cuellar is continuing the tradition established by his predecessors.

Collective Security

The founders of the League of Nations promoted the concept of collective security on the assumption that all nations share a common interest in preserving peace: thus the slogan "Peace is indivisible." They claimed that any act of aggression should be confronted by all other sovereign states, united in their determination to restore peace. Faced with the collective response of all other members, the aggressor nation would have no alternative but to end hostilities and pull back.

The theory appeared plausible, provided certain conditions were present:

1. All members should be willing to live up to their commitments and support collective action against the aggressor

2. All members should agree that the circumstances justified collective action

3. All members should agree on the identity of the aggressor

Reaching such near-universal agreement is not an easy matter. No government ever admits that it is guilty of aggression. Governments invariably claim that they have been forced to act in self-defense, to protect vital interests against threatened encroachments, or to respond to unacceptable provocation. Even when the facts of aggression are fairly clear, other governments may not act with impartiality: they have their own interests to protect.

Chapter VII of the UN Charter provides for "action by air, sea, or land forces" by the member-states "to maintain or restore international peace and security." With the single exception of the UN "police action" in Korea between 1950 and 1953, no collective military action of the type envisaged by the Charter has been undertaken by the members. One reason for this is the inability of the five permanent members of the Security Council to agree on taking joint action. Even under the Uniting for Peace Resolution, no majority has ever advocated or supported collective military action to restore peace.

Collective security, as initially envisioned by the Charter, has proved unattainable, but the practical need of defusing international conflicts and preserving peace remains. Responding to this need, the United Nations has shifted the emphasis to a less-controversial and demanding form of action: peacekeeping operations.

Peacekeeping operations differ from collective security measures in at least four basic aspects:

1. When the United Nations decides on a peacekeeping operation, it does not need to deal with the question of aggression. There is no need to determine the identity of the aggressor or the facts of aggression in a given dispute.

2. The peacekeeping forces are not used to inflict punishment; they cannot even enter the territory of the states involved in the dispute without the permission of the governments. By contrast, the collective security measures as seen by the Charter were clearly directed *against* an aggressor state and were to be imposed against that state's will.

3. Peacekeeping forces usually have come from smaller countries that have no interests of their own in the dispute. By contrast, the armed forces envisaged in the Charter for collective security were to be provided primarily by the major powers, which, as permanent members of the Security Council, had a major responsibility for collective security.

4. In a peacekeeping operation, the objective is to act as a buffer between the opposing sides, to keep order, or to oversee compliance with a cease-fire—not to force an aggressor to surrender.[5]

Peacekeeping operations differ in size, type of activities, duration, and objectives. In a number of cases, they have not involved military forces at all: they have consisted of small observation teams authorized to patrol a certain area and report any violations. Illustrations include the UN Truce Supervision Organization established in 1949 to report on cease-fire violations by Israel or its Arab neighbors; the UN Military Observer Group in India and Pakistan patrolling the cease-fire line in Kashmir; the UN Yemen Observation Mission, which supervised the disengagement of military forces during the 1962–1964 civil war in Yemen; and the Truce Supervision Organization for the Suez Canal after the 1967 war.

In other cases, military contingents ranging from 3,000 to 20,000 troops have been used to keep warring parties apart, to restore order, to protect defenseless populations, or even to settle through diplomacy any disputes that may arise in the area between the feuding sides. Illustrations include the UN Emergency Force stationed in Egypt from 1956 to 1967; the UN Congo Operation (ONUC) between 1960 and 1964; the UN Force in Cyprus, in existence since 1964; the UN Security Force in West Irian in 1962 and 1963 during the dispute between Indonesia and the Netherlands; the UN Disengagement Observer Force stationed in the Golan Heights in 1974 as a buffer between Israel and Syria; and the UN Interim Force in Lebanon (UNIFYL) stationed in southern Lebanon since 1978.*

Equipped with only light arms, these military contingents are not expected to engage in fighting (except in self-defense). When confronted by superior forces they have no alternative but to step aside. The UNIFYL, for example, did not prevent the Israeli forces from pouring into Lebanon in the summer of 1982. Moreover, UN peacekeeping forces cannot remain in place without the express permission of the state on whose territory they are stationed. In 1967, for example, Egypt asked for the removal of the UN Emergency Force stationed in the Sinai. Secretary General U Thant tried to persuade the Egyptian government to reverse its decision; when he failed he had no alternative but to comply. Within days, Israel, fearing that Egypt was planning to attack, launched what became known as the "Six-Day War."

Toward a More Orderly System

In the continuing quest for a more orderly international system, the UN has been much more helpful than most of us realize. Even those who advocate the unrestrained pursuit of national interest cannot totally ignore the cold realities of interdependence. Beyond ideological, cultural, ethnic, political, or economic differences, all sovereign states, large and small, wealthy or poor, find that in one way or another their interests are entwined with those of other countries. In the last four decades, the world has witnessed the proliferation of international arrangements and structures dealing with economic, social, legal, technical, and other issues that no single country could tackle effectively by itself. Whereas some of those arrangements, such as the EEC, were not tied directly to the United Nations, the list of international agreements, arrangements, organizations, legal rules, and other cooperative developments initiated by the United Nations is long and impressive.

The International Law Commission, established by the General Assembly, has conducted studies that led to the adoption of important conventions (multinational treaties) including the Vienna Convention on Diplomatic Relations (1961); the Vienna Convention on Consular Relations (1963); the Vienna Convention on the Law of Treaties (1969); and the most recent and comprehensive Convention on the Law of the Sea (1982), dealing with navigation and overflight, exploration and exploitation of resources in the open seas and on the seabed, the extent of territorial waters (12 miles), exclusive economic zones extending beyond a country's territorial waters (200 miles beyond the coastline), fishing and shipping, pollution and conservation, and a machinery for settling disputes, including an international authority to supervise and control the extraction of minerals found on the ocean floor and its subsoil.

---

* The "multinational peacekeeping force" composed of American, French, Italian, and British forces, which was stationed in Lebanon between September 1982 and February 1984, was not a UN operation.

Other international conventions that have resulted from the initiative of the General Assembly, the International Law Commission, or the Economic and Social Council (ECOSOC) include the Treaty Governing the Exploration and Use of Outer Space (1967), the Genocide Convention (1948), and the Covenant on Human Rights (1966). The means of enforcement and the extent of compliance have not been perfect, yet violations are not commonplace and when they occur they are frowned on even by those who are not directly affected. More important, it is possible to speak of a violation only if there is a rule. The United Nations, by expanding the scope of international law and bringing under generally accepted rules activities that previously were left to the discretion of a sovereign government, has cut down the degree of arbitrariness that always has been the hallmark of the international system.

As the world economy has become increasingly interdependent, the United Nations has been used as a major forum for the discussion of issues and for the initiation of international arrangements designed to aid the handling and solution of problems. Trade, monetary relationships, economic development and growth, technology transfers, communications, and access to resources and markets involve activities, relationships, and problems too complex to be tackled separately by individual countries. World trade has achieved phenomenal growth since the end of World War II, expanding almost 700 percent in constant (1970) dollars under the liberalizing rules of GATT.

To deal with trade problems affecting the less-developed countries, the UN Conference on Trade and Development (UNCTAD) sought in 1964 new trade arrangements that could help economic development and narrow the gap between the industrial states and the LDCs. Out of this initial conference UNCTAD emerged as a new organ of the General Assembly, with its own permanent structure and administration (see chapter 10, The LDCs and International Trade).

Very important, although not widely publicized, work is being done by the Specialized Agencies. Under the UN Charter, these agencies are endowed with "wide international responsibilities, as defined in their basic instruments, in economic, social, cultural, educational, health, and related fields" (Article 57). Although they cooperate closely with the UN, legally they exist and operate outside its framework, which allows them greater flexibility. For all practical purposes, they owe their legal existence to treaties or other agreements signed by the states that compose their membership. Each agency has its own charter, which defines the responsibilities of the agency and prescribes its organizational structure. Each agency has its own budget, financed primarily by the contributions of its members.

Although the specialized agencies have many features in common, they also differ in certain important aspects. Certain agencies, such as the Food and Agriculture Organization (FAO), the World Health Organization (WHO), or the UN Educational, Scientific, and Cultural Organization (UNESCO), have fairly large bureaucracies and offices in many parts of the world. Others, such as the Universal Postal Union (UPU), the International Telecommunications Union (ITU), the World Meteorological Organization (WMO), and the International Civil Aviation Organization (ICAO), have smaller staffs and are primarily concerned with technical matters. To facilitate the performance of their functions—which are of practical utility for the movement of mail, international communications, weather prediction, and international travel—the member-states have granted them certain regulatory functions. The International Monetary Fund (IMF), the International Bank for Reconstruction and Development (the World Bank), the International Finance Corporation (IFC), and the International Development Association (IDA) play significant roles in the areas of economic development and economic stability. The IMF and the World Bank have large financial resources with which to carry out their responsibilities.

Although most of the Specialized Agencies have fairly modest financial resources, they provide valuable services in the fields of health, farm production, pollution control, communications, transportation, technical assistance, pest control, education, nutrition, and many other areas (see Digest at the end of this book).

These are some of the arrangements and structures the UN has helped to promote. The list is by no means exhaustive.

The Politics of the United Nations

Of the UN membership of 157,* over 120 belong to the Third World (also referred to as LDCs or the South). In the General Assembly and in those agencies or organizations having worldwide membership and voting arrangements based on one vote for each member-state, the Third World group enjoys an overwhelming majority. This is evident especially in the General Assembly, in which important resolutions can be easily passed by the LDCs against the objections of the major powers.

Although the principle of one vote for each member may appear equitable, in reality it conceals major inequities. For example, 107 members have populations totaling 1,304 million people with a total GNP of approximately $900 billion. Their 107 votes represent a two-thirds majority in the General Assembly. Contrast this voting strength to that of Britain, China, France, the Soviet Union, and the United States (the five permanent members of the Security Council), which have only five votes in the General Assembly. These five countries have populations totaling 2,604 million and a GNP of $5,112 billion.

The voting predominance of smaller and poorer countries becomes even more evident when one focuses on a simple majority. Eighty LDCs, constituting a majority in the General Assembly, represent only 755 million people and a total GNP of $325 billion. Another revealing statistic is that sixteen member-states with only 10 percent of the votes in the General Assembly contribute more than 60 percent of the Organization's total expenses.

This uneven distribution of voting power in the General Assembly has not contributed to its effectiveness or influence. With its artificial majorities, the General Assembly may pass resolutions, especially on critical economic issues, but such resolutions remain moot if their implementation depends (as it often does) on the cooperation of the major powers: passing a resolution against the will of these powers does not contribute to practical solutions. One ill-fated attempt by the developing nations to push through a UN Capital Development Fund in 1966 succeeded in establishing the Fund but

---

* This number includes the Ukraine and Byelorussia, the two Union Republics of the Soviet Union, which were initially included by special arrangement at Yalta between Roosevelt and Stalin.

failed to make it a viable institution. Most of the wealthy countries did not contribute funds, and the agency withered on the vine. This problem could be resolved by adopting, for example, a new voting arrangement based on a formula that takes account of population size and GNP. However, given the present political realities within the UN, there is no likelihood that this or a similar change in the Charter will come about. The voting arrangements in the General Assembly are strongly favored by the Third World countries. Many of these countries tend to be critical of policies espoused by the West, especially the United States. This tendency inevitably becomes entangled in the rivalry between the United States and the Soviet Union. Not surprisingly, influential people in the United States often express disillusionment with the UN.

Another weakness of the General Assembly is its preference for open, public debate. Most international disputes require quiet diplomacy. Because delegates tend to play to the galleries or to the home audiences for applause, a debate in the General Assembly is more likely to raise the level of controversy than to smooth the way toward reconciliation. The secretary general drew the attention of the delegates to this in his report to the 1982 annual meeting of the General Assembly:

> Obviously, a parliamentary debate may generate rhetoric, and sometimes even a touch of acrimony. But negotiations and the resolution of urgent problems require a different approach. Debate without effective action erodes the credibility of the Organization. I feel that in the United Nations, if we wish to achieve results, we must make a more careful study of the psychological and political aspects of problems and address ourselves to our work accordingly. It is insufficient to indulge in a course of action that merely tends to strengthen extreme positions.[6]

The attitude of the United States toward the UN has undergone changes that reflect the political developments within the Organization. Initially, the United States placed the primary emphasis on the Security Council, which was seen as the pivotal organ. With the advent of the Cold War, the prospects for Soviet cooperation vanished, and the repeated use of the veto by the Soviet Union (as the only means at its disposal to overcome the pro-Western majorities in the Security Council) cooled considerably the United States' reliance on the Council. During the Korean War (1950–1953) the United States pushed through the Uniting for Peace Resolution, which gave the General Assembly authority to deal with security issues previously reserved exclusively for the Security Council. In the 1950s, the Security Council declined in its importance as an increasing number of political issues were submitted to the veto-free General Assembly. This shift of activity to the General Assembly continued into the early 1960s. The pendulum swung again back to the Security Council after the middle 1960s, when the General Assembly membership showed a dramatic change with the influx of the newly independent countries, particularly from Africa.

The UN has not fulfilled the more optimistic expectations of some of its most ardent proponents. It has not eliminated war, poverty, or injustice. Neither has it become, however, a superfluous institution. As the UN approaches its fortieth anniversary, it can be said with considerable justification that it has helped dampen conflicts, shorten the length and destructive intensity of armed confrontations, and defuse crises by providing a neutral ground and an opportunity for adversaries to clarify their perceptions of one another's intentions and to move away from the path of war to the safer avenues of diplomacy. With instant communications the world has become virtually a global village, with the UN as its town meeting hall. Complete harmony is likely to remain an elusive ideal, but the United Nations system provides a forum where opponents can use arguments instead of armaments to resolve a dispute, and where compromise can be a more realistic option than the uncertain expectations of victory on the battlefield. On the other hand, the Organization can be only as effective as its members—especially the major powers—are willing to make it.

The Rules of International Law...

International law consists of written and customary rules sovereign governments accept as binding in their relations with one another. Most of these rules are of fairly recent origin: contemporary rules of international law go back to no more than five centuries. Until very recently, most of those rules originated in Europe. The making of rules continues.

Whereas international law, as we know it today, is of recent vintage, rules regulating relations among sovereign entities can be found in the records of the earliest civilizations. An agreement between two Mesopotamian kingdoms to submit a boundary dispute to arbitration dates back to around 3100 B.C. Assyrian, Babylonian, Hebrew, Hindu, and Chinese records contain many references to alliances, boundary settlements, peace treaties, and the treatment of envoys. The Bible is a rich source of similar material, and the same holds true for the writings of Herodotus, Xenophon, and Thucydides among the ancient Greeks. Some of the rules in the ancient sources appear strikingly familiar to us today. However, modern international law cannot trace a direct and unbroken descent from those ancient rules.[7]

The early origins of contemporary international law can be traced to the early centuries of this millenium. The Catholic Church played a significant role in this, as it tried to use its spiritual authority to reconcile rivalries among the Christian rulers in Europe, arbitrate disputes, authorize the conquest of lands across the seas (lands inhabited by non-Christians), or limit the cruelty of warfare. The rise of the Protestant movement undermined the authority of the Pope at the very time strong national states—starting with Britain, France, and Spain—emerged during the fifteenth and sixteenth centuries. These new sovereigns did not always turn to the Pope as the supreme arbiter.

To regulate somewhat their relations with one another, these states gradually developed practical rules of conduct, adding new ones as necessity demanded. Many of these initial rules were in the form of customs that had grown over the years out of repeated practice and imitation.

With the advent of the Soviet Union and the other socialist states and the emergence of many new sovereign states carved out of the former colonial empires, new demands have been raised for a reappraisal of the current rules of international law.

Although both the socialist and the Third World governments have found most of the rules of international law acceptable and have abided by them, they have sought adjustments to make some of the rules more equitable. For example, the generally accepted rule that the high seas do not belong to any sovereign entity has not been challenged with regard to the freedom of navigation; but the developing countries have insisted that mineral resources found at the bottom of the oceans should be exploited for the benefit of humanity, not solely for the benefit of those countries that have the technical means of bringing those resources to the surface. It is generally agreed that, for a long time to come, only the highly industrialized states will have the technology and the financial means to take advantage of these seabed resources. In the new Law of the Sea, approved in April 1982 under the auspices of the United Nations, the overwhelming majority of the participating states agreed to establish an international authority to regulate the exploitation of these resources "for the benefit of all."[8]

The Problem of Enforcement

The rules of international law suffer from a serious institutional handicap: there is no superior authority empowered to enforce them and to punish those who violate them.

Our conception of law is that as citizens we have an obligation to comply with its provisions whether or not we like a specific rule; if we violate a rule, there is an elaborate machinery to penalize us—a police officer, a judge, a jailer, even an executioner. As citizens, we are subject to the domestic laws of our country. International law is different from domestic (municipal) law in one crucial aspect: the subjects of international law are primarily the sovereign states. These states are expected to abide by the rules, but if they ignore or violate them there is no machinery to punish them or enforce compliance. The sovereign states are not subject to any superior machinery of enforcement.

True, an International Court of Justice exists at The Hague, and all the member-states of the United Nations are "parties to the Statute of the International Court of Justice." Does that mean that all UN members accept automatically the jurisdiction of the court? Do they accept an obligation to submit any dispute to the Court and are they prepared to abide by its decision? Most governments are not eager to entrust the protection of their national interests to others, however impartial those others may be. The Statute itself includes one article known as the *optional clause,* which serves as an escape hatch. In effect, this article provides for the "ipso facto and without special agreement" acceptance of the *compulsory* jurisdiction of the Court. However, this article is not automatically accepted; it is *optional.* A government may state that its adherence to the Statute does not include this article. A country may even qualify its acceptance of the optional clause by stating certain reservations or limitations. The United States, for example, accepted the clause in 1946, but to pacify conservative and isolationist elements in the U.S. Senate, a declaration was attached stating that "matters which are essentially within the domestic jurisdiction of the United States of America *as determined by the United States of America*" (italics added) were not subject to the compulsory jurisdiction of the Court.[9] Many other countries have used a similar reservation. Even a government that has accepted the optional clause may claim that a dispute arises from an issue that *in its view* is domestic and therefore outside of the Court's jurisdiction.

The victim of a violation cannot seek redress of its grievances by turning to the United Nations either. A country may appeal to the UN and its plea may be answered with a comforting resolution by the General Assembly or the Security Council, but the UN has no enforcement machinery to turn a punitive resolution from a piece of paper into an effective instrument to punish an aggressor or even restore peace in a troubled area. The UN peacekeeping forces that have been used to keep adversaries apart have a limited function, which certainly does not include punitive action. Such peacekeeping forces first must be accepted by the warring sides before they enter the sovereign territory of any of the combatants, and their mission is limited to preserving a modicum of nonviolence or checking compliance with agreements for temporary pacification.[10]

The bottom line is that in our contemporary international system (as in centuries past) the defense of a country's national interest is left largely to its own military force or the protection of powerful friends. Even when a government comes to the assistance of an embattled friend, it does so not so much to uphold the rules of international law as to serve its own national interest or strategic aspirations. One can hardly think of a weaker system of law in terms of enforcement. Even the fear of divine retribution—a powerful restraint in earlier centuries—is no longer present.

Reciprocity

The absence of effective enforcement does not mean that the rules of international law are meaningless; far from it. The rules exist because governments consider them useful, reasonable, practical, and basically beneficial to their interests. They are not forcibly imposed by a superior authority; they result from the consent of sovereign governments that freely decide to respect these rules because to do so is in their best interest—at least most of the time. They respect and apply those rules on the basis of *reciprocity:* because other governments are doing the same. They protect, for example, a foreign embassy in their capital because they expect their own embassy to be protected by the other government. This element of reciprocity is central to the actual implementation of the rules of international law. When a government, however, decides that violation will serve its interests *more* than compliance, it may opt to break a rule. The daily headlines tend to give the impression that violation of the rules is the norm; the opposite is true. Violations merit a headline precisely because they are rare compared to the multitude of international transactions and peaceful settlements of disputes that occur every year. Moreover, the demands international law makes on states are so limited that governments can pursue their national interests without the need to ignore or violate existing rules.

Limited Scope

Much more significant a handicap than the absence of enforcement machinery is the limited scope of international law. To see how limited this scope is, you need only glance through the table of contents of any textbook on international law.[11] The contents are likely to include, in addition to a general discussion of the nature, subjects, and sources of international law, such topics as the recognition of states and governments, extinction and succession of states, territorial jurisdiction, rules of maritime and air transportation, status and immunities of state officials and diplomatic agents, methods for the peaceful settlement of disputes, and rules related to the conduct of war, neutrality, military occupation, or the treatment of prisoners, the wounded, and civilians. These traditional topics reflect the actual scope of international law.

There are many other areas of equal or even greater importance that are beyond the pale of international law. Although they seriously affect the safety, wellbeing, economic development, physical environment, or security of others, they are considered to be within the domestic jurisdiction of a country and therefore outside the scope of international law. The following illustrations will help make the point.

Economic Actions. Between 1973 and 1980, the members of OPEC increased the price of oil more than 1,100 percent, setting off worldwide inflation exacerbated by persistent stagnation. These decisions by the OPEC governments played havoc with the economies of many countries, especially the poorer developing countries that did not have oil resources of their own. However destabilizing, the OPEC actions did not violate any rule of international law.

In a world of growing economic interdependence, many economic decisions of major importance still remain outside the scope of international law unless governments agree to limit their own discretion by signing bilateral or multilateral treaties. The General Agreement on Tariffs and Trade (GATT) is one such multilateral agreement that was designed to expand international trade, primarily among the advanced industrial countries. Although some progress has been made, many crucial economic decisions that seriously affect the wellbeing of other countries remain beyond the scope of international law.

Armament Sales and Use. International law has no jurisdiction over the production, acquisition, or marketing of conventional weapons. [The treaties against the use of exploding (dum-dum) bullets or against the use of bacteriological or chemical weapons may be cited as exceptions, if such weapons were regarded as "conventional."] With regard to nuclear weapons, we can identify several international agreements designed to introduce some control: the treaty banning atmospheric tests of nuclear weapons, the nuclear nonproliferation treaties, the treaties banning the use of space or celestial bodies for military purposes, and the Strategic Arms Limitation Treaties (SALT I and SALT II). These agreements, however significant, still leave to the discretion of the various governments—especially those of the superpowers—a great many decisions of grave importance to the world community. The current discussion in the United States and in the Soviet Union regarding the development of space vehicles with military capabilities not covered by agreements already signed by them is an illustration of the wide discretion governments still have in the area of armaments.

Pollution of the Environment. The natural environment usually does not follow the artificial boundaries that delineate the territories of the various states. In Latin America, Africa, Europe, and South Asia, where the land is parceled among several states, rivers cross national boundaries. Pollution can be carried downstream. Industrial pollutants may be carried by the wind across national borders.[12] Acid rain is a vexing issue between Canada and the United States. Decisions related to such problems are normally within the domestic jurisdiction of each government, no matter how much such decisions may affect neighboring countries. Unless neighbors sign a treaty regulating such matters, actions by one government, however damaging to others, do not violate international law.[13]

Domestic Policy Decisions. The urgent need to improve the living standards in the developing countries cannot be met by international aid alone; the problem also calls for positive steps on the part of the LDCs' own governments. Wrong decisions by domestic officials can play havoc with the development prospects or may introduce elements of dangerous instability in a strategically important area, yet no government can be accused of violating international law because it happens to follow counterproductive policies.

Food Production and Population Control. Experts in food production predict that we will lose the race between the expansion of the Earth's population and the rise in food production. They argue that unless the birth rate is brought under control, especially in the poorer developing countries, the world will face mounting problems of famine, unrest, and revolution in the coming decades. These dire predictions may turn out to be unfounded because of improving techniques in food production. Nevertheless, the rapid growth of population (figure 8-2) presents a problem for many countries, undermining their development efforts. Eventually, discontent may explode into conflicts with worldwide repercussions. Yet, little can be done under international law to induce governments to adopt birth-control policies or change the structure of their farm production to make it more effective. Efforts by the United Nations and its specialized agencies, or through special treaties, have been helpful—but the ultimate authority for making the necessary decisions rests with the sovereign governments.

Although the current scope of international law is limited on many crucial areas, it is equally true that its scope is constantly expanding. Activities and relations that prior to World War II were left outside the purview of international law have since become subject to international regulation. The proliferation of multinational treaties and the activities of a growing number of international organizations illustrate rising awareness that we live in a world of highly interdependent entities. Prudence and common sense call for cooperative efforts to deal with problems the consequences of which do not remain within a state's territory but spill across national frontiers.

The Sources of
International Law...

Before we can say that a rule of international law has been violated we must be able to say that such a rule actually exists. In domestic (municipal) law we have legislatures and other state institutions that produce binding rules. No comparable institutions exist in the international system. How can we tell then what is included among the rules of international law? One way to answer this question is by identifying the sources of international law. This approach is reflected in Article 38 (i) of the *Statute of the International Court of Justice*. The Court's function, the statute reads, is "to decide in accordance with international law such disputes as are submitted to it." To carry out this function, the Court has to rely on three primary and two secondary sources:

a. international conventions, whether general or particular, establishing rules expressly recognized by contesting states;

b. international custom, as evidence of a general practice accepted as law;

c. the general principles of law recognized by civilized nations;

Figure 8-2

World population growth, 10,000 B.C. to A.D. 1982.

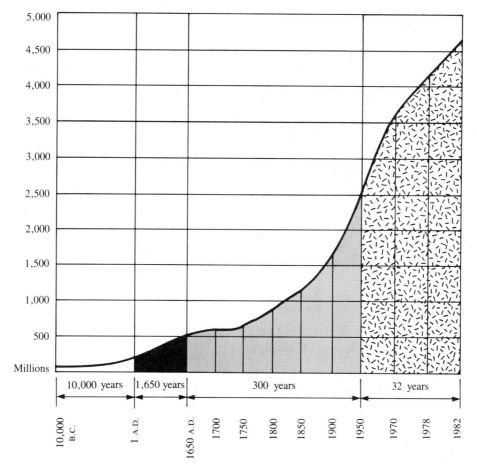

d.   . . . judicial decisions and the teachings of the most highly
   qualified publicists of the various nations, as subsidiary means for
   the determination of rules of law.

Let us take a brief look at these sources of international law.

....Customary Rules

Not long ago, most of the rules of international law that applied throughout the
international community were unwritten, customary rules that had grown out of prece-
dent, continuous practice, and general acceptance. In more recent times, governments
have shifted their preference to written treaties, the content and meaning of which can be
clearly established. Many customary rules of earlier times have been put in writing as
international *conventions*.

Even with the tremendous expansion of written agreements in recent times,
customary rules retain their significance. Treaties are primarily binding on only their
signatories; customary rules, by contrast, enjoy a wide, near-universal acceptance.

A customary rule is the product of necessity and convenience. It emerges gradually over a fairly long period, as one government after another finds it useful to follow a
given practice in dealing with similar situations. Most of the existing customary rules
resulted from practices initiated and applied by the European powers.

The major weakness of customary rules is their rigidity; they cannot be changed
quickly to adjust to new needs and requirements. The solution, theoretically at least, is
for governments to revise a customary rule by signing a "law treaty." The familiar rule of
the three-mile limit for territorial waters was increasingly challenged during the last fifty
years. Eventually, in 1982, the Convention on the Law of the Sea adopted a twelve-mile
limit in most cases, and even a 200-mile *economic zone* extending beyond a country's
seashore into the ocean, including the ocean floor.[14]

The emergence of many new states in the last thirty years has raised questions
about their obligation to abide by customary rules that existed before they acquired their
sovereign status. The prevailing view is that governments are expected to observe
well-established customary rules. This applies particularly to new states that have
become members of the United Nations. The Charter requires new members to settle
disputes "in conformity with the principles of justice and international law" (Article 1(i))
and "to establish conditions under which justice and respect for the obligations arising
from treaties and other sources of international law can be maintained" (Preamble). In
fact, most new states have automatically accepted the customary rules because they find
them to be convenient, and because of the central element of reciprocity. Nevertheless,
certain customary rules have been challenged by the actions of several non-Western
states. For example, the rule that foreign property should be protected no longer holds its
former validity. The takeover of foreign properties is no longer regarded as a violation of
international law; the generally accepted rule now is that some compensation should be
paid for nationalized foreign assets. In practice, revolutionary regimes have nationalized
foreign assets without offering more than a token compensation or none at all. In most
cases, however, such a cavalier attitude is counterproductive; even the most intransigent

regimes agree in the end to pay a partial indemnity in exchange for foreign credits or trade arrangements.

Because customary rules, being unwritten, can be subject to challenge or conflicting interpretations, governments today turn more and more to the signing of written international agreements.

·· **Treaties**

International agreements may be given various labels: conventions, covenants, charters, protocols, and most frequently treaties. Whatever the title, all international agreements signed by sovereign governments or IGOs are *treaties*. The International Law Commission has defined a treaty as "an international agreement entered into by two or more states or other international persons, and [which] is governed by international law."[15]

The importance treaties have in our international system is illustrated by the number of such instruments that have been registered and published by the UN Secretariat in its Treaty Series. As of 1981, over 18,000 treaties, filling more than 1,000 volumes, had been signed by sovereign governments. No less striking than their number is the variety of relations they cover: political, military, economic, commercial, cultural, financial, and administrative. A treaty, as an instrument for regulating relations among states, possesses great versatility. It also has the advantage of relative precision, because its terms are set in writing (differing interpretations of a treaty's provisions do occur). Moreover, whereas customary rules take a long time to emerge, treaties can introduce new rules within a short period to meet changing circumstances.

A treaty is a useful device because it enables governments to assume obligations and make commitments while keeping their sovereignty intact. Every time a government signs a treaty, it agrees in effect to curb its sovereign right and conform with the terms of that treaty. It accepts those limitations precisely because it is sovereign and can freely decide which arrangements to accept and which to refuse.

Types of Treaties

When a treaty is signed by only two governments it is called a *bilateral* treaty; if signed by more than two, it is *multilateral*. Treaties signed by two or more countries, the legal effects of which are limited to the signatories, are usually classified as *contract treaties* (*traités-contrats*) to distinguish them from treaties of general applicability, which are known as *law treaties* (*traités-lois*).

Contract treaties, as the term implies, involve some special agreement of concern to only the signatories. Law treaties, on the other hand, deal with problems of broad interest, are signed by a large number of states, and are open to other states that may join later. The Geneva Convention on the treatment of prisoners of war, the Vienna Convention of Diplomatic Relations, the Charter of the United Nations, the Statute of the International Court of Justice, the 1982 Convention on the Law of the Sea, the General Agreement on Tariffs and Trade (GATT), the Nuclear Non-Proliferation Treaty, and agreements on copyright, international flights by civil aircraft, and the movement of international mail are familiar illustrations. Not all law treaties have universal application. Some relate to one region, such as the Charter of the Organization of African Unity or the Treaty of Rome that created the European Common Market.

Pacta Sunt Servanda

Whatever the number of participants or the content of a particular treaty, its provisions must be respected and faithfully implemented. *Pacta Sunt Servanda* (agreements must be kept) is a time-honored customary rule. The terms of a treaty must be interpreted in good faith, and the various provisions must be read in the context of the entire document and in light of the objectives established by the participants during the negotiations.[16] A disagreement over the meaning of a particular clause may be resolved through negotiations or submitted to arbitration or to the International Court of Justice.

A vexing question in international law is whether a treaty can be terminated unilaterally because fundamental circumstances have changed since the time it was signed. This doctrine of *rebus sic standibus* (things being as they are) has been generally accepted, but under two conditions that were spelled out in Article 62 of the Vienna Convention on the Law of Treaties, signed in May 1969:[17] (1) the circumstances that have changed "must have constituted an essential basis of the consent of the parties," and (2) the effect of changes must be such that they "radically transform the extent of obligation to be performed under the treaty."[18] The same article specifically states that the doctrine *rebus sic standibus* cannot be invoked if the treaty has established a boundary between the states, or if the change of conditions is due to "a breach by the party invoking it." Needless to say, widespread implementation of this doctrine would completely destroy the validity of all treaties.

General Principles

Although customary rules and treaties are universally accepted as primary sources of international law, the "general principles recognized by all civilized nations" are not, even though they are identified as such in Article 38 (i) of the Statute of the International Court of Justice.[19]

Most of these general principles can be traced to municipal law. For example, the principles that one should not benefit from one's own wrongdoing, that agreements should be fulfilled in good faith, or that one should respect the rights of another are certainly useful and, in the absence of any other more specific rule, they may be taken into account by an international tribunal such as the ICJ. In other words, the general principles can serve as an auxiliary, not a primary, source.

Judicial Decisions and the Writings of Experts

It is generally agreed that the decisions of the International Court of Justice do not *create* new rules of international law in the strict sense of law making, but they do help strengthen and clarify the meaning of rules created by custom or treaty. In this regard, they may be *subsidiary* but by no means *secondary*. The decisions of domestic courts also may contribute indirectly to the development of international law, especially when they deal with litigation over the implementation of a treaty.

The second subsidiary source under Article 38(i) is "the teachings of the most highly qualified publicists of the various nations." As long as the rules of international law were in most part customary, only a few individuals had adequate expertise. Those who wrote authoritatively about the rules provided a most vital, if not the only, source to those who wanted to know the meaning or the validity of a rule. Today our knowledge of international law has expanded greatly; however, the number of experts still remains limited and their influence on the verification and interpretation of rules is considerable.

···Resolutions and Decisions

The Statute of the ICJ does not make special reference to the resolutions passed by the UN General Assembly or Security Council or the decisions of other international bodies. Such actions, however, certainly contribute to the development of international law: concerned parties invoke such rulings as proof of the existence of obligations or rights.

What is the legal effect of those resolutions? Do they constitute another source of international law left out of Article 38(i)? Many UN resolutions have been ignored by governments that found their prescriptions unwelcome and damaging to their interests. On the other hand, even those resolutions that have been rejected by recalcitrant governments are not thrown into the waste basket; many other governments consider them as binding and invoke their provisions on every occasion. The fact that, in the absence of the necessary machinery, such resolutions cannot be enforced does not mean that they are without legal or political consequences. Resolution 242, for example, was incorporated in the 1979 Israeli–Egyptian peace treaty and was mentioned more recently, in 1982, by President Reagan in his proposal for an autonomous Palestinian entity federated with Jordan, and again in 1984 during the withdrawal of the U.S. force from Lebanese soil. (Resolution 242, passed by the UN Security Council in 1967, calls for the withdrawal of Israel "from territories" it seized during the Seven-Day War.)

Despite the refusal of governments to abide by the UN resolutions they dislike, such resolutions, which reflect a wide consent or even consensus, are no less binding than other rules of international law—at least for the UN members—and should be regarded as another source.[20]

However, the decisions, resolutions, or recommendations of international organizations should be regarded as only a subsidiary source of international law, contributing to its overall development either by reaffirming the existence of a rule or by setting the stage for the eventual growth of a customary rule or the signing of a multilateral treaty. For example, Resolution 242 did not *create* a new rule but *reaffirmed* the rule that military conquest of foreign territory does not convey title of ownership to the conqueror.

The Subjects of International Law..

The subjects of any legal system include those who:

1. Have certain duties and obligations

2. Have rights

3. Can enter into contractual or other legal relationships with other parties having the same capacity under the system

....Sovereign States

Initially, only sovereign states were considered to be subjects of international law. Individuals were not, except when they engaged in a crime against humanity, such as piracy. This traditional identification of the subjects of international law has undergone some change in recent times.

.... IGOs

For over one-hundred years, international organizations formed by sovereign states have enjoyed a separate legal personality. The Universal Postal Union is one of the earliest illustrations. Today dozens of IGOs are treated as subjects of international law. The United Nations is the best known. Article 104 of its Charter requires all member-states to accord to the UN, within their territories, "such legal capacity as may be necessary for the exercise of its functions." Since 1946, the UN has signed many treaties both with individual states and with other international institutions. The Specialized Agencies also have entered into agreements with sovereign states or other entities. Regional IGOs, such as the EEC, also have done so. All such organizations are legitimate subjects of international law, and have both duties and rights.[21]

.... Nonsovereign Entities

Another category of subjects includes nonsovereign entities such as colonies, possessions, protectorates, mandates, or trust territories. Colonies are considered to be legally an extension of the colonial power and under its sovereign authority. However, under the mandate system of the League of Nations and more recently under the trusteeship system of the United Nations, former colonial territories came under rules of international law providing for certain rights and obligations. As the number of nonsovereign entities diminishes with the emergence of new sovereign states, this category becomes marginal.

.... Political Groups or Movements

Of greater current interest is the increasing acceptance of rebellious or national liberation movements as potential subjects of international law. Normally, a rebellious movement is primarily a domestic affair; nevertheless, certain rules of international law apply to them. For example, under international law, other governments are expected to stay neutral, abiding in this by the rules governing neutrality in time of war.[22] They may extend recognition to an insurgent movement, but only if it has gained control of a substantial piece of territory inhabited by fairly large groups of people. This, however, is not always the case. Liberation movements such as the PLO have entered into international agreements, thereby becoming subjects of international law, in a limited sense.

Private Entities and Individuals

Are individuals or private entities or associations subjects of international law? Only indirectly, in the opinion of most experts.[23] The citizens of a state cannot present claims before an international tribunal even though such a claim may arise from a treaty violation. The Charter of the ICJ (Article 34) explicitly states that "only States may be parties in the case before the Court." A private claim must be embraced by the government, which alone has the capacity to bring the case before the international tribunal. This applies no less to multinational corporations. A dispute between an MNC and a foreign government may be subject to the domestic laws of the host state or, if the dispute has international overtones, it may be brought before the Court. In the latter case, the MNC must rely on the willingness of the government of its country of origin to bring the case to the international tribunal.

One illustration of individuals becoming subjects of international law directly is provided by the trials of the Nazi leaders after World War II. The agreement signed in August 1945 by the United States, the United Kingdom, France, and the Soviet Union established an International Military Tribunal vested with the authority to try high officials of the Axis Powers accused of crimes against peace, crimes against humanity, and violations of international treaties renouncing war. Later, the UN General Assembly declared that genocide—the massive extermination of populations—is a crime under international law and that the perpetrators, whether government officials, public servants, or private individuals, are punishable. These basic principles were incorporated in the Genocide Convention (Convention on the Prevention and Punishment of the Crime of Genocide), which came into force in 1951. Persons charged with actions designed to exterminate physically a national, ethnic, or racial group may be tried by a competent tribunal of the state where the acts were committed or by an international tribunal. No such international tribunal has been established yet. An illustration reflecting current technological advances is the treaty on the Rescue and Return of Astronauts, which was drafted by the UN Committee on Outer Space and has been in effect since December 3, 1968.[24]

War and the
International Law

For thousands of years, war was regarded not only as a legitimate course of action for sovereign governments but as one of their most basic rights. Until recent decades, international law did not ban war; rather, it viewed war as an acceptable method of self-help to enforce one's rights in the absence of an effective machinery for impartial protection and enforcement. Theologians like St. Augustine or Thomas Aquinas did not condemn war unequivocally: they spoke of *just* and *unjust* wars.[25]

Technological developments in the destructive capacity of weapons and the emergence of mass armies led by the turn of the nineteenth century to the first serious discussion of steps to make war more humane or even to limit it as an acceptable way to protect or advance a state's national interests. Prominent thinkers already had condemned war as inhumane and uncivilized. The French writer Victor Hugo had written in an eloquent passage:

> A day will come when the only battlefield will be the market open to
> commerce and the mind open to new ideas. A day will come when
> bullets and bombshells will be replaced by votes, by the universal
> suffrage of nations, by the venerable arbitration of a great sovereign
> senate which will be to Europe what the Parliament is to England, what
> the Diet is to Germany, what the Legislative Assembly is to France. A
> day will come when a cannon can be exhibited in public museums just
> as an instrument of torture is now, and people will be astonished how
> such a thing could have been.[26]

Some cannons have been confined to museums, but only because new and infinitely more powerful machines of war have made them obsolete. Still, Victor Hugo was echoing humanity's longing for peace and international order.

....The Hague Conferences

In 1899, the first Hague Conference, convened on the initiative of the czar, produced certain rules for the more humane conduct of warfare. Eight years later, in 1907, the Second Hague Conference addressed the same concern.[27] The two Hague conferences reaffirmed and expanded several customary rules while adding some new regulations relating to the conduct of hostilities. Special agreements prohibited the use of expanding (dum-dum) bullets or poisonous gases, and the laying of automatic contact mines. Other conventions dealt with the status of merchant vessels found in enemy ports at the outbreak of hostilities, imposed restrictions on the seizure of merchant vessels and the conversion of merchant vessels into warships, and on the bombardment of civilian targets. Other provisions defined the rights and duties of neutral states in time of war.[28]

Although limited in scope and purpose, the Hague conventions did establish some practical limitations on the hitherto virtually unlimited rights sovereign states enjoyed. More important, they gave official sanction to the idea that warfare should be controlled.

Shortly before the outbreak of World War I, U.S. Secretary of State William Jennings Bryan negotiated bilateral treaties that provided for a "cooling-off period," calling on governments engaged in a dispute to refrain from military action until an international commission had ascertained the facts.

These initial efforts to promote the peaceful settlement of international disputes did not prevent the use of force. Following the tragic carnage of World War I, antiwar sentiments found expression in the Covenant of the League of Nations. In its Preamble, the Covenant imposed on the signatories an obligation to avoid resort to war and, under Article 12, the members agreed that they would submit to arbitration or to a commission of inquiry under the League Council "any dispute likely to lead to rupture" and that they would "in no case" resort to war "until three months after the award by the arbitrators or the report to the Council"—a provision reminiscent of the "Bryan Treaties." The Covenant, however, did not outlaw war. Except for specific limitations of a rather technical and legalistic nature, the Covenant left the League members free to resort to war, while nonmembers retained the right to war in its unrestricted pre-1919 form.

The Kellogg–Briand Pact

The first attempt to outlaw war was made in 1928 on the initiative of the United States and France. The General Treaty for the Renunciation of War (also known as the Kellogg–Briand Pact, after the names of its architects, the American Secretary of State Frank B. Kellogg and the French Foreign Minister Aristide Briand), signed in Paris on August 27, 1928, by representatives of fifteen states and eventually ratified or accepted by a total of sixty-five nations, was uncommonly broad and specific.[29] In Article 1, the signatories solemnly stated that "they condemn recourse to war for the solution of international controversies, and renounce it as an instrument of national policy in their relations with one another." In Article 2, they agreed that "the settlement or solution of all disputes or conflicts of whatever nature or of whatever origin they may be, which may arise among them, shall never be sought except by pacific means."

Under the wording of the treaty, any government that sought to settle a dispute by military action was technically in violation, whatever excuses or justifications it might invoke. The treaty was much more sweeping, clear-cut, and unequivocal than the League Covenant. It also was many years ahead of its time: many wars have erupted since 1928. Nevertheless, the Kellogg–Briand Pact did outlaw all wars of aggression. The Pact, despite its bold language, had a major weakness: no machinery was provided for its implementation.[30] It was not without practical effect, however. After World War II, German and Japanese officials were tried, and several were executed, because they were found guilty of waging an aggressive war. The Pact has no termination date: it continues to be in effect.

The Geneva Conventions

During the interwar period (1919–1939) additional efforts were made to regulate the activities of states in time of war—an oblique indication that few people expected war to become a thing of the past. In 1925, a protocol prohibiting the use of poison gases and bacteriological warfare was signed by several countries (and was generally observed during World War II); in 1929, the Geneva Convention on the treatment of the sick and wounded, as well as of the prisoners of war (the familiar "Geneva Convention"), became the basic document that guided the treatment of prisoners during World War II. By contrast, the 1936 London Protocol concerning the use of submarines against merchant ships was completely discarded by all belligerents during the war. Submarine warfare was used extensively by Germany, which was less dependent on the use of the high seas for its war effort and therefore less exposed to allied retaliation. By contrast, poison gases and bacteriological warfare, as well as the humane treatment of the wounded and prisoners, were matters of equal importance to all belligerents: reciprocity induced compliance.

After the war, the Geneva Conference of 1949 succeeded in developing more precise rules, which were incorporated in four major conventions: Treatment of Prisoners of War; Amelioration of the Conditions of Wounded, Sick in Armed Forces in the Field; Amelioration of the Condition of Wounded, Sick and Shipwrecked Members of Armed Forces at Sea; and Protection of Civilian Persons in Time of War.

The United Nations Charter on War

The experiences of World War II gave new impetus to the drive for imposing limits to the use of military force. The Charter of the United Nations went beyond the provisions of the Kellogg–Briand Pact, because the members of the organization not only assumed the obligation, under Article 2, "to settle their international disputes by peaceful means in such a manner that international peace and security, and justice, are not endangered"; they also agreed to refrain "from the threat or use of force." The members have not only renounced under the Charter their right to go to war but even to *threaten* the use of force. At face value, the provisions of Article 2 give the impression that the members of the United Nations—and the membership includes almost every sovereign state—have solemnly committed themselves to the peaceful settlement of disputes. However, under other provisions of the Charter, members still can use force in self-defense or for collective action in the event of armed attack.

Wars of aggression are, of course, clearly outlawed by the Charter; except that no government has ever admitted that it is guilty of aggression. In addition, there is no universal agreement on the meaning of *aggression*. In 1974, a Special Committee, originally set up by the UN General Assembly in 1967, adopted by consensus a definition of aggression as "the use of armed force by a State, against the sovereignty, territorial integrity or political independence of another state, or in any other manner inconsistent with the Charter of the United Nations, as set out in this definition."[31] Unfortunately (in this context), most wars do not start with such a clear-cut "act of aggression." They are preceded by a deterioration of relations, border incidents, charges and countercharges, and mutual protestations of innocence. In fact, virtually every government that goes to war swears that it has done so in self-defense or with the noblest of objectives. Whether a war is aggressive or defensive is a matter of subjective interpretation, not only by the countries directly involved but also by others. To a country's friends, its actions are usually defensive; to its enemies, aggressive.

Summary

• The search for a more orderly international system has a long history. Some believe that a peaceful world is a utopian dream and that peace can be protected only through military preparedness. Some argue that only a world government can safeguard peace.

- Between these two extremes, three major alternatives have been tried: (1) the order imposed within the domain of large empires; (2) the order promoted by international organizations established by sovereign governments; and (3) the order of generally accepted rules (the rules of international law).

- The United Nations is the most universal organization ever created. It has neither fulfilled the most optimistic expectations nor proven to be a wasteful and ineffectual institution. To assess its record, we must look into the three major areas of its activity: conflict resolution, collective security, and the development of international arrangements to promote peace, stability, and the general welfare.

- The UN provides a useful channel for contacts among those governments engaged in a conflict and often has helped defuse a dangerous controversy.

- The UN has only once (during the Korean War) tried to act as an instrument for collective security. Collective security requires unanimity among the major powers against an aggressor state; such unanimity is not likely under the prevailing international realities. The UN therefore has shifted its emphasis to peacekeeping operations. These operations are not designed to punish an aggressor but to keep two adversaries apart until solutions can be found. The presence of UN peacekeeping forces must be accepted by the warring parties.

- The UN has been very helpful in promoting cooperative international arrangements and structures dealing with economic, social, legal, technical, and other issues.

- Among the weaknesses of the UN is the one-state, one-vote principle prevailing in the General Assembly and other UN structures. Many countries whose combined total populations and GNPs are relatively small can outvote the major countries.

- Composed of sovereign states, the UN can be only as effective and useful as its members want to make it.

- International law is the other major instrument for a more orderly international system. It consists of written or customary rules sovereign governments accept as binding in their relations with one another.

- The major weakness of international law is the absence of a machinery to enforce the rules and punish violators. Nevertheless, governments respect the rules because of the element of reciprocity.

- The scope of international law is limited and does not cover important areas with international significance. The scope is gradually expanding, however.

- The primary sources of international law are customary rules and treaties. Other sources are the general principles of law, judicial decisions, and the writings of experts.

- Until a few decades ago, war was considered to be a legitimate course of action. At the end of the nineteenth century, the first steps were taken to establish rules of conduct designed to lessen the inhumanity of war. The first attempt to outlaw war was made in 1928 under the Kellogg–Briand Pact; the Pact did not prevent World War II. The UN

Charter clearly prohibits wars of *aggression* and *the threat or use of force* except in self-defense or for collective action. Identifying the aggressor, however, is not an easy matter.

Notes

1. Emerson, Rupert. *From Empire to Nation*. Cambridge, Mass.: Harvard University Press, 1960; Eisenstadt, S. N. *The Political Systems of Empires*. London: Free Press, 1963.
2. Chi, Tsui. *A Short History of Chinese Civilization*. London: Victor Gallancz, 1942.
3. Perez de Cuellar, Javier. *Report of the Secretary General on the Work of the Organization*. New York: The United Nations, 1982.
4. For a very good discussion of the UN structure, see Goodspeed, Stephen S. *The Nature and Function of International Organization*. 2nd ed. New York: Oxford University Press, 1967, pp. 105–134.
5. Stoessinger, John G. *The United Nations and the Superpowers*. New York: Random House, 1965, pp. 63–89.
6. Perez de Cuellar, *op. cit.*, p. 10.
7. Von Glahn, Gerhard. *Law Among Nations*. 3rd ed. New York: Macmillan, 1976, p. 34.
8. The United States voted against the Convention on the grounds that the international control of such activities was in conflict with the principles of free enterprise. The Soviet Union and its allies, as well as seven Western industrial states, abstained. The overwhelming numerical majority of positive votes should not obscure the fact that twenty-one countries accounting for roughly 60 percent of the UN budget were not prepared to endorse the new Convention for a Law of the Sea.
9. De Cain, Vincent F. "The Connally Amendment." *National Review*, March 11, 1961, pp. 143–147; Briggs, Herbert W. "The United States and the International Court of Justice: A Re-Examination." *American Journal of International Law*, 1959, pp. 301–318.
10. Goodspeed, Stephen S. 1967, pp. 183–284.
11. See, for example: Brierly, J. L. *The Law of Nations*. 6th ed. London: Oxford University Press, 1963; Bishop, William W., Jr. *International Law: Cases and Materials*. 2nd ed. Boston: Little, Brown, 1962; Fenwick, Charles G. *International Law*. 4th ed. New York: Appleton-Century-Crofts, 1965; Von Glahn, Gerhard. *Law Among Nations*. 3rd ed. New York: Macmillan, 1976; Svarlien, Oskar. *An Introduction to the Law of Nations*. New York: McGraw-Hill, 1955.
12. Wolman, Abel. "Pollution as an International Issue." *Foreign Affairs*, Vol. 47, 1968, pp. 164–175.
13. Kneese, Alan V., et al., eds. *Managing the Environment: International Economic Cooperation for Pollution Control*. New York: Praeger, 1971.
14. *Convention of the Law of the Sea*, UN Document, Part II, Section 1; Part VI.
15. *International Law Commission (ILC) Yearbook*, 1962, Vol. ii, p. 31.
16. Kunz, Josef L. "The Meaning and the Range of the Norm *Pacta Sunt Servanda*." *American Journal of International Law*, Vol. 39, 1945, pp. 180–197.
17. See text of the Vienna Convention on the Law of Treaties in the *American Journal of International Law*, Vol. 63, 1969, pp. 875–908.
18. In justifying the abrogation of the May 17, 1983 treaty between Lebanon and Israel, Lebanese President Amin Gemayel is quoted: "When the choice is between an agreement and a nation, we have no doubt to choose the nation." *The Washington Post*, March 13, 1984.

19. Von Glahn, *op. cit.,* p. 19. For an opposing view see Schlesinger, Rudolph B. "Research on the General Principles of Law Recognized by Civilized Nations." *American Journal of International Law,* Vol. 51, 1957, pp. 734–753.
20. Higgins, Rosalyn. "The United Nations and Law-Making: The Principal Organs." *American Journal of International Law,* Vol. 64 (Proceedings, 1970), pp. 37–48; Castafieda, Jorge. *Legal Effects of United Nations Resolutions.* New York: Columbia University Press, 1970.
21. Bishop, William W., Jr. *International Law: Cases and Materials.* 2nd ed. Boston: Little, Brown, 1962, pp. 614–620.
22. Von Glahn, *op. cit.,* p. 85.
23. *Ibid.,* pp. 187–196.
24. Lay, S. Houston, and Taubenfeld, Howard J. *The Law Relating to Activities of Man in Space.* Chicago: University of Chicago Press, 1970.
25. Stratmann, Franziskus. *The Church and War.* New York: Sneed and Ward, 1928; Tooke, John D. "The Development of the Christian Attitude to War before Aquinas." In *The Just War in Aquinas and Grotius.* London: Society for the Propagation of Christian Knowledge, 1965, pp. 1–20.
26. Quoted in Goodspeed, Stephen S., *op. cit.,* p. 3.
27. Von Glahn, *op. cit.,* p. 543.
28. *Ibid.,* pp. 625–646.
29. Morris, Roland S. "The Pact of Paris for the Renunciation of War: Its Meaning and Effect in International Law." *Proceedings of the American Society of International Law,* 1929, pp. 88–91.
30. Wright, Quincy. "The Meaning of the Pact of Paris." *American Journal of International Law,* Vol. 27, 1933, pp. 39–61; Kaplan, Morton A., and Katzenbach, Nicholas deB. *The Political Foundations of International Law.* New York: Wiley, 1961, p. 210.
31. *The New York Times,* April 13, 1974.

THE
GREAT
ISSUES

9

....................The East—West
Rivalry

MX missile being tested at Vandenberg, California

Rivalry has been the prevailing pattern in the relations between East and West—primarily between the United States and the Soviet Union—for more than thirty-five years. The pendulum may have swung at times from Cold War to détente and back again, but the deep-seated antagonism continues, changing only in its outward intensity. Both sides spend staggering sums on armaments to keep each other at bay, and in large measure they determine the direction of their foreign policies by the dictates of this rivalry. In the past, similar feuds almost invariably erupted in war. In the nuclear age, a war between the superpowers is a chilling prospect.

We must assume that such a costly and dangerous rivalry would not have gone on for so long unless it were grounded on overpowering causes—on conflicting interests so irreconcilable that solutions cannot be found in compromises, reciprocal accommodations, and a mutually advantageous cooperation.

In the following pages we shall try to identify and evaluate these conflicting interests, and to touch on the key dimensions of this antagonistic relationship in the hope that such an overview will yield a balanced and realistic picture.

The Economic Aspects ....

Marxists claim that economic factors determine political relationships and actions. On this basis, the momentous antagonism between East and West should be provoked largely by unbridgeable economic conflicts. Can we identify economic interests that are presently or potentially in such a fundamental and uncompromising disparity?

Prior to World War II, both Germany and Japan could claim that their economies were in dire need of resources located outside their borders and that the survival and prosperity of their peoples could be assured only by expanding their control over the areas where the coveted resources were located. Those who controlled the targeted areas had no alternative but to resist such encroachments. Even in the absence of ideological or nationalistic ambitions, the economic antagonisms provided a powerful impetus for a military confrontation. Are there conflicting economic interests of a comparable magnitude dividing the two camps today? More specifically, is the Soviet Union in dire need of resources that can be obtained only through conquest or the expansion of its imperium and political control?

Natural Resources. It is an established fact that the Soviet Union is rich in minerals and energy resources, and will not become heavily dependent on foreign sources until some time in the next century. By then, technology may have reduced the critical importance of many of those minerals and fuels. In any event, a potential scarcity so far in the future cannot explain or justify the present confrontational relationship between the United States and the Soviet Union.

Foreign Markets. If the United States and the Soviet Union are not in competition for scarce and vital minerals and fuels, are they engaged in a dire contest for markets? The Soviet economy has increased its output for consumer products in the last thirty years, but it has yet to reach the high levels of productivity that would create large surpluses for exports. Currently, it cannot even satisfy the needs of the Soviet people. Soviet consumers still have to cope with scarcities and long waiting periods for the delivery of durable goods such as automobiles or appliances. The quality of goods, although improving, is mostly inferior to comparable Western products. A drive for foreign markets is not a pressing concern for Soviet economic planners. Currently the Soviet Union and its COMECON partners account for only 8.3 percent of world trade. In 1980, the import–export trade of the United States, West Germany, the United Kingdom, France, and Japan totaled $1,690 billion compared to a COMECON total of $208 billion (table 9-1).

Competition for markets between the Soviet Union and the United States (or between East and West) is not a realistic cause for conflict, and it is not likely to become one for a long time. In fact, confrontations due to economic rivalries for markets would be more justifiable among the Western industrial powers.

Access to Resources and Markets. A third economic reason for rivalry and confrontation could be an attempt by the Soviet Union to hinder Western access to foreign markets or sources of raw materials and fuels. An overview of the major areas reveals that thus far the Soviet Union has not been able to interfere effec-

Table 9-1

Basic Figures from United Nations Statistics* on the Import–Export Trade of the Major Powers

Country	1970	1980	Increase (percent)
United States	82	471	574
West Germany	64	380	593
United Kingdom	41	235	573
Japan	38	369	971
France	36	245	679
Soviet Union	30	145	483

*Figures in billions of dollars; real percent increase was less than indicated because 1970 and 1980 figures are in current dollars and percent increase has not been adjusted for inflation.

tively with Western access to such areas—assuming that such interference was a Soviet policy goal. In Latin America and the Caribbean, only two countries (Cuba and Nicaragua) are not fully open to Western trade or economic influence. Soviet efforts for economic penetration in this region directly or through Cuba have been spasmodic, limited, and far from successful. In black Africa, only Ethiopia and to some extent Angola and Mozambique are under Soviet influence. (Angola and especially Mozambique showed signs of veering away from Soviet tutelage in 1984.) Ethiopia's economy is of marginal importance. Oil-producing Angola is cooperating with the West in the extraction and marketing of oil. Mozambique needs Western benevolence more than vice versa. In north Africa, Libya continues to export to the West its only important resource—oil—despite Colonel M. Quaddafi's vociferous anti-Western rhetoric. In the Middle East, South Yemen is strategically important because of its location but economically of little significance. Iraq and Syria have been critical of the United States because of its stand on the Palestinian question and have accepted Soviet influence, but both countries have remained accessible to Western trade and economic relations most of the time; Iraq in particular has been moving away from Soviet influence recently. Even Iran, under the Islamic Republic, is gradually opening up to the West, where it can find customers for its oil exports. Iran, although unfriendly to the United States, is not politically under Soviet influence. Vietnam, Laos, and Cambodia are mostly cut off from the world economy by their own choice, but their economic importance has been marginal for the past twenty years. Afghanistan's participation in world trade was miniscule (0.004 percent) even before the Soviet invasion.

Even if these countries were induced by the Soviet Union to deny economic access to the West, the effect on the Western economies would be marginal. In a world total of $3,691 billion of import–export trade in 1980, these countries represented a total of $73.6 billion, or less than 2 percent. This percentage would be even smaller if the revenues of Libya, Iraq, and Iran (from their oil exports, mostly to the West) were not included. Soviet influence, even in those countries where it is fairly strong, has not interfered seriously with Western trade or economic access. The most important countries in this group (the oil exporters) would likely resist such interference because they have to sell their major export primarily in the West.

Clearly, the two rival camps are not in dire economic competition. One may even argue that they are to a certain extent *interdependent*.

Interdependence between East and West

That such seemingly implacable adversaries can also be interdependent merely points to the complexity of international relations and the unreality of simplistic, black-and-white, one-dimensional perceptions.

One peculiar aspect of the interdependence between East and West relates to their capacity to annihilate one another in a nuclear holocaust; they depend on each other's ability to act rationally and avoid actions that could precipitate a nuclear war. This is particularly pertinent to the United States and the Soviet Union, which, principally, have this capability.

Another aspect of this interdependence, which is becoming increasingly evident, is primarily economic. Although not yet vital, this economic interdependence is increasing in importance, as the following illustrations show.

Import–Export of Foodstuffs. The increasing Soviet population, the inefficiency of Soviet agriculture, and the difficult climatic conditions have turned the Soviet Union into a net importer of grains and other foodstuffs. By contrast, the United States and Canada, with their highly efficient and productive agriculture, can supply the Soviet needs for a long time to come. At the same time, the American farmers need additional markets for their surpluses. This economic interdependence was dramatically highlighted in 1982, when President Reagan set aside ideological considerations and approved the lifting of the embargo imposed by the Carter administration, so that large quantities of grain could be sold to the Soviet Union.

Import–Export of Fuels. The large territory of the Soviet Union is richly endowed with natural resources that the West can use. Public attention was drawn in 1981–1982 to the controversy over the construction of a 3,000-mile pipeline from the Yamal Peninsula in northwest Siberia to Western Europe to pipe forty billion cubic meters of natural gas annually to the industries and homes of West Germany, France, the Netherlands, Belgium, Austria, and Italy for a period of twenty years. These European countries favor the project because they will gain access to an additional source of energy. The Soviet Union on its part will use the hard currency proceeds from its annual sales of gas to purchase food and other products from the West. The United States initially objected to the pipeline project because it thought that this supply of gas would greatly increase West European dependence on the Soviet Union as a source of energy. This form of economic dependence, American policy makers feared, would increase Moscow's political leverage. Because the gigantic undertaking depends heavily on Western technology, Washington tried to slow down the project by blocking the shipment of pipeline equipment. This effort failed because of West European objections and the economic effects on the prospective suppliers of the equipment. The pipeline project moved on in an incongruous symbiosis with nuclear-tipped missiles on both sides of the Oder–Neisse line.

Import–Export of Technology. Less symmetrical is the Soviet dependence on American and Western technology. The Soviet system of command economy does not provide strong incentives for the invention of new products. The overwhelming majority of technological innovations in the last hundred years occurred in the Western market economies, which provide incentives to individual initiative and inventiveness. In this area, the Soviet Union needs the West more than vice versa.

Neither Interdependence Nor Competition Is Critical. One more observation is in order. The economic interdependence between the advanced capitalist countries and the Soviet camp may not yet be vital to both; but neither are the two sides confronted with a life-and-death competition over the control of vital resources that one side can have only by denying them to the other side.

It is difficult to find substantial economic reasons for the ongoing rivalry between East and West. The foregoing review seems to indicate that if a global war breaks out between East and West in the remaining part of this century, its real causes will not be primarily economic. Other factors that may be responsible include ideology, nationalistic ambitions, domestic politics, or the vested interests of individuals and groups that benefit from the perpetuation of the rivalry. We shall explore these factors after a brief comment on the People's Republic of China.

The Chinese Factor ....

The People's Republic of China with its large population (which has already surpassed the 1 billion mark) could face problems in providing adequately for its people in the future. However, increasing productivity in agriculture, the introduction of modern technology, and population control policies could ease such economic pressures.

Statistically speaking, China does not have an extremely high population density: with 283 persons per square mile, it compares favorably to Bangladesh, which has 1,660, or to India, which has 549. However, the bulk of the Chinese population is crowded in a fairly narrow area along the Pacific coastline. More than two-thirds of the Chinese territory is not suitable for cultivation, as it consists of mountains, arid plains, and deserts.

If overpopulation in China ever becomes a cause for an expansionist policy, the potential outlets will be more likely in Siberia, Soviet Central Asia, or possibly Australia. Other neighbors such as Korea, Japan, the Philippines, Vietnam, Malaysia, Cambodia, Indonesia, or India could not ease China's population problem; they have too many people of their own. Thus, for purely economic reasons, China and the Soviet Union are potential rivals; China and the United States are not. The only important bone of contention between China and the United States is the status of Taiwan. This island is not economically vital to China; the dispute is political, related to nationalistic principles and questions of national prestige. The current Chinese leadership, which has a pragmatic approach to international relations, appears to have decided to combine a verbal reaffirmation of China's sovereign claims on Taiwan with a prudent avoidance of any effort to try to change the status of the island by force. The Chinese leaders are aware that the use of force to retake Taiwan would jeopardize relations with the United States—a potential supplier of food and technology and a countervailing factor against Soviet pressure. China also lacks at the present the naval forces and the advanced weapons needed to mount an invasion of Taiwan.

The expected benefits from economic cooperation have played a key role in the improvement of Chinese relations with the United States, Japan, and other OECD countries since the mid-1970s. To develop its economy, China needs Western technology. On the other hand, China could become an important market for Western products, including foodstuffs. Trade currently continues to be limited because China has few items for export and insufficient hard currency earnings to increase its imports. The potential is there, however, as any visitor can readily see.

The Roots of Conflict ··

As we have pointed out, the United States and the Soviet Union do not have major economic interests that are so antithetical that they could justify a potentially suicidal confrontation. Why is it then that the two superpowers and their allies spend together more than $500 billion per year for armaments and for the maintenance of large armies they consider vital to their defense against the threat posed by the other side? What is the essence of the threat? Are the United States and its NATO allies threatening to invade Eastern Europe and the Soviet Union as Hitler did four decades ago? Is the Soviet Union planning to invade Western Europe or the oil fields of the Middle East at the risk of nuclear war? What is the threat facing the United States, considering that this country is beyond the physical reach of Soviet military power (with the exception of nuclear ICBMs)? Can one visualize a Soviet amphibious operation against the United States? In any case of aggressive military action taken by either side, the risk of mutual annihilation in a nuclear exchange cannot be ruled out. How realistic is the threat under these circumstances? We have discussed war as "the continuation of politics by other means." Politics is a fairly rational process.[1] People engage in politics because they wish, through influence and the exercise of power, to gain certain benefits or advantages. For centuries, leaders have been trying to gain by force what they were unable to obtain through political (diplomatic) means in the international arena; however, a nuclear war that threatens the very survival of the warring parties and promises hardly any gains at the end of the conflict is no longer a rational alternative or an "extension of politics."

If the two rival camps are not engaged in a deadly competition over the control of economic resources vital to their existence, and if they have no rational incentive to seize territories vital to the other side and so risk annihilation, what other factors might explain their protracted and costly rivalry?

··· Assessing the Soviet Threat

Government officials, politicians, journalists, analysts, educators, and other opinion leaders in the United States and in other countries routinely speak of the *Soviet threat;* we seldom see a concrete description of this threat.

What is the essence of the Soviet threat under conditions of mutual nuclear deterrence? Such a threat, to be realistic, must not carry with it the risk of nuclear war; it must consist of actions that will promote changes detrimental to Western interests without provoking a nuclear confrontation. Under these conditions, the most realistic (risk-free) form the Soviet threat can take is the promotion of Marxist-oriented, pro-Soviet, or at least anti-Western regimes in one country of the Third World after another, through the activities of domestic revolutionaries assisted in some way by the Soviet Union but generally without the direct involvement of Soviet military forces.

Promotion of Pro-Soviet Regimes

Even during the 1970s, when the two superpowers toned down their Cold War rhetoric and embraced the policy of détente, neither side stopped its efforts to win friends and expand its area of influence. The results at the end of the decade were mixed and inconclusive, to say the least. The Soviet Union lost its foothold in Egypt and Somalia, Iraq drifted away from the Soviet orbit, and China normalized its relations with the United States. We witnessed the emergence of Marxist-oriented, largely pro-Soviet, and anti-Western regimes in South Yemen, Ethiopia, Afghanistan, Mozambique, Angola, and Nicaragua. South Vietnam, Laos, and Cambodia passed into the socialist camp. Iran was politically lost to the West, but it did not come under Soviet control because of the religious orientation of the revolutionary group that came to power. Practically all of these shifts resulted from the actions of local activists and leaders. With the exception of the current military involvement in Afghanistan, no Soviet forces were used to bring about the changes that benefited the Soviet side. Local leaders, subscribing to some version of Marxism (often a vague one) spearheaded the drive for change, exploiting local conditions that served their purpose: in Vietnam they relied mainly on nationalist aspirations for unification; in South Yemen they exploited tribal rivalries; in Ethiopia they benefited from public disenchantment with a traditional monarchy unable to deal with pressing economic and social problems; in Mozambique and Angola they used the widespread public opposition to a colonial power that had retained control much too long; in Nicaragua they took advantage of popular discontent with an oppressive and corrupt dictatorship. The extent of Soviet influence in each of these countries varies, and so does the Marxist–Leninist content of their institutions, the permanence of their ties with the Soviet Union, and their economic or strategic significance. Nevertheless, for the time being, the Soviet leaders can list these countries among their "client states."

In mobilizing public support for their revolutionary operations, the local leaders relied heavily on the "weapon of ideology" and the techniques of propaganda, but they seldom used the ideology of Marxism–Leninism as the main instrument for popular mobilization; their emphasis was on local causes of popular discontent.

If the promotion of pro-Soviet regimes is the most realistic form the expansion of Soviet control can take and is the essence of the Soviet threat, how successful has this process been in practical terms? A review of the countries that have moved into the socialist camp will provide the answer. Most of these countries—Cuba, Nicaragua, Ethiopia, Angola, Mozambique, South Yemen, Cambodia, Laos, and Vietnam—are not economically vital to the West; they are more of a burden than an economic benefit to the Soviet Union.[2] Their importance is mostly political and in some cases strategic, but there is hardly any country among them that might be considered vital to the security of the United States. Cuba is undoubtedly an irritant, Ethiopia and South Yemen could conceivably affect the access to the Red Sea in time of war, and Vietnam provides one of two American-made bases for the Soviet navy; but in general the process has not brought any spectacular gains to the Soviet Union. The Soviet expectations and predictions of the 1950s and 1960s that "wars of liberation" would bring the countries of the Third World to the Soviet camp did not come true.

Of 122 states that are usually classified as Third World countries, only fourteen can be considered as Soviet *satellites* or client states. Moreover, during the last forty years, Marxist-oriented revolutionary groups have failed in their efforts to force radical changes in at least sixteen countries, whereas extensive Soviet influence was drastically reduced in at least five others (table 9-2).

Although the number of Soviet client states remains limited, a continuing and unchallenged emergence of anti-Western, Marxist-oriented, pro-Soviet regimes would certainly pose a double threat: (1) success in one country might encourage similar developments elsewhere; (2) if the process is left unchecked, the number of Marxist regimes may reach a "critical mass" and enable the Soviet Union to attain a predominant position in the world.

The countries of the industrial West, the United States in particular, have a vital interest in this ideological struggle, which may be more real in the long run than the threat of Soviet military aggression or nuclear confrontation.

Dealing with the Challenge

The ideological challenge of the Soviet Union involves much more than mere ideological arguments and propaganda techniques. It is multidimensional, and has political, economic, social, and military aspects. In our discussion of guerrilla warfare and terrorism, we touched on the political and military elements of the conflict (chapter 6). In chapter 10, our discussion of the problems facing the developing countries will highlight

Table 9-2
List of Marxist–Leninist Setbacks in the "Ideological" Conflict

Year	Case
1946	Soviet-backed rebellion in the Iranian province of Azerbaijan fails
1948	Soviet-backed insurgencies in India (Telengana) and Indonesia (Madium) fail
1949	Communist-led guerrilla campaign in Greece is crushed
1953	Communist-led (Huk) rebellion in the Philippines is put down
1960	Communist rebellion in Malaya defeated after twelve years
1962	Marxist-oriented rebels are defeated in the Congo
1962	Pro-Communists are ousted in Guiana
1963	Communist rebels are defeated in Venezuela
1965	Communist-led coup in Indonesia fails
1966	Communist-backed Nkrumah regime in Ghana is overthrown
1967	Insurgents under Marxist revolutionary leader Che Guevara are defeated in Bolivia
1968	Communist setbacks occur in Colombia, Sarawak, France
1971	Communist coup fails in the Sudan
1971	Marxist revolutionary agitation in Mexico and Brazil fails
1972	Marxist terrorists are crushed in Uruguay
1972	Soviet advisors are expelled from Egypt
1972	Marxist rebels are crushed in Sri Lanka
1975	Pro-Marxist coup is foiled in Portugal
1975	Mass arrests of Communists are made in Syria; Soviet-backed insurgents are defeated in Oman
1976	Pro-Soviet government is ousted in Peru
1977	Soviet advisors are expelled from Somalia
1983	Communist guerrillas are defeated in Thailand
1983	Removal of Marxist regime in Grenada is accomplished by United States forces

many of the economic and social factors that are relevant to the ideological struggle and can be exploited by Marxist-oriented revolutionaries.

To counter this multidimensional challenge, Western policies also must be multi-dimensional.

Use of Local Leaders. Any effort to combat the revolutionary and propaganda activities of Marxist-oriented groups in a given country must be undertaken primarily by local leaders. Foreigners cannot generate popular support and lead the effort; they can only assist the local leadership, and this they may have to do with discretion to avoid creating the impression that the local pro-Western leaders are foreign puppets.

Military Countermeasures. The military might of the United States is largely irrelevant in preventing revolutionary changes in the Third World countries. The American experience in Vietnam and the Soviet difficulties in Afghanistan indicate that, without strong political and emotional support by the local population for their own government and institutions, foreign military intervention is not effective in combating a local insurgency.

Military countermeasures can be effective if undertaken by the government of the target country *in conjunction* with social and economic measures that are likely to generate popular support. A military response becomes necessary when the revolutionary challenge takes the form of a protracted, guerrilla-type drive for power. Even then, success or failure will depend in large measure on the ability of the government to isolate the insurgents *politically*. As we pointed out in the discussion of guerrilla warfare, this type of conflict is above all political in nature and the outcome will depend on whether the government of the target country inspires public confidence.

Domestic Political Measures. To win public confidence and support, the government of the target country must show genuine concern about and take serious steps to remove or at least tone down social and economic cleavages that lead to alienation and discontent. In this regard, experience shows that a widely held belief in the country that the government is making a sincere effort to improve conditions is no less important than improvement itself. What measures will be most effective cannot be determined in the abstract or by a sweeping formula: conditions vary and so do the appropriate remedies. A government, however, that allows provocative disparities and inequities between rich and poor to go on unchecked may be paving the ground for revolutionary upheavals. Note that poverty is not as destabilizing as provocative ine-quality—poverty is relative. In the United States the *poverty line* is at $3,000 annual income; in India around $30! Discontent does not come from comparing one's economic conditions with those that prevail in another, faraway country; it comes from compari-sons with other socioeconomic groups *within* one's country.

Support for LDCs. Efforts to improve economic and social conditions require above all appropriate policies by the government of the target country. The success of such local initiatives, however, may depend on the assistance the wealthier countries can provide. Self-centered economic policies on their part may play into the hands of revolutionary groups. The OPEC members—especially conservative governments such as that of Saudi Arabia—did not serve their long-term interests by undercutting the economic development of many LDCs by increasing the price of oil. That the economic hardships now facing so many heavily indebted LDCs have not erupted into violent revolutionary upheavals shows that revolutionary agitation does not easily succeed and that adroit and realistic policies can effectively blunt the ideological weapon as an instrument of Soviet foreign policy. The refusal of the United States to sign the 1982 Convention on the Law of the Sea (because of its provisions granting the Third World countries a share in the benefits from the exploitation of mineral resources found on the ocean bed and the establishment of an international authority to control such mining) may be another illustration of an erroneous strategy. If the ideological conflict is the most pragmatic challenge facing the United States, policies that strengthen cooperation with the developing countries and help remove the conditions on which Marxist-oriented agitation thrives should form a cardinal feature of United States foreign policy.

Cultivating Relationships: Preventive Measures. The Soviet Union appears to be very conscious of the practical significance of the ideological conflict and takes advantage of every opportunity to cultivate relations with revolutionary groups abroad and, when conditions permit, even to encourage and assist their activities. In the West, the tendency is to react when a challenge is fairly obvious and advanced; preventive medicine is seldom practiced. There are several reasons for this approach.

1. Most of the measures that are needed to improve economic, social, and political conditions in target countries must be initiated and carried out primarily by their governments. The Western governments cannot force such measures on the local leaders. Even advice has to be given discreetly lest it offend the recipients.

2. The measures that the West can take may be in conflict with the interests of important domestic constituencies, especially those that are economic measures. Liberal trade policies, economic aid, commodity agreements, technology transfers, economic cooperation through multilateral or bilateral agreements, despite their long-term strategic utility, do not always receive wide support in the industrial Western countries. In fact, they often face subtle or overt opposition from economic groups that wish to protect their own particular interests.

3. Many Western governments—as well as the governments of many LDCs—tend to view the North–South dialogue as an adversary relationship rather than as a cooperative endeavor. The developing countries want improved access to the Western markets for their exports and would like much larger resource transfers on lenient, concessional terms. They also want a larger voice in the councils of major international economic institutions such as the IMF and the World Bank. To achieve these objectives, they call for a fundamental restructuring of the existing international trade and monetary system

under a New International Economic Order (NIEO). The United States and other industrial states do not favor such a drastic restructuring and prefer instead specific measures on a "case-by-case basis,"[3] mostly through bilateral, regional, or multilateral agreements, depending on the actual circumstances. While the more sweeping features of the NIEO may be unrealistic, a conscious effort to integrate the LDCs more closely into the international economic system (which we may note is *not* under Soviet control) is the most effective way for undercutting the expansion of Soviet influence and preventing the emergence of anti-Western, Marxist-oriented regimes.

4. Reliance on military instrumentalities has the advantage of being in line with traditional thinking. After all, for countless centuries, when all else failed, conflict was resolved by the sword. Western legislators who are reluctant to approve large outlays for economic aid or complex measures of economic cooperation seldom reject proposed expenditures for the military (box 9-1). Support for such expenditures is seen as a patriotic duty and usually has the concurrence of large and influential constituencies. Such constituencies are not often present in support of the subtle measures that are needed to combat the conditions that play into the hands of revolutionary activists, before conflict breaks out into the open.

Box 9-1
Economy and Defense

In fiscal year 1982, prime defense contracts—those over $10,000—pumped over $4 billion into the Virginia economy. This figure represents a $471 million increase over the previous year. Virginia ranked eighth of the fifty states in terms of its share of the total amount spent by the Department of Defense on prime contracts. Payments in wages and salaries to Virginians working as civilian employees of the departments and agencies of the Defense Department represented a further injection into the Virginia economy.

As a result, when defense appropriations come to the House floor, I am always supportive of the bulk of the programs necessary to the restoration of the national defense because the support of Northern Virginia is important to this effort. . . .

SOURCE: Excerpts from letter by U.S. Congressman Stan Parris of the Eighth District of the State of Virginia to his constituents, February 1984.

Despite these negative influences and attitudes, the importance of a broad economic, political, and ideological strategy to foster improved conditions in the developing countries and *to integrate them on an equitable basis into the international economic system* cannot be overemphasized.

The foregoing comments indicate that the Soviet threat is neither as potent nor as deadly as our preoccupation with it implies. On the other hand, the West certainly faces a challenge from a Soviet Union formally dedicated to an ideology that claims to hold the key to a future world to be erected on the ruins of capitalism. In this sense, the causes for the rivalry are real enough. However, the East–West conflict may be sustained for other, less obvious reasons related to its *utility*.

.... The Utility of the Conflict

On both sides of the East–West rivalry, we can identify elements that contribute to the perpetuation and the exacerbation of the conflict because they find it useful to them. This may appear to be a cynical statement, but those who are familiar with the inner workings of international politics will find it to be sound. The following illustrations may be instructive.

Soviet Motivations. A number of factors influence the utility of the conflict on the Soviet side:

1. The imperialist threat is a convenient excuse for repressive measures and economic shortcomings that might not be acceptable if that "threat" were to disappear.

2. Important segments of the ruling elite in the Soviet Union—party officials, military officers, managers of defense-oriented industries and scientific institutions, the officials of the security apparatus, and others—who derive material benefits personally from the perpetuation of the conflict would probably oppose and undermine (subtly, to be sure) any genuine effort to end the conflict. A leader seriously determined to seek such an end probably would be accused by a rival in the Politburo of betraying the cause of Marxism–Leninism, or even of being an agent of the "imperialists." Although the ordinary people certainly want peace, those in power find advantages in a protracted conflict, as long as its intensity can be controlled. This explains why the Soviet leaders are manifestly reluctant to push the rivalry to a point where it might ignite a nuclear war, yet they are equally unwilling to promote genuine accommodation.

3. Without the protracted rivalry and the specter of an imperialist threat, the Soviet control over Eastern Europe would have virtually no justification. The Soviet leaders have too many indications that the ordinary people in the countries of Eastern Europe are not happy with their governments and that an end to the rivalry could make

control even more difficult. The perpetuation of the rivalry also serves the interests of the local governing elites, whose privileges and power depend on the present state of affairs.

4. Soviet hopes to promote wars of liberation and Marxist-oriented revolutionary changes in the Third World will suffer in a climate of genuine peace. The revolutionary activists who now find in the Soviet Union a potential mentor will be left without sources of ideological inspiration and material support. For the Soviet leaders this aspect of ending the conflict will appear as an abdication of their claims to a superpower status for their country. No doubt the rest of the world will interpret such a development in a similar vein.

Western Motivations. In the United States and the Western nations in general, comparable considerations make the continuing rivalry useful and even necessary:

1. United States and West European cooperation has survived conflicting economic interests because every disagreement has been dwarfed by the overriding issue of the perceived Soviet threat. The same applies to the relations between the United States and Japan. In the absence of the Soviet challenge, the inevitable differences might have been less manageable.

2. The East–West rivalry contributes to national cohesion within the Western countries. It provides an intellectual and ideological focal point overshadowing political, economic, and social differences that otherwise might be disruptive.

3. The challenge of Marxism–Leninism to the democratic institutions highlights the superiority of these institutions and strengthens popular allegiance to them. Because of the incessant ideological attacks on these institutions, routine acceptance, which might result in their atrophy, is replaced by vigorous support and determined defense.

4. Although we may argue that the resources diverted to military and other efforts related to the East–West rivalry could be used to meet other needs, the fact remains that industries have grown to service the needs of defense and they now exert their own political influence in ways that tend to perpetuate the conflict. In the United States, and in other Western countries, many localities depend on military installations for their economic prosperity and efforts to eliminate such installations are strenuously resisted by the local people and their representatives. There are also influential public and private bureaucracies—the military, defense-oriented scientific entities, and the like—the survival and prosperity of which depend heavily on the perpetuation of the rivalry. Like their Soviet counterparts, these domestic entities in the West have a vested interest in a continuing rivalry provided the intensity of the conflict does not escalate to a

nuclear war. Although there are some strategists in the United States who speak of a *winnable* nuclear war (as we shall see in greater detail later in this chapter) their arguments are designed more to justify greater outlays for weapons than to advocate seriously a nuclear war.

The Military Dimension

Whatever the real or imagined causes for the East–West rivalry, both sides find it sufficiently serious to spend tremendous sums to maintain military forces of unprecedented destructive capacity. Collectively, the member countries of NATO and the Warsaw Pact spent more than $500 billion in 1983 on armaments and the military, and the total seems to grow larger every year, not only because of inflation but also in adjusted figures. With such emphasis on military means to keep the other side at bay, the East–West rivalry has acquired a military dimension that has now its own momentum, imperatives, and logic and in many ways overshadows all other aspects of the conflict (figure 9-1).

This is hardly surprising; the weapons possessed by both sides can literally obliterate the human race. Under the circumstances, there are legitimate fears that, regardless of the actual causes, a confrontation may escalate out of control—and then it will be too late for even historians to try to analyze the reasons that led to the clash.

The Preeminence of the Military Dimension

The peculiar preeminence of the military dimension is reflected not only in the vast sums of money spent on weapons but also in the tremendous amount of intellectual effort devoted to the development of new weapons and to the study of questions of strategy. One might argue that strategy and weaponry historically have been used most of the time to serve nonmilitary objectives such as territorial aggrandizement, plunder, personal ambitions, revenge, or the pursuit of glory. In the East–West rivalry it sometimes seems that the nonmilitary reasons for conflict often take the back seat while the military dimension moves to the center of the stage. The governments of the two protagonists spend more time worrying about the effectiveness of their military hardware and the wisdom of their strategies than about the nonmilitary (economic, political, ideological) aspects of their relationship. In the end, the military threat takes on a life of its own, dwarfing in the process the more mundane causes of the rivalry.[4] In view of the special significance and complexity of the military dimension, we must devote to it a considerable portion of our discussion of the East–West rivalry.

The Nuclear Equation

At dawn on July 16, 1945, the New Mexico desert rumbled as the first atomic bomb exploded with a blinding flash. Three weeks later, a B-29 bomber dropped an atomic bomb on Hiroshima. Three days after that, another atomic bomb was dropped on Nagasaki. The United States had at the time one more atomic bomb in its arsenal, although more were in production. This was the opening of a technological revolution in the development of weapons that by far exceeded anything achieved in the past.

Figure 9-1
Key United States bases abroad.

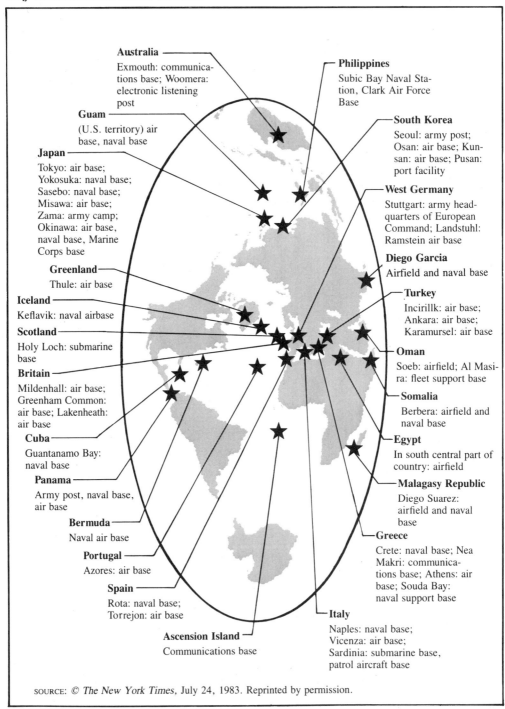

Australia
Exmouth: communications base; Woomera: electronic listening post

Guam
(U.S. territory) air base, naval base

Japan
Tokyo: air base; Yokosuka: naval base; Sasebo: naval base; Misawa: air base; Zama: army camp; Okinawa: air base, naval base, Marine Corps base

Greenland
Thule: air base

Iceland
Keflavik: naval airbase

Scotland
Holy Loch: submarine base

Britain
Mildenhall: air base; Greenham Common: air base; Lakenheath: air base

Cuba
Guantanamo Bay: naval base

Panama
Army post, naval base, air base

Bermuda
Naval air base

Portugal
Azores: air base

Spain
Rota: naval base; Torrejon: air base

Ascension Island
Communications base

Philippines
Subic Bay Naval Station, Clark Air Force Base

South Korea
Seoul: army post; Osan: air base; Kunsan: air base; Pusan: port facility

West Germany
Stuttgart: army headquarters of European Command; Landstuhl: Ramstein air base

Diego Garcia
Airfield and naval base

Turkey
Incirillk: air base; Ankara: air base; Karamursel: air base

Oman
Soeb: airfield; Al Masira: fleet support base

Somalia
Berbera: airfield and naval base

Egypt
In south central part of country: airfield

Malagasy Republic
Diego Suarez: airfield and naval base

Greece
Crete: naval base; Nea Makri: communications base; Athens: air base; Souda Bay: naval support base

Italy
Naples: naval base; Vicenza: air base; Sardinia: submarine base, patrol aircraft base

SOURCE: © *The New York Times*, July 24, 1983. Reprinted by permission.

Since that day, tremendously more powerful nuclear bombs and delivery systems that can span the oceans in minutes have revolutionized warfare and have raised fundamental questions about the rationale of war itself. A nuclear exchange between the United States and the Soviet Union would result in tens of millions of dead and incapacitated within a matter of hours or days in both countries; the destruction of their major urban and industrial centers; the radioactive contamination of their food and water supplies; the breakdown of government authority; and the end of their capacity to function as organized social entities. Such a war, obviously, cannot be regarded as "the continuation of politics by other means." No gains can possibly offset losses of such staggering magnitude.

Not surprisingly, both superpowers view their nuclear arsenals as a means of preventing war rather than as the instruments for military victory. Despite occasional statements by American or Soviet strategists giving the impression that a nuclear war is a realistic option, deterring the other side from seriously contemplating a nuclear confrontation has been and continues to be the primary objective of both the American and the Soviet policy makers.

The Strategy of Deterrence...............................

On the American side, the policy of deterrence is designed primarily to raise the level of potential damage to the Soviet Union to such a point that any Soviet gains from an expansionist venture will be overwhelmingly exceeded by the destruction that inevitably will be inflicted on Soviet society.

Figure 9-2
Nuclear buildup in the United States and the Soviet Union.

THE ARMS RACE		
Year in which Superpowers Acquired Weapons		
	United States	Soviet Union
Atomic Bomb	1945	1949
Intercontinental Bomber	1948	1955
Hydrogen Bomb	1954	1955
Intercontinental Ballistic Missile	1958	1957
Satellite in Orbit	1958	1957
Submarine Launched Ballistic Missile	1960	1968
Multiple Warhead	1966	1968
Anti-Ballistic Missile	1968	1972
Multiple Independently–Targetable Warhead	1970	1975
Long Range Cruise Missile	1982	?
Neutron Bomb	1983	?

SOURCE: "World Military and Social Expenditures," *The Washington Post*, May 27, 1984.

Because the Soviet Union now has a comparable capability to damage the United States, deterrence from the American viewpoint rests squarely on the ability of the American strategic forces to survive a Soviet attack, launch a counterattack, and penetrate Soviet defenses to inflict cataclysmic destruction. This is the essence of *second strike* capability.

.... Strategic Deterrence

No atomic or thermonuclear weapon has been exploded in war since 1945. Initially, the deterrence was political and psychological rather than strategic. Between 1945 and 1953, the United States had overwhelming superiority in the nuclear field. Until 1949, it had a monopoly of atomic weapons. Even after 1949, when the Soviet Union acquired atomic bombs, the U.S. Air Force was much stronger than its Soviet counterpart. The prevalent strategic view during those early years was that long-range bombers carrying atomic weapons could attack and defeat any nation hostile to the United States or any power threatening its vital interests. In theory, no country could risk the terrible devastation exemplified by the leveling of Hiroshima and Nagasaki. The outbreak of the Korean War in June 1950 shattered this certainty. Although the United States had the military means to annihilate the North Koreans by using atomic weapons—and this with virtual impunity given the Soviet limitations in delivery systems—no such action was taken by the Truman administration. The reasons were primarily political. World public opinion was against the use of atomic weapons. When President Truman, replying to a reporter in November 1950, said that "there has always been active consideration of [the bomb's] use," the reaction was very negative. In London, one-hundred Labour Members of Parliament signed a letter protesting the possibility of using the atomic bomb. Even Churchill expressed "disquiet" over the prospect.[5] The reluctance to use the "ultimate weapon"—Truman's assurances of "active consideration" notwithstanding— was not abandoned, even when the Chinese troops intervened massively in the war. When Eisenhower became president, discussions about a possible use of atomic weapons to end the war in Korea continued on a purely pragmatic basis, as shown by recently declassified documents.[6] Eventually, the war ended without the use of atomic weapons.

During the Eisenhower years (1953 to 1960) the United States continued to have clear superiority, especially in the means of delivery—despite Kennedy's allegations of a "missile gap" during the 1960 presidential campaign. The Soviet ability to attack the United States with nuclear weapons [by then both superpowers had developed thermonuclear (hydrogen) bombs] depended on a fairly small number of long-range aircraft, which would have to penetrate a complex warning and air defense system to reach their targets on American soil. The American strategy in those years was known as *massive retaliation*—a warning that an attack on the United States or its NATO allies would be countered with massive nuclear strikes against the aggressor. During the Eisenhower administration, Secretary of State John Foster Dulles coupled this strategy with a string of alliances with countries located around the Soviet heartland as part of a *containment* strategy designed to prevent further Soviet expansion. The Soviet Union, of course, branded this strategy *capitalist encirclement* and made every effort to undermine it by diplomatic means.

During the Truman and Eisenhower years, the Joint Chiefs of Staff and the National Security Council on several occasions discussed the military advantages of attacking the Soviet Union while the United States held a decisive superiority. However, as Eisenhower reflected in a 1956 entry in his diary: "Since this would not only violate national tradition, but would require rapid, totally secret congressional action and immediate implementation, it would appear impossible that any such thing would occur."[7]

In the 1960s, the strategy of massive retaliation was replaced by the doctrine of "strategic deterrence." The Soviet Union shifted its support to the so-called wars of liberation—usually guerrilla operations against colonial regimes or pro-Western governments in the underdeveloped nations of the world. It was hard to see how any of these military conflicts could be countered with the massive use of nuclear weapons. A threat is effective only if it is believable under the circumstances; massive retaliation against wars of liberation was not credible. The doctrine of strategic deterrence was equally inapplicable to lower-level, localized conflicts. Only a Soviet attack against the United States or NATO could possibly trigger a nuclear exchange. This was manifested during the ten years of the war in Vietnam. As in the Korean War, nuclear strength proved irrelevant.

Strategic deterrence came into play very successfully during the Cuban missile crisis. When the Soviet Union tried to install in Cuba medium-range missiles capable of striking American targets within minutes, the Kennedy administration used only conventional countermeasures but it made clear that it would resort to nuclear weapons if all other means failed to achieve the removal of the offensive missiles. The Soviet Union was forced to capitulate.

In the 1960s, the Soviet Union embarked on a serious drive to develop its nuclear weapons and delivery systems. Although the United States retained superiority in the accuracy of its delivery systems until the end of the decade, the Soviet Union made considerable strides in developing high-yield (throw-weight) nuclear bombs capable of destroying missile silos and other hardened facilities. The Soviets also improved the accuracy of their ICBMs, especially the SS-9, a very large, liquid-fueled missile. By 1970, both superpowers had a second strike capability against the other. The United States could no longer rely on strategic deterrence.

Mutual Deterrence

The new reality—both superpowers capable of inflicting devastating blows on each other—dictated a new strategy based on *mutual deterrence*. The possibility of mutual devastation is the foundation of mutual deterrence. At present, both the United States and the Soviet Union continue to have a *second strike capability,* despite continuing technical developments in the accuracy of delivery systems (missiles); the improvement of guidance systems; the use of several, independently targeted nuclear warheads on a single missile (MIRVs); the submarine-launched ballistic missiles (SLBMs); cruise missiles; reconnaissance satellites; fractional orbital bombardment systems (FOBS);[8] or other devices not publicly known. This means that although either superpower can launch a nuclear strike and inflict heavy damage on its opponent, neither is now capable of preventing a devastating *second strike* by the other. Even if we were to assume that the Soviet missiles could destroy all land-based strategic missiles on American soil, the other components of the strategic triad—the aircraft of the Strategic Air Command, consisting of approximately 80 B-52Ds, 165 B-52Gs, 90 B-52Hs, and 66 FB-111s, and the Poseidon and Trident nuclear-powered submarines carrying 544 SLBMs—could deliver such a catastrophic blow to the Soviet Union that any elation from the success of a first strike would be very short-lived.

The doctrine of mutual deterrence assumes that:

1. The top decision makers in the governments of both superpowers are rational individuals

2. No accidents or miscalculations will trigger a catastrophe

3. Both sides have the opportunity and willingness to engage in negotiations to defuse a crisis

4. Both sides are sufficiently and reliably informed about their mutual capabilities and intentions

Mutual deterrence also depends on the ability of the superpowers to monitor through electronic means the deployment of nuclear weapons and to detect any threatening preparations for war. The reconnaissance satellites have played a stabilizing role because of their extraordinary capabilities. Efforts by both superpowers either to neutralize the effectiveness or nonvulnerability of space satellites or to conceal the location of land-based ICBMs are likely to increase uncertainty and undermine mutual deterrence. When either superpower cannot be fairly sure what the other side is doing, the need to react swiftly (launch-on-warning) increases exponentially.

The strategy of mutual deterrence is still used, although some strategists have questioned its effectiveness. Under conditions of mutual deterrence, an increase in the number of warheads or improvements in the sophistication of certain systems do not alter the deterrent capability of either side provided that each side can deliver a second, devastating strike. In other words, the essence of mutual deterrence is the assured destruction of the aggressor. This *mutual assured destruction* (MAD) doctrine does not require that the arsenals of the two superpowers be equal: the element of superiority is virtually irrelevant. The key is that neither side has the capacity of eliminating the other's *retaliatory* capability. In the early 1970s, President Nixon spoke of *nuclear sufficiency,* a phrase that signaled a move away from the concept of nuclear superiority, which had remained at the core of United States strategic thinking since 1945. The doctrine of sufficiency implied also that because both superpowers had an oversupply of nuclear weapons, sufficient to deter each other effectively, an arms race to augment the existing arsenals made no sense; the additional expenditure would neither essentially alter the strategic balance nor increase the security of either side. This practical thinking led the governments of the two superpowers to conclude agreements designed to introduce some control over the further development of strategic weapons. The Antiballistic Missile Treaty (ABM) and the Strategic Arms Limitation Talks (SALT) agreements were the end products of these strategic considerations.

The Reagan administration, reflecting in this the views of its more conservative and defense-oriented constituencies, embarked on a costly defense program, claiming that the Soviet Union had achieved superiority in critical areas of strategic weaponry. Especially by improving the accuracy of its ICBMs, the Soviet Union had presumably gained the capability of destroying in a first strike most of the Titan and Minuteman land-based ICBMs.

American strategists urged the development of a new missile system dubbed the MX (missile experimental). Several modes of deployment were suggested, all designed to assure the survival of most of these missiles in the event of a first strike by the Soviet Union. Defense experts disagreed on the best deployment mode; some argued that it was virtually impossible to eliminate the vulnerability of these missiles; others pointed out that the possibility of the destruction of all land-based missiles in a single, massive Soviet attack was fairly remote for a number of technical reasons—such a strike would require a degree of coordination in launching the missiles that was nearly impossible to achieve. Moreover, the thirty minutes of flying time needed by the incoming missiles to reach their targets would allow time for launching most of the land-based U.S. missiles before they were destroyed by the Soviet warheads. Others pointed out that as long as the nuclear-armed submarines and the aircraft of the Strategic Air Command could deliver more than 1,500 nuclear warheads on Soviet targets (both military and civilian), a Soviet first strike would be suicidal regardless of its effect on the land-based missiles.

....War-Winning Strategy

In this connection, belligerent statements by superpower officials should be used with extreme caution. In 1983, for example, certain officials in the Reagan administration publicly stated:

> The Administration's objective within the current five-year plan is to
> build a nuclear deterrent that could survive in a protracted nuclear
> conflict and, in the long run, be capable of forcing the Soviet Union to
> end such a war in terms favorable to the United States.[9]

Such a strategy, of course, went beyond the level of deterrence and contemplated a protracted nuclear war and a *victory* against the Soviet Union. A *war-winning strategy* would require superiority, not mere sufficiency. It would also mean that the United States government was prepared to accept the devastation inevitable in a protracted nuclear conflict as the price for a victory over the Soviet Union. Assuming that the Soviet Union would not accept such nuclear inferiority on its part, the war-winning strategy would simply usher in a renewed arms race that brought no improvement in the security of either superpower.

The United States had the capability of "winning" a nuclear war in the 1950s and 1960s, but it deliberately refrained from using its atomic and nuclear weapons to pressure or blackmail the Soviet Union. In the 1970s, when the Soviet Union gained parity, mutual deterrence prevented the Soviet Union from embarking on any actions threatening vital American interests. As long as the realities of assured mutual destruction continue, the Soviet Union will have no incentive to initiate dangerous provocations. However, if the certainty of a second-strike capability (and the uncertainty of a nuclear response) is removed, the possibility of miscalculation, bluff, or blackmail by either side can expose the world to unnecessary and potentially disastrous risks. Mutual deterrence will be weakened and may even become irrelevant if further technological developments neutralize the surveillance systems, end the invulnerability of the nuclear submarines, or introduce new weapons or antimissile defense systems that will make a second strike impossible or ineffective, thus encouraging the strategic assumption that a nuclear war is *winnable*.

For this reason, the most cautious decision makers on both sides appear to concur that agreements designed to prevent the development of destabilizing weapons systems and to reduce the strategic arsenals are desirable and necessary. However, obstacles are still raised by vested interests, political pressures, and the controversies that accompany the detailed evaluation of specific weapons systems.

....A New Strategic Perspective

In this era of mutual deterrence, the officials who deal with the nuclear equation face, in addition, a basic distortion in traditional strategic thinking. For centuries, governments amassed armies and weapons to conquer neighbors, create empires, or defend their domain against hostile intruders. Any advance in weaponry or military tactics promised tactical or strategic advantages and greater success in war. In the nuclear age, the strategic weapons cannot be used to decide a conflict, to gain territory, or to impose the will of a superpower on other weaker states.

Throughout history, potential opponents did not discuss their respective arsenals; they did not set limits to their efforts to improve their war-making capabilities. Now, the negotiators for the SALT agreements or the new round of START talks are asked to do precisely that. It is hard for modern theorists to abandon the traditional mode of strategic thinking (which saw weapons in terms of "combat-related" advantage and victory on the battlefield) and embrace a strategy in which the weapons are most useful when they are not used!

However difficult it may be for traditionally thinking decision makers to adjust to the novel realities of the nuclear age, such adjustment is not impossible, as the SALT I and SALT II and other arms limitations agreements testify.

.... The Credibility of Deterrence

It is a historical fact that the strategy of deterrence in its various configurations has prevented a war between the two superpowers and their allies. Nevertheless, certain strategists raise disturbing questions about deterrence:

- Is the doctrine of mutual assured destruction (MAD) a practical foundation for deterrence?

- Will an American president risk the extermination of millions of United States citizens if faced with a determined Soviet pressure in the absence of effective means to protect the land-based missiles or to provide realistic protection to the American cities?

- Will an American threat to unleash a nuclear attack restrain the Soviet leadership when they, too, can deliver a devastating blow on the United States? In other words, will they believe such a threat and call off their aggressive move?

The corollary of this line of strategic reasoning is that unless the United States has an effective defense against a Soviet attack (and the ability to inflict on the Soviet Union punishment that far exceeds anything the Soviets can do to the United States), the threat of nuclear retaliation will not be believed and therefore it will not be effective. The implication is that for the strategy of deterrence to be effective, it must be based on the assured survival of the U.S. nuclear arsenal.

Assured Survival

Assured survival refers primarily to the United States land-based missiles, which are currently vulnerable to a Soviet counterforce[10] nuclear attack. (*Counterforce attack* is a nuclear strike directed primarily against missile silos, not against civilian targets.) Some strategists believe this vulnerability gives the Soviets a first strike capability.

A first strike capability is meaningful only if the attack deprives the victim of second strike capability. The Soviet Union could be regarded as having a first strike capability if the United States relied only on its land-based launchers (assuming, of course, that the Soviet Union can destroy them all in one grand sweep). However, the United States has at the present time (1983) approximately 9,850 warheads with 3,505 total megaton yield in its arsenal. (This megaton yield equals the explosive force of 3,500,000,000 tons of TNT or the yield of 159,000 atomic bombs of the type dropped on Hiroshima). Of these, approximately 1,650 warheads are carried by the United States nuclear submarines. In addition, the B-52s of the Strategic Air Command are being equipped with air-launched cruise missiles (ALCMs), which can be launched far away from the Soviet airspace and antiaircraft defense systems. The cruise missiles are small and can easily avoid satellite detection. They have their own built-in guidance system, including a highly accurate target identification system, and because they fly beneath the range of conventional radar detection systems they can penetrate the Soviet airspace undetected. Even without these awesome additions to the American Triad, it would take the missiles on only four Poseidon-class submarines to devastate over one-hundred Soviet cities. Even if a Soviet counterforce strike on the Titan and Minuteman III missiles were totally successful, the other two elements in the strategic Triad—aircraft and submarines—could deliver in a second strike more than 300 bombs of one-megaton yield each on Soviet cities. Each one-megaton-yield reentry vehicle (RV) can destroy a city the size of Detroit, killing instantly over 460,000 people and injuring up to 600,000. The Soviet Union does not even have 300 cities with 1,000,000 inhabitants. Virtually every major urban center in the Soviet Union could be pulverized. Given that such destruction is a distinct possibility we may question the utility of any Soviet attempt to destroy in a first strike the land-based strategic forces of the United States.

Certain strategists and government officials in the United States do not agree that a nuclear war will be so devastating and they claim that even a *protracted nuclear war* can be *survived* by enough people to achieve *victory* and rebuild the nation. It is hard to calculate precisely the effects of a nuclear war; for obvious reasons there are no true experts on the subject and no past experience to draw on. Our only experience was the bombing of Hiroshima and Nagasaki, and the two explosions there cannot provide valid guidance: the devices used were of a fairly low yield and, however devastating to the two cities, they left the rest of Japan untouched and therefore able to provide care for the survivors.

The logical corollary of a war-winning strategy is that the United States must have the capacity to reduce with its first strike the Soviet retaliatory capabilities to a point that a Soviet counterattack will inflict on the United States only *tolerable* damage, thus allowing the United States to impose its terms on a devastated Soviet Union. This war-winning strategy is seen as the proper replacement for the doctrine of mutual assured destruction, which is viewed as lacking in credibility and realism.

The advocates of a war-winning strategy as a new foundation for deterrence are in effect trying to restore the strategic equation that existed in the 1950s and early 1960s when the United States was fairly immune to a Soviet nuclear attack. A return to such an "updated" version of massive retaliation is no longer feasible, however. Both superpowers have the capacity of delivering devastating blows to one another, whereas neither has the means to protect its territory and its people from the effects of a nuclear attack. Nor is there any indication that such defensive measures will become available and effective in the foreseeable future.

Even if such defensive systems were feasible, they would be destabilizing, especially when combined with superior attack systems on one side. No defense was ever so effective as to render totally irrelevant the offensive means of the other side. In addition, the record of the past thirty years conclusively proves that every American advance in the development of strategic weapons was soon matched by the Soviet Union and vice versa. In the end, both sides are likely to reach the point when a *first use* will appear as the only way to blunt the strategic forces of the other side and reduce the effects of a second strike. This would lead to a launch-on-warning strategy, cutting down even further the time for verification or consultation.

The launch-on-warning doctrine may be inching already into United States strategic thinking. Undersecretary of Defense Richard DeLauer said in November 1982: "We can fly the MX out before [the Soviets] can fly their missiles in."

The principal danger of a war-winning strategy, as opposed to the MAD doctrine, is that technological innovations on both sides will increase the incentive to launch first; more accurately, they will increase the penalties for *not* launching first. A preemptive strike will become not only tempting but imperative. In the face of these realities, we may question whether it is realistic and beneficial to discard the strategy of deterrence based on MAD as obsolete and replace it with a strategy of "winning" even a protracted nuclear war. The major advantage of the current doctrine of MAD as the basis for mutual deterrence is that both sides fear the dangers of uncontrollable escalation and are uncertain as to each other's reaction: this uncertainty is the foundation of deterrence.

At the present time, both sides have second strike weapons systems that are virtually invulnerable. If technological developments lead to *mutual vulnerability* of their second strike systems, each side will have a strong motivation to shoot first rather than wait to retaliate. This would be the most dangerous and unstable of all possible worlds, increasing the risks of mutual devastation and in no way strengthening the security of the United States.

.... Deterrence and Vulnerability

Weapons that are vulnerable to an adversary's attack cannot be convincing as the means for deterring such an attack. For a number of years, the vulnerability of land-based ICBMs has been the focal point of a strategic debate in the United States. In the early 1980s, the Reagan administration spoke of a *window of vulnerability*. It implied that the Soviet Union had the capacity to destroy most of the land-based U.S. ICBMs in a surprise nuclear strike. The further implication was that this *window* had to be *closed* quickly. Whether such a window actually existed and whether the land-based missiles could indeed be made invulnerable to a Soviet attack remained open questions.

Vulnerability, of course, is not a new development. Some of the strategic forces of both superpowers have been vulnerable to a surprise attack by the other side since the early 1950s. In fact, up to the end of the 1950s, the Soviet strategic forces were relatively more vulnerable in view of the superiority of the U.S. aircraft of the Strategic Air Command (SAC) both in terms of quality and in the number of aircraft. With the advent of the ICBMs at the end of the 1950s, the Soviet Union acquired a limited capacity to destroy some U.S. strategic forces in a surprise attack, but the Soviet delivery systems lacked the pin-point accuracy required for a truly effective first strike. With almost one-third of the SAC aircraft kept continuously in the air, the United States had at its disposal tremendous retaliatory capabilities throughout the 1960s, regardless of the results of a surprise nuclear attack. In addition, with the development of the nuclear submarines capable of carrying initially the Polaris and later the Poseidon missiles, the United States acquired a virtually invulnerable system as part of a triad comprising the SAC aircraft, the land-based Titan and Minuteman ICBMs, and the submarine-launched ballistic missiles (SLBMs). Even the introduction of multiple independently targeted reentry vehicles (MIRVs) (in effect missiles carrying several warheads that can be directed to different targets once the missile has reached its destination) first by the United States and soon after by the Soviet Union in the 1970s did not radically alter the equation, as the possession of MIRVs by only the Soviet Union might have done during the previous decade. Although the land-based Titan and Minuteman missiles were admittedly vulnerable to a Soviet surprise attack, the other two legs of the triad continued to provide the United States with retaliatory capabilities of cataclysmic proportions.

Whatever the varied views on the extent of vulnerability or the prospects and the methods of defense, the land-based missiles of both superpowers are vulnerable and will remain so for the foreseeable future. Of course, it may be technologically possible to

Table 9-3
Soviet Nuclear Stockpile (1984)[1]

System	Launchers	Force Loadings	Total Warheads[2]	Additions since 1979[2]	Remarks
Strategic:					
ICBMs					
SS-11 Mod 1	100	100	200	0	Down 30 from 1983
Mod 2/3	420	422–540	844–1354	some	As many as 60 Mod 3 deployed
SS-13 Mod 2	60	60	60–120	0	
SS-16	some	some	some	0	None deployed according to U. S. Air Force
SS-17 Mod 3	150	600	750–1200	600–1200	Full MIRV assumed; some single RV deployed
SS-18 Mod 4	308	3080	3388–6160	3080–6160	Full MIRV assumed
SS-19 Mod 3	360	2160	2520–4320	2160–4320	Full MIRV assumed; some single RV deployed
	1398	6422–6540[3]	8362–13354	5840–11680	358–522 up from 1983 estimates
SLBMs					
SS-N-5	45	45	45	0	Down 15 from 1983
SS-N-6 Mod 1/2	368	368	368–736	0	Down 16 from 1983; in production
SS-N-8 Mod 1/2	292	292	292–584	0	In production
SS-N-17	12	12	12–24	0	In production
SS-N-18 Mod 1/3	224	1568	1792–3136	1120	Full MIRV assumed; in production
SS-N-20	40	360	360–720	360–720	Up 180 from 1983; full MIRV assumed; in production
	981	2645	2869–5245	1480–1840	944 up from 1983 estimates
Bombers					
Tu-22M *Backfire*	130	390	390–650	249–498	SALT assumes 4 weapons per bomber
Tu-95 *Bear* A/B/C/G	115	200–210	370–420	5–10	30 *Bear A*; 85 *Bear B/C/G*.
Mya-4 *Bison*	45	45	45–90	0	
	290	635–645	805–1170	254–508	

1. Based on information in DoD, SMP 1984 and other DoD/NATO documents. Full documentation is available from the authors.
2. Total warheads based on full MIRV force loading, plus 1 reload/spare per launcher. Variation depending upon the breakdown of modifications on the reload missiles.
3. DIA states that current force loading is actually below 6400, taking into consideration actual single warhead deployments.

Table 9-3 (*continued*)
Soviet Nuclear Stockpile (1984)[1]

System	Launchers	Force Loadings	Total Warheads[2]	Additions since 1979[2]	Remarks
ABM					
ABM-1B *Galosh*	32+	32–64	34–64	some	(Antiballistic missiles) New missiles may have been deployed
Theater:					
Tac Air					
Tu-16 *Badger*	316	316–948	316–948	0	(Tactical aircraft) SALT assumes 2 weapons per plane
Tu-22 *Blinder*	139	139–278	139–556	0	
Tactical Fighters	1795–2545	2495–3245	2495–5790	1100–1850	
	2250–3000	2950–4471	2950–7294	1100–1850	
Naval Aviation					
Tu-22M *Backfire*	105	315	315–525	268	SALT assumes 4 weapons per *Backfire*
Tu-16 *Badger A*	34	34	68	0	SALT assumes 2 weapons per other planes
Badger C/G	245	245–735	245–1225	0	
Tu-22 *Blinder A*	39	78–117	78–234	0	
Tu-142 *Bear F*	51	51–102	102	0	
Be-12 *Mail*	94	94	94–188	0	
	568	817–1397	902–2342	268	
LRINF					(Long-range intermediate nuclear forces)
SS-4	224	224	224	0	Down 8 from 1983
SS-20	378	1134	1134–2268	822–1824	Up 165 from 1983
	602	1358	1358–2492	822–1824	
Battlefield					
SS-12/22/23/SCUD	650–975	650–975	650–1950	150–162	SS-22/23 newly deployed
FROG 7/SS-21	744	744	1488–2232	150+	SS-21 newly deployed
152-mm T/SP	600–900	600–900	600–1800	600–900	180-mm nuclear may be deployed
203-mm/240-mm	300–450	300–450	300–900	300–450	
SS-C-1b	10–100	10–100	10–100	0	One coastal division deployed

(*table continues*)

Table 9-3 *(continued)*
Soviet Nuclear Stockpile (1984)[1]

System	Launchers	Force Loadings	Total Warheads[2]	Additions since 1979[2]	Remarks
Land-Based SAM	84–990	84–990	84–990	84–990	SA-2s at Front level thought nuclear; SA-1/3/5/10 also possible
ADM	?	some	some	?	(Atomic demolition munitions)
	2388–4159	2388–4159	3132–7972	1334–2652+	
Sea-Launched: **ASCM**					(Anti-ship cruise missiles)
SS-N-1/3 A/B/C	313	313	318–353	0	In production; 6-9 SS-N-1 deployed
SS-N-7	96	96	96.	0	In production
SS-N-9	122	122	122	32	In production
SS-N-12	64	64	64–112	48	In production
SS-N-19	88	88	88	88	In production
SS-N-22	40	40	40	40	In production
	723	723	688–811	208	
ASW					(Antisubmarine weapons)
SS-N-14/15	314	314	314–324	38–46	14 SS-N-15 deployed
SUW-N-1	12	12	10–20	12	
	326	326	324–344	50–58	
AAW					(Antiaircraft weapons)
SA-N-6	20	20	20–160	20–160	Aboard 1 *Slava*, 2 *Kirov* cruisers
TOTAL STOCKPILE	**9,578– 12,099**	**18,316– 22,316**	**21,442– 41,248**	**11,385– 21,048**	

SOURCE: *Arms Control Today*, Vol. 14, No. 5, June 1984.

decrease vulnerability to some extent, but the cost both economically and politically may be prohibitive, as the disagreements over the "basing mode" for the MX and over Reagan's Strategic Defense Initiative (SDI) have amply shown.

Currently most experts accept the vulnerability of the land-based missiles (including the MX) as a given. In May 1983, a report submitted to the U.S. Congress by the Pentagon estimated that by 1989 the Soviet Union could have so many accurate nuclear warheads that as many as 99 percent of American land-based missiles could be destroyed by "a well-executed Soviet first strike." More specifically, the report (which was prepared by the Air Force) stated that the "Soviets probably possess the capability to destroy almost all of the 1,047 U.S. ICBM silos, using only a portion of their own ICBM forces."

Although the land-based missiles may be theoretically as vulnerable as the report claims, these predictions cannot be properly evaluated without reference to the overall *composition* of the U.S. strategic arsenal and the *political* and *technical* problems involved in a *counterforce first strike;* that is a Soviet missile attack directed almost exclusively on strategic military targets (mainly the ICBM silos), not on population centers.

Composition

For the remainder of this decade and even into the 1990s, the U.S. strategic forces will consist of land-based missiles (the present Titan and Minuteman, and possibly the planned ten-warhead MX or the smaller one-warhead Midgetman, still on the drawing board); submarine-launched ballistic missiles (SLBMs), with the more advanced Trident class coming increasingly into service; and long-range aircraft (the existing B-52s and possibly the B-1 or the Stealth) armed with air-launched cruise missiles (ALCMs).

One advantage of this composition is its *diversity,* not only in terms of basing modes (land, sea, air) but also in terms of *penetration* modes and *endurance* (the ability to pass through enemy defenses and the ability to remain "usable" over a long period after a nuclear war has started). As a result of the diversity of the arsenal, even a surprise attack capable of wiping out in one blow 99 percent of the land-based missiles would not deprive the United States of its second strike capability.

The second advantage of the present composition is its *redundancy*. The different weapons systems have overlapping missions and capabilities. Even if one portion of the U.S. strategic force were to be eliminated or rendered incapable of carrying out its assigned mission, other weapons systems will be able to fulfill theirs. The retaliatory capabilities of the surviving systems would be more than adequate to inflict unimaginable devastation on the Soviet Union.

The third element that must be taken into account in any discussion of vulnerability is the destructive capacity of the weapons. Each leg of the triad—even a fraction of each—possesses destructive capabilities sufficient to inflict devastating losses on the other side. Because it is technically impossible for the Soviet Union to eliminate in a single blow the entire strategic arsenal of the United States, the evident vulnerability of the land-based missiles is politically and strategically of questionable relevance and cannot be used effectively by the Soviet Union to blackmail the United States into accepting undesirable changes in the status quo.

There is one more feature of the current strategic triad that affects the reality of vulnerability: *synergy*. The combination of forces is more effective than the statistical sum of the parts. Each leg of the triad has different characteristics, which require a different mode of attack by the Soviet strategic forces. A massive counterforce strike "out of the blue" (in a sort of nuclear Pearl Harbor) cannot succeed because of the different elements involved and the different reaction modes of the various elements in each leg of the triad. An attack on one element will trigger the activation of other elements before they can be eliminated. For example, Soviet ICBMs directed against land-based U.S. ICBMs require a flight time of approximately thirty minutes. If such an attack were in progress, the SAC aircraft would have more than twenty minutes lead-time to take off and become invulnerable. On the other hand, if Soviet submarines, poised close to the American shores, were to strike the SAC bases, the flight of the Soviet SLBMs would take only ten minutes, thus revealing that a surprise attack is in progress long before the ICBMs reach their targets. This would give sufficient time to launch the U.S. ICBMs before the silos were hit by the incoming Soviet ICBMs. In short, a first strike against the land-based missiles, however possible it may appear theoretically—and the 1983 Air Force report seems to imply such capability—loses a great deal of its practical validity when examined in the overall context of the strategic triad.

Political and Technical Aspects

The vulnerability of the land-based missiles also must be assessed in conjunction with the political realities. If a *surprise* attack will not have the effect that could possibly justify it (and we explained why it would not), a nuclear exchange is more likely to occur after a period of mounting confrontation. Even a few days of crisis will set in motion steps leading to a high level of readiness (with at least most of the SAC bombers on alert or in the air and most of the submarines poised for missile launching). In other words, the deterioration of the political climate will act in itself as a signal for taking the preparatory steps needed to reduce vulnerability and assure retaliation.

The vulnerability of the land-based missiles also must be assessed in terms of the purely technical problems involved in a counterforce strike. Considering that both the targets and the attacking missiles are located over different areas, calling for different flight times to cover the corresponding distances, it will take a degree of split-second timing that most experts agree is difficult to achieve under combat conditions. It also appears that if several warheads arrive simultaneously over a target they may destroy each other; more accurately, the first exploding warhead may destroy not only the missiles on the ground but also other incoming warheads destined for nearby targets (called *fratricide* by weapons specialists). Some experts have further pointed out that it is one thing to test *one missile* and reach a point with admirable accuracy and another to launch simultaneously enough missiles to destroy in one fell swoop 1,042 land-based ICBMs.

The vulnerability of elements of the U.S. strategic arsenal thus does not affect the validity of deterrence because it does not—and there is no indication that it will in the foreseeable future—assure the Soviet Union that it can reduce to acceptable levels the devastation it would experience in retaliation for a first strike.

....Vulnerability of Other Targets

Vulnerability is not limited to the strategic forces. The population centers, the major industrial and energy installations, and the conventional forces of the United States and of the Soviet Union are extremely vulnerable to nuclear attack. There is no indication that effective protection can be devised in this decade or in the next. The futility of defense was recognized by both superpowers in 1972 when they signed the Antiballistic Missile (ABM) Treaty.

Numerous studies have shown that there are no practical ways to protect effectively these targets from incoming nuclear warheads. The evacuation of cities within a few hours or even days under conditions conducive to panic is an unrealistic option. Even if evacuation were possible, the radioactivity from such a massive deluge of nuclear explosions could reach even those who were able to escape the immediate effects of the blast. Moreover, the physical destruction of urban and industrial centers will disintegrate the country's economic, governmental, and social fabric.

The C^{3}I System

Another important sector that is vulnerable to a nuclear attack is the so-called strategic command, control, communications, and intelligence system—the C^{3}I, in Pentagon parlance. This C^{3}I system is regarded as the weakest link in the United States deterrence structure. Basically speaking, the C^{3}I system enables the president of the United States to control and direct the actions of the strategic forces. In time of crisis or imminent attack, the president needs absolutely reliable information on which to base his or her decisions, and also the means to communicate those decisions to the appropriate military authorities so the desired action can be taken in the form and at the time determined by the president.

During the years of the massive retaliation doctrine, the United States needed:

1. *Sensors* to detect and verify that an attack on the United States was in progress

2. *Command centers* to evaluate the sensor data

3. *Communication links* to connect the sensors and the command centers with the president and the other appropriate authorities, and links to connect the decision makers with the strategic forces

During the 1950s and 1960s, the U.S. C^{3}I system was based on the assumption that the U.S. nuclear forces should be able to respond quickly in the event of a Soviet attack. To assure such swift, massive retaliation, the C^{3}I system had the mission of:

1. Providing *early warning* to alert decision makers and give them sufficient time to react

2. Enabling the president to make a decision on retaliatory action as early as possible and to transmit such a decision as effectively and as quickly as possible to the strategic forces for implementation

3. Providing the means of directing the SAC bombers to take off toward their assigned targets

4. Ensuring safeguards against unauthorized action by the strategic forces (fail-safe)

These tasks of the C^{3}I reflected a strategic doctrine that focused essentially on a massive retaliatory attack on the entire Soviet target system (both military and civilian).

In 1974, the Pentagon modified its basic strategic doctrine to provide the president with additional choices short of a full-fledged retaliation. The rationale was that Moscow could be deterred more effectively if the United States had the ability to respond at different levels of escalation. This shift to what could be called a *doctrine of controlled escalation* placed different requirements on the C³I system. The sensors, in addition to providing early warning, would have to establish the type and extent of attack to enable the president to decide on the size of retaliatory action and the set of targets appropriate to the initial strike. The system also was required to have the capability of monitoring and reporting the status of the surviving U.S. forces. Finally, because the response was to be initially limited, the president should have the means of communicating not only with allies but also with the Soviet leaders to prevent further escalation. In 1980, President Carter signed Presidential Directive 59 (PD-59), which reflected this doctrine of controlled escalation, and which sought to enhance deterrence by presenting the Soviet leaders with the fact that the U.S. government retained the option to respond to different types of attack by launching large-scale or limited retaliatory strikes, and to conduct protracted nuclear exchanges if necessary to deny the Soviet Union of victory. This approach, labeled *countervailing strategy,* placed even greater demands on the C³I system. Not only should the early warning facilities survive but the command structure also should be able to retain its effectiveness over a much longer period, to accommodate the requirements of a protracted nuclear war and to continue functioning well beyond the ordering of an initial response to an attack. In addition, the C³I system should have the capability to verify and assess the damage already inflicted on Soviet targets, to enable the U.S. forces to direct additional blows at undamaged targets. This meant that under the requirements of the countervailing strategy, the C³I system should be able to *survive* and *endure,* at least to a degree necessary to perform its most essential functions.

There is no indication that the present C³I system can be made invulnerable to a massive nuclear attack. Heavily dependent as it is on electronically transmitted signals, it is vulnerable to the effects of nuclear explosions on such electronic transmissions even when facilities are not physically destroyed by a direct hit. The overall vulnerability of the system can be reduced, but it cannot be eliminated. The Soviet C³I system is no less vulnerable to enemy action.

Extended Deterrence

Our discussion on the effectiveness of mutual deterrence has focused primarily on one of the two key problems that currently preoccupy American strategic thinking: the so-called counterforce problem—the vulnerability of U.S. land-based ICBMs to a concerted Soviet attack. The other central issue of major concern to U.S. and NATO strategists and political leaders deals with the credibility of *extended deterrence*.

The principal objective of extended deterrence is to prevent a Soviet attack by conventional or nuclear forces against Western Europe or Japan—and, one may argue, against the oil-producing countries in the Middle East, under the Carter Doctrine—or a Soviet effort to force major concessions on the United States by threatening such action against those regions. The implication of the extended deterrence strategy is that any

Soviet action threatening seriously the status quo in those key areas is likely to lead to U.S. nuclear retaliation against the Soviet Union.

Credibility of the Strategy

In recent years, some strategists have voiced doubts about the willingness of U.S. leaders to use nuclear weapons in the event of a Soviet attack or a serious threat against the key areas. Such concerns are not new. The credibility of the U.S. commitment to defend those countries was questioned even during the 1950s. Such doubts did not receive wide acceptance in those early years because, until the late 1960s, the United States enjoyed a degree of superiority that would have enabled the U.S. government to confront effectively and without excessive risk any Soviet threat directed against Western Europe or Japan. In the 1970s, however, the Soviet Union gained parity with the United States in strategic nuclear forces, raising serious questions with regard to the credibility of extended deterrence. The fear has been expressed that the United States may be inclined to separate the conflict on Allied territory from an attack on its own soil, and accept a Soviet pledge that no Soviet strategic weapons will be used against American targets unless the United States uses its own strategic weapons against the Soviet Union. This is known among strategists as the problem of *decoupling*.

Credibility Remedies

Those who have raised doubts about the credibility of extended deterrence do not agree on the remedies. One line of reasoning holds that the United States is not likely to use medium-range or strategic weapons to defend Western Europe without first reestablishing the conditions of supremacy it previously enjoyed in strategic weapons and without first improving the survivability of its nuclear arsenal against a Soviet counterforce strike. In this view, only if the punishment to be inflicted on the Soviet Union were to exceed by far anything the Soviets could inflict on the United States would Moscow see the strategy of extended deterrence as credible and realistic.

The logical corollary of this argument is that the United States must solve the counterforce problem by making its land-based ICBMs invulnerable to a Soviet first strike. The inability to assure a high degree of invulnerability for the MX has revealed that a solution to the counterforce problem is not in sight. As efforts in this direction have been frustrated by technical and political problems, certain strategists have revived proposals for an extensive system of antiballistic missiles (ABMs) for the defense of the missile silos. Such a program, needless to say, would require a repudiation of the ABM Treaty by the United States. President Reagan's Strategic Defense Initiative, which apparently envisions non-nuclear means for the destruction of incoming missiles, is not expected to become a reality soon.

Other strategists argue that a more likely scenario evolving from a Soviet thrust against the United States' allies will include gradually escalating countermeasures—conventional forces, battlefield atomic weapons, theater nuclear forces (TNFs),[11] and finally strategic weapons. The outcome of the conflict, they say, will depend on *escalation dominance* by the United States—that is, on the ability to "win" at each level—and on a Soviet perception that the United States possesses and is prepared to take advantage of this ability. They add that escalation dominance on the part of the United States may require the massive deployment of SDI means to defend cities as well as ICBM silos, in conjunction with a substantial improvement in the ability of U.S. strategic and TNF forces to destroy most Soviet forces in a first strike. The advocates of this strategy justify such a tremendous buildup of forces by saying that without it, U.S. political leaders, caught in an escalation of tensions and threats at a time of severe crisis, and being aware of their forces' vulnerabilities, may be inclined to make serious concessions to avoid a nuclear exchange. The fear, in other words, is not so much that the Soviets will actually unleash their missiles but that they may "win" a confrontation without firing a shot. These strategists further argue that the likelihood of such a surrender is greater if the Soviet pressure does not involve directly the United States; that is, any U.S. concessions will be at the expense of its allies.

Other strategists argue that whether the United States could develop the type of defense envisaged by Reagan remains open to question in view of the tremendous technical problems involved, not to mention the crippling costs. Besides, the Soviet Union would undoubtedly match such defensive measures; the entire exercise will only usher in a new round in the arms race without buying more security or more-effective deterrence. These strategists add that, assuming a credibility problem exists with regard to extended deterrence, the most effective way to deal with it is by modernizing the TNF weapons in Europe and by maintaining and improving the diversity and capabilities of the strategic triad. Extended deterrence, they argue, depends on the many uncertainties a Soviet government contemplating aggression in Europe must confront. First of all, there is no assurance that a conventional attack will not escalate to the use of battlefield atomic weapons; in fact, the use of such weapons is an integral part of NATO defense planning. Once the barrier that has so far averted the use of nuclear weapons in war is broken, escalation to medium-range weapons and eventually to strategic weapons cannot be ruled out with any degree of certainty. If such an exchange is unleashed, the Soviet Union will be exposed to annihilation in the absence of any effective defense. Can the Soviet leaders seriously assume that the United States will concede the loss of Western Europe without taking countermeasures? Such a concession would reveal to the world that the United States is no match for the Soviet Union. The rise of the Soviet Union to worldwide preeminence would be inevitable. But if the United States takes the necessary steps to avert such a disastrous outcome, the risk of escalation becomes very real.

It is the risk of nuclear war itself that will deter any Soviet attack on Western Europe or Japan, or even any political pressure carrying with it the serious risk of nuclear war. In other words, extended deterrence is an integral part of the overall strategy of deterrence; its credibility rests on the ability of the United States to deter an attack on itself by maintaining assured destruction capabilities. In brief, this view holds that the credibility of extended deterrence rests primarily on political, not technological, considerations. The Soviet leaders will not press for a change in the status quo as long as they perceive the potential cost to themselves as exceeding by far any potential gains. Under current conditions, the U.S. leaders have the necessary cards to call a Soviet bluff without being forced to make damaging concessions; the Soviet leaders are not unaware of this.

Nuclear Arms Control ....

Although at the present time mutual deterrence remains credible despite the reservations discussed in the preceding pages, the unceasing developments in mass destruction weapons and auxiliary systems tend to increase uncertainty and instability. This is a problem that affects the security of both sides. Not surprisingly, for more than twenty years both superpowers have taken steps to scale down uncertainty and instability by applying mutually agreed restraints on the types, numbers, and capabilities of their nuclear arms.

....The First Treaties

The first major step was taken in 1963, eight months after the Cuban missile crisis, which had brought the two superpowers closer to a nuclear war than they had ever been. In June 1963, the United States, the Soviet Union, and Britain signed a Limited Test Ban Treaty, which prohibited all nuclear tests except those conducted underground. Four years later, the superpowers signed a treaty that banned the placement of nuclear weapons in space. The following year they signed the Treaty on the Non-Proliferation of Nuclear Weapons (which has since been ratified by 116 countries), realizing that in a world rife with nations hostile to one another the possession of nuclear weapons by many governments would expose the world—and themselves—to unacceptable risks.

.... SALT I

Steps initiated the same year to limit the strategic arsenals of the two superpowers came to a halt following the Soviet invasion of Czechoslovakia in August 1968. The process was revived three years later under President Richard M. Nixon and his policy of *détente*, which was designed to lower tensions and expand trade, scientific, and cultural relations between the United States and the Soviet Union. After fairly long and complex negotiations, the two governments signed the first Strategic Arms Limitation Treaty (SALT I) in May 1972.

In 1974, President Gerald R. Ford met with the Soviet leader Leonid Brezhnev in Vladivostok and agreed on the general guidelines for a second round of talks to reach a new SALT pact to last until 1985. The key element in their understanding was that both sides should have equal numbers of strategic missile launchers.

.... SALT II

When the negotiations started, a number of disagreements arose over the proper classification of certain weapons systems that did not fit neatly into the definition of "strategic launchers." The American side, for example, wanted to include in the total number of launchers the Soviet aircraft known in the West as Backfire, a swept-wing aircraft designed primarily for missions against Europe or China. It could conceivably reach the United States, but only on a one-way mission with no capability to return to base. The Soviets insisted that the Backfire bomber could not be regarded as a strategic weapon. On their part, the Soviet negotiators wanted to place restrictions on U.S. cruise-missile technology. The cruise missile that was then being developed by the United States was in effect a highly accurate pilotless aircraft that could travel short, medium, or intercontinental distances and could be launched from air, land, or sea. Cruise missiles could fly close to the ground below the detection range of enemy radar.

The negotiations had difficulties for other reasons as well. The U.S. Senate objections to the 1972 trade agreement extending most-favored-nation status to the Soviet Union because of Soviet restrictions on Jewish emigration, and in 1975 the Soviet-sponsored dispatch of Cuban troops to Angola in support of the Marxist regime there cast a chilling shadow over American–Soviet relations. President Ford decided to shelve further discussion on SALT II.

Following the election of Jimmy Carter to the presidency, discussions were resumed, after an initial bad start, in May 1977. This time the negotiations reached a satisfactory conclusion and a new treaty was signed in Vienna in June 1979 by Carter and Brezhnev. The treaty met with strong criticism by conservative circles in the United States and when, seven months later, the Soviet Union invaded Afghanistan, President Carter decided not to press for ratification by the Senate. Nevertheless, the U.S. government let it be understood that it would abide by the terms of SALT II provided the Soviet Union did the same. This understanding was later embraced by President Ronald Reagan, despite his long-standing opposition to SALT II.

....The START Negotiations

The Reagan administration, claiming that the Soviet Union had taken advantage of the period of détente to build up its strategic forces in an effort to achieve a first strike capability, embarked on a massive armaments program. Faced, however, with strong public opposition to its nuclear weapons policy, the Reagan administration proposed a new round of negotiations not only to limit the growth but actually to reduce the number of weapons. In 1982, President Reagan proposed that the two superpowers hold strategic arms reduction talks (START) to reach "verifiable, equitable, and militarily significant" agreements. In his initial proposal, Reagan suggested that each superpower reduce its missile launchers to 850 and nuclear warheads to 5,000. He added that, to enhance stability, no more than one-half of the 850 launchers on either side could be land based. Reagan further suggested establishing in a second stage "an equal ceiling on other elements of our strategic nuclear forces including limits on the ballistic throw-weight." He added, however, that these were only suggestions and that "nothing is excluded" as a subject for the proposed negotiations.

The initial Soviet reaction was far from positive. One of the Soviet objections was that the proposed limits on land-based missiles would require severe reductions on their part, considering that land-based missiles account for 75 percent of Soviet warheads and striking power. The United States could comply with the proposed ceilings by retiring all 450 single warhead Minuteman II missiles (the oldest in the arsenal) and 50 Minuteman III, and replacing them with one hundred MX missiles with ten warheads each.

....TNF Negotiations

Side by side with the START talks, the two superpowers opened negotiations for the reduction of the theater nuclear forces (TNF); specifically, the talks centered on the reduction of the medium-range SS-20s targeted on Europe and the cancellation of the Pershing II and cruise missile deployment in Western Europe. When the negotiations on the TNF reached a stalemate in the fall of 1983, NATO went forward with the deployment of Pershing II and cruise missiles in Europe. The Soviet Union walked out on the negotiations on both TNF and START. In January 1985 the two governments resumed negotiations over both defensive and offensive strategic weapons.

....Three Crucial Aspects

The brief review of the steps thus far taken by the superpowers to reach agreements bringing under some control their nuclear arsenals shows that their efforts were complicated and often frustrated not only because of technical problems or international developments but also because of the mutual distrust, which has remained a constant factor, and because of the desire of each side to retain its superiority in one type of weapon or another. Neither side could expect to reach an arms control agreement that would leave its opponent in a strategically vulnerable or inferior position. Agreements on arms control are feasible only when they are *balanced*.

Being balanced, however, is only one aspect. The problem goes beyond numbers. To be truly beneficial in the long run, agreements should be aimed at reducing uncertainty in three crucial areas:

1. The weapons allowed under the agreement should be capable of deterring the other side from deliberately initiating a first strike or from engaging in political or military ventures that could lead to nuclear escalation. In other words, the agreement should enhance *deterrence stability*.

2. Arms buildup should be restrained by setting limits to the numbers of weapons or by prohibiting weapons—as in the case of the ABM Treaty—that could fuel the arms race by introducing an element of uncertainty or vulnerability. This is the element of *arms race stability*.

3. Weapons systems that will give each side a low incentive and a low capability to initiate—or even contemplate or threaten—a first strike at a time of severe crisis should be allowed or promoted. This is the element of *crisis stability*.

Arms control proposals and counterproposals do not always reflect a genuine desire to reach agreements that will increase stability in all three areas. Instead both superpowers have sought strategic advantages in each agreement, although in the end they had to accept more balanced arrangements. This search for strategic advantage has been a major handicap through the years and is likely to remain so for the foreseeable future.

Why Agreements Are Needed

The governments of the two superpowers have concluded several arms control agreements in the last twenty years and are likely to conclude more in the future for compelling practical reasons. The technological advances of the past few years (MIRVs, accurate ICBMs, cruise missiles) and developments that are expected in the not too distant future (antiballistic laser beams, the stealth bomber, antisatellite weapons in space, depressed trajectory SLBMs, FOBs) are likely to reduce crisis stability, and the reliability of deterrence while accelerating the arms race. The arms race is automatically fueled, in the absence of mutually agreed restraints, because each side wants to make the "last move" and offset the other side's perceived advantage. This is an endless process, as the experience of the last three decades has shown. Every technological advance made by one side was matched before long by the other. The arms buildup becomes itself a source of conflict because it arouses suspicions in the other side and because each government, to justify the huge costs involved in the arms race, exacerbates the political climate by focusing on elements of conflict and by exaggerating the threat it presumably faces. At the same time, the military, civilian, and industrial bureaucracies that benefit from the arms race are likely to press for new weapons unless limits are set by arms control agreements.

Increasing Stability

Technological developments do not automatically undermine deterrence or crisis stability; in fact, they may increase stability. For example, the development of the nuclear submarine provided the United States with an invulnerable weapon that made deterrence a realistic strategic option at a time when Soviet advances in land-based ICBMs might have raised doubts about the wisdom of a deterrence strategy. On the other hand, the development of MIRVs—initially by the United States—presumably has increased crisis instability because it has made the American land-based ICBMs much more vulnerable to a Soviet first strike by the MIRV Soviet ICBMs, according to the report presented by the U.S. Air Force in 1983. In deciding to develop new weapons systems or to limit or ban existing systems under an arms control agreement, policy makers should ponder what the effect will be on preserving and strengthening—or undermining—deterrence, crisis, and arms race stability.

Verification

Given the mistrust between the two superpowers, it is not surprising that verification has been a major concern from the early days of arms control negotiations. This concern has been more evident on the American side because of the differences between United States and Soviet society. The Soviet Union is a closed society in which little becomes public without official permission. This complicates Washington's efforts to verify that the Soviet government is complying with the terms of an arms control agreement. In fact, the early efforts to reach such agreements in the 1950s failed not only because the Soviet leaders were unwilling to have their country locked in a strategically inferior position (given the American superiority at the time) but also because they were unwilling to allow on site inspections within the Soviet Union to verify compliance. This did not necessarily mean that they were planning to cheat; rather, they wanted to prevent opening their borders to outsiders who could "spy" on other aspects of Soviet life. The 1963 Test Ban Treaty became possible only when the development of technical means made detection of violations possible without on site inspection. Other arms control agreements became possible in the 1970s only when satellite technology developed to the point that each side could monitor the other without intruding into its territory. Prior to the development of national technical means (NTMs) of verification, arms control negotiations could not move beyond the starting gate.

Since the late 1960s, the monitoring capabilities of space satellites and other electronic NTMs have advanced to the point that Harold Brown, the U.S. secretary of defense in the Carter administration, could say in 1979: "It is inconceivable to me that the Soviets could develop, produce, test, and deploy a new ICBM in a way that would evade this monitoring network."[12] Of course, verification is not absolutely foolproof; but existing technology provides "adequate capabilities" to identify "attempted evasion if it occurs on a large enough scale to pose a significant risk," and to do so in time for countermeasures to be taken.[13]

There is general agreement that both sides have observed SALT I and SALT II (even though SALT II has not been ratified) because the advantages of compliance obviously outweigh any benefits that may come from violations, which may be detected and duplicated by the other side. The Standing Consultative Commission (SCC)—a little known agency, made up of U.S. and Soviet representatives, established under Article XIII of the ABM Treaty—has been instrumental in examining quietly any reports by either government on suspected violations and clearing up any questions. The U.S. delegates to the SCC have testified in Congress that the Commission has "never had to deal with a case of actual noncompliance."[14]

The main problem is not the verification but the signing of agreements that promote stability in the three critical areas we identified earlier: deterrence, crisis, and the arms race. What matters most is the content and the guiding philosophy of the agreement. After all, "a fully verifiable bad agreement is still a bad agreement," to quote Paul Nitze, the arms control negotiator for the IMF talks under the Reagan administration.[15]

Conventional Forces ....

In a conventional war between the two superpowers, the United States would enjoy at least one advantage because of its location. The United States is not vulnerable to an invasion of Soviet conventional forces; the two oceans form an insurmountable barrier. By contrast, the Soviet Union is potentially vulnerable to an invasion by land with conventional means. Soviet strategic planners and political leaders cannot overlook the fact that Soviet territories can be subject to penetration by conventional forces either from the West (NATO) or from the East (China). To offset the disadvantages of geography, the Soviet Union has developed in the last forty years a large conventional force of approximately 3,673,000 troops with an additional 560,000 in paramilitary units. Even with conscription, such a large force places a heavy burden on the Soviet economy. The savings realized from paying the draftees a pittance are minimal. The troops have to be fed, clothed, and equipped with costly armaments. The Soviet leadership, however, appears determined to maintain such a large force regardless of cost because they want:

1. To be able to deter, and if necessary beat down, any conventional threat from the West or the East

2. If deterrence fails and war breaks out, to be capable of expanding Soviet control over key areas such as Western Europe or the Persian Gulf and over the straits through which the Soviet navy must pass to reach the oceans

3. To keep the East European satellites under effective control

4. To preserve the party's control within the country itself

In the last two decades, the Soviet Union has devoted a great deal of effort to developing a sizeable and modern naval force. The mission of the Soviet navy in peacetime is to remind governments in key regions that Moscow has interests in those regions and the military capability to defend them. The expectation is that this presence will reinforce the image of the Soviet Union as a major power and will reduce the effectiveness of the corresponding American presence. In times of severe crisis or war, the mission of the Soviet navy is to challenge the use of the world's seaways by the West. Considering the critical dependence of the United States, Western Europe, and Japan on unhindered access to the raw materials and fuels that are located overseas, control of the oceans and of the vital straits that connect the major bodies of water is a matter of survival. The ability of the Soviet navy to pose an effective threat is circumscribed, however, by certain inescapable geographic realities. All major home ports of the Soviet navy either are located inside "bottled-up" seas, or are too far to the north for year-round, all-weather use. To reach the oceans, the Soviet naval units have to pass through the Straits of Kategat between Denmark and Norway, which block the access from the Baltic Sea to the Atlantic. The Black Sea fleet has to pass through the straits of the Bosporus and the Dardanelles and then the Aegean to reach the Mediterranean, which also is blocked at two ends, Gibraltar and the Suez. In the Far East, Soviet naval units fanning out from Vladivostok will have to sail through the Sea of Japan and pass through either the La Pérouse Straits between Sakhalin and the Japanese island of Hokkaido or through the Korean Straits dominated by South Korea and the Japanese island of Tshushima. The ports of Murmansk and Arkhangelsk on the northern coast of European Russia have direct access to the open seas, but they are ice-locked for more than seven months each year. Even during the ice-free months, Soviet naval forces from these bases will have to pass between Greenland and Iceland and between Iceland and the United Kingdom, the so-called GIUK gap. Petropavlovsk on the Kamchatka Peninsula is the only Soviet port in the northern Pacific not constrained by choke-points; however, it is remote and has no land transportation links adequate to serve large Soviet forces.

In general, the routes the Soviet navy will have to use to reach the Atlantic, the Pacific, or the Indian Ocean are highly vulnerable, very long, or both.[16] It is true that current Soviet influence in Ethiopia and South Yemen, in Angola and Mozambique, or in Vietnam, Cuba, Libya, or Syria may enable the Soviet navy to use local facilities for refueling, repairs, and crew rest, but without unhindered access to the home bases such naval units will be vulnerable and their effectiveness will be seriously handicapped. In times of peace, access to the world's oceans is open; the Soviet navy, carrying the Soviet flag and providing a visual presence of Soviet might, is a valuable political and propaganda tool in the hands of the Soviet foreign-policy makers.

The mission of the American conventional forces differs materially from that of the Soviet Union. The United States is not exposed to an invasion by conventional forces, as the Soviet Union certainly is. Russia has a long history of foreign invasions: Mongols and Tartars from the East, Swedes and Poles from the West. In the last two centuries, Napoleon's Grand Army and Hitler's invasion have left a legacy that bears heavily on the thinking of Soviet leaders and strategists.[17] By contrast, the United States does not need a large conventional ground force to defend its frontiers or its territory. Both its neighbors, Canada and Mexico, pose no threat. In all the wars in which the United States participated during this century, its forces were used overseas in Europe, in the Pacific, in Korea, and in Vietnam. This historical fact reflects the perception Americans have of their role in world affairs and their worldwide interests. Although U.S. territory may be technically beyond the reach of hostile conventional forces, the United States cannot afford the loss of free access to most parts of the world, especially to those regions that are economically or strategically important.

In light of these realities, the U.S. conventional forces have complex and demanding missions. They must be able to deter any aggressive designs by the Soviet Union against Western Europe and to raise the potential cost of a Soviet expansionist move into the vital region of the Persian Gulf, thereby discouraging any such designs. In the event of war, they must be able to defend the territory of Western Europe in cooperation with the NATO allies; prevent extension of North Korean control over South Korea and frustrate a threat to Japan; prevent the Soviet forces from seizing control of the choke-points the Soviet navy must pass to reach the open seas from its home ports in the Baltic, the Black Sea, or the Sea of Japan; and repel or at least interdict and thwart a Soviet conventional attack in the Persian Gulf. Moreover, in time of war, the U.S. Navy in particular will have the mission to protect the sea lines of communication between the United States, Europe, the Persian Gulf, and the Far East against Soviet submarine and land-based air attacks with nonnuclear means: the West cannot fight a prolonged conventional war in Europe or Asia without the ability of the United States to use sea routes to reinforce its military contingents and resupply its forces and those of its allies. (It is estimated that the supplies and matériel currently available in Central Europe for the NATO forces will be exhausted within thirty days.)

One may be tempted to conclude that the U.S. conventional forces, totaling 1,881,000 men and 168,000 women, will not be able to fulfill adequately all these difficult missions. However, any attempt to assess the balance of conventional forces between East and West must take into account a number of practical considerations.

1. Numerical comparisons alone will not provide a realistic understanding of each side's capabilities or weaknesses; we have to look at the missions each contingent or type of weapon is designed to accomplish and its ability to do so when engaged in combat with the corresponding forces of the adversary.

2. We must take into account all the different types of forces that will be used in combat; to count the number of tanks one side can throw against the tanks of the other side without reference to number and effectiveness of antitank missiles or aircraft designed to attack and destroy armored vehicles is meaningless.

3. We cannot limit comparisons to Soviet and U.S. conventional forces; the contribution of their allies must be included in any assessment.

4. We cannot ignore questions of morale, training, reliability, and leadership. How will the conventional forces of Moscow's allies in Eastern Europe behave in time of war? Will the Western governments in Europe act quickly and in unison in the event of Soviet pressure or an outright war threat?

Finally, no discussion of the East and West conventional forces and their missions can be divorced from the possibility that a war involving the superpowers directly against one another may not remain at the conventional level. The possibility of the NATO forces resorting to battlefield atomic weapons to repel a Warsaw Pact advance through the territory of West Germany is very real. Once nonconventional weapons are thrown into the battle, there is no certainty that further nuclear escalation can be avoided. In today's world, the risk of nuclear war cannot be left out of the calculations of either side. To view a war between East and West as merely an updated version of World War II would be a dangerous and unrealistic approach.

The Rapid Deployment Force

In view of the risks inherent in a nuclear escalation, the conventional forces of the two superpowers are not likely to be used in combat directly against one another. However, changes detrimental to U.S. and Western interests can occur piecemeal, without the direct participation of Soviet conventional forces (they could happen through Soviet proxies, as in the case of Cuban troops sent to Africa). To cope with such contingencies, the United States has organized a Rapid Deployment Force (RDF). Conceivably, this force can be useful in helping friendly governments in the Middle East, Africa, or Latin America facing a serious threat from a hostile neighbor. The RDF would be less effective, however, in dealing with domestic upheavals resulting in the overthrow of pro-Western or nonaligned governments and their replacement with pro-Soviet or at least anti-Western regimes.

Revolutionary changes spearheaded by domestic groups pose a challenge the United States will find difficult to meet by using its conventional forces. It is evident that in the event of a domestic coup or uprising in a Latin American, African, Middle Eastern, or Asiatic country, the U.S. conventional forces, including the RDF, will find it difficult to intervene and prevent or reverse the change, mostly for political and legal reasons. For example, could a U.S. military intervention by the RDF or other forces have prevented the fall of the Shah of Iran, the rise of a pro-Soviet regime in Ethiopia, or the rise of the Sandinista regime in Nicaragua? In a purely technical sense, we may argue that a strong and determined deployment of U.S. conventional forces in those countries might have altered the outcomes, although others may counter that, as shown in Vietnam and elsewhere, it is extremely difficult for a foreign military force to fight off domestic revolutionary forces, especially when the local government has lost the support and confidence of large segments of its population.

Such changes also present a serious legal problem. They are portrayed as *internal* affairs, falling within the domestic jurisdiction of the countries involved. Under the Charter of the United Nations and the rules of international law, military forces cannot enter the territory of another country without the invitation or permission of its government. This means that only if a pro-Western government, facing a revolutionary challenge, calls for United States help can the RDF move in (provided Congress does not object). If the pro-Western government faces a widespread and massive opposition, a U.S. conventional force will face the risk of becoming involved in another Vietnam-type situation (as the Soviets have also found in Afghanistan). It will further face the additional legal handicap that its transit through or over the territory of other countries will require their permission. In the past, even NATO allies have been reluctant to allow the transit of U.S. forces to areas that are outside the NATO defense perimeter.

Another serious problem is that a threatened government may not even have time to call for help. The leaders of a coup seldom advertise their plans in advance. When a sudden change occurs, the United States or the West in general can do very little. As we pointed out in the earlier section on The Roots of Conflict, such domestic upheavals can be averted more effectively through complex measures of a political, economic, and social nature, assisted by the West but initiated and carried out primarily by the threatened government.

....Showing the Flag

In peacetime, the conventional military forces can serve as an instrument of foreign policy. This is particularly true of the U.S. Navy, which, with its mobility and high visibility, can project a U.S. *peacetime presence* in many parts of the world. It is generally assumed that perceptions of U.S. military strength encourage friends and allies to cooperate with Washington and adopt policies supportive of U.S. policies on a variety of issues. Conversely, governments unfriendly to the United States or its allies may be less likely to act against Western interests than they otherwise might be.

To establish this peacetime presence, the U.S. Navy routinely operates in various regions. The Sixth Fleet in the Mediterranean and the Seventh Fleet in the Western Pacific are familiar illustrations. A two-carrier task force has been stationed in the Indian Ocean, and naval units regularly visit foreign ports and conduct exercises jointly with the navies of other friendly countries. In the event of a serious international crisis, the United

States uses this presence to underline its concern and its capability to intervene if its interests are threatened seriously. Although such intervention is not always politically feasible, the perception of the United States as a superpower, in the eyes of friends, foes, or neutrals, depends in some measure on this visible peacetime presence.

The presence of the Soviet navy also is used to remind other countries in key regions that Moscow has interests in those regions, and the military capability to defend those interests. The expectation is that this peacetime presence will reinforce the image of the Soviet Union as a superpower and will reduce the effectiveness of the corresponding U.S. presence.

Without underrating excessively the effectiveness of this peacetime presence, the political realities of our time have lessened the effect of such forces (whether U.S. or Soviet) compared to earlier times when the major powers used naval units or other conventional forces to impose their will on others. Today, this peacetime presence is more effective as an instrument of *influence*.

Conventional weapons play another role in expanding the influence of the major powers. Both sides supply several countries with conventional armaments. Many governments rely on such supplies to improve their military potential or to discourage real or imagined threats to their security from unfriendly neighbors.

Political influence is expected to follow *military aid* from a major power to a client state. The perceived need for more and newer weapons and the practical need for spare parts to maintain those already in place help strengthen and perpetuate political ties and the dependence of client states on one or the other major power. The training of military officers, a part of military aid, is expected to forge ties likely to serve over time the interests of the major power. Historical experience, however, shows that a revolutionary change in one or the other direction may quickly wipe out all political gains—as happened to the Soviet Union in Egypt in 1972 and to the United States in Iran in 1979, to mention only two cases. Nonetheless, both sides consider such aid to be a worthwhile investment.

A Closing Note..

The bewildering complexity of the military aspects of the East–West rivalry has given rise to problems that will be difficult to solve even with the best of intentions on both sides. These problems have an existence of their own, proliferating not as a consequence of unbridgeable economic or political cleavages but as the offspring of other military problems and developments. With the military dimension of the East–West rivalry overshadowing all other aspects, each side devotes vast resources to improve its military capabilities and match the capabilities of the other side. However, the military capabilities of both sides have less-than-marginal relevance to the solution of the economic, social, and political problems facing humanity today. When they do not exacerbate those problems with their very existence—or their cost—they can do little if anything to help improve the conditions that make life miserable in so many parts of the world. Although extensive evidence shows that this is indeed so, our preoccupation with the threat presumably posed by the other side and with the military aspects of the rivalry has become a mindset, a way of thinking that dominates our assessment of world problems.

A dispassionate, hard-headed assessment shows that the United States is not engaged in a life-and-death economic struggle with the Soviet Union over scarce resources that one can have only by denying them to the other. Nor is there any rational basis for a drive for "world domination" either by the Soviet Union or by the United States. The world is much too diverse for such simplistic notions. Even the ideological struggle is no longer as relevant as it appeared to be in the early part of this century. Nevertheless, countless conflicts of local or regional nature tend to become entangled in the wide web of the East–West competition. In turn, such conflicts tend to feed and exacerbate East–West antagonism.

Not as militarily dangerous, but no less real and potentially disruptive, is the economic disparity between the affluent, industrialized North and the underdeveloped South. In fact, the North–South interaction cannot be dissociated from the East–West conflict; the two affect each other in a variety of ways. For a more comprehensive view of the major patterns of contemporary international relations, we will focus in chapter 10 on the North–South relationship.

Summary

- Rivalry has been the prevailing pattern in the relations between the East and West—primarily between the United States and the Soviet Union—for more than thirty-five years.

- The economic interests of the two camps are not in such fundamental conflict as to justify the antagonism. The Soviet Union is not in dire need of energy resources or raw materials it can obtain only through conquest of other lands. Nor is there a deadly competition for markets between the two camps.

- Important elements of economic interdependence between the two sides are evidenced by the Soviet purchases of grain from the United States or the construction of the natural gas pipeline from the Soviet Union to Western Europe.

- The *Soviet threat,* to be realistic, must not carry with it the risk of nuclear war. Such a threat lies primarily in the emergence of Marxist-oriented, pro-Soviet, or at least anti-Western regimes in Third World countries through the activities of domestic revolutionaries, who have the assistance but not the direct military involvement of the Soviet Union.

- Soviet efforts to promote pro-Soviet regimes in Third World countries have not been overly successful.

- To deal with this form of the Soviet threat, the West needs multidimensional policies, which require the participation of local leadership elements, with effective policies of their own, in the target countries. These policies have economic, social, political, humanitarian, ideological, and military aspects.

- Regardless of the causes of the East–West rivalry, we find elements in both camps that contribute to the perpetuation of the conflict because it serves their interests.

- The military dimension has become a central element in the rivalry between the United States and the Soviet Union and now has a life of its own, dwarfing the more mundane causes of the conflict.

- Both sides rely on their nuclear arsenals to deter one another from attempting serious changes in the status quo. This strategy of mutual deterrence is based on the ability of both sides to inflict devastating losses on the other.

- Both sides now have a second strike capability; that is, their forces are not vulnerable to a surprise attack (first strike) and can survive to retaliate. The effects of such retaliation, both sides agree, make "victory" in full-fledged nuclear war meaningless.

- Deterrence and its corollary doctrine of Mutual Assured Destruction have come under criticism by observers who believe the threat of retaliation at the risk of one's own destruction is not credible. However, as long as a second strike capability exists, the uncertainty regarding the opponent's reaction will remain as effective a restraint as it has been in the past.

- Other critics of the strategy of deterrence speak of the vulnerability of specific systems to a first strike. Although individual systems may be vulnerable, their vulnerability is reduced substantially by the fact that they are part of a complex, synergistic mechanism.

- Some people doubt that the United States will use its nuclear arsenal to repel a Soviet attack on Western Europe at the risk of provoking a Soviet nuclear attack on its own soil. However, the Soviet leaders cannot lightly decide to find out how the United States will respond by launching such an attack. The uncertainty of the United States' reaction is the foundation of extended deterrence.

- In addition to mutual deterrence, the superpowers have reached arms control agreements. Such agreements are useful and effective if they enhance (1) deterrence stability, (2) arms race stability, and (3) crisis stability.

- The question of how to verify observance is central in arms control agreements. Technological developments have improved the means of verification, reducing the necessity for on site inspection, which in earlier years was a major stumbling block.

- In conventional ground forces, the Warsaw Pact has a numerical advantage in Europe, but the Soviet Union faces the problem of guarding its 3,000-mile border with China. The Soviet navy is handicapped by the geographic location of its home ports, which are located either in the arctic circle or in areas that have access to the oceans only through narrow passages controlled by potentially hostile states.

- The U.S. Rapid Deployment Force has military capabilities but it is handicapped by political and legal limitations.

- The military dimension overshadows all other aspects of the East–West rivalry; however, the military capabilities of both sides, acquired at great expense, have less-than-marginal relevance to the solution of the economic, social, and political problems facing humanity today, and to the influence potential of the superpowers.

Their nuclear arsenals, in particular, are of little use in the exercise of power; in fact, their most practical utility lies in keeping the two superpowers within the confines of the transactional approach in their relations with one another.

Notes

1. For a definition of "politics" see Kousoulas, D. G. *On Government and Politics*. 5th ed. Monterey, Calif.: Brooks/Cole, 1982, p. 21.
2. We did not include here the East European satellites or Afghanistan because the extension of Soviet control over those countries is due to special Soviet needs and does not necessarily imply a worldwide drive for territorial expansion in the traditional fashion.
3. President Reagan's statement at the Cancun conference October 1983.
4. This is reflected in the recent book by the former U.S. Secretary of Defense. Brown, Harold. *Thinking About National Security: Defense and Foreign Policy in a Dangerous World*. Boulder, Colo.: Westview Press, 1983.
5. Truman, Harry S. *Memoirs,* Vol. II. New York: Doubleday, 1956, p. 451.
6. In 1953, President Eisenhower implied the possible use of atomic weapons in Korea to break the stalemate. Again there was no specific policy decision. See Blechman, Barry M., and Powell, Robert. "What in the Name of God Is Strategic Superiority?" *Political Science Quarterly,* Vol. 97, Winter 1982–83, p. 591.
7. *The Washington Post,* May 16, 1983.
8. The FOBS missile is fired in a fairly low trajectory in the opposite direction from the target, enters a partial Earth orbit, and, when it reaches the target from the opposite side, turns downward, and strikes the target. Soviet FOBS presumably would be fired toward a southward orbit and approach the United States from the direction of Latin America, thus avoiding the early warning system located along the Canadian north. Such a flight, however, still could be detected by the reconnaissance satellites.
9. *The New York Times,* January 9, 1983.
10. *The Washington Post,* May 19, 1983.
11. Theater nuclear forces include tactical weapons with ranges of less than 1000 miles as well as intermediate nuclear forces (INF) with ranges from 1,000 to 3,000 miles, such as the Soviet SS-20 or the American Pershing II.
12. U.S. Congress, Senate, Committee on Foreign Relations. *The SALT II Treaty,* Part 2, 96th Congress, First Session. Washington, D.C.: U.S. Government Printing Office, 1979, p. 242.
13. *Ibid.,* p. 241.
14. *Challenges for U.S. National Security*. Washington, D.C.: Carnegie Endowment for International Peace, 1983, p. 53.
15. U.S. Congress, Senate, Committee on Foreign Relations. *Op. cit.,* p. 446.
16. *Challenges for U.S. National Security,* Part II. Washington, D.C.: Carnegie Endowment for International Peace, 1981, pp. 101–109.
17. United States Presidents Nixon and Carter have written that in their meetings with the Soviet leader Leonid Brezhnev repeatedly recalled "the 20,000,000 dead" suffered by the Soviet Union during World War II.

10
North–South:
Dialogue
or Confrontation? ....

Nomadic Masai in Sub-Saharan Africa face serious problems because of drought

Those who live in a European or a North American city cannot easily envision the conditions that are a way of life for hundreds of millions of people in Africa, Asia, and Latin America. Only a personal visit can transform academic descriptions into living images of deprivation, squalor, and helplessness. The term *less-developed countries* (LDCs) used in current literature resembles a decent garment thrown over the emaciated shoulders and the swollen belly of a sickly, malnourished child. It may conceal some of the ugliness but it does not quite give an accurate image of reality.

Diversity and Common Traits...............................

The countries that are considered to be "less developed" are not as uniform as the common label seems to imply. Among the 122 members of the United Nations that belong to the so-called Group of 77, we find a great variety of religions and cultures, ideologies and political systems, forms of economic organization, levels of productivity, and per capita income. Some of these countries have an arid climate but have rich underground resources such as oil; others have only an arid climate and little hope of overcoming their poverty; some have large and rapidly growing populations that devour any economic gains and prevent genuine improvement; some have great potential, others only modest prospects. Already we find it necessary to invent new labels to reflect this diversity. Some of the LDCs have moved to the category of *newly industrializing countries* (NICs), whereas others are so poor and have such dismal prospects for economic development that they are labeled as *least developed,* and some authors already place them in a *Fourth World* made up of countries that will have to remain for a long time dependent on aid from the affluent countries just to survive.

Nonetheless, practically all LDCs—or Third World countries—share certain common historical memories. The overwhelming majority of them were until recently under the colonial or semicolonial control of foreign powers. Their former masters were almost invariably white, whereas the people in most LDCs are nonwhite. Most of the people in the LDCs seem to share an ambivalent love–hate attitude toward the affluent, industrialized countries in the West. They resent their former masters for past humiliations, but they also recognize that most of the practical help for their economic development can come only from the affluent market economies.

Whatever their differences in religion, traditions, or political institutions, they all seem to share an impatience to break out of the bondage of poverty and stagnation. This is accelerated by the effect of the current revolution in communications; the ignorance that in earlier times served as a protective shield against frustration is now eroded daily by the increasing awareness of what the world is like elsewhere. Finally, in practically all LDCs we find a wide gap between a small minority enjoying a comfortable or even affluent lifestyle—because of the possession of either property or political and state power—and a mass of peasants and manual laborers going through a drab, hard life unrelieved by the conveniences people in the industrialized North take so much for granted.

Changing these conditions for the better is a colossal undertaking and is one of the major challenges facing humanity as we approach the twenty-first century. Although *economic development* is the key objective, the issue is not purely economic. It has momentous political overtones, which intertwine with the other central issue of our time: the East–West rivalry. Although most LDCs espouse a policy of *nonalignment,* trying to remain outside the arena of the East–West contest, they cannot divorce themselves from the realities of this world and retreat into a comfortable and safe isolation. Their economic development depends on assistance from the advanced countries; on the other hand, their resources are of vital importance to the industrialized North.

References to *North* and *South* in this context suffer from geographic imprecision. Australia and New Zealand, for example, are grouped with the North; India, China, and the Republic of Korea fall under the South. The Soviet Union and the other industrialized states in the Soviet bloc, which are certainly located in the Northern hemisphere, are somehow left out of the North. The *North* actually is a code word referring to the members of the Organization for Economic Cooperation and Development (OECD), and especially to the major industrial states that have market economies, such as the United States, Japan, West Germany, Britain, and France. The *South* is another code word, standing for the countries that usually identify with the Group of 77. Whether we use *South, Third World,* or the more neutral *less-developed countries,* we refer to this group.

Regardless of the precision or accuracy of these terms, the countries that consider themselves to be members of the South give top priority to the development of their economies. Admittedly, the problems involved in this quest for economic development are complex, as our comments in the following pages will show.

Both North and South are in this venture together. Their interaction may be channeled into a constructive dialogue or may degenerate into a sterile and self-defeating confrontation. This is the second megaissue of our time.

Conflicting Perceptions ·····································

Common sense may suggest a joint effort by North and South, but ideological perceptions tend to fuel confrontational attitudes. In politics, perceptions create reality, and whatever the factual merit of the Third World ideological perceptions, they are there and cannot be ignored.

To be sure, the ideology of the Third World is not shared with equal fervor by all the countries in this group. Nigeria does not speak in the same tones used by Libya or Ethiopia; Brazil has different views from those of Mexico and (even more so) those of

Cuba; India does not agree on all matters with Indonesia or Zaire, let alone with Pakistan. Despite different nuances and even conflicting overtones, however, we can distill certain ideological propositions that all Third World countries seem to embrace.

1. With different degrees of forcefulness, practically all LDCs tend to argue that their underdevelopment is the result of past exploitation by the colonial powers whose imperialist policies distorted economic priorities to serve the latter's interests.

2. The difficulties the LDCs face today are largely created by an international economic system that is dominated by the rich countries and deliberately tilted in their favor at the expense of the poor, underdeveloped countries in the South.

3. To compensate for past injustices, the North has an obligation to give the LDCs massive amounts of capital.

4. To remove the imbalances of the present international economic system, the affluent countries in the North (and primarily the leading OECD members) must accept extensive reforms in the context of a New International Economic Order.

5. Capitalism is an economic system that unleashes the basest instincts of greed and ruthlessness and leads to the exploitation of those who are economically weak. (This bias against free enterprise owes much to the historical experiences of most of these countries; it surfaces often, at least in their rhetoric in international forums, even though many of them allow the activities of private enterprises.)

6. Economic development must be combined with social measures to alleviate poverty and to distribute more equitably the benefits of economic growth. (Social justice, often seen as synonymous to socialism, is given a high place in their value system at least in an ideological sense. In many instances, civil and political rights take a back seat.)

These core propositions of the Third World ideology cast the "capitalist" and "imperialist" giants of the industrialized North in the role of the villains, whereas the Soviet Union is often treated with benevolent moderation. The Marxist overtones of the Third World ideology encourage this attitude, and the Soviet Union understandably takes advantage of it at every opportunity. On the other hand, it must be noted that most developing countries show no interest in adopting the Soviet model of command economy. They prefer a vague *Third Way,* which usually tilts toward socialist forms of economic organization and has a strong bias in favor of state-owned enterprises.

Most of these ideological perceptions, with their open or implied criticism of the West, inevitably generate negative Western responses, particularly from the United States. The records of the United Nations and of other international forums are full of rhetorical recriminations reflecting the Third World ideological arguments and the responses of Western representatives.

The Western representatives reject the argument that *capitalism* is synonymous with *exploitation* by pointing to the benefits of their economic system, which, by encouraging private initiative and providing people with productivity incentives, has raised the living conditions of the masses of their peoples to levels unsurpassed in history and unequaled by any other contemporary economic system (see table 10-1).

They question the claim that colonialism impoverished the Third World countries and distorted the latter's economic development. There is no clear evidence, they say, that the major colonial powers, such as Britain or France, put into their colonial possessions less than they took out. The affluence of most OECD countries hardly can be attributed to colonial exploitation; most of them never had any colonies. Although economic aid may be justified for humanitarian reasons or may be viewed as a form of mutually beneficial cooperation, it cannot be given as *compensation* for alleged past injuries.

Heatedly debated is the argument that the obstacles to development are external, created by an international economic order that serves the interests of the rich and powerful countries. Those opposing this view argue that any conditions unfavorable to the developing countries in their dealings with the North stem from their weaker bargaining position. As they need the resources and the assets of the advanced countries more than the latter need theirs, they find themselves in the position of the weaker side in any transaction. This is unfortunate but it is a fact of life as old as humanity. That this is not a malicious plot to exploit or hold them back is evidenced by the improving bargaining position of the newly industrializing countries. Proponents of this view add

Table 10-1

Per Capita Income in Selected Countries

OECD[1]		COMECON[2]		Third World[1]	
Belgium	10,760	Bulgaria	2,800	Algeria	2,350
Canada	11,320	Czechoslovakia	4,500	Bangladesh	140
Denmark	12,470	Germany, Dem. Rep.	3,700	Bolivia	570
Germany, Fed. Rep.	12,460	Hungary	2,270*	China	310
Italy	6,840	Romania	2,560*	Ghana	360
Japan	10,080	Soviet Union	4,600	India	260
New Zealand	7,920			Indonesia	580
Norway	14,280			Malaysia	1,860
United Kingdom	9,660			Nigeria	860
United States	13,160			Peru	1,310

[1]Figures quoted in *World Development Report 1984*, pp. 218–219, published for the World Bank by Oxford University Press, 1984.
[2]Estimates based on annyal state budgets and other data.

that there is no question that those who have a stronger bargaining position will take advantage of it. This is exactly what the OPEC members did when they raised the oil prices, even though their action hurt their fellow Third World countries even more than the countries of the affluent North. Western commentators add that the major obstacles to development are domestic; above all, they point to the economic and political systems that impede productivity, smother individual initiative, and subordinate economic development to ideological and political priorities.[1]

Although we should not underestimate the influence of these conflicting percep-tions, acrimonious rhetoric, however satisfying emotionally, does not do much to help feed the hungry, irrigate the fields, or turn the wheels of industry. Certainly there is some truth in the allegations and recriminations voiced by both sides, but trying to find out who is "right" will not have much practical utility. In the following pages we will make an effort to explore the current realities as objectively as possible.

Levels of Development...

The World Bank has recognized for some time the diversity of the underdeveloped countries and has established several categories based on economic criteria (figure 10-1). Twenty-four countries with a population totaling 2,210 million (a figure that includes 1,700 million for China and India) have an annual per capita income (PCI) of less than $410 (1983) and are classified in the Bank's literature as *low-income econo-mies*. Even within this group we find notable differences. China and India have very large populations and an annual PCI of $300 and $260, respectively, but they also have great potential for economic development. By contrast, countries such as Afghanistan, Chad, Mali, Niger, and the Central African Republic have small populations and fairly large territories, but they possess few natural resources underground, and their arid climates make the growing of food an uncertain enterprise.

Another thirty-nine countries with a population totaling 663 million are classified as *lower-middle-income* and have an annual PCI ranging from $420 to $1,630. This group includes three oil-exporting countries: Indonesia, Angola, and Nigeria. Although these three nations' oil resources improve their chances for economic development, their large populations and extensive needs minimize the ameliorative effect of their oil revenues. The overwhelming majority of countries in this group are oil *importers,* and the vulnerability of their economies to rising energy costs was shown dramatically during the 1970s when they had to borrow heavily just to pay their oil bills. Their mounting foreign debt continues to create vexing problems, not only for them but for their lenders as well.

The diversity found in this group of lower-middle-income countries in race, religion, historical background, ideology, and political and economic institutions re-sembles a multicolored mosaic. The group includes such countries as Kenya, Bolivia, Thailand, Cuba, Mongolia, Morocco, Lesotho, Jordan, Syria, Egypt, and the Philip-pines. Even the differences in their annual PCI (ranging from $420 to $1,630) show that the countries with the higher PCI levels differ markedly in economic development and living conditions from those at the lower end of the continuum. Life in Turkey or Paraguay, which have annual PCIs of $1,540 and $1,630, respectively, is quite different from that in Senegal or Liberia, which have annual PCIs of $430 and $520.

The next group, identified as *upper-middle-income,* includes countries with a population totaling 464 million and an annual PCI ranging from $1,700 to $5,670. In this group of twenty countries we find five major oil exporters: Iran, Iraq, Mexico, Algeria, and Venezuela. Their oil revenues are substantial, but are not sufficient to meet the complex needs of their large populations. Other countries included in this group are South Korea, Portugal, Argentina, Chile, Yugoslavia, Greece,[2] Israel, and Trinidad and Tobago. Several of these countries have developed their economies to the point that they can now attract foreign investments and engage in diversified trade exchanges under fairly equitable terms and conditions. Those in the higher PCI levels are classified as newly industrializing countries (NICs) to reflect their considerable progress.

A special group is composed of Libya, Saudi Arabia, Kuwait, and the United Arab Emirates. These countries are classified as *high-income oil exporters.* Not only are their revenues from oil exports sizeable; they are also high in relation to their small populations. This accounts for their extremely high (statistically, at least) annual PCIs, which reach $24,660 in the United Arab Emirates, $20,900 in Kuwait, $12,600 in Saudi Arabia, and $8,450 in Libya (compared to the $12,820 annual PCI in the United States).

The overwhelming majority of the countries in the low-income and lower-middle-income categories—over seventy countries, accounting for almost two-thirds of world population—face widespread poverty and slow economic growth. Their quest for rapid economic development is understandable.

The diversity of the conditions and potentials of the LDCs requires that we use caution in identifying common problems or advancing suggestions for their solution. Nevertheless, we can focus on certain external factors and domestic problems that affect the development of all these countries to a greater or lesser degree.

Figure 10-1
LDCS: Population and per capita income. Categories established by the World Bank.

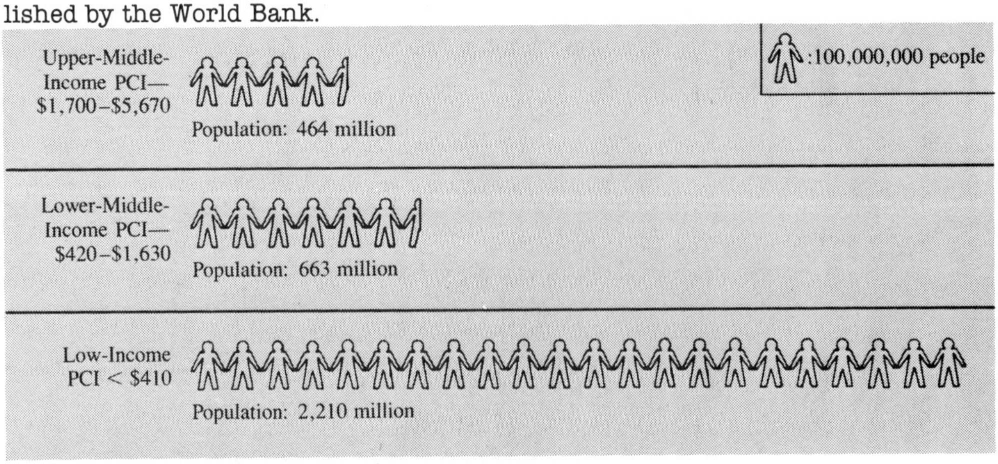

External Factors ....

The external factors that affect a country's rate of development include the trade policies of the advanced market economies, capital flows and technology transfers to the developing countries, cost of energy, and rate of growth in the industrial states of the North.

....................................The LDCs and International Trade

However reluctantly, influential economic circles in the OECD countries, including the United States, increasingly recognize that the developing countries cannot expand their imports from the advanced countries unless they have the hard currency to pay for such goods. One way for them to acquire such currency is by expanding their own exports. Trade, most economists agree, plays a pivotal role in promoting economic development and growth because it enables countries to concentrate on items they can produce more efficiently and economically than can other countries (*comparative advantage*) and to produce such items in larger quantities, thereby cutting costs and making their products more competitive in the international market (*economies of scale*). Although special interest groups occasionally pressure for protectionist measures—which inevitably reduce trade opportunities—there is widespread agreement that expanding trade is essential for prosperity and growth.

This positive attitude about the role of trade has been evident in the policies that have been adopted by the advanced market economies since the end of World War II in their own relations. It has not been evident, however, in their relations with the developing countries. The American and British architects of the postwar international trading order did not accept the argument that the LDCs required special treatment. A large part of the world was then still under colonial rule, and the few sovereign LDCs had too little influence to impose views at the international conferences that created the new trading arrangements. For the industrial market economies led by the United States, liberalization of trade was the guiding principle. For the underdeveloped countries, special treatment to protect them against foreign competition and allow time for their fledgling industries to grow, and special arrangements to protect the marketing of their key commodities against disruptive price fluctuations, were more critical issues than was the liberalization of trade, which favored the countries that were already strong, or had great potential, in international trade.

Because the industrial states that prepared the Havana Charter needed the approval of the participating LDCs (see chapter 7), the Charter incorporated provisions that took into account some of the LDCs' special needs. Moreover, the International Trade Organization (ITO) opened the possibility for LDC participation in the management of international trade. The Havana Charter and the ITO, however, never came into effect. GATT, which took their place, had no provisions concerning economic development, no provisions for special commodity agreements, no provisions to protect the industries of the LDCs during the early stages of development, and no instrumentalities for the effective participation of the LDCs in future negotiations. In addition, the concept of reciprocity, which was so central to the GATT system, worked against the LDCs, which, with their small markets, had little to exchange for concessions. Moreover, the practice of having negotiations among the principal suppliers and then extending the new liberalizing arrangements to other GATT members left most LDCs out of the negotiating process (they were not principal suppliers).

The Formation of UNCTAD

As the number of sovereign LDCs increased dramatically during the 1960s with the dismantling of the colonial empires, pressures for new arrangements grew. GATT was not an effective forum for the LDCs, so they turned to the United Nations, in which they held a numerical majority. In July 1962, a Conference on Problems of Developing Countries, held in Cairo, marked the first major step by the Latin American, African, and Asian LDCs to formulate a joint policy on questions of trade and development. Faced with the possibility of alienating the LDCs to the benefit of the Soviet Union, which was becoming vocal in its support of the Third World, the Northern industrial states abandoned their opposition and, in 1962, agreed to a decision by the UN Economic and Social Council (ECOSOC) to convene a UN Conference on Trade and Development (UNCTAD), which met in Geneva in 1964.

Relying on their numerical majority in the UNCTAD, the Southern states decided to press for trade reform within this new forum. To coordinate their activities and policies, they formed the Group of 77, named after the number of the cosponsors of a Joint Declaration of the Developing Countries presented to the UN General Assembly in 1963. In their declaration, the signatories charged that "the existing principles and patterns of world trade still mainly favor the advanced parts of the world" and that "the present tendencies in world trade frustrate the efforts" of the developing countries "to attain more rapid growth" instead of helping "the developing countries to promote the development and diversification of their economies." The LDCs asked that international trade become "a more powerful instrument and vehicle of economic development not only through the expansion of the traditional exports of the developing countries, but also through the development of markets for their new products and a general increase in their share of world exports under improved terms of trade."[3] They proposed more specifically the introduction of new machinery and methods and the reduction of barriers to LDC exports without reciprocal concessions as required by GATT; stabilization of prices for their exports of primary commodities to the developed countries; expansion of markets in the North for manufactured and semimanufactured products from the South; financial assistance with easy terms to facilitate capital imports by the LDCs and thus promote their economic development; and reduction in shipping and other costs affecting adversely the South's trading position.

Soon after 1964, UNCTAD became a permanent organization with a secretary-general and a secretariat composed of an international staff. Under its first secretary-general, Raul Prebisch, UNCTAD became an active and forceful forum for the LDCs. The UNCTAD structure includes, in addition to the secretary-general and the secretariat, the conference, which is composed of representatives from all member-states and meets every three years; the Trade and Development Board, which serves as the standing committee of the conference and meets twice each year; and four permanent committees, which deal with specific matters and meet at least once a year.

The combined influence potential of the LDCs in UNCTAD is no match for that of the industrial market economies; nevertheless, joint efforts have proved somewhat more effective than individual pressures: joint action has improved the South's bargaining position and has resulted in changes favoring the LDCs. The management of international trade, however, is still dominated by the advanced market economies.

One problem the LDCs face results from their difficulty in maintaining unity because of the many political and economic cleavages among them. The LDCs have differing levels of economic development, trade potentialities, investment needs, and capacity to absorb economic aid, loans, or investments. The oil price increases in the 1970s—imposed by countries that belong to the Group of 77—played havoc with the economies of most other LDCs, which are oil importers. Moreover, extreme demands raised by governments with a strong anti-Western political orientation tend to politicize confrontations within the UNCTAD framework and prevent serious bargaining.[4]

UNCTAD's record is uneven. However, as the dependence of the industrial states on the potential markets of the Third World countries becomes more evident, UNCTAD may provide a useful forum where new arrangements can be discussed and put into effect.

The Generalized System of Preferences

The economic viability, development, and sustained growth of the LDCs are matters of concern not only to the LDCs themselves but also to the developed countries. The random distribution of natural resources in the world, the economic and political problems that arise when the expansion of population is not accompanied by adequate opportunities for productive employment, and the increasing capacity of the developing countries for production and their need for expanding markets all point to the necessity for a positive approach to economic development. Currently, the best customers of the advanced market economies are other members of the OECD, the NICs, and the upper-middle-income LDCs. Poor countries are not good customers. Moreover, if the past record means anything at all, economic development and increased trade will benefit most those countries that already are rich and productive.

Because of these practical considerations, changes are being introduced, however reluctantly. GATT has found it necessary to add to Part IV, its Agreement which came into effect in 1965 and provides for economic development and trade with the LDCs. Part IV calls on states to refrain from increasing trade barriers to imports from LDCs and to give high priority to the reduction and eventual elimination of such barriers. After several years of negotiations, partial agreements, delays, and revisions, a generalized system of preferences (GSP) was agreed upon in 1971; it did not come into force, however, until 1976. The initial agreement was that the new GSP arrangements would remain in force for ten years; in 1980, the UNCTAD members agreed to extend them indefinitely. This preferential treatment for products from LDCs was limited in scope and could be altered through the implementation of "safeguards" against damaging effects on the economy of an advanced country. The major weakness of the GSP is that many LDCs have too few products for export to take full advantage of the GSPs. Another drawback is that the extensive reductions of trade barriers under GATT make the preferential treatment accorded to LDCs less meaningful in practical terms.

The Lome Agreements

The LDCs in UNCTAD also have pressed for commodity agreements to control price fluctuations in the LDC commodity exports. During the 1960s and early 1970s, the North resisted any serious arrangements for the protection of such primary commodities. But the oil crises of the 1970s and an increasing awareness among U.S. strategy-conscious circles of the North's dependence on raw materials located in the South, plus the apparent increase of Soviet influence among frustrated Southern elites, forced a shift in the attitudes of the industrial states. In May 1975, at a meeting of the Commonwealth Heads of Government in Jamaica, then British Prime Minister Harold Wilson spoke of a general agreement on commodities as well as of specific commodity agreements and of the need to stabilize the export earnings of the LDCs.

The EEC also took the initiative during a conference in Lome, Nigeria, in 1975, with the participation of forty-six African, Caribbean, and Pacific (ACP) countries associated with the EEC to sign a treaty (convention) that provided for preferential access to the EEC markets for the products of the ACP countries without reciprocal concessions on the part of EEC members, and formulated a price stabilization plan (Stabex) with a fund for compensating ACP countries facing disruptive price changes in the world market for a commodity critical to the economy of a given ACP country.

A second treaty (Lome Convention II) was signed in 1979 between the EEC and fifty-eight ACP countries; it provided for even greater cooperation between the EEC and the ACP participants.[5] A third Lome Convention was discussed in 1984.

The Lome agreements were only a partial effort by a group of countries—both North and South—to introduce some order in the trade of certain commodities. On a worldwide basis, however, UNCTAD has been a principal forum for promoting price stability in the exports from developing countries. UNCTAD Resolution 93 on an "Integrated Programme for Commodities," passed in June 1976, set as the objective of future action "the achievement of stabilization of commodity prices at levels which would be remunerative and just to producers and equitable to consumers." As in Lome I and II, the focus was on a "common fund" to compensate countries facing serious losses due to demand fluctuations in the world market. After several conferences in the succeeding years, an Agreement Establishing a Common Fund for Commodities was signed in Geneva by eighty-two states, including the United States and the Soviet Union.

The New International Economic Order

Although these moves were constructive, they hardly satisfied the demands and needs of the LDCs. The Group of 77 developed in the mid-1970s a broad set of proposals for a New International Economic Order (NIEO). This NIEO, as outlined in various statements, declarations, and resolutions, covers virtually all areas of international economic relations and seeks changes that would protect the interests of the LDCs and promote their development through bold programs in economic aid, technology transfers, trade reforms, sharing of resources, control of the multinational corporations (MNCs), and monetary arrangements to improve exchange rate stability and the flow of capital.

The North–South exchanges over the NIEO proposals often have been marred by acrimony and extremist rhetoric reflecting the frustration of many developing countries as they encounter what they consider to be a negative attitude on the part of the advanced countries, especially the United States. But the inability of the South to bring about the radical changes contained in the NIEO cannot be attributed only to their weak bargaining position (which is improving) or to a self-centered negativism on the part of the North. A new element has been added in the last decade. Several LDCs have been forging ahead, moving into the new category often identified as the newly industrializing countries (NICs); such countries include Argentina, Brazil, South Korea, Mexico, Portugal, Spain, and Taiwan. In a few more years, these countries may be advanced enough to qualify for membership in the OECD.[6] Already their representatives occasionally show signs of annoyance with the more radical rhetoric of some of their colleagues.

As we pointed out, the LDCs are disparate in levels of economic development, significance of resources, economic potential, population characteristics, geographic location, and several other important variables. Nevertheless, despite the many differences among them, they continue to display a high degree of cohesion when they confront the North in international forums. Even when they disagree among themselves on a particular point, they are in agreement that the Northern industrial states should accept greater and more effective participation of the South in the management of the international economic system.

There are signs of a more responsive attitude on the part of the North. The meeting of President Reagan with key leaders of the Third World at Cancun, Mexico, in 1982, the increase in the resources of the IMF in 1983 to help LDCs meet their serious foreign debt problems, and the Caribbean Basin Initiative are steps—however small—in the right direction.

We mentioned the Lome Conventions between the EEC and a large number of African, Caribbean, and Pacific states. There also appears to be increasing recognition in the United States that its large balance of trade deficits ($90.6 billion in 1984) cannot be reversed unless demand for its products increases, especially in the unsaturated markets of the Third World. Imports by the LDCs, however, cannot expand without economic development and increasing exports to provide the means to pay for imported goods.

Another serious consideration is the increasing dependence of the North on the raw materials and other primary commodities and resources found in the Southern sovereign countries. The asymmetry of interdependence, which has affected the bargaining position of the South, is gradually becoming less pronounced as access to such supplies becomes increasingly important to the major industrial states in the Northern hemisphere. Access to vital supplies is and will remain a key issue in international trade negotiations.[7] The oil crises, caused by the OPEC decisions, offer a lesson that will not be forgotten despite a temporary lessening of demand due in part to more efficient use of oil and in part to the worldwide recession of the late 1970s and early 1980s. Another oil crisis cannot be ruled out. Measures to regulate the supply of oil are in the interest not only of developed countries but also of the oil-importing LDCs, which suffered even more than the North and have a parallel interest in any arrangements that will prevent future shocks. This is just one more illustration of the complexity of international economic relations today and of the necessity for cooperative solutions (see figure 10-2).

Although there are hopeful signs, there is no justification for excessive optimism. The "global negotiations" on trade, energy, raw materials, economic development, and international monetary problems that have been suggested by the South, to be conducted under the auspices of the United Nations, have not achieved much progress, partly because of American reservations about the desirability of a new negotiating forum that would have a Southern majority and presumably a greater role for the Soviet Union. The need to update the international trade order is there, however, and cannot be wished away.

Figure 10-2
The interdependence of LDCs and industrial countries is graphically shown by the real gross domestic product (GDP) of industrial countries and the export volume growth of developing countries, 1966–1982.

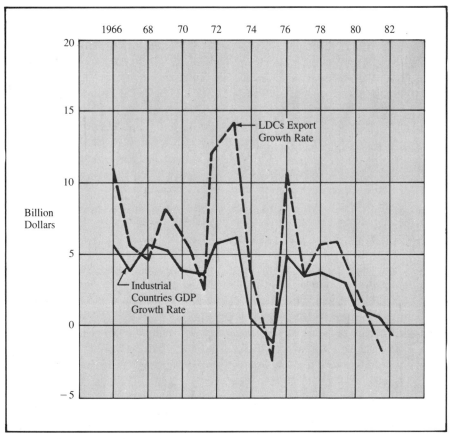

SOURCE: IBRD: World Development Report 1983.

.... Capital Flows

No international arrangements to promote expanded and "fairer" trade exchanges between North and South can be effective unless the developing countries: (1) are able to produce items others, especially the industrial states, are interested in buying, and (2) have the means (foreign exchange) to pay for expanded imports from the North or from one another. In other words, in addition to improving the terms of trade, sustained efforts to promote economic development are needed if LDCs are to move from their present stage of underdevelopment and reliance on a limited and vulnerable cluster of commodities to the level of modernization, productivity, and diversification that characterizes the economies of the OECD countries.

Economic development can be accelerated with outside assistance in the form of grants, loans, and technology transfers. In the sphere of technology, the LDCs enjoy an unplanned advantage; technological developments in the advanced countries (developments that require considerable research and a great deal of expenditure before they become commercially profitable) are routinely transferred to LDCs through equipment imports, technical assistance, or overseas training.

Foreign Aid

Although technology transfers certainly are beneficial, most LDCs need large amounts of *capital* from abroad to supplement their inadequate domestic resources. The needs are staggering. It is estimated that 800 million people live at a mere subsistence level in the Southern hemisphere. This figure accounts for almost 30 percent of all the people in the LDCs. In many cases, the prospects for improvement are dim; in others, the potentials are encouraging. However, in all LDCs, much depends on the inflow of capital from abroad. For all practical purposes, the primary source for such assistance is the group of countries with advanced market economies that form the OECD. A few key figures will illuminate the dimensions of the problem. Of the world's population of 4,550 million (estimated), approximately 23 percent live in the advanced countries of the Northern hemisphere; 77 percent live in the less-developed South. The 23 percent that live in the advanced countries of the North produce approximately 90 percent of all manufactured goods, 82 percent of all grains, and 78 percent of all livestock products. They use approximately 6,360 units of commercial energy per capita (each unit equals the energy produced by one kilogram of coal), whereas the developing countries use 463 units per capita. The disparity becomes starkly evident when we compare specific countries in the North to certain countries in the South. The per capita energy consumption in Canada is 13,453 units; in the United States, 11,919; in West Germany, 6,627; in the Soviet Union, 6,122. Contrast these figures to the per capita consumption in Mali, 41; Bangladesh, 41; Tanzania, 53; Pakistan, 218; India, 242; and Egypt, 565.

It is a fact of life that, for the foreseeable future, certain developing countries cannot rely exclusively on direct investments, external borrowing, or hard currency earnings from their exports. In such cases, economic aid becomes a critical source of funds. According to the International Bank for Reconstruction and Development (IBRD) studies, approximately forty Third World countries will continue to rely almost totally on foreign aid at least for this decade. Most of these countries are in Sub-Saharan

Africa. Another fifty countries that now rely heavily on aid are expected to reduce gradually their dependence on grants and low-interest loans. The bulk of this aid (official development assistance, ODA) comes from the industrial countries that are members of the Development Assistance Committee (DAC) of the OECD[8] and, to a lesser extent, from some of the oil-exporting countries, especially the Arab countries, which, however, channel their aid almost exclusively to Moslem LDCs.

Official development assistance comes to the developing countries either through bilateral arrangements or through multilateral institutions. In either case, we can identify three interrelated elements:

1. Not all developing countries are equally in need of aid; they are at different stages of development

2. Most ODA is channeled to the countries that are poorest and are at the lowest levels of the development process

3. Bilateral and multilateral efforts must complement each other

During the early postwar years, the industrial democracies, the United States in particular, supported the view that economic development should depend primarily on private capital transfers (lending and investments) and domestic capital resources, not on public financing from abroad. The liberalization of trade was expected to provide the developing countries with the opportunity to earn foreign exchange that could be used for development purposes.

Moreover, with the outbreak of the Cold War, Washington's concern focused on the reconstruction of the European economies through the Marshall Plan. The developing countries were told that European reconstruction had an obvious priority because it would restore the vitality of the European economies and open up renewed opportunities for trade, borrowing, and investment. The International Bank for Reconstruction and Development (IBRD) was designed to be more active in promoting reconstruction than development. Even when the IBRD made loans to developing countries, the terms were based on prevailing market rates and conditions.

In 1953, the LDCs advanced a proposal for a Special United Nations Fund for Economic Development (SUNFED) to provide soft loans to developing countries. Despite its optimistic acronym, SUNFED never came into being because of the opposition of the industrial states. However, the persistent pressures of the LDCs and certain political developments led to a shift in the policies of the North and especially of the United States.

Just as the initiation of the Marshall Plan in Europe was powerfully encouraged by the perceived Soviet threat to this vital region in the late 1940s, the change of U.S. policy on the question of aid to the developing countries owed a great deal to the Soviet efforts to gain political influence in the Third World. Following the 1955 Bantung Conference of the Non-Aligned states and the 1956 Twentieth Congress of the Communist Party of the Soviet Union, in which Nikita Khrushchev told the developing countries that they no longer needed to go "begging to their former oppressors for modern equipment" because "they can get it in the socialist countries, free from any political or military obligations," the United States began to view the Third World as an arena of competition with the

Soviet Union in the context of an expanding Cold War.[9] It seems that many constructive U.S. policies resulted only from the prodding of a Soviet initiative.

To deal with the Soviet challenge in the Third World, the United States, as the leading industrial power, had two alternatives: either reform radically the international trade order to provide the LDCs with the arrangements they demanded or change U.S. policies on the question of economic aid. Changes in the trading system under the GATT were more difficult to accept because they would undermine the liberalization that Washington considered the primary necessity and the major feature of the system. Moreover, changes such as those demanded by the LDCs would affect adversely domestic interest groups in the United States. Aid was politically less troublesome. The proponents of economic aid pointed out that most of the LDCs were unable to generate domestic savings in sufficient amounts because of their low per capita incomes, and that they also were unable to obtain sufficient foreign exchange from exports because their economies were not diversified and productive enough. Economic aid should thus supplement the meager domestic resources and promote economic development and growth. Such development would in turn encourage social progress, political stability, and closer ties with the "free world."[10] One result of this linkage between U.S. foreign policy objectives and economic aid was the expansion of aid arrangements and programs:

- In 1958, the United States established its own Development Loan Fund (DLF) with an initial endowment of $300 million

- Also in 1958, Washington reversed its position and agreed to the establishment of the Inter-American Development Bank, contributing $350 million to the Bank's initial $1 billion capital fund

- In 1959, a United Nations Special Fund (UNSF) was established to use voluntary contributions by UN members to finance infrastructure projects in developing countries

- In 1961, President Kennedy proposed an ambitious program of economic aid for Latin America under the label *Alliance for Progress*

- Despite congressional reservations, appropriations for foreign economic aid became a routine component of the federal budget

- With American encouragement and prodding, the OECD members established the Development Assistance Committee (DAC)

- Washington further revised its position on the role of the IBRD; with European reconstruction already accomplished, the Bank was encouraged to turn its attention to development

- In 1958 the lending capacity of the Bank was increased from $10 to $20 billion

- In 1960, again on U.S. initiative, the International Development Association (IDA) and the International Finance Corporation (IFC)

were established within the IBRD system to serve as vehicles for economic assistance to developing countries

Britain and France also became more active in the area of economic assistance,
albeit for different reasons. The dismantling of their colonial empires did not end the
economic ties between the metropole and the former colonies. London and Paris wanted
to preserve their influence in the newly independent countries: economic aid was one of
the principal means to achieve their goal.

Considering the need for infrastructure development and the time lag in reaching a
satisfactory yield from new projects and enterprises, a significant portion of the capital
flow into the LDCs had to take the form of either grants or *concessional* loans (that is,
loans with easy terms for servicing and repayment). Private financial institutions
obviously were in no position to make such loans; only governments and government-
supported international institutions could provide this type of assistance [official development assistance (ODA) in the established terminology of the United Nations]. In
the last thirty years, ODA took several forms:

1. Loans from the World Bank, its affiliates, and the government-
   supported regional banks

2. Government-guaranteed loans for specific projects

3. Loans or grants from one country to another

4. Technical assistance either through international organizations or
   directly by an advanced country to an LDC

Assistance also came in the form of food supplies or other key commodities. In the early
1980s, the World Bank increased its capital stock to approximately $80 billion, and the
International Development Association added another $12 billion to its reserve funds.
Needless to say, these additional funds came primarily from the major market economies
in the North. The World Bank used these added resources to expand its assistance to
projects relating to the production and storage of food, the production of energy, and the
development of infrastructure facilities (see figure 10-3 on p. 287).

In the 1970s, ODA constituted 43 percent of the net capital flows into the LDCs.
By 1979, the portion was down to 35 percent, mainly because the volume of regular
loans to LDCs increased tremendously during the same period. In fact, ODA from the
OECD countries showed a 4 percent annual real increase in net aid disbursements: these
countries increased their total ODA contributions from $6.9 billion in 1970 to $25.4
billion in 1981. Moreover, several oil-exporting countries with large dollar surpluses in
the 1970s devoted a sizeable fraction to ODA. Aid from OPEC countries jumped from
$350 million in 1970 to $5.9 billion in 1977, and to over $7 billion in 1980. As a
percentage of GNP, the ODA contributions varied widely from country to country, as
table 10-2 indicates.

Few donor countries have raised their annual contributions to 0.7 percent of their
GNP, as the Commission on International Development of the United Nations recommended in 1969, and even fewer to the 1 percent sought by the Group of 77. The United

States in particular has been reducing the ratio of ODA to its GNP. In 1960, the United States contributed $2.7 billion, 0.53 percent of its GNP at the time. By 1970, the contribution was down to 0.32 percent of GNP. By 1980, after a brief increase in 1979 when it amounted to $7.1 billion, or 0.27 percent of GNP, U.S. ODA decreased to $5.7 billion, 0.20 percent of GNP. Foreign aid, of course, has no powerful lobby to pressure the U.S. Congress for increased outlays (except for a number of export industries that benefit directly). This is regrettable because the security and prosperity of the United States depend to a large extent on resources located in key regions of the Third World.

The LDCs tried to counter this negative trend by using their numerical majority in the United Nations. In the General Assembly and in UNCTAD, they pressed for foreign assistance outlays equal to 1 percent of the GNP of the developed countries. They later scaled down this demand to 0.7 percent, but still the North did not cooperate. In frustration, the LDCs made a key plank of their plan for a New International Economic Order the demand for greater participation in the World Bank and IMF decision-making bodies and in the management of aid flows.

The resources available for economic aid certainly are inadequate in light of the tremendous needs. For this reason, it is generally agreed that ODA should go to the countries in greatest need, especially those that cannot rely on direct investments or regular borrowing from abroad. Two types of aid, bilateral and multilateral, should complement one another to maximize the effectiveness of each. For example, multilateral institutions, especially the development banks, are particularly effective in providing financial assistance for large, infrastructure projects such as roads, dams, irrigation and land reclamation works. Multilateral aid often is more acceptable, because it is viewed as free of political motivations or "strings." Bilateral aid usually is more effective when the donor country can provide special expertise or has a special relationship with the recipient country. Of course, countries offering aid in the context of bilateral arrange-

Table 10-2
Selected Donors of ODA

OECD	%of GNP	OPEC	% of GNP
Italy	.19	Nigeria	.05
United Kingdom	.43	Iraq	2.12
Japan	.28	Venezuela	.22
Austria	.48	Libya	.92
United States	.20	Saudi Arabia	2.60
Netherlands	1.08	Kuwait	3.88
France	.71	United Arab Emirates	3.96
Norway	.82	Quatar	4.80
West Germany	.46		
Sweden	.83		

SOURCE: The World Bank, World Development Report 1982 (New York: Oxford University Press, 1982), p. 140.

ments often do so with the objective of building closer political ties with the recipient country.

....The Expansion of Lending

In the 1970s, new problems exacerbated the capital needs of most LDCs. Following the drastic increases in the price of oil, the oil-importing LDCs had to pay for the higher costs of their oil imports by borrowing from Western banks at market interest rates. The Western banks were glad to provide the loans; they needed outlets for the deposits of the OPEC members. As a result, the influx of loans into the LDCs increased from an annual volume of $9.1 billion in 1970 to $57.3 billion in 1980 and $81 billion in 1982 (table 10-3 shows the major borrowers). World Bank projections anticipate an annual inflow by 1990 ranging from $99.2 (low case) to $151.1 billion (high case).[11]

The foreign debt of LDCs currently is more than $550 billion, with $364 billion owed to private banks and other financial institutions mostly in the industrial market economies, and $191 billion owed to official lenders such as governments and international agencies. Merely to service these loans (interest and amortization) required in 1982 an annual outlay of $81 billion.

Although this transfer of capital by far exceeded the sums envisaged by the proponents of foreign aid, it has been a mixed blessing for the developing countries. A large portion was used to pay for the increased cost of oil imports and could not be used for development projects. The terms of these loans were determined by market con-

Table 10-3

Latin America's Public and Private Debt (in Billions of Dollars, 1983)

Country	Total Debt	Debt to U.S. Banks
Argentina	38.5	11.2
Bolivia	3.0	0.4
Brazil	84.0	23.0
Chile	17.0	5.3
Colombia	10.3	3.2
Costa Rica	3.5	0.5
Ecuador	6.5	2.0
El Salvador	1.5	0.3
Guatemala	1.5	0.14
Honduras	2.0	0.3
Mexico	80.0	29.4
Nicaragua	2.5	0.4
Panama	2.3	1.0
Paraguay	1.5	0.3
Peru	11.0	2.3
Uruguay	3.5	0.6
Venezuela	28.5	2.2

SOURCES: Federal Reserve Board; the World Bank.

ditions; they were not *concessional* (soft) loans. In the late 1970s and early 1980s, high interest rates, a world recession that reduced trade opportunities, and the high cost of imported oil placed several developing countries in a liquidity squeeze (see table 10-3). Even a country such as Mexico, which has considerable earnings from its oil exports,

Figure 10-3
Amount and distribution of World Bank loans.

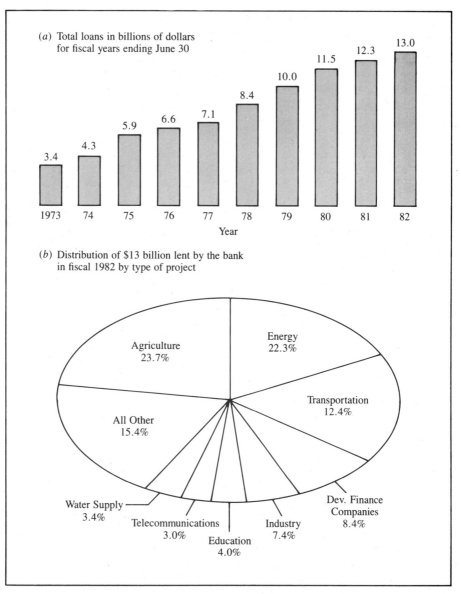

(a) Total loans in billions of dollars for fiscal years ending June 30

(b) Distribution of $13 billion lent by the bank in fiscal 1982 by type of project

SOURCE: © *The New York Times*, March 8, 1983. Reprinted by permission.

found itself in a serious financial bind in 1982 because of extensive borrowing. Several other developing countries had to renegotiate with their lenders the repayment of loans through "recycling"—in effect, adding interest already due to the principal of the loan—or by arranging for new loans just to keep up with interest payments. Liberia, Malagasy, Pakistan, Senegal, Togo, Uganda, and Zaire all had to sign multilateral agreements in 1981 to extend repayment of loans. Particularly pressed were those developing countries that are oil importers.

This new development may induce certain positive and constructive policies on the part of the United States and the OECD countries. For the most part, the problem is manageable.[12] The impression that the developing countries are at the mercy of their lenders is rather misleading. There is a peculiar relationship in borrowing, especially when large sums of money are involved: the lender has a vested interest in the financial health of the borrower. The lenders (both private and governmental) have no incentive to push a borrower country to bankruptcy. If Brazil is unable to make the interest payments due on its loans, the United States government may come to the rescue with a sizeable additional loan. Obviously, there is an aspect of interdependence between lenders and borrowers: a massive default on these loans could bring the collapse of the Western banking system.[13]

A Balance Sheet

The highly optimistic expectations of some foreign aid advocates that economic aid would lead to rapid development of the LDCs, and their political alignment with the West have not been fulfilled; still, there has been progress. Several countries have benefited from the inflow of foreign capital, in the form of both aid and investment, and have forged ahead moving to the category of newly industrializing countries. On the other hand, several have profited only marginally, and others not at all.

Critics, from the LDCs primarily, argue that the quantities of aid were insufficient and unevenly allocated, with the bulk of the aid going to a few selected countries of particular interest to the West. Other commentators blame the LDCs for a variety of misdeeds ranging from corruption and mismanagement of aid to inept bureaucracies, excessive governmental controls, the emphasis on grandiose industrial projects at the expense of agriculture, or the absence of certain qualities and attitudes among the people, as well as the lack of appropriate political and social institutions, The Marshall Plan, some argue, succeeded precisely because the European people already possessed the skills, attitudes, and traditions that are necessary for economic growth. All these arguments have some basis in fact. Despite disappointments, however, it is clearly in the interest of the advanced democracies, and particularly the United States, to promote and assist the development of the LDCs.

Political Motivations
for Supplying Aid

Although economic development does not necessarily lead to the emergence of democratic institutions or pro-American governments and publics, it can prevent domestic discontent from reaching the boiling point. Extensive experience shows that anti-

Western regimes often came to power when revolutionary elites were successful in exploiting public disaffection.

Historically, we find that economically strong and politically stable countries do not willingly embrace Soviet tutelage or the communist model of economic and political organization. Those developing countries that have registered the most impressive progress appear to be least susceptible to a communist takeover. In this regard, the West in general and the United States in particular can only benefit from the steady and balanced development of the Third World countries—at least of those that have the potential to develop strong economies.

Economic assistance can serve important *political* objectives. It is in the interest of the West to assist the Third World countries (1) to gain political stability by reducing the causes of social friction, and (2) to maintain their independence so that they remain open and accessible to the West for peaceful economic, commercial, and cultural relations.[14]

It is also in the interest of the United States and the other market economies to assist and encourage the integration of the LDCs into the international economic system, which, for all practical purposes, is the Western system. Such integration, of course, calls for a more equitable and effective participation of the LDCs in the management of the system, within the practical limits imposed by the realities of their economic strength and level of development.

A judicious and generous contribution of economic assistance can serve political objectives in addition to promoting a healthier world economy and expanded markets for Western products. To be beneficial, long-term loans to developing countries, whether concessional or regular, must be based primarily on economic criteria. Both lenders and borrowers should ask the question: "Will the finished project generate sufficient income to be profitable?" The answer should determine whether the loan should be sought or given. In practice, however, the structuring of development assistance programs as well as the use of the aid by the receiving countries do not always live up to expectations or declared intentions.

Not infrequently, the aid is too limited to be effective or does not fully take into account the actual needs of the receiving country. At times, the selected form of aid suits the needs or the objectives of the donor rather than those of the recipient. In other cases, the government of the prospective recipient may press for certain spectacular or politically impressive projects expected to strengthen the leaders' prestige or popularity. In the Cold War years of the 1950s and 1960s, both the Soviet Union and the United States responded to such requests in the hope of winning client states in their ideological rivalry. During the same period, most developing countries placed emphasis on industrialization. Factory smokestacks were seen as the irrefutable sign of progress. Without the human infrastructure of skilled personnel and managerial and technical know-how, many such projects became monuments to misplaced good intentions.

Development of Agricultural Resources

Sobered by numerous disappointments, several LDC governments began to pay greater attention to agriculture in the 1970s. Convincing evidence from agricultural projects already underway showed that rapid growth of productivity and production in agriculture was possible. Improved nutrition is a first step toward a healthier, more productive labor force. Large segments of population in many LDCs still suffer from hunger and malnutrition, so the increasing recognition of the importance of agriculture is a positive development in international economic thinking.

At the same time, problems previously ignored now receive greater attention. In Sub-Saharan Africa, for example, river blindness (onchocerciasis; infection with a parasitic worm) and sleeping sickness (trypanosomiasis; carried by the tse-tse fly) prevent the cultivation of large, fertile areas in Zaire, Gambia, Nigeria, Cameroon, and Botswana. Efforts to eradicate these diseases now are being financed by the World Bank, WHO, FAO, and individual countries from the OECD group, but progress is slow because available insecticides do not seem to be effective: the tse-tse fly especially shows remarkable resistance.

The development of new farmland is not an easy matter even in the absence of disease-carrying insects. New farm areas can be cleared, but cutting down forests requires costly machinery and fuels. Even when farmland is opened for cultivation, the farmers need roads to carry their produce to the market and storage facilities to prevent spoilage and waste. We may add that several countries, especially along the southern fringes of the Sahara, have too arid a climate to develop successful agriculture without expensive irrigation works.

Education and Training

Regardless of the volume or direction of outside economic assistance, many LDCs are handicapped in their development efforts by a shortage of people with technical and administrative skills. Although expanding educational opportunities have already reduced the levels of illiteracy in many LDCs, improvements in education take almost a generation to reflect themselves in economic gains. Literacy is a key element in the development process because technical training and the use of equipment usually require the ability to read instructions.

Social attitudes and traditions also may seriously interfere with economic development. In India, for instance, religious superstitions and cultural taboos may be a greater handicap than any of the purely economic shortcomings. Punctuality, precision, careful implementation of instructions, and labor discipline are indispensable traits in a modern industrial society; they are not always present in LDC labor forces. Many state employees do not display as yet the necessary competence, administrative ability, discipline, or diligence in carrying out their assigned tasks. In agriculture, farmers are often reluctant to cast aside traditional methods of farming and embrace novel but more productive techniques.

Corruption in Government

Critics of foreign aid frequently point to another problem: corruption. In many LDCs, government employment is one of the few sources of somewhat stable and certain income. Because foreign aid is normally administered and, more important, distributed by government officials and employees, the temptation to use one's official position for personal enrichment is strong. The opportunity to dispense favors to relatives, friends, political supporters, or those who are willing to pay or barter a return favor is a source of power and influence that many officials find difficult to neglect. Complaints that foreign aid does not reach the ordinary people as intended are not always unfounded. Corrupt practices present a problem that is hard to combat; however, it is unrealistic to over-emphasize the element of corruption in evaluating the record of foreign aid.

.... Military Aid

One form of external aid calls for special comment. Foreign *military* aid is sought by many LDCs that cannot afford to pay for all the armaments they consider necessary for their defense or foreign policy objectives. Their requests seldom go unheeded. Weapons that are considered outmoded by the major powers for their own purposes are coveted additions to the arsenals of some LDCs. Giving them away to "friendly" governments is an inexpensive way to curry favor. Both the United States and the Soviet Union use foreign military aid as a means of keeping or gaining friends; they know that in many LDCs the military either is in power or is the most cohesive and influential group. At the same time, they tend to avoid the transfer of overly sophisticated weapons or excessive quantities that may be used to create dangerous situations. The Soviet Union, for example, for several years has supplied the Syrian army with weapons, but never to the point that the latter could seriously threaten Israel's existence. Moscow knows that a crisis caused by such action could precipitate a serious confrontation of the two superpowers. The United States has limited its military aid to Greece and Turkey so that the forces of these two countries—both NATO allies but regional adversaries because of the Cyprus dispute and Turkish claims on the Aegean—will be fairly balanced, with neither side gaining overwhelming superiority over the other.

The Soviet Union provides both military and economic aid to a few LDCs, but the bulk of the Soviet aid goes to eleven states closely associated to the Soviet Union. In 1980, approximately $4.7 billion in economic aid and $350 million in military aid went to six countries where pro-Soviet communist governments are firmly established: Cuba, Mongolia, Vietnam, Cambodia, Laos, and North Korea. Most of the economic aid, nearly $3 billion, went to Cuba. About 87 percent of the assistance given the Cubans was in the form of commodity subsidies. The Soviet Union reportedly bought Cuban sugar at 42 percent above world prices and sold oil to Cuba at about 40 percent below the world price. Thirteen percent of the aid was in the form of economic and technical support for specific development projects. Five countries with Marxist-oriented governments—Angola, Ethiopia, Mozambique, Afghanistan, and South Yemen—received a total of $900 million in arms and military equipment and approximately $300 million in economic and technical aid.

To what extent can foreign aid be used as an instrument of foreign policy? The record is inconclusive. Economic or military aid may increase the dependence of weaker countries on major donors, especially for spare parts for equipment received from a certain country. However, there seem to be limits to the compliance a donor can obtain by suspending or threatening to cut off economic or military aid. The U.S. Congress threatened El Salvador in the early 1980s with the suspension of military aid unless human rights violations were stopped. Improvement was slow and marginal, although in this case the recipient country could not easily find alternative sources of aid.

Direct Investment and
Multinational Corporations ....

Normally loans (even those that are concessional) have to be repaid with interest. Direct investments do not carry a similar burden. Such investments in the developing countries come primarily from private, profit-seeking investors from the advanced market economies. Private investors require, as a rule, a political and economic climate that inspires confidence and security. Because many developing countries were until recently under colonial rule, they tend to be ambivalent about their relations with the industrial states. On the one hand, long-established economic, political, even cultural ties with their former colonial masters favor economic cooperation; on the other, latent resentments and antagonisms undermine such cooperation. Direct investments, in particular, are often viewed with suspicion, and foreign companies willing to establish local subsidiaries are criticized as agents of neocolonialism and exploitation. The political and ideological climate that prevails in many developing countries and the possibility that foreign investments may be nationalized discourage private investors.[15]

.... Weaknesses of LDCs

In view of the uncertainties and complexities inherent in investing in a foreign country, it is not surprising that few individuals or small companies venture into the Third World. The bulk of direct foreign investment in the LDCs is carried out by large, multinational corporations (MNCs).

Critics of the MNCs claim that because of the latter's economic resources and preeminence in certain critical sectors of an LDC's economy (manufacturing, mining), they are able to make decisions that have a bearing on the overall development of the host country without taking into account its interests and preferences.[16]

The developing countries, the critics argue, are in a weak bargaining position when dealing with the MNCs. The governments of many LDCs are anxious to develop certain sectors of their economies—expand industrialization, extract and process their mineral resources and the like—by having foreign companies invest directly, but they are also concerned with the economic and even political influence these corporate giants may be able to exert. They want to regulate the activities of the MNCs so that their country will derive from the association maximum benefit at the lowest political and economic cost. Excessive regulations, however, may discourage prospective investors. Faced with this dilemma, the governments of LDCs are often forced to allow MNCs a virtually free hand. Moreover, even when the host governments establish regulations, they often lack the experienced professionals (lawyers, accountants, statisticians) needed to put such regulations into effect.

The bargaining position of LDCs is further weakened by the ability of MNCs to find alternative outlets for investment. The latter are likely to find sources of raw materials and cheap labor, or countries with greater political stability, elsewhere. Not infrequently, a few major MNCs dominate internationally a given industry or the processing and marketing of a given product. When necessary, such companies may work together to reduce competition among themselves in making direct investments abroad, thus improving their bargaining position in negotiations with an LDC.

.... Selected Countries

Considerable evidence shows that MNCs are not overly anxious to invest in the Third World. More than three-fourths of all foreign direct investment is in the advanced market economies. Even the money that has gone to LDCs is concentrated in a small number of countries. In 1980, five countries—Brazil, Mexico, Venezuela, Indonesia, and Nigeria—accounted for 36 percent of all private foreign investment in the Third World. Nine other countries—India, Malaysia, Argentina, Singapore, Peru, Hong Kong, the Philippines, Trinidad and Tobago, and Iran—accounted for another 22 percent.[17] There is no indication that the situation has changed substantially in the years since. One reason for this selectivity, and one more factor that affects the bargaining position of LDCs, is the uncertainty involved in investing in the Third World.

.... The Element of Risk

All investments carry a risk, but those made in the LDCs often involve greater uncertainty about the eventual success of an enterprise. The foreign investor has to face, in addition, the risk of political instability, abrupt policy changes, nationalization, or popular hostility and labor unrest in the host state. Such political uncertainties tend to offset the economic advantage of local production factors or of a promising local market. Uncertainty translates to costs the investor has to consider when making a decision to invest or evaluating the profit margins of an enterprise. Inevitably, such costs are passed on to the host country. It has been estimated that the average return on book value of direct investments by American MNCs in the advanced market economies between 1975 and 1978 was 12.1 percent, whereas the average return in LDCs was 25.8 percent.[18] Nonetheless, most direct investment by MNCs goes to the advanced market economies.

.... Negative Aspects

Critics of the MNCs list several other negative aspects of their activities in the Third World. The MNCs, they claim, make only a limited contribution to local employment because their operations are not usually labor-intensive and they often use foreign personnel in key positions; in addition, they often hurt local enterprises by competing with them in the local capital markets. MNCs are also charged with siphoning off too much capital from the host country through high profits, manipulation of import and export prices, royalties and fees paid by the local subsidiary to the parent company for technology, and through other practices. MNCs, the critics add, often create small enclaves of development, which do not benefit the host economy as a whole. These enclaves employ few local citizens, acquire supplies from abroad, manipulate earnings to avoid taxes, and distort production by creating inappropriate consumer demand at the expense of socially desirable patterns.

Finally, the critics raise the question of MNC involvement in local politics. One of the most notorious examples they mention is the intervention of the International Telephone and Telegraph Company (ITT) and its Chiltelco subsidiary in Chile against

Salvador Allende Gossens in the early 1970s. There have been other incidents of illegal or improper political involvement.[19]

....Advantages for the LDCs

Supporters of MNC direct investment in developing countries do not dispute that some of the points raised by the critics may have a basis in fact. No international interaction of such magnitude and complexity, they say, could be free of shortcomings and drawbacks. But the bottom line is the overall effect of these projects.

MNCs, they argue, bring into the LDCs otherwise unavailable financial resources. Considering the liquidity problems facing several LDCs that are heavily in debt (a fact that may cut into their ability to borrow) the influx of capital in the form of direct investment becomes even more important.

Direct investments are productive. The investors make every effort to ascertain that the venture has a good chance of being profitable. Whereas an LDC government may promote a project for political reasons without due consideration of economic realities, foreign investors keep their eyes on economic factors and the profitability of the enterprise they contemplate.

Benefits to the host country also come in the form of crucial foreign exchange earnings through exports. The MNCs, with their international marketing connections, open trading opportunities that may be beyond the grasp of local entrepreneurs. The quality of MNC products normally are up to international standards, and the name-recognition these products enjoy worldwide increases their marketability and makes them more competitive than similar products turned out by small, little-known local companies.

The production of the MNC subsidiaries not only helps the host country earn foreign exchange through exports; it also enables the country to save on imports. Items produced locally by the MNC subsidiary replace products that otherwise would have to be imported. In addition, these products are produced by local citizens, and this creates greater employment opportunities.

Although a relatively small percentage of the labor force is employed by the MNC subsidiaries (after all, the majority of people in most LDCs are still engaged in agriculture) those employed learn skills and acquire work attitudes that tend to become the local standards as the economy develops.

Critics who recognize the validity of these points argue nevertheless that the MNCs are primarily interested in profits and have no concern for welfare and social programs (in housing, health, and education) that are desperately needed given the poverty and low living standards prevailing in most LDCs. The supporters of the MNCs counter that social programs tend to remain on paper in the absence of increased production. To carry out social programs, governments need financial resources; without more production and greater revenues little can be accomplished even with the best intentions of the LDC governments. By contributing to greater production and a country's development, and through the housing, health, and education programs they provide for their employees, the MNCs help improve the overall standard of living in the host country.

With regard to the bargaining advantages the MNCs have in their dealings with the developing countries, supporters of the MNCs argue that such advantages lose much of their effectiveness once an MNC has started operations. The host country has legal jurisdiction over the local subsidiary, whereas the foreign company has a valuable asset to protect. The sovereign government of the host country can do much to benefit or harm the foreign enterprise. Not infrequently, the host government takes advantage of these changing conditions and seeks to revise earlier agreements that gave the MNC too many privileges.

....A Balance Sheet

Without ignoring the arguments of the critics or accepting in toto the claims of the proponents, we must recognize three well-established facts:

1. Most LDCs seek foreign direct investments because they believe that the advantages outweigh the drawbacks

2. Most of the LDCs with large foreign investments already have moved into the category of either the newly industrializing countries or the upper-middle-income group

3. MNCs do not appear to be too eager to invest in the Third World, apparently unconvinced that investments in the LDCs are as profitable and one-sided as the MNC critics claim

Foreign direct investment in the LDCs has its drawbacks but, on balance, it tends to be beneficial to the host country. As time goes on, the LDCs, especially those with large foreign investments, are likely to improve their bargaining position and strengthen their control over foreign companies through new regulations, competent personnel, and participation in joint ventures. Already, several developing countries that in the past were reluctant to accept foreign private investments are changing their policies. By creating a more favorable environment, they are likely to bring in more private direct investment—especially if this positive approach proves to reflect a long-term orientation.

Domestic Determinants
of Development ....

The domestic factors that affect the pace of economic development include the ratio of domestic savings to the gross domestic product (GDP); the productivity of labor and the level of efficiency in using resources; the role of the government as a regulator and as an entrepreneur; the availability of skilled personnel; the effectiveness of the bureaucracy; the degree of internal political stability; the effect of religious, cultural, or ideological constraints; the rate of population growth; and the availability of exploitable resources within a country's territory.

Our discussion has focused primarily on the effect the policies of the industrial democracies of the North have on the developing countries in the South. Those policies unquestionably play a pivotal role. We should not underrate the effect of those policies or the constraints imposed by the international economic environment, which is largely dominated by the advanced countries; however, in the long run, it is the domestic policies of the developing countries that hold the key to their economic development and future growth.

With the possible exception of the countries on the southern fringes of the Sahara and in other areas with meager natural resources, which will continue to rely heavily on ODA for a long time, most developing countries have the potential to combine improvements in trade conditions and increased capital flows from the North with more effective domestic policies and thus bring their economies nearer the take-off point.

Such domestic policies should be designed to advance two basic objectives: (1) mobilization of domestic resources, and (2) greater efficiency in resource use. Past experience shows that improvements in the use of resources are the most critical for the development process, but they also are the most difficult to achieve because they require policy reforms and the promotion of management structures and practices that often conflict with traditions, social attitudes, and the government's political goals or ideological orientations.

Even with improvements in domestic policies, the outlook for some of the poorest LDCs is not bright. World Bank studies estimate that even with an annual GDP growth of 5 to 6 percent between now and the year 2000, more than 600 million people in LDCs will continue to live in conditions of abject poverty.[20] Many of the low-income countries will need effective policies not only to stimulate economic development but also to curb population growth (figure 10-4). China has taken drastic steps in an effort to slow its population growth by imposing salary cut-backs on couples giving birth to more than one child. Chinese reports claim that the population increase during the last decade was 70 million less than it would have been without the drastic measures. (These measures, incidentally, have created a peculiar problem because of the traditional Chinese preference for sons. There have been incidents of female infanticide, apparently sufficiently widespread; in a speech in May 1983, Chinese Premier Zhao Ziyang is quoted saying "The whole society should resolutely condemn the criminal activities of female infanticide . . . and the judicial department should resolutely punish the offenders according to law.")[21] Although restraints on population growth may be helpful in many instances, they may not be enough to overcome other drawbacks. Many of the low-income countries will continue to need outside aid to cope with the effects of widespread poverty.

In the case of the more advanced middle-income and newly industrializing countries, endeavors to improve resource mobilization and especially to upgrade the efficiency of resource use may be stymied by external factors beyond the government's control, as our discussion on trade and capital flows has shown. Nevertheless, external impediments should not serve as an excuse for failing to take the necessary domestic steps. The interaction of external factors and domestic policies is a fact of life that underlies the complexity of the development process and points to the need for realistic, nonideological, open-minded approaches.

.... The Necessity for Efficiency

Over the past two decades, governments in most developing countries have played an active role in promoting economic development. Although these efforts have been fairly successful in several countries that are now moving into the category of upper-middle-income, or the even higher category of the NICs, in the majority of LDCs—especially those of low-income or lower-middle-income—progress has been slow and largely unsatisfactory, held back at least in part by weak institutions and inefficient economic management. This lack of progress, even retrogression, varies greatly from one country to another and is due to differences in population, natural resources, political systems, and traditions. In many countries, a serious handicap is the shortage of experienced and well-trained personnel. This problem may ease as education improves, but the immediate need is to use available skills efficiently and to develop institutions and procedures that will provide incentives for further efficiency.

Figure 10-4
Actual and predicted world population growth.

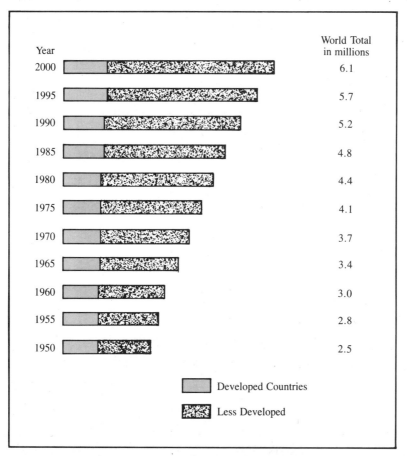

SOURCE: The Hunger Project P.O. Box 789, San Francisco, California.

Prescriptions for greater efficiency are easily drafted on paper, but governments have to deal with domestic institutions, which have their own traditions, vested interests, and a built-in resistance to change. Reforms can be imposed by fiat—but they can still fail, smothered slowly by public inertia and subtle resistance. Reforms can be the product of negotiation and compromise, in which case they may fall short of what is actually needed. In either case, change does not come easily.

Regardless of a country's political and economic system, and its ideological underpinnings, efficiency has two distinct and related aspects: (1) resource allocation efficiency, through pricing, markets, and administrative manipulation; and (2) operational efficiency, through proper organization and incentives to maximize the yield of capital and labor in both the private and public sectors at the lowest possible cost.

Generally speaking, inefficient use of resources results from several practices that are equally detrimental to both developing and advanced countries. They include distorted pricing, counterproductive incentives, low-yield investments, administrative ineffectiveness and inadequate training, and slipshod behavior at the operational level. Endeavors to deal with such problems have to come largely from government initiative, especially in the developing countries. It is the government that has to chart the policies, create the institutional and political environment in which economic activities take place, build the physical infrastructure, and decide whether to encourage private initiative or shift the emphasis to state-owned enterprises (SOEs) and the public sector. Such policy decisions have a direct bearing on the effective mobilization of resources and, even more, on the efficient use of those resources.

To improve efficiency and accelerate economic development, governments—regardless of their ideological orientation or the political system of their country—need to deal realistically with the counterproductive practices we mentioned. The following comments may show why.

Efficient Pricing

It should be obvious that the prices of goods should reflect their relative scarcity and production costs. If the "right price" for a bag of potatoes is one dollar and the government imposes a price of seventy cents, farmers will have hardly any incentive to produce potatoes; if they have a choice, they are likely to shift to some other crop or cut down production to serve their family needs only.[22] Before long, a serious shortage of potatoes is almost inevitable.

Although the deleterious effect of distorted pricing on production is well established, governments ignore this and impose artificially low prices on certain products and services because they are eager to provide their lower-income groups with low-priced goods and services to ease poverty and economic hardship. The results do not often correspond to their good intentions. An often overlooked fact is that without increased *production* even the most equitable *distribution* will not improve living conditions significantly. Price controls expected to benefit the lower-income groups may end up by reducing, instead of increasing, the availability of goods. For similar reasons, government-imposed low interest rates tend to discourage savings, thus reducing the availability of funds for investment. Rent control discourages new construction and leads to the neglect and disrepair of existing housing.

Many price-distorting practices in the developing countries can be traced to the early years after independence. Faced with high popular expectations, widespread poverty, shortages of capital and commodities, and the lack of foreign exchange for imports, many LDC governments adopted internally oriented policies and ambitious social programs that resulted in extensive price distortions. In more recent years, an increasing awareness of the effect sound pricing has on the efficient allocation of resources and especially on stimulating economic activity has led several countries to adopt policies that have resulted in more efficient pricing. Many of these countries are now found among the NICs or the upper-middle-income group.

Price distortion is not the only problem responsible for lower growth rates. Other economic, social, political, and institutional factors also account for variations. The negative effect of distorted pricing may be minimized somewhat if a country is well-endowed with natural resources; nevertheless, even in such countries, the economy could grow faster without the drawback of distorted pricing.[23]

The Role of Incentives

Human beings are not robots. They produce more when they have a good reason to make an effort. This is why incentives are so effective. Farmers will not work hard to produce more if the government purchases their products at artificially low prices. Workers will not reach high levels of productivity if wages are held artificially low or if they find few goods to buy with their income. Investors will not risk their capital in a climate of uncertainty or official hostility against their efforts or if they face heavy taxation that cuts into their profit beyond reasonable limits. The managers of state-owned enterprises (SOEs) will not perform effectively if they are hamstrung by stifling regulations, if they can cover inefficiency and deficits by going to the public treasury for bail-out assistance, or if their job security and promotion depend more on political and bureaucratic criteria than on the economic performance of the enterprise they manage. Citizens will not put their savings in the banks if the official interest rates are artificially low; they will find outlets in a black market of lending, reflecting the actual scarcity of and demand for money. Even centrally planned command economies (as in the Soviet Union, Eastern Europe, or China) are now coming to grips, however reluctantly, with the importance of sound economic incentives.

Low-Yield Investments

Governments in developing countries often undertake for political reasons projects whose economic viability is questionable. In other instances, wrong choices may be due to inadequate studies and false projections. In the late 1970s, for example, Ivory Coast built six large sugar complexes, which turned out to have production costs three times higher than the world market price for sugar. During earlier years, when steel mills and cement plants were seen as evidence of progress, several developing countries invested scarce resources in such projects only to find that production costs were much higher than the world market prices or that the return on their investment was low or even negative because of inefficient management, shortages in skilled labor, lack of infra-structure facilities, or the wasteful use of resources.[24]

Past disappointments have induced the governments of several LDCs to strengthen their evaluation and planning procedures. In this, they have been assisted by the World Bank and other institutions that participate actively in the evaluation of proposed projects before they approve financing.

....Operational Drawbacks

Unused productive capacity causes a lower return on a given investment, be it private or public. Low-capacity use is not uncommon in both advanced and less-developed economies. In the industrial market economies, most excess capacity results from demand fluctuations, economic recessions, and the technological obsolescence of equipment. In the LDCs, low-capacity use usually is due to inadequate infrastructure facilities, shortages of materials or skilled labor, distorted pricing affecting the marketability of products, and unsound projections (which often lead to oversized facilities).

When a production facility is not used adequately, the loss often has a *ripple effect* on the rest of a country's economy. According to World Bank reports, the Indian fertilizer industry operated in 1981 at 67 percent of capacity. Because of lower output, India spent some $400 million of foreign exchange to import fertilizers, thus cutting down on other imports. Frequent breakdowns reduce the availability of locomotives in African and Asian rail systems by 30 to 70 percent. The returns of irrigation facilities in South and Southeast Asia often are much below their potential. One recent study suggested that with better water use these areas could produce an additional 20 million tons of rice, enough to provide minimum food requirements for 90 million people each year.[25]

Delay is another common cause of inefficiency, especially delays in the completion of projects, in the arrival of supplies, or in production and marketing. In most developing countries, governments are actively involved in the investment process. Faced with public pressures to develop the economy, they tend to start several projects simultaneously; their ambitious investment programs may exceed their financial resources or the availability of managerial personnel or skilled labor. When difficulties arise, they are forced to stretch out the completion time over longer periods than initially projected, revise plans midstream, or even leave projects half-finished, with the inevitable losses in capital and output.

Delays are costly everywhere. In the advanced countries, a two-year delay in the completion of a project is likely to increase the cost of investment by more than 20 percent. The same is true in the LDCs, where one- or two-year delays are common. Some delays, of course, are justified by changed circumstances or external factors beyond the control of the LDC: delays in the arrival of supplies from abroad, delays in the disbursement of funds from foreign or international sources, or unforeseeable domestic contingencies. However, many delays are due to poor planning and overoptimistic scheduling. The need for better project selection, planning, and implementation is obvious. Just one year less delay worldwide could save billions of dollars in LDC investments.

Once a project is in operation, delays in the arrival of supplies or delays in the production schedule because of inefficient practices, management incompetence, or labor slackness are not uncommon. Most of the delays in this area can be avoided by local action, as can those in the movement of products from the production site to the market. Delays in marketing are especially costly in agriculture because of the high risk of produce spoilage; a poor road network, shortage of trucks, or irregular availability of rail transport can offset production gains in agriculture by causing costly delays. The profitable marketing of many manufactured products depends on their seasonal availability. Repeated delays in shipping such products tend to discourage not only domestic but also foreign buyers, thus damaging a country's exports. (In this regard, MNCs are helpful because they are less prone to suffer or condone delays.)

Another cause for delays is the breakdown of equipment due to poor maintenance. Because of inadequate maintenance, facilities often run down much faster than they would have done had proper maintenance been carried out routinely. This is particularly true in state-owned enterprises (SOEs) and in public facilities such as roads. Underfunding for maintenance is not uncommon even in the advanced countries. In the United States, for example, critics often complain that poor maintenance of the highway system is becoming a major problem. In Nigeria, roads constructed in the 1970s had to be virtually rebuilt three to five years later because of poor maintenance. In many cases, the managers of state-owned factories assign low priority to equipment maintenance because the benefits of maintenance are not directly visible as output. Moreover, the managers of SOEs usually have recourse to state financing for new equipment and for this reason they have less incentive to protect the equipment and prolong its useful life.

Personnel Shortages

A serious problem for many LDCs is the shortage of experienced personnel at both the managerial/administrative and the production level. Although incompetence is always harmful, the peculiarities of the public sector and the counterproductive incentives often found in it tend to exacerbate any technical inadequacies in the staff or the production-line workers. Bureaucratic rather than commercial and business criteria for judging performance, lack of incentives linked to cost-effective production, reliance on the public treasury to cover deficits, and stifling regulations and controls magnify the effects of technical shortcomings. This is particularly true in the case of the SOEs.

Both in the SOEs and in the civil service, the tendency is to overstaff at the lower levels to provide employment for a larger number of job-seekers. On the other hand, both face shortages at higher levels in managerial and technical personnel. Skill shortages are hard to measure precisely; nevertheless, studies indicate that most developing countries face serious difficulties in finding competent personnel to fill posts in the public sector, particularly openings for administrators, engineers, managers, accountants, and other professionals. Not infrequently, the shortage is exacerbated by the tendency of professionals to go abroad, where they can find better-paying positions or more-satisfying conditions of work. This so-called *brain drain* is an additional problem for many LDCs.[26]

To reduce the skill shortage, between 20 and 25 percent of all ODA goes to technical-assistance programs designed to transfer knowledge and skills to developing countries.[27] Such assistance is valuable, but it must be accompanied by domestic policies to establish career-development programs, improve pay and working conditions in the public sector, and link rewards to performance. In many countries, however, personnel policies are geared more to administering an ingrained system of counterproductive bureaucratic rules than to improving public sector management.

The Role of Government ....

In most LDCs, the role of government is extensive. In fact, recent studies indicate that in many developing countries the expansion of the public sector has reached a point where serious inefficiencies emerge.[28] Certain economic activities generally are recognized as being the responsibility of the state; others, however, can be carried out more effectively by private individuals or institutions making their own decisions to invest and produce on the basis of what they think will be profitable in the prevailing market conditions. In the countries based on the Soviet model, virtually all economic activities are carried on by government enterprises, public institutions, or closely controlled units such as the collective farms. By contrast, in the market economies, most financial activities are left to private initiative. The volume and direction of production generally is determined not by government planners and bureaucrats but by businesspeople who hope to make a profit by judging correctly the realities of supply and demand in the marketplace, domestically and internationally.

Without embracing the extremes of the Soviet model, most LDCs in the past twenty-five years have shown a tendency to expand the public sector. Despite this, 60 to 70 percent of the gross domestic product (GDP) in developing countries comes from the private sector; this is not surprising. Most farming is done by private farmers, usually working their small plots; with over one-half of the population in most developing countries living in the countryside, a significant part of the economy is in the private sector. Most services also are privately owned.

.... State-Owned Enterprises

The LDC governments have concentrated their involvement mostly on major industrial enterprises (manufacturing, mining), public utilities, banking, and major services such as rail, air, and truck transport. Investments in those areas are usually large, and this explains why often 50 to 60 percent of total investment in developing countries goes to the public sector.

The LDCs emphasize state-owned enterprises (SOEs) for a variety of reasons. Quite often, few local citizens have the capital resources or the experience needed for a large investment; the state is the only one that can initiate major new enterprises; it can use public revenues or foreign loans to finance the project. In other instances, the LDC government wants to take over control of existing enterprises from their foreign owners or from minority ethnic groups; to reactivate facilities abandoned by their foreign owners after a revolution; or to take control of bankrupt private firms. Not infrequently, there is a strong popular bias against private enterprise.

During the colonial period—or the era of foreign economic penetration in countries that were not under colonial control—the major enterprises in manufacturing, mining, or farming were in foreign hands. These foreign firms were seldom concerned with the development of a local market for their products. Their aim usually was to maximize their profits by paying low wages to their local employees and low prices for local supplies or other resources. These practices have given a bad name to private enterprise in most developing countries. As a result, there has been public pressure on the governments to take steps to protect the public from foreign or domestic "capitalists." There also has been public pressure for government action to promote economic growth and social welfare. In response, most governments have taken an active economic role by establishing extensive controls over the economy and by engaging in production directly.

Despite this emphasis on the public sector, the majority of LDCs have mixed-market economies; a gradual shift away from SOEs does not face insurmountable ideological or institutional barriers. Such a shift is becoming increasingly necessary. Many developing countries suffer water shortages, unreliable telephone services, frequent power stoppages, breakdowns in rail transport, deteriorating highways, and poor health and education facilities, not to mention inefficient and cumbersome administrations. Governments, by further assuming the role of the producer, stretch their managerial capacity to the breaking point. Efforts to improve the essential services, which are normally the responsibility of government, are hampered by the fact that the state is involved in activities that could be managed outside of the state bureaucracy. It is not possible to determine the most appropriate mix of private enterprise and SOEs by a rigid, universal formula; the mix has to be based on a pragmatic assessment of local conditions and potentials, as free as possible from ideological stereotypes and commitments.

It is useful to keep in mind that the incentives motivating the managers of an enterprise and the way it is managed determine in large measure the efficiency of an enterprise, whether it is private or public. In theory, an SOE can be run efficiently. A large bureaucratic structure is not necessarily an impediment. After all, in the advanced market economies, big private corporations or the MNCs also have large bureaucracies. Their success, however, is mainly due to the sound incentives given their personnel to produce. If an SOE were run as a commercial entity, subject to the effects and the imperatives of the marketplace, it could be theoretically as effective as a private entity of similar size and organization. There is, however, a great difference between what is theoretically possible and what happens in practice. Most SOEs in the developing countries are operated as public bureaucracies; their managers are more concerned with procedure than output and, with easy access to state subsidies, they have little incentive to minimize costs. Moreover, government pressures on the SOE managers to hire people merely to relieve unemployment cut into their productivity and further distort SOE production.

Although private enterprise has practical advantages, it would be misleading to suggest that it can be universally beneficial, especially in the poorer LDCs where entrepreneurial and managerial talent is scarce. However, the greater potential for competition and the impetus to initiative and careful management given by the expectation of material gain (as well as the ever-present threat of bankruptcy—a threat that seldom confronts the SOEs) tend to instill a degree of diligence and discipline not always found in the public sector.

.... **Regulating the Economy**

In every country today, the government exercises some control over the economy and affects economic activities in a variety of ways. At one extreme lies centralized planning in the Soviet model, at the other, a totally unregulated market system; the latter is today virtually nonexistent. Between the two extremes we find different combinations of market mechanisms with varying degrees of government intervention.

Planning Difficulties

These *mixed-market economies* reflect two conflicting considerations. On the one hand, experience shows that no planning organization with a nationwide scope can calculate accurately the relative scarcity of goods or the availability of resources over a number of years and prescribe specific production goals without introducing damaging distortions in the process. On the other, the market mechanisms can neither correct by themselves inequalities in income and wealth nor automatically deal with certain social priorities such as environmental protection or public health. The challenge facing every government, regardless of its ideological complexion, is how to prevent market excesses without creating bureaucratic strangleholds. In many developing countries, the cure often has been worse than the disease.

Since 1945, agencies for long-range economic planning have been commonplace in developing countries. These agencies, however, have not lived up to expectations. In recent years, people familiar with the realities of development have suggested that multiyear development plans have little influence either on investments in the public sector or on economic policy in general. At the root of the problem, they say, is the lack of reality that is often inherent in such plans. The complexity of economic change, the unreliability of forecasts and projections, and the effects of international developments that cannot be foreseen or prevented play havoc with the most impressively constructed plans. Many now argue that economic plans can be useful only if applied as flexible guidelines, not as rigid blueprints.

Nevertheless, a certain fascination with the drafting of multiyear economic plans remains strong. To minimize the inherent weaknesses of long-term planning, however, developing countries may have to take certain practical steps. Plans for the allocation of national resources must take into account the availability of these resources and the overall financial position of the public sector. Quite often, governments in LDCs find that the public expenditures are out of control because the central authorities were not aware of the spending programs of different public agencies or other existing commitments. Moreover, multiyear plans require accurate projections of public revenues or of foreign borrowing over a comparable number of years; yet seldom if ever are such multiyear plans linked to and integrated with multiyear budgets.

Planning agencies also tend to concentrate on developing future projects rather than on completing projects already in progress or on providing financing for the maintenance of those that have been completed. In six out of ten World Bank borrowers in the early 1980s, this bias had assumed serious proportions.[29] In several countries, projects were left unfinished because the funds anticipated by the planners did not materialize.

Planning further suffers from the paucity of information. It is impossible to plan without facts, yet all too often this is attempted. During the early 1980s, for example, the external debt crisis was compounded by the lack of comprehensive data on the affected countries' obligations, potentials, and shortages. A midcourse correction that might help revise unrealistic plans is difficult to achieve in the absence of effective means for monitoring and evaluating implementation. The gathering and evaluation of reliable data can be done only by competent professionals; the shortage of experts in most developing countries further weakens the effectiveness of planning.

Implementation Problems

Planning is one side of the coin; the other side is implementation of the specific programs. How projects and programs are carried out, how implementation is managed, and how problems are solved will affect the ultimate success in reaching the targets set by the planners. The growing number of projects has placed a heavy burden on the limited number of capable managerial experts in all developing countries. The prospect is that this trend will continue during the remainder of this decade.

Matters become worse when managers are saddled with several (often conflicting) goals by the government, and when they are encased in a web of regulations drafted by officials who have only passing familiarity with the operational problems and needs of the project. Imagination and common sense could help a great deal in this regard. For example, in Kenya, Colombia, and elsewhere, rural road maintenance is entrusted to local citizens who are hired as part-time contractors responsible for a small section (one-half to two kilometers) of road in their vicinity. Every month, the road is inspected and the contractor is paid if the job is done. The system has additional advantages; the need for machinery is reduced to a minimum, bureaucratic involvement is also reduced, while the fact that the contractor is known to the local people who use the road and have an interest in seeing that the work is done (community concern) reinforce the formal supervision by the government inspector.

The managers of physical projects—those who operate industrial plants or utilities or direct the building and maintenance of roads and other infrastructure facilities—have the advantage that the technology for the construction, maintenance, and operation is already available and cannot be easily ignored by the regulators. There are, however, problems that stem from local conditions. We have already mentioned the shortages of skilled labor. In many instances, we also find cultural barriers that prevent workers from accepting the discipline required for effective production (for example, religious rites and holidays often interfere with the production routine). The performance of a factory or other production unit also is affected by what is happening in other sectors of the economy and this undermines the efforts of even the most competent manager. Timely delivery of supplies or raw materials depends not only on transportation but also on the output of the suppliers. Such linkages are beyond the control of a given manager regardless of her or his competence. Problems of this type are common to all economies, but they are more difficult to solve in developing countries because of the uneven development of the various sectors and the varying levels of efficiency from one unit to another. Even more difficult is management of social programs designed to improve the living conditions of the low-income, often illiterate "masses." The success of such programs quite often requires radical changes in traditional patterns of individual and community behavior. Programs dealing with health, nutrition, birth control, farming techniques, or sanitation often fall short of expectations because of subtle or open resistance by the intended beneficiaries. In other cases, programs may encounter the opposition of local groups that do not want to change social patterns that are to their benefit, especially when such changes give a stronger voice to disadvantaged, low-influence groups.

The Remedies

Many if not all of the shortcomings discussed in the preceding pages can be corrected by changing the way the central bureaucracies of most developing countries operate. Greater flexibility, less centralization of decision making, use of productivity incentives, avoidance of stifling overregulation, more modest and realistic selection of projects and programs, and greater reliance on common sense could help. In countries in which educational levels are low, poverty widespread, and the supply of competent bureaucrats limited, improvement requires external assistance; nevertheless, even in such countries the main effort has to be made by the country itself.

For the past three decades, most developing countries expanded their public bureaucracies not only in the areas of conventional civil service but also in industry, commerce, and social development. The cost has been considerable; the results often disappointing. People in and out of government are beginning to have second thoughts about the excessive reliance on the public sector, but the alternatives are not easy to implement. Many developing countries brought some of their industries under public ownership to assert national control and assure that their economic activities would serve the government's social priorities. Changing the status of these enterprises is a politically sensitive issue, especially because in many developing countries public opinion is hostile to "capitalist exploitation." A rational employment policy to promote higher productivity or base selection and promotion on merit may be difficult to implement because of a country's ethnic, racial, religious, or linguistic divisions. Moreover, in many countries influential groups favor bureaucratic growth or oppose reduction in public employment. With the public sector providing a large portion of nonfarm employment, any effort to streamline the existing public bureaucracies is likely to be resisted by those who may lose their job or by those who use patronage as a source of political influence. It may also be said that "overstaffed bureaucracies and cumbersome procedures often have even more powerful beneficiaries—those who control the flow of patronage or who profit from the corruption that comes from administrative restrictions."[30]

Past failures have shown that effective management of the economy requires pragmatic policies, well-functioning institutional structures, and competent personnel. When the public sector is overloaded with responsibilities it cannot handle effectively, governments may consider greater reliance on markets to do what experience has shown that markets generally do best. In the face of political and practical barriers, however, administrative reforms may have a better chance to succeed if they are pursued through selective, step-by-step endeavors instead of grandiose schemes that threaten vested interests, which are likely to block and neutralize them.

In any event, the need for a pragmatic, nonideological approach is evident. Improvement can come primarily from domestic policies and programs; external assistance can only help the process along.

The Realities
of Interdependence ....

A discussion of the North–South relationship cannot leave out the question of interdependence. Economic dependence is usually *asymmetrical* in the sense that some countries depend more heavily on other countries than vice versa. A normal feature of the international system, economic dependence is seldom entirely one-sided and this is the essence of interdependence. This applies to virtually all countries regardless of the level of their economic development. Most industrialized states, for example, depend on foreign investments, technology, or supplies from other advanced countries. Canadian or Belgian industries depend as much on foreign patents as do LDCs such as India or Brazil. Japan is extensively dependent on foreign sources of raw materials and fuels as well as on markets in both advanced and developing countries for its products. African or Latin American LDCs depend on foreign loans, economic assistance, and trade opportunities with the industrial states. (In chapter 9, we discussed aspects of the East–West economic interdependence.)

.... Dependency Theory

The type and degree of economic dependence we have discussed differs from that in the dependency, or *dependencia,* theory, as understood by a school of thought initially developed by Latin American economists of Marxist leanings. This theory holds that during the U.S. economic domination in Latin America and the colonial era, the controlling powers deliberately distorted the development of the subject territories to tie them to the economic interests of the *metropole*. As a rule, the colonial territories or dependent countries were forced to concentrate on the production of one or two agricultural commodities for export or the extraction of minerals needed by the industries of the dominant power. There were few attempts to introduce economic diversification or to develop skilled labor forces. In the opinion of the dependency theorists, the economies of the developing countries are still tied to the dominant industrial states, which continue to control the direction of the former's economic development (neocolonialism).[31]

According to this school of thought, the dependency relationship prevents most LDCs from charting their own development policies. The political implications of this theory are obvious. The LDCs cannot break out of the confines of underdevelopment without revolutionary action to sever the restrictive ties.

The dependency theory seems to offer a plausible explanation for the underdevelopment of the former colonies and dependent countries, but a closer look shows that economic realities are much too complex for such a simple explanation. The economic development of the Third World countries is a gigantic undertaking. Because the countries in this group differ greatly in resources, social characteristics, geographic factors, racial composition, historical background, economic organization, and educational and training levels and traditions, the pace and direction of their development vary. Some countries, such as Brazil, South Korea, India, and Nigeria, are moving ahead; others, such as Zambia, Tanzania, Mozambique, and Burma, are struggling to take off. Still others, such as Mali, Niger, and Ethiopia, are just trying to survive. Inadequate levels of economic development are due to a variety of factors, both domestic and international. These factors range over the weak demand for the products of certain countries, unwillingness of private businesses to invest, inefficiency of local bureaucracies, counterproductive traditions, lack of key resources, inadequate foreign assistance, and ideological commitments of political leaders. The dependence theory may be a source of emotional satisfaction for the critics of the advanced countries, but it is of little help as a source of insight into the real problems of economic development.

Asymmetry of Dependence

The asymmetry of resources, the rate of development, and the degree of dependence resulting from actual circumstances offers a more realistic insight into the obstacles to development. There are several causes for asymmetry.

Differences in National Resources. Surface and underground natural resources differ greatly from one country to another. Some countries are rich in valuable minerals, others have fertile land and a good climate, others have both, and some have neither. A country's national endowment of resources combined with the skills and productivity of its people, the efficiency of its economic system, and the stability and efficacy of its political and social institutions eventually affect its gross domestic product (GDP) and the per capita income (PCI) of its people. The differences are staggering. The PCIs of selected countries given in table 10-4 provide an indication of the tremendous diversity.

Table 10-4
Diversity in Wealth among Selected Countries as Indicated by Per Capita Income

Country	Per Capita Income*	Country	Per Capita Income*
Switzerland	$17,430	Zambia	$600
Germany, Fed. Rep.	13,450	Indonesia	530
United States	12,820	Kenya	420
France	12,190	Tanzania	280
Japan	10,080	India	260
Mexico	2,250	Zaire	210
Paraguay	1,630	Ethiopia	140
Jordan	1,620	Laos	80
Nicaragua	860	Bhutan	80

*In 1983 United States dollars.
SOURCE: UN Statistics.

We find significant differences not only in the per capita income of individual countries but also in the gross domestic product (GDP) of the major groups of countries identified as the First, Second, and Third Worlds. For example, the twenty-four OECD countries, with 17.41 percent of the world's population, account for 63 percent of the world's goods and services. The COMECON countries, with 9 percent of the world's population, account for only 15.8 percent; the First World, with only twice as many people as the Second, produces six times as much. The difference between the First and the Third World is even more dramatic. The LDCs, with 74 percent of the world's population, account for only 22 percent of the world's goods and services. The percentage would be even lower if the oil-exporting Arab countries, with their extremely high GDPs, were excluded (table 10-5).

Differences in Trade. The trade among the OECD countries is much more extensive than their trade with the rest of the world. Total world trade (both imports and exports) was valued in 1980 at approximately $3,700 billion ($1,860.7 billion in imports; $1,831 billion in exports). The twenty-four OECD countries imported approximately $1,345 billion and exported $1,251 billion, mostly to each other. This means that the OECD countries, with 17.41 percent of the world's population, accounted for more than 70 percent of world trade. These figures imply (1) that the industrialized market economies are much better customers and suppliers for each other, and (2) that the developing countries have a long way to go before they expand sufficiently their capacity to produce and export and thus increase their hard-currency earnings for more imports as well as for their further economic development.

Dependence on Price and Demand Stability. Several LDCs will continue to depend for exports on a narrow array of products until their economies reach higher levels of diversification. Until then, their economies will remain vulnerable to demand fluctuations for their commodities in the world market. Not surprisingly, most LDCs are anxious to assure stable prices and fairly constant demand levels for their products. Price and demand stability is particularly crucial for LDCs with only one or two major products—usually mineral or agricultural—for their export trade. When demand and world prices for these products fluctuate, the effects are much more destabilizing for the LDCs producing them than for the industrial states, which have multifaceted economies. The price of copper, which represents almost 95 percent of Zambia's total export earnings, is of vital importance to that country but of limited significance

Table 10-5
World Population and Gross Domestic Product (1980)

	Population	Gross Domestic Product
World	4,548,530,000	$11,706,000,000,000
OECD	792,200,000	7,372,000,000,000
COMECON	391,340,000	1,837,150,000,000
LDCs	3,364,980,000	2,499,850,000,000

SOURCE: World Bank statistics.

for the economy of the United States, which imports only 13 percent of its consumption needs in copper. A drop in the demand for coffee, cocoa, copper, or bauxite inevitably results in lower prices and a serious shortfall in the foreign exchange earnings of the supplier countries. Stable prices and fairly constant demand levels are of obvious importance to the countries exporting such minerals or agricultural products—just as uninterrupted supplies are to the importing countries. The modest efforts in Lome to increase price and demand stability were discussed earlier.

Need for Capital and Technology. The developing countries need large sums of capital for their economic development; the major source for that capital is the advanced North. They also need technology not only to raise their productivity and improve the quality of their products but also to diversify their economies. Technology transfers also will have to come primarily from the North.

These are facts of economic reality that inevitably affect the relationship between North and South and underscore the asymmetry of dependence.

Interdependence

Asymmetry of dependence does not mean, of course, one-sided dependence. The North is also dependent on the South. Decisions made by the governments of the LDCs, as well as political, economic, and social developments—which may not be necessarily planned by them—have a far from negligible effect on the short-term and long-range interests of the countries in the North. The industrialized market economies depend heavily on minerals and fuels that are found largely in the territory of Third World countries. The significance of these resources for the First World industries cannot be questioned. The dependence of North on South for the resources was succinctly stated in a recent Congressional hearing: "Complete stoppage or even a significant reduction in the flow of these materials to the United States, the nations of Western Europe, and Japan, could generate economic and therefore political catastrophe."[32] Figure 10-5 illustrates the dependence of the U.S. economy on imported raw materials.

Less obvious is the long-term dependence of the North on expanded exports to the South.

From the end of World War II until recently, the economies of the advanced countries, including that of the United States, were faced with extensive consumer needs within their own area. Oversupply of goods was certainly not a major problem. The economies of Western Europe and Japan had first to recover from the consequences of war. Gradually, however, they reached such levels of production that their output exceeded what their own consumers could absorb. Inevitably, competition became keen and was a matter of serious concern. Japanese automobiles flooded the U.S. market, cutting into the sales of American cars. The consumer market could absorb only so many cars, whether made in the United States or Japan. A key element of the problem was that the U.S. consumers had too many cars available to them for purchase: abundance allows choice. It also leaves cars unsold. The case of the automobile industry is not unique. In many other areas of production, we witness an excess of productive capacity in the advanced economies; at the same time, people in most LDCs lack even simple necessities.

Economists have pointed out that the problems facing certain industries in the advanced countries are due to structural changes. The *comparative advantage* for certain industries is shifting to other countries—including some of the LDCs. The United States produced 39 percent of the world's steel in 1955, but only 15 percent in 1981. New products and new services are opening up new employment and new trade opportunities while they are changing the economic landscape. Some advocate protectionist measures to shield tottering industries from foreign competition. Others reject such measures and advocate instead even greater liberalization of trade in the GATT context. The LDCs on their part seek protection for their fledgling industries and liberal trade arrangements

Figure 10-5

U. S. dependence on foreign sources of raw materials: Percentage from different countries.

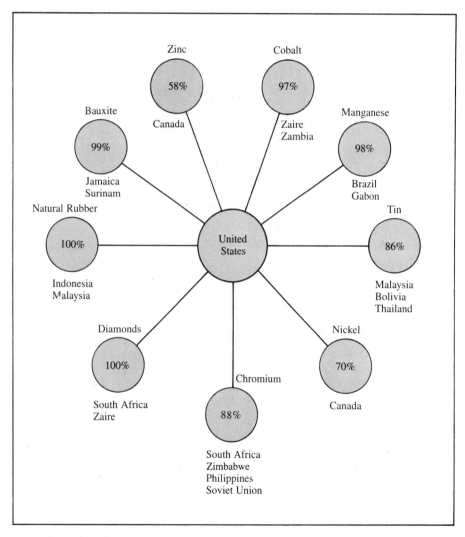

SOURCE: Department of Commerce, Bureau of the Census, Office of International Economic Research.

with the advanced countries without reciprocation. There is a great deal of disagreement and confusion as to the best course of action.

We may search for insight in the economic record of the advanced market economies during the last hundred years. Around the turn of the century, the industrialized economies of Europe and North America began to move gradually into the era of mass production. Increasingly efficient machines and methods of production raised productivity to undreamed of levels. The massive output of goods called for a mass consumer market capable of absorbing the abundance of commodities. It was not enough for potential consumers to desire the goods; they needed to have money to buy them: a mass consumer public could not exist without mass purchasing power; a mass consumer market could not rest on a thin layer of well-to-do customers. The masses had to become potential consumers. For the past eighty years, the industrial states introduced—fitfully and haphazardly to be sure—a series of private and public measures that resulted in the emergence of a mass consumer public, the familiar "consumer society" that has become the hallmark of the OECD economies.

We may be fast approaching a stage in world economic development when our automated, mass-production, high-technology, and high-volume economies will need a global mass consumer public to survive. As in the case of our domestic economies, a global mass consumer market will require mass purchasing power on a global scale. Increasing numbers of people in the LDCs will need to have the money to buy our products. Their purchasing power will certainly have to come from their own increased domestic production. If they are to become consumers of our products and services, the LDCs must have the foreign exchange to import them. One way to obtain the needed foreign exchange is by exporting their own products.

Beleaguered industries in the United States and other OECD countries raise objections to trade policies that could result in expanded imports from LDCs, in which labor costs often are much lower. Protectionist or discriminatory policies may be attractive in the short run, but they will not address the structural changes that are already visible. However undesirable to certain economic groups, the forthcoming structural changes are no less inevitable than the passing, in the early part of the nineteenth century, of the canal boats as a prime means for the transportation of coal.

The dependence of the advanced market economies on a global mass consumer market is another major aspect of the interdependence between North and South. In the short run, concessions on the part of the North may be painful, but the economic development of the LDCs in conjunction with expanding trade between them and the advanced market economies is the most promising course for the future. Closer cooperation between North and South also is the most effective way to forestall Soviet expansion and resolve the protracted East–West rivalry favorably for the West.

Summary

- The countries included under the label *less-developed countries* (LDCs)—or *the Third World,* or *the South*—differ in political systems, religion, culture, ideology, economic organization, productivity, and resources. Nevertheless, they share certain common historical experiences; they are impatient to develop economically; they have large parts of their population living at a subsistence level; they attribute their underdevelopment to past policies by the former colonial powers and to present inequities in the international economic system. With varying degrees of intensity, they favor a New International Economic Order (NIEO).

- Through the UN Conference on Trade and Development (UNCTAD), the Lome Conventions, and other instrumentalities, the LDCs are trying to change the terms of international trade to improve their position. Slowly, changes are being introduced in cooperation with the North.

- Expanded trade goes hand in hand with increased capital flows to the LDCs through foreign aid, lending, and direct investments, which are made mostly by multinational corporations (MNCs).

- The role of the MNCs has been criticized, but on balance their net effect appears to be beneficial to the LDCs. Most LDCs welcome foreign direct investments, provided they can establish safeguards against abuses by the MNCs. For political as well as economic and operational reasons, however, MNCs are not too eager to invest in the Third World. Most such investments are in the advanced market economies.

- Economic development is hampered by several domestic factors such as low efficiency, inadequate material resources, lack of proper incentives, operational drawbacks, shortages in skilled labor, and counterproductive governmental policies.

- The view that underdevelopment may be due in large measure to domestic factors and domestic policies is challenged most forcefully by the dependency (*dependencia*) theorists, who claim that the former colonial powers and the other industrial states of the North continue to control and determine the direction of the economies of the LDCs to continue exploiting them.

- Those who do not subscribe to the radical theory of dependency argue that there is in fact interdependence between North and South: the North needs the resources of the South, and the South needs the help of the North to develop economically. There is, however, an asymmetry to this mutual dependence: under specific circumstances, one side may be more heavily dependent on the other, and this affects bargaining positions.

- The dependence of the advanced market economies of the North on a global mass consumer market suggests that the economic development of the LDCs is in the interest of the advanced countries; only by developing economically will the LDCs become active customers.

- Closer cooperation between North and South also is the most effective way for the OECD countries to forestall the emergence of anti-Western regimes in the Third World and to counter Soviet influence in the protracted East–West rivalry.

Notes

1. Berger, Peter L. "Speaking to the Third World." In Stack, John F., Jr. *Policy Choices*. Guilford, Conn.: Dushkin, 1983, pp. 174–184.
2. Greece already is a member of the OECD and of the European Economic Community (EEC).
3. UN General Assembly, 18th Session, Official Records, Supplement no. 7 (A5507), pp. 24–25.
4. Spero, Joan Edelman. *The Politics of International Economic Relations*. 2nd ed. New York: St. Martin's Press, 1981, pp. 193–195.
5. "The New Lome Convention." *The Economist*, October 22, 1979.
6. Frank, Isaiah. "The 'Graduation' Issue for the Less Developed Countries." *Journal of World Trade Law*, July/August 1979.
7. Bergsten, C. Fred. *Completing the GATT: Toward Rules to Govern Export Controls*. Washington, D.C.: British North American Committee, November 1974; Roessler, Frieder. "GATT and Access to Supplies." *Journal of World Trade Law*, January/February 1975.
8. The DAC comprises Australia, Austria, Belgium, Canada, Denmark, Finland, France, the Federal Republic of Germany, Italy, Japan, the Netherlands, New Zealand, Norway, Sweden, Switzerland, the United Kingdom, the United States, and the Commission of the EEC.
9. Goldman, Marshall I. *Soviet Foreign Aid*. New York: Praeger, 1967, p. 63.
10. Millikan, Max F., and Rostow, W. W. *A Proposal: Key to an Effective Foreign Policy*. New York: Harper and Brothers, 1957.
11. World Bank. *World Development Report, 1982*. New York: Oxford University Press, 1982, p. 35.
12. World Bank. *World Debt Tables*. 1982–83 ed. Washington, D.C.: 1983, p. xi.
13. Aronson, Jonathan D., ed. *Debt and the Less Developed Countries*. Boulder, Colo.: Westview Press, 1979; International Monetary Fund. *World Economic Outlook*. Washington, D.C.: International Monetary Fund, 1980, p. 29.
14. Nelson, Joan M. *Aid, Influence, and Foreign Policy*. New York: Macmillan, 1968, pp. 69–70.
15. Lall, Sanjaya, and Streeten, Paul. *Foreign Investment, Transnationals and Developing Countries*. London: Macmillan, 1977; LaPalombara, Joseph, and Blank, Stephen. *Multinational Corporations and Developing Countries*. New York: The Conference Board, 1979.
16. For a critical view see Müller, Ronald, *Global Reach: The Power of the Multinational Corporations*. New York: Simon and Schuster, 1974.
17. Spero, *op.cit.*, p. 222.
18. *Ibid.*, p. 228.
19. Kugel, Yerachmiel, and Gruenberg, Gladys. *International Payoffs: Dilemma for Business*. Lexington, Mass.: D.C. Heath, 1977.
20. World Bank. *World Development Report, 1983*. New York: Oxford University Press, 1983, p. 39.
21. *China Reconstructs* vol. XXXII, no. 6, 1983.
22. According to Peter McPherson, Administrator of the U.S. Agency for International Development (AID), the farmers in Sub-Saharan Africa "are paid by their government between 25 and 50 percent of the true value of most export crops in most countries. . . . In short, in many countries in Africa, poor farmers are essentially paying inexplicit taxes at 50 percent or higher. It is understandable that food production on a per capita rate has been dropping for many years in Sub-Saharan Africa. Peasant farmers are rational decision makers . . . when prices are such that most agricultural activity is not profitable, farmers will tend to grow only

enough for their own consumption. . ." Speech delivered to the 1983 International Development Conference, quoted in *World Development Forum,* July 15, 1983.

23. World Bank, *World Development Report, op.cit.,* p. 63.

24. Wrong decisions are not the exclusive prerogative of LDC governments. Advanced governments can make mistakes, too. The supersonic Concorde, developed jointly by Britain and France, is used today only by their national airlines and does not cover even their operational costs. The development costs may never be recovered.

25. World Bank, *op.cit.,* p. 45.

26. Serageldin, Ismail, et. al. *Manpower and International Labor Migration in the Middle East and North Africa.* New York: Oxford University Press, 1983.

27. It is estimated that in 1981 approximately $8 billion, mostly in the form of grants, went to technical assistance. More than one-half was given by OECD countries on a country-by-country (bilateral) basis. The rest came from the UN Development Program (UNDP), other UN agencies, the World Bank, the IMF, and the regional banks. Smaller amounts came from private voluntary agencies, the countries of Eastern Europe, and some developing countries such as China and India.

28. Shepard, William G., ed., *Public Enterprise: Economic Analysis of Theory and Practice.* Lexington, Mass: Lexington Books, 1978.

29. World Bank, *op.cit.,* p. 71.

30. *Ibid.,* p. 116.

31. Amin, Samir. *Accumulation on a World Scale.* New York: Monthly Review, 1974. Also by the same author, *Unequal Development: An Essay on the Social Formation of Peripheral Capitalism.* New York: Monthly Review, 1976. See also *International Organization*, Vol 32, Winter 1978; entire issue on "Dependence and Dependency in the Global System."

32. Subcommittee on Mines and Mining, Committee on Interior and Insular Affairs, U.S. House of Representatives, No. 96–99 Part III, September 1980, p. 22 (Testimony by Admiral Robert J. Hanks).

International Relations Digest

Accretion A legal addition to the territory of a state through the gradual deposit of soil by a river to the river bank or by the sea to a seacoast. The concept of accretion dates back to Roman law, which held that an addition follows the fate of the principal object. Soil added by the river becomes part of the territory of the riparian state. Land added to the coast not only becomes part of the national territory but also extends the state's maritime frontier. The same applies to islands formed within the territorial waters of a given state.

Alliance An agreement by two or more countries to use jointly military means to defend or advance their interests. The members of an alliance usually are required under the terms of their treaty to come to the aid of any other alliance member facing an attack by a country outside of the alliance. NATO and the Warsaw Treaty Organization are contemporary illustrations.

Anarchism The doctrine that rejects political authority in all its forms. The anarchist claims that the individual is suppressed by the institutions of social and state control—bureaucracies, courts, police, the military, as well as the institutions of private property and religion—and cannot be free until all those institutions are abolished and oppression is replaced by voluntary cooperation and equitable sharing of economic benefits. Some branches of anarchism openly espouse the use of violence both in theory and as a tactical necessity.

Antiballistic Missile (ABM) A missile carrying a nuclear warhead designed to explode at a high altitude and destroy incoming enemy nuclear missiles in flight before they reach their targets. The deployment of ABMs by the United States and the Soviet Union was limited under the 1972 Strategic Arms Limitation Treaty (SALT).

Apartheid The legal rules enacted by the government of South Africa to separate the nonwhite from the white citizens by imposing special restrictions on the former with regard to political participation, housing, education, employment, sports, recreation, marriage, and other social activities and relationships.

Appeasement A policy in which one country is willing to give up a vital interest of its own to avoid a confrontation with another country without receiving a commensurate and reciprocal concession.

Arbitration One of the methods used under international law for the peaceful settlement of disputes. The parties to a dispute agree to submit their case to a third party and pledge to accept the verdict of the arbitrator as binding. The document signed by the parties, which defines the essence of the dispute, is known as *compromis* and the verdict as *arbitral award*. The 1899 Hague Peace Conference established a Permanent Court of Arbitration, which is not actually a court but a panel of jurists from which interested governments can select arbitrators.

Arms Control Efforts to reduce the risk of war by imposing limitations on the type, features, or quantity of armaments. Such efforts may be unilateral, but as a rule they take the form of bilateral or multilateral agreements for partial disarmament, stabilization of forces at agreed levels, limits on the testing of new weapons, a complete or partial ban on the deployment of weapons in certain environments—such as outer space or the seabed—or in certain geographic areas or localities—such as the Antarctica.

Arms Race   Competition between two hostile countries or groups of countries in increasing their weapons arsenals and military forces to maintain superiority over their opponent. In an arms race the real or imagined preparations of A are seen by B as evidence of offensive intentions, even when they are defensive in character and taken only in response to a military buildup by B. The result is a continuous escalation in the development, procurement, and deployment of weapons and the mobilization of forces.

Balance of Payments   The difference between the value of foreign exchange a country receives from other countries (for their purchase of goods and services in the form of investments, loans, remittances, and as a result of any other private or public transactions) minus the value of foreign exchange transferred to other countries as a result of private or public transactions.

Balance of Power   A concept central to the study of international relations, although the term itself has acquired more than one connotation. It basically means that a sovereign state may improve its power potential and protect or advance its interests more effectively by joining other states or by shifting its support from one group of states to another so that the balance will tilt in its favor. One of the uses of the balance of power concept relates to the British policy of shifting support to one or another group of European powers so that no state or group of states could gain such overwhelming superiority as to place the continent under its control. Another use of the term focuses on the aspect of equilibrium and on the notion that a country's security and the protection of its national interests call for a relative balance with the power potential of a probable opponent. Other meanings refer to *any* distribution of power. This uncertainty about the actual meaning of the term has caused concern to international relations theorists.

Balance of Terror   This term, coined by Winston Churchill, refers to a system of preserving peace in which the two superpowers and their allies (in NATO and in the WPO) avoid military conflict by threatening one another with mutual annihilation in a nuclear exchange. (See also Mutual Assured Destruction.)

Balance of Trade   The difference between the value of foreign exchange received from other countries for the purchase of commodities minus the value of foreign exchange paid to other countries for the purchase of commodities.

Bandung Conference   A conference convened in 1955 in Bandung, Indonesia, by a number of former colonial dependencies and other underdeveloped countries. The participants declared their determination to remain "nonaligned" in the Cold War, proclaimed the "five principles of peaceful coexistence" *(Pancha Shila)*, and expressed their preference for a version of socialism that focused primarily on social justice and a more equitable distribution of the domestic product. The participants saw themselves as representatives of a Third World, separate from the capitalist First World and the Soviet-dominated Second World.

Baruch Plan   Named after Bernard Baruch, this plan was presented to the UN Atomic Energy Commission in 1946. Its objective was to place the possession of atomic weapons under international control by creating an international authority that would control the use of fissionable materials, conduct inspections to prevent violations, and regulate the distribution of atomic plants for peaceful purposes in the various countries. The plan further provided for the destruction of existing atomic bombs. At the time, only the United States possessed such bombs; the last stage in the process was the elimination of the American atomic bomb monopoly. The Soviet Union rejected the Baruch Plan because, in the Soviet view, it would prevent Moscow from developing its own atomic weapons, leaving the United States with a monopoly of atomic weapons technology.

Berlin Blockade   In June 1948, the Soviet authorities imposed restrictions on travel among the three zones in divided Germany, which were occupied by the United States, Britain, and France, and the western sector of the city of Berlin, located approximately one-hundred miles inside Soviet-occupied zone of Germany. The United States responded by initiating an airlift to Berlin. For nearly ten months after the Soviets sealed off land access to Berlin, U.S. aircraft flew into Berlin with food and other supplies. The blockade was lifted in May 1949. By imposing the blockade, the Soviets actually hastened exactly what they wanted to avoid: a rearming of West Germany.

Biological Weapons   Devices designed to carry and spread among the enemy troops (or polulation) bacteria and viruses that can cause severe epidemics. A multilateral treaty was signed in 1972 (the Convention on the Prohibition of the Development, Production and Stockpiling of Bacteriological and Toxic Weapons) outlawing the possession of such weapons and calling for their destruction. Compliance, however, is left mostly to self-restraint. Regardless of any treaty obligations, combatants may refrain from the use of such weapons because an epidemic starting in the enemy camp may well spread over into the user's own territory.

Bipolarity   A situation in international relations in which two states or two groups of states have such a preponderance of power that the course of international affairs in general is determined by their actions, interactions, decisions, or omissions. Other states in such a bipolar system either join one or the other of the two power centers (poles) or, if they remain nonaligned, are likely to have minimal effect on global affairs and especially on matters of war and peace. During the early years after World War II (roughly between 1946 and 1960), the United States and the Soviet Union were the two centers of power and the international system at the time could be regarded as bipolar. This bipolarity has since given way to a multipolar situation as other states have recovered from the effects of war and become influential in world affairs.

Bretton Woods Agreements   Treaties, developed at the international conference hosted by the United States in July 1944, that set the foundations for a postwar international economic order. Two major contemporary institutions were produced by this conference: the International Monetary Fund (IMF), which was designed to regulate international monetary relations, and the International Bank for Reconstruction and Development (IBRD or World Bank), designed to assist the task of postwar reconstruction and economic recovery.

Capitalism   An economic system based on the private ownership of the means of production, a market economy, the pursuit of profit, the pricing of goods on the basis of supply and demand, the channeling of investments on the basis of what promises to be profitable, the unrestricted movement of capital and labor with employment and remuneration determined by profitability and productivity, and the unhindered accumulation of wealth by private individuals. Although the basic tenets of capitalism always existed in human society—and the incentives for personal gain that capitalism espouses seem to be part of human nature—the sophisticated economic theories that underlie modern capitalism trace their origin to Adam Smith and his celebrated book *Wealth of Nations*. Today, there is no country with an "orthodox" form of unrestrained laissez faire capitalism. Capitalism today is combined with government regulation and active government involvement in economic affairs. The result is a mixed-market economy.

Chemical Weapons   Weapons carrying toxic chemical substances that under certain conditions may cause health damage or death when inhaled or when the substances come into contact with the victims' body. The problem with such weapons is that gases or other air-carried substances released in enemy territory may be transported by wind into friendly areas.

Clark Amendment   Legislation enacted by the U.S. Congress in 1976 prohibiting American military involvement in Angola.

Club of Rome   An international group of thirty scholars who met in Rome in 1968 and discussed the problems facing humanity as a result of the population explosion and the depletion of arable land, fresh water, ocean fisheries, fossil fuels, and strategic minerals. The first report of the Club of Rome was published in 1972 under the title *The Limits of Growth*. The pessimistic assessment of the report and of subsequent studies inspired by the Club were criticized by other experts who argued that if a similar assessment had been made in the eighteenth century it would have included coal but not petroleum as a fuel and iron ore but not bauxite. In any event, the Club of Rome has generated greater awareness for the conservation and less wasteful use of resources.

Coercive Diplomacy   The use by one government in its interactions with another of political, economic, or military threats. The objective is to induce the other government to comply to avoid certain deprivations or losses.

Cold War   The conditions of protracted and acute tension and confrontational diplomacy that characterized the relations between the United States and the Soviet Union and their allies between 1946 and 1963. During the Cold War period, the two antagonistic camps engaged in psychological warfare, ideological hostility, diplomatic confrontations, military engagements in peripheral areas without the direct involvement of both superpowers, an escalation in the arms race, and other forms of unfriendly interactions short of global war. The Cold War situation reached its climax during the Cuban missile crisis (1963). After this confrontation, which brought the two superpowers closer to a nuclear war than ever before, sobering thoughts led the leadership in both countries to tone down their hostility. Eventually, the Cold War gave way to a new situation which became known as détente. Détente faded after 1980, following events in Poland and Afghanistan, and a situation resembling that of the Cold War of the early postwar years reemerged in the early 1980s.

Collective Security   In its more technical meaning this term applies to a situation in which several sovereign states agree (1) not to use force against each other to settle any disputes that may arise among them; and (2) to jointly use force against any aggressor. The assumption is that a potential aggressor faced with such overwhelming concentration of power will be reluctant to use force and disturb the peace. The United Nations was envisaged initially as an organization of collective security, with the main responsibility assigned to the Security Council. However, this function of the UN has not been operative because any collective security action would require unanimity of the major powers (the five permanent members of the Security Council). Only once, during the 1950 North Korean invasion of South Korea, did the Security Council take collective action—made possible by the accidental absence of the Soviet representative.

Colonialism   The rule of an area and of its inhabitants by an external sovereign entity that treats the subject area as part of its imperial possessions. Historically colonial possessions resulted from (1) the emigration of nationals of one state to sparsely populated areas, as in North America or South Africa or (2) the conquest of militarily weak entities, as in Asia, Africa, and Latin America. The sovereign ruler claimed the unhindered right to administer the colony and exploit its resources.

Command Economy   The model of economic organization introduced by Joseph Stalin in the 1930s. It remains in effect in the Soviet Union and has been applied with variations in the countries of Eastern Europe, Cuba, and China. In this model, the industrial and commercial enterprises are controlled by economic ministries, managed by state-appointed personnel, and operated on the basis of an annual plan drafted by a central planning agency. The agricultural sector is organized in collectives or similar nonprivate units. All decisions relating to investments, production targets, selection, quantity, and quality of products, employment, compensation, and other critical economic matters are controlled by the government.

Communism   The contemporary ideology of communism is based primarily on the doctrines of *scientific socialism* developed by Karl Marx and supplemented by Vladimir Ilyich Lenin, Joseph Stalin, and Mao Tse-tung. Communism is formally identified by the term *Marxism–Leninism*. The doctrinal tenets of Marxism–Leninism include a belief that the transition from capitalism to socialism is inevitable, that the prime mover of history is the class struggle, and that a party of dedicated militant revolutionaries representing the working class (the proletariat) is the vanguard and the guiding force of this struggle. The aim of the class struggle is to establish a "dictatorship of the proletariat"—the social class of propertyless workers who will eventually overthrow capitalist society and end the conditions of "capitalist exploitation of man by man." Marxism–Leninism calls for the collectivist ownership and control of the means of production and for a centrally planned economy. In practical terms, Marxism–Leninism as practiced by the Soviet Union is the underlying ideology of a political/social/economic system in which the elite of the Communist party controls virtually all the economic sources of powers, determines political and social interactions and developments, and for all practical purposes maintains monopoly control over the entire state structure.

Conciliation   As one of the methods that can be used under international law for the peaceful settlement of disputes, this term refers to the process of submitting a given dispute by the parties to a commission or a single person for the purpose of examining all aspects of the dispute and suggesting a solution to the parties concerned. Either or both parties are free to accept or reject the proposals of the conciliators.

Containment   The postwar foreign policy of the United States, which was designed to raise obstacles to a perceived Soviet drive for territorial expansion. The theoretical formulation of this policy was presented by George F. Kennan in 1947. The basic assumption was that the Soviet Union was bent on expansion by fomenting disorder and revolutionary movements in adjacent areas. The U.S. reaction under the containment policy was first to halt Soviet expansion in countries such as Greece, in which a Communist-led guerrilla campaign was underway, and second to erect a system of alliances from Norway to Turkey and on to the Middle East and Asia. NATO, CENTO, SEATO, and ANZUS were the alliances that reflected this policy. The Soviet Union denounced this policy as *capitalist encirclement* and made every effort to undermine it. Of the early alliances, CENTO and SEATO are no longer in existence.

Council of Mutual Economic Assistance (CEMA or COMECON)   A regional organization established in 1949 by the Soviet Union and its East European satellites. Its objective is to coordinate the economies of the participating countries, to introduce a division of labor among them, and to tie more closely the economies of the smaller members to the economy of the Soviet Union. The organization has a Council, which functions as the major decision-making body, and an Executive Committee, which implements the decisions of the Council. The Executive Committee is assisted by a Secretariat headquartered in Moscow. Several specialized committees assist the Council and the Executive Committee in the area of planning and in technical fields. In addition to the Soviet Union, CEMA includes Bulgaria, Czechoslovakia, East Germany, Hungary, Poland, and Romania. Albania, which was an original member, has not participated in CEMA since 1961. The only non-European member is Mongolia.

Counterforce Strategy   A deterrence strategy that relies on the ability of a superpower to deter its opponent by threatening devastating blows on its military targets only. This, in effect, requires that the nuclear weapons and delivery systems have the necessary accuracy and destructive power to eliminate the opponent's offensive nuclear weapons. A counterforce strategy differs from a *countervalue* strategy, which relies on the devastation of cities and other civilian targets to deter the opponent.

Counterinsurgency   The military strategy and tactics employed by a government trying to combat a guerrilla campaign.

Countervalue Strategy   A strategy of nuclear deterence that relies on the threat to destroy cities, industrial installations, and other civilian targets. (See also, in contrast, Counterforce Strategy.)

Coup d' Etat   A sudden, rapid takeover of governmental power by a small military or political group acting clandestinely from within the political structure. The organizers of a coup almost always use fairly small military contingents to seize governmental buildings, telecommunication and mass-media facilities, harbors and airports, and other key installations and to capture or eliminate high government officials and other individuals of potential threat to the organizers of the coup.

Crisis   In international relations, a development or situation affecting the international environment that requires decisions with potentially far-reaching consequences to be made while conditions are changing rapidly and information is fragmentary.

Decision-Making Approach   In international relations, this is the shift of emphasis from the more abstract level of the nation-state to the individuals who actually make the decisions in the name of the state. The decision makers choose among various alternative courses of action on the basis of their perception and definition of the specific situation as well as of their perception of the wider context of their country's historical background, place in the international environment, and the "realities" of the international relations pertinent to their country. On the basis of these perceptions, they formulate a policy that they believe to be in the *national interest*. Their final decision is further affected by domestic factors that have a bearing on their own political standing or interests. Finally, the outcome reflects the constraints imposed on the decision makers by the constitutional and political institutions of their country. The proponents of the decision-making approach as a level of analysis expect decision makers to reach choices through rational analysis; nevertheless, they realize that emotional, subjective, and even irrational elements enter the decision-making process. The major usefulness of the decision-making approach for the study of international relations and foreign policy is that it shifts the focus from the state level ("France did") to the more specific level of the individuals who make the decisions, and to their motivations and perceptions.

Détente   A French term indicating a lessening of protracted tension between two antagonistic countries or groups of countries. Détente may evolve gradually without formal agreements between the antagonists, as a result of a recognition by the respective decision makers that the continuation of tension and hostility is not in the best interest of their countries. *Détente* as a political term became familiar during the latter part of the 1960s and the decade of the 1970s, when the relations between the Soviet Union and the United States (and their allies) shifted gradually away from the tension of the Cold War period to more relaxed, businesslike forms of interaction. During the period of détente, several arms control agreements were signed. This period of détente came to an end in the early 1980s.

Diplomacy   (1) The operational techniques and methods of interaction employed by the representatives of sovereign states or other international actors in their relations with the representatives of other actors; (2) the practice of using official representatives stationed abroad to conduct exchanges with the officials of the host state on a routine basis; and (3) the entire process of the formulation and implementation of foreign-policy decisions. Diplomacy in a general sense involves a nonviolent approach to the handling of problems or issues that exist between international actors. Diplomatic exchanges may be formal or informal, open or secret, direct or through signals, bilateral or multilateral, at the ambassadorial, ministerial, or head-of-state or government (summit) level. Although diplomacy is a nonviolent form of interaction, diplomats may, on occasion, use direct or implied threats to influence the thinking of the other side, a form known as *coercive diplomacy*.

The status of diplomatic representatives, their privileges and immunities, their ranks and other matters pertaining to their functions (matters determined mostly by customary rules of international law) were formalized under the 1961 Convention on Diplomatic Privileges and Immunities (the Vienna Treaty).

Domino Theory   The assumption that the fall of one country under hostile control will lead to the successive fall of neighboring countries to the opposing camp. The domino theory frequently was invoked during the Vietnam War to justify the U.S. involvement. The argument was that if South Vietnam were allowed to fall under communist control, one after another the countries of southeast Asia also would pass under communist control.

Dumping   The selling abroad of commodities in large quantities at prices deliberately set far below cost to disrupt the world market for the commodity and gain certain political or economic advantages.

Embargo   The banning of exports to another country as a means of forcing a desired course of action by the country subjected to the embargo.

Eurocommunism   The tendency in the communist parties of West European countries to act independently of Soviet tutelage and to accept the pluralistic character of the Western European political systems. Eurocommunism traces its origins to the *polycentrism* advocated in the 1960s by the leader of the Italian Communists, Palmiro Togliati. The movement toward greater independence from Moscow intensified and spread after the Soviet invasion of Czechoslovakia in August 1968.

European Economic Community (EEC or Common Market)   A regional economic organization was established in 1958 under the Treaty of Rome by six European countries: Belgium, France, Italy, Luxemburg, the Netherlands, and West Germany. It became the next step in the process of European cooperation and integration that had started with the 1952 Treaty of Paris, which established the European Coal and Steel Community (ECSC) for the joint exploitation of the iron and coal resources of the Ruhr. Since 1958, the EEC has reached the highest degree of economic integration among sovereign states ever achieved. Under the EEC, trade barriers among the member-states have been virtually eliminated. Moreover, the EEC agencies and institutions have contributed to the cooperative solution of common economic problems. The most important organs of the EEC are the Council of Ministers and the Commission. The Council is a decision-making body composed of representatives from the member-states. Decisions usually require unanimity, but certain issues can be decided by majority. The Commission is a supranational organ with considerable authority to carry on the day-to-day operations of the Community. The membership of the EEC was expanded in 1973 with the admission of Britain, Denmark, and Ireland, and in 1981 with the admission of Greece. Combined with the Euratom and the ECSC, the EEC forms the European Community. In addition to the organs of the EEC, Euratom, and ECSC, the Community has a Parliament which serves as a deliberative and consultative body, with deputies elected since 1979 by the voters of each member-state and a ten-member Court of Justice.

European Free Trade Area (EFTA)   This organization was established in 1959 on British initiative to eliminate tariff and other trade barriers among its member-states. The initial members were Austria, Britain, Denmark, Norway, Portugal, Sweden, and Switzerland. Finland joined as an associate member in 1961. The highest organ is a Council of Ministers, which settles disputes and makes policy recommendations to the governments of the member-states. A Secretariat has its headquarters in Geneva. In 1973, Britain, Denmark, and Ireland left EFTA and joined the EEC. EFTA continues to be active. In 1977, the members agreed to abolish all tariffs and other trade barriers applying to industrial products traded among the member-states.

First World   The industrially advanced countries that have mixed-market economies and pluralistic political systems. For all practical purposes, the First World includes the member-states of the Organization of Economic Cooperation and Development (OECD).

Foreign Aid   The transfer of resources from one country to another in the form of grants, low-interest (concessional) loans, commodities free of charge, or technical knowledge. Assistance may also be in the form of military equipment or training (military aid). Foreign aid may be channeled through international organizations both public and private. A major illustration of an ambitious and successful foreign aid program was the so-called Marshall Plan. Foreign aid to developing countries has become a major feature of contemporary international economic relations.

Fourth World   The least-developed countries, which have very low per capita incomes and a scarcity of resources—fuels, minerals, arable land, and so on. This category was introduced to indicate that among the Third World countries (the LDCs) there are countries that have very dismal prospects for economic development and require economic aid for a much longer period to cope with the conditions of widespread poverty among their people.

Free Trade   The free flow of goods from one country to another, unhindered by governmental regulations, controls, and other barriers. The advocates of free trade favor a reduction in tariffs, quotas, and other nontariff barriers. GATT is an international organization dedicated to promoting free trade.

Geneva Convention   One of the most widely familiar rules of international law on the conduct of war, the Geneva Convention on Prisoners of War was signed in 1929. It provided that prisoners of war should not be tortured or mistreated, but could be required only to give their captors their name, birth date, rank, and serial number. They were entitled to food comparable in nutritional value to that given the captor's troops, and they could not be made to work in war-related production. The Convention was revised in 1949 to update the rules applying to the treatment of prisoners and the sick and wounded, and to the protection of civilians. The Geneva Convention was generally observed by the combatants during World War II. In the postwar decades, however, the Geneva Convention has been violated in many instances.

Geopolitics   In a very general sense, this term refers to the relationship between geography and international relations. Geopolitics is more specifically associated with certain theorists who attempted to construct global explanations of international developments, based on worldwide geographic considerations. British geographer Sir Harold J. Mackinder (1869–1947) postulated a series of propositions. He claimed that Eurasia (East Europe and Russia) constituted the *heartland* of the international system. Europe, Asia, and Africa (combined with the inner heartland) constituted the *world island*. North and South America and Australia were the *insular* power bases or the *outer crescent*. According to Mackinder, whoever controlled the heartland would eventually control the world island, and whoever controlled the world island would rule the world. At the time—prior to World War I and, later, prior to World War II—the practical thrust of the theory was that Germany should not be allowed to extend its control over East Europe and Russia. Later, Mackinder turned his theory around to apply it to the dangers of Soviet control over East Europe and Germany. The American geopolitician Nicholas J. Spykman (1893–1943) revamped the Mackinder theory by shifting the emphasis to the rimlands of Western Europe, the Middle East, Africa, South Asia, and the Far East, which surround Mackinder's heartland. Spykman argued that the security of the United States would be threatened if the powers controlling the heartland were allowed to bring under their control the *rimlands*. Another American, Admiral Alfred Thayer Mahan (1840–1914), saw the world's oceans as connecting rather than separating the continental land masses. The acquisition and defense of overseas empires, therefore, required control of the high seas through strong naval forces. Mahan saw the United States as an imperial power that could play a worldwide role. Mahan's theories remain relevant in the sense that states with worldwide interests must be able to project their power and influence at great distances from their homeland. The German Karl Haushofer (1869–1946) embraced Mackinder's heartland theory and advocated a German–Russo–Japanese bloc in which Germany was to play the dominant role. Such a bloc would eventually achieve, in his view, a preponderance of power and bring under its control the periphery of the world island thus isolating the insular areas, especially the United States.

Globalism   In U.S. foreign policy, the tendency to reject isolationism and accept international responsibilities on a global scale. Globalism may be pushed to extremes by those who advocate the role of world policeman for the United States. Since the Vietnam War, the prevailing tendency is to view globalism in a more moderate and limited context.

Good Offices   One of the methods used under international law for the peaceful settlement of disputes. A third party offers its good offices to the countries involved in a dispute and tries to bring them together so that they can carry on direct negotiations by themselves. Normally, the party offering its good offices meets separately with each of the parties. This practice is particularly useful when the disputing parties do not have diplomatic relations or are each reluctant to take the first step in initiating talks for fear of giving an impression of weakness.

Guerrilla Warfare   Hit-and-run type of military action by fairly small armed bands fighting against a foreign invading army or against the established authorities of their country. The advantage of guerrilla warfare is that the bands can move swiftly, preselect targets and launch surprise attacks, and avoid capture by melting into the population. The disadvantage of guerrilla warfare is that it cannot bring under permanent guerrilla control important inhabited areas and cities unless the bands grow in number and eventually pass to conventional types of warfare. This transition is a most critical step for the guerrillas, because under conventional warfare the numerical strength and fire-power of the guerrillas must be comparable to that of the regular army opposing them.

Gunboat Diplomacy   The dispatch of naval units by a major power to the coastal waters of a smaller country with the objective of intimidating the latter's government and obtaining compliance. This is an extreme form of coercive diplomacy.

Hot Line   The communications link between the American and Soviet governments, established under an agreement signed by the two superpowers in June 1963. It consists of teletype machines printing in the Cyrillic and the Latin alphabet. Initially, the machines were connected by land and sea cable, but now they are linked through communication satellites. In September 1971, the two superpowers signed an Agreement on Nuclear Accidents, which requires both countries to use the hot line in the event of accidents involving their forces or in the event that either of them track unidentified flying objects by their early warning systems. The 1971 agreement further obligates each country to give advance notice to the other on missile tests that will extend beyond its own territory in the direction of the other. Such notice, however, is not normally given over the hot line, but is passed through regular diplomatic channels.

Human Rights   In political science; the right of human beings to be free of arbitrary interference by state authorities in their daily lives. These include the right of personal freedom and protection against arbitrary arrest, the right of unrestricted selection of domicile, the right to travel, the right of equal protection under law, the inviolability of correspondence, and the like. Many nations also include social and economic rights, such as the protection of health, the right to leisure, or the right to employment. In 1948, the UN General Assembly adopted the Universal Declaration of Human Rights. In 1953, the West European states adopted a Convention on Human Rights and established a Commission of Human Rights, which reviews complaints and reports its findings and recommendations to the Committee of Ministers of the Council of Europe. In 1975, the Conference on Security and Cooperation in Europe (CSCE), which met in Helsinki with the participation of the United States, the Soviet Union, and most Western and Eastern European states, approved the Helsinki Accord, which provides for the protection of human rights. Violations of human rights, however, occur in many countries that are legally bound by such international agreements.

Ideology   A cluster of beliefs, assumptions, and prescriptions relating to the basic organization of society, its core values, and an individual's place in it. An ideology is concerned with the nature of the political and social system, the distribution and exercise of power, the role and place of the individual, and the basic objectives of society. To be regarded as an ideology, such a cluster of beliefs must acquire a fairly wide popular following.

Imperialism   In a broad sense, a long-range policy of a sovereign entity to extend its rule over different sovereign or other entities, covering an extended geographic area. The objectives of an imperialist policy vary: (1) it may result from economic necessity to assure the imperialist power raw materials for its industries, food for its people, markets for its products, or precious metals for its treasury; (2) it may be traced to security needs—to subjugate potential adversaries, to bring under control strategically important areas, and to create a "buffer zone" between the center of the imperialist power and potential enemies; (3) it may be inspired by considerations of prestige and power, because size alone can serve as a source of prestige and power; finally (4) it may be rationalized in humanitarian terms as a civilized mission (the "white man's burden") carried by the imperialist nation—often against the will of the "beneficiaries." A different version of imperialism was presented by Lenin in his pamphlet *Imperialism: the Ultimate Stage of Capitalism* (1917), in which he rationalized the survival of capitalism in the industrial states and the relative improvement of the workers' standard of living despite Marxist predictions to the contrary. Lenin argued that the capitalist states were exploiting their colonial possessions, bringing their profits to the metropole, and giving some crumbs to the workers to keep them quiet. Moreover, investment opportunities in the industrial countries were diminishing while capital was accumulating from the exploitation of the colonial areas. The competitive search for markets and investment opportunities led to imperialist policies and imperialist wars, which would hasten the inevitable downfall of capitalism.

Inquiry   Parties to an international dispute may agree to appoint a fact-finding commission to review the disputed facts and thus help them reconcile their differences. Such commissions have been particularly useful in determining boundary lines. In 1967, the UN General Assembly unanimously adopted a resolution urging the members to make more effective use of the fact-finding procedures envisioned in Article 33 of the Charter. Nevertheless, governments are not eager to entrust to third parties the determination of the "facts" in a dispute.

Intangible Assets   In international relations, the assets affecting power and influence that cannot be measured. They include a country's leadership, prestige, ideology, population loyalty, and cohesion.

Integration   In the international arena, the process whereby two or more sovereign states accept limitations to their freedom of action and establish joint institutions and procedures to coordinate their activities for their common benefit. The highest degree of integration is reached when two sovereign actors become one; this level is rarely achieved through voluntary renunciation of sovereignty. Less-extensive forms of integration are more likely. International integration is promoted when international actors share common values and interests.

Intercontinental Ballistic Missiles (ICBMs)   Liquid- or dry-fueled rockets capable of carrying nuclear warheads and covering a distance of over 5,000 miles within approximately thirty minutes from the moment of launching; they fly in a ballistic arc.

Interdependence   In international relations, countries are interdependent when the interests of one can be seriously affected by the decisions of the other and vice versa.

Intervention   Interference in the affairs of a state by another, designed to force the former to take measures or forego actions according to the wishes of the latter. Intervention may involve the use of military force or other forms of coercion. Intervention is a likely form of action when one actor is much stronger than the victim of intervention. If the opposing parties are fairly equal in military strength, the result may be war instead of intervention.

Irredentism   Under this policy a country, claiming to have ethnic brethren in neighboring territories under the sovereign control of another country, embarks on a campaign to bring the kindred groups—and the land they inhabit—under its sovereign control. Irredentist policies may be limited to propaganda efforts to strengthen the ethnic loyalties of the kindred groups or to foment a revolutionary movement in favor of uniting with the *mother country,* or may extend to a military campaign by the mother country to seize the areas inhabited by its ethnic brethren. Such a military campaign is likely to be resisted by the state that has control of those areas. Many wars in the last one-hundred years can be traced to irredentist policies. Even when the irredentist government is successful in the war, the transfer of territory does not become legitimate and permanent until an international agreement is signed by the two countries and possibly by other interested parties.

Isolationism   The general thrust of U.S. foreign policy during the nineteenth century and prior to the two world wars in the twentieth century. The central theme of this policy was that the United States should not become directly involved in disputes of the European powers (primarily). This policy, however, did not exclude active U.S. interest in the Pacific, and especially in Latin America and the Caribbean.

Kellogg—Briand Pact   The popular name for the General Treaty for the Renunciation of War signed in Paris on August 27, 1928, by representatives of fifteen states and ultimately ratified or accepted by sixty-five nations, virtually all existing sovereign states at the time. Under the terms of this treaty, the participating states "solemnly" declared that "they condemn recourse to war for the solution of international controversies" and they renounced war "as an instrument of national policy in their relations with one another." The signatories also agreed that "the settlement or solution of all disputes or conflicts of whatever nature or of whatever origin they may be, shall never be sought except by pacific means." The treaty had no date or provisions for its termination: technically, it is still in force. The familiar name of the treaty comes from Frank B. Kellogg, then U.S. Secretary of State, and Aristide Briand, French Foreign Minister at the time.

Kennedy Round   The negotiations carried out between 1963 and 1967 under the auspices of GATT with the objective of widening and accelerating the reduction of trade barriers. The negotiations were initiated as a result of the U.S. Trade Expansion Act of 1962, which was passed at the urging of President John F. Kennedy. In previous GATT negotiations, the basic procedure was to agree on reciprocal tariff concessions among countries on a commodity-by-commodity basis. The aim of the Kennedy Round was to introduce reductions across the board. The agreement signed in 1967 set substantial duty reductions on dutiable imports with the exception of certain agricultural and dairy products. The less-developed countries complained that the tariff reductions would be of limited benefit to them because of their inadequate production of industrial goods for export. Primary products were not given much attention by the negotiators of the Kennedy Round. Nevertheless, the liberalization of trade proved beneficial in the long run, especially for the advanced market economies.

Kiloton Weapon   An atomic or nuclear weapon with less than 1 million tons of TNT equivalency of explosive yield. One kiloton equals the force of 1,000 tons of TNT.

Latin American Free Trade Association (LAFTA)   This regional organization was established by the Treaty of Montevideo in 1960 to liberalize trade relations among the participating countries: Argentina, Brazil, Chile, Colombia, Ecuador, Mexico, Paraguay, Peru, Uruguay, and Venezuela. Unlike the European Economic Community, the LAFTA members had to negotiate periodically for further reductions because the agreement made no provision for automatic, across-the-board tariff cuts. In addition, the similarity of the participating countries in their exports contributed more to competition among them in trying to find markets abroad than to cooperation to increase trade with each other. In 1980, Bolivia joined the ten LAFTA members to establish the Latin American Integration Association (LAIA). Under the new arrangement, the richer and more-developed countries in the group are expected to make greater trade concessions.

Lebensraum   A term used by Adolf Hitler to identify his claim that the German nation needed "living space" (*Lebensraum*) to develop economically and that such living space could be found primarily in the fertile plains of European Russia.

Less Developed Countries (LDCs)   Countries whose economies are characterized by low productivity, inefficient agricultural production, limited and uneven industrial development, extensive poverty, and ineffective production practices. These countries are also identified as the Third and Fourth Worlds. In international forums, they often act together as the Group of 77 (although the membership has grown to 122). Currently the LDCs are developing at different rates and therefore, under the LDC label, we find different categories determined by the level of development already achieved and by other economic factors such as the existence of certain resources on their soil (for example, oil).

Limited War   In a general sense, an armed conflict having limited objectives and conducted with a limited application of military power. In a limited war, neither side throws into the battle all its power assets and neither sides aims at the complete destruction or subjugation of the other. Limited war differs in this respect from total war. In the nuclear age, limited war between the superpowers and their allies involves the use of only conventional forces or at most only battlefield (theater) atomic weapons—not the use of ICBMs and SLBMs and similar mass-destruction weapons against military and civilian targets.

Linkage   In a broad sense, the consequences the developments in one area of interaction between two international actors may have on other areas of interaction. During the 1970s, Henry Kissinger promoted a linkage strategy in the relations between the United States and the Soviet Union. This strategy rested on the assumption that Soviet expansionism would be moderated by increasing Soviet dependence on a more-stable relationship with the United States and other Western nations. Expanded trade relations, agreements on the control of nuclear weapons, cultural exchanges, and a toning down of mutual recriminations, would, under the linkage strategy, create a vested interest in mutual restraint and strengthen the process of détente. The validity of this strategy came under attack following the Soviet invasion of Afghanistan, the events in Poland, the alleged Soviet military buildup, the stationing of SS-20s aimed at Western Europe, and the downing of the Korean airliner in 1983. Nevertheless, the validity of linkage was proven, albeit in a reverse fashion. Even actions not directly affecting the interests of the United States contributed to the deterioration of U.S.–Soviet relations in the early 1980s.

Lome Convention   The first Lome Conference met in 1975 in the city of Lome, Nigeria, with the participation of the EEC member-states and forty-six countries from Africa, the Caribbean, and the Pacific (the ACP group). The participants signed the Lome Convention (Lome I), which ensured aid to the ACP countries and gave them a greater voice in aid management. It also provided for preferential access of ACP products to EEC markets without reciprocal concessions by the ACP countries. In addition, it created a fund (Stabex) to be used as a cushion for stabilizing the export earnings of the ACP countries from twelve key commodities that are crucial to their economies. A second accord (Lome II), signed in 1979, which now covers fifty-eight ACP countries expanded the Stabex fund, increased foreign aid outlays by nearly 70 percent and provided for greater cooperation between the EEC and ACP members, especially in the industrial sector. Although these agreements did not go as far as the ACP states wanted, they were steps in the direction of greater cooperation between the advanced and the developing countries.

Marshall Plan   The popular name for the European Recovery Program enacted by the U.S. Congress in 1948. The legislation provided grants and low-interest loans to the European countries that were willing to participate. It was named after George C. Marshall, who as the U.S. Secretary of State proposed in 1947 a vast American-financed program of economic aid to help the reconstruction of war-shattered Europe. The sixteen countries that participated in the program formed the Organization of European Economic Cooperation (OEEC). In 1961, the OEEC was replaced by the Organization for Economic Cooperation and Development (OECD) with the admission of several other advanced market economies outside of Europe. Currently OECD has twenty-four members.

Mediation   One of the methods for the peaceful settlement of disputes. It should not be confused with *good offices*. In mediation, the mediator participates actively in the negotiations for the settlement itself. Mediation can be undertaken by a third state, a group of states, an individual, or an international organization. The mediator is expected to offer specific proposals and assist the disputing parties directly in negotiating a settlement. The mediator may meet with the parties separately or in joint sessions. To perform the mediation function, the mediator must be acceptable to the disputing parties. Mediation is used fairly frequently in contemporary international relations.

Megaton Weapon   Nuclear weapons having explosive power equivalent to at least 1 million tons of TNT. (Each megaton represents an explosive yield equivalent to 1 million tons of TNT.)

Military-Industrial Complex   A term used by President Eisenhower in his farewell address, referring to the military services, defense industries and their executives, labor union leaders, academic and scientific experts, intelligence analysts, and politicians who benefit financially from the continuation of international tension and the resulting perception that extensive outlays for defense are needed. The implication is that all those groups and individuals who benefit from high levels of defense spending are part of a conspiratorial cabal working behind the scenes to undermine any improvement in international relations. Whether the conspiratorial image is accurate or not, such a complex does exist in the sense that there are many individuals in every country, including the Soviet Union, whose personal interests are served by greater outlays for defense, and such individuals are likely to support defense-oriented policies.

Montreux Convention   The 1936 multilateral treaty that recognized exclusive Turkish sovereignty over the straits of Bosporus and the Dardanelles, and gave Turkey the right to fortify the area. The Montreux Convention reaffirmed the right of free passage of commercial ships of all nations. With the exception of aircraft carriers and submarines, all warships of states bordering on the Black Sea are allowed to pass unrestricted through the straits in peacetime. On the other hand, only light warships of non–Black Sea powers may pass through the straits to enter the Black Sea, and then under limitations in terms of tonnage, duration of cruising time, and number of naval units present at one time. In time of war, the straits are closed to all belligerents if Turkey is neutral; if Turkey is one of the combatants, she can decide what ships may or may not go through.

Multinational Corporation (MNC)   A private corporation that establishes subsidiary companies in various countries through direct investment. The subsidiaries are normally subject to the laws of the host country, although cooperation with the parent company is close. MNCs are controversial because of their economic power and the possibility that they may interfere in the affairs of the host country. Nevertheless, MNCs may benefit the host country with the inflow of capital, the opportunities for employment they create locally, their worldwide connections for the marketing of products produced by the subsidiaries, and so on. Three-fourths of MNCs operate in the advanced market economies.

Multiple Independently Targeted Reentry Vehicles (MIRVs)   A ballistic missile (ICBM or SLBM) carrying in its cone several nuclear warheads (bombs). The warheads are released once the missile has approached the target area, and each warhead then continues its independent flight to the assigned point of impact, guided by its own preprogrammed equipment.

Multipolarity   In international relations, a situation in which several major states or groups of states possess assets that enable them to influence decisively the course of international developments and to counterbalance the power or influence potential of other states or groups of states. Multipolarity differs from the situation that prevailed in the early period after World War II, when the United States and the Soviet Union were the two effective power centers. In a multipolar (as contrasted to a bipolar) system the participants may enter new alignments, shift their support, or constrain one another with greater flexibility.

Mutual Assured Destruction (MAD)   The doctrine at the heart of nuclear deterrence: Both sides have the capacity to destroy one another and neither side can prevent its own destruction by first destroying the retaliatory weapons of the other. The proponents of this doctrine in the United States argue that the Soviet Union will not attempt an aggressive move against areas vital to the Western alliance if such a move can trigger a nuclear response that will lead to the devastation of the Soviet Union. From the U.S. point of view, the key is that the United States must always maintain a devastating second strike capability and that the Soviet Union must be convinced that the United States will use this capability if necessary.

MX Missile   A ten-warhead, land-based ICBM, originally planned for deployment in a *mobile basing system*. The mobile deployment was expected to reduce the vulnerability of the missiles to a counterforce strike by Soviet ICBMs and to make it necessary for the Soviet Union to use a greater number of missiles in a first strike, thereby reducing its second strike capability.

National Interest   Whatever the decision makers and opinion leaders in a given state consider to be vital or beneficial to their nation-state as it interacts with other international entities. The preservation of a country's territorial integrity, prestige, political independence, and economic wellbeing is undoubtedly in the national interest. Disagreements emerge over the wisdom of specific policies and over the effect such policies will have on the protection of these fundamental interests.

Nationalism   The aggregate of feelings, beliefs, illusions, prejudices, and convictions that bind an individual to a group of people considering themselves to constitute a nation. Nationalism may be related to a shared historical background, a common language, a religion, or an ethnic heritage. Nationalism is closely associated with the institution of the sovereign state as it has emerged in the last 600 years. A national group that does not have sovereign control over the territory it inhabits is likely to struggle until it achieves such control by creating its own sovereign state. A nation that already has control over its own state is likely to fight to preserve its independence and territorial integrity. Its citizens are taught through political socialization to be loyal to their nation and to its nation-state. Nationalism makes the nation-state the primary focus of an individual's loyalties. Nationalism has proved to be the most powerful and most enduring force in international relations. The nationalist loyalties of the Chinese or of the nations in Eastern Europe have proved much more powerful than the principles of "proletarian internationalism" proclaimed by Marxism–Leninism. Nationalism, of course, also can take a highly intolerant, ethnocentric form and become the motivating force for military expansion and aggressive policies.

Neutralism   The policy of individual states or groups of states to refrain from joining rival camps and becoming the allies of one or the other opposing side. In the contemporary East–West conflict, many countries, especially those in the Third World, have opted for a policy of neutralism, more often identified by the term *nonalignment*.

Neutrality   A legal status under international law, claimed by a state that is in no way involved in a war between other states. A neutral state has certain rights as well as obligations. The rights of a neutral state include the inviolability of its territory, the right of its citizens to trade freely with the warring states, the right of its ships to travel unmolested, the right to take any steps to protect its neutrality. On the other hand, a neutral state cannot supply one of the fighting states with arms and munitions, it cannot receive in its territory and give shelter to the troops of any of the belligerents and allow them to return to combat, and it cannot take actions that can benefit the war effort of one of the belligerents. Warships of the belligerent countries may enter neutral ports for refueling and reprovisioning, but their stay must be short and their supplying of food and fuel must be only sufficient to allow them to reach the nearest port of their country.

Neutron Bomb   A nuclear weapon, formally known as the enhanced radiation device, designed to minimize the blast and heat effects of the explosion and instead emit intense radiation over a large area, killing all living organisms but leaving buildings and other inanimate objects intact. The American-proposed deployment of such weapons in Europe in the late 1970s was not carried out because of strong objections by the Europeans.

New International Economic Order (NIEO)   A set of proposals advanced by the Third World countries in 1974 at the Sixth Special Session of the UN General Assembly and incorporated in the Declaration on the Establishment of a New International Economic Order approved by a majority of the participants. The NIEO proposals aim basically at the restructuring of the international economic system so that the developing countries will have more effective influence on decision making in key areas such as trade, aid, monetary policies under IMF, capital flows for investment, technology transfers, distribution of resources from the ocean seabed and other environments, and the like. More specifically, the proponents of NIEO claim that the international economic system is controlled by the major industrial powers, the policies of which prevent the development and modernization of the LDCs.

New World Information and Communication Order (NWICO)   A highly controversial proposal made in 1980 by the Commission for the Study of Communication Problems sponsored by UNESCO. The Commission proposed "effective legal measures designed to circumscribe the action of transnationals by requiring them to comply with specific criteria and conditions defined by national development policies." The *transnationals* referred to in this proposal are the major news agencies; namely, the Associated Press and the United Press International (United States), Reuters (Britain), and Agence France-Press (France) and other Western broadcasting companies. This proposal was interpreted by the Western governments as an attempt to legitimize state censorship of foreign news media by Third World countries.

Nonaligned Movement (NAM)   A group of Third World nations that have chosen not to become politically and militarily associated with either the West or the Soviet bloc. From a nucleus of twenty-five nations, NAM has now 101 members. Since the first meeting in Bantung in 1955, the nonaligned countries have held seven summit meetings: in Belgrade (1961), Cairo (1964), Lusaka (1970), Algiers (1973), Colombo (1976), Havana (1979), and New Delhi (1983). Between summit meetings, the chairperson of the group is chosen from the country that hosted the previous meeting.

Nonalignment   See Neutralism.

Nuclear Non-Proliferation Treaty   Signed on July 1, 1968, this treaty was designed to prevent the development and acquisition of nuclear weapons by countries that were not already in possession of such weapons in 1968.

Essentially, the treaty provides that (1) the powers already having nuclear weapons will not supply nuclear weapons or weapons technology to nations not having nuclear weapons; (2) the nonnuclear countries will not undertake to acquire nuclear weapons by any means; and (3) the nonnuclear nations will cooperate with the IAEA and provide full and accurate information. To strengthen their monitoring effectiveness, the IAEA inspectors have at their disposal certain technical means enabling them to detect at least the more serious attempts at cheating. In 1977, the Nuclear Suppliers Group, which includes the United States, the Soviet Union, and thirteen other advanced countries, agreed on new guidelines to supplement the provisions of the Nuclear Non-Proliferation Treaty. The 1977 guidelines (1) made export sales conditional on the recipient's acceptance of international safeguards; (2) required buyers to refrain from reexporting nuclear technology or materials that could contribute to the production of nuclear explosives, except under the same safeguards that applied to the initial acquisition; (3) required suppliers and customers to take specific physical measures to protect nuclear plants, equipment, and materials; and (4) called on suppliers to show restraint in the sale of sensitive technologies, such as uranium enrichment and plutonium reprocessing.

In 1978, the U.S. Congress passed a law, the Non-Proliferation Act, which stated that nonnuclear weapon states receiving U.S. fuel and equipment for their nuclear plants would face a cutoff of such supplies unless they accepted "full-scope" safeguards on all their peaceful nuclear activities.

A major weakness of the Nuclear Non-Proliferation Treaty is that countries likely to develop their own nuclear weapons are not among the signatories: Argentina, Brazil, Cuba, Israel, North Korea, Pakistan, Saudi Arabia, and South Africa. Moreover, three countries having nuclear weapons—France, China, India—have not signed. Another weakness of the treaty is that any signatory can terminate its adherence by giving ninety-day notice.

Nuclear Proliferation   The acquisition of atomic and nuclear weapons by one country after another. The assumption is that if several countries have the capability of using nuclear weapons in a military confrontation with another international actor, the likelihood of a nuclear war will increase exponentially.

Occupation   The acquisition of title over territory not belonging to any other state. The Europeans used this legal concept to take over as colonial possessions lands inhabited by nomads or by people judged by them to be primitive.

Oder–Neisse Line   The present boundary between Poland and East Germany. It takes its name after the two rivers that delineate the frontier from the Baltic Sea in the north to the Czechoslovakian border to the south. Originally this was a provisional boundary agreed by the World War II Allied Powers at the Potsdam Conference in 1945. The Potsdam agreement allowed the Soviet Union to annex East Prussia and placed the German territories east of the Oder–Neisse line under Polish administration. The Helsinki Accord of 1975, which formalized the postwar division of Europe, also made the Oder–Neisse line at least the accepted de facto boundary between East Germany and Poland.

Open Skies Proposal   A proposal presented by President Eisenhower to Soviet Premier Nikita Khrushchev at the 1955 Geneva summit meeting. It was an effort to overcome Soviet objections against on site inspections to verify any arms control agreement. Under the open skies plan, both superpowers would have the right to fly over each other's territory to verify compliance and also to reduce the dangers of surprise attack. The Soviet Union eventually rejected the proposal, claiming that its main purpose was to facilitate American espionage.

Opium War In 1839, Chinese troops surrounded the European enclave in Canton and seized large quantities of opium, the major commodity marketed by the Europeans in China at the time. The British claimed that the action constituted unacceptable interference with the freedom of international trade and took military action: the Chinese forts in Canton were destroyed. Although the Chinese losses were minor in military terms, China was forced to sign the Treaty of Nanking in 1842, giving up Hong Kong to Britain, opening Canton to the opium trade, paying a huge sum in reparations, and giving to the European powers four more treaty ports, which were placed under European jurisdiction. The Opium War and the Treaty of Nanking signaled the onset of the *century of humiliation,* which ended for the Chinese in 1949.

Organization of African Unity (OAU) An association established by African states in 1963 to speed up the end of colonialism in Africa, promote economic development for its members, and encourage unity and the peaceful settlement of disputes among them. The membership includes every independent African state except South Africa, which is excluded because of its apartheid policies. The OAU structure consists of an assembly of heads of government meeting annually and a secretariat with headquarters in Addis Ababa. The presidency of the OAU rotates among the fifty member-states annually. The organization has encountered serious problems of unity because of political and ideological rivalries among the members and conflicting views on their relations with the advanced countries. The members, however, have cooperated effectively especially in the United Nations and other international forums, where they have often supported joint efforts for a New International Economic Order, increased aid for economic development, and reduced tensions between the superpowers.

Organization of American States (OAS) An association established in 1948 to coordinate political, economic, and social policies by the countries of the Western hemisphere. Canada was not a participant. In 1962, Cuba was excluded from participation in the OAS because of the pro-Soviet orientation of the Castro government. The highest organ of the OAS is the Inter-American Conference, which meets every five years to consider matters of interest to the member-states. The OAS Council, headquartered in Washington D.C., serves as the coordinating agency in the five-year intervals between the Conferences. The Pan-American Union, also headquartered in Washington, functions as the secretariat of the OAS. The OAS also has several Specialized Organizations dealing with health, agriculture, education, and other social or technical issues. The Inter-American Development Bank is affiliated with the OAS. The OAS has been active in promoting the peaceful settlement of disputes among its members and their collaboration in economic and social matters. The OAS also oversees the implementation of the Rio Treaty provisions.

Organization of Economic Cooperation and Development (OECD) An association that replaced in 1961 the Organization for European Economic Cooperation (OEEC), initially established to administer the European Recovery Program (Marshall Plan). The twenty-four members of OECD include virtually all the economically advanced countries that have market economies and pluralistic political systems. The objective of this organization is to coordinate the policies of the member-states on economic matters to promote economic growth, free trade, and monetary stability, and also to expand the contribution of the members to the economic development of the LDCs. In the North–South Dialogue, the OECD is the counterpart of the Group of 77. The OECD membership includes the ten members of the EEC, the five members of EFTA, plus Australia, Iceland, New Zealand, Finland, Spain, Turkey, Canada, the United States, and Japan. Yugoslavia (which does not have a market economy and a pluralistic political system) is given special status as an associate, mostly for political reasons. The OECD has a council composed of representatives from all member-states, an executive committee of ten members elected annually by the council, and a secretariat headed by a secretary-general.

Organization of Petroleum Exporting Countries (OPEC)   A producers' cartel established by oil-exporting countries in 1960 to counter primarily the power of major oil companies. The initial membership of Saudi Arabia, Iran, Kuwait, Iraq, and Venezuela expanded in the following years while their own government control over their oil resources was considerably strengthened. The first major attempt to use their control over petroleum supplies for political purposes took place in 1973. Although the embargo failed to gain any of OPEC's political objectives, the cartel initiated price increases that within seven years raised the price of oil per barrel from $2.50 to $30.00. OPEC is currently composed of the original members plus the United Arab Emirates, Qatar, Algeria, Libya, Ecuador, Gabon, Nigeria, and Indonesia.

Östpolitik   The *Eastern Policy* adopted by West Germany in the late 1960s. Under this policy, West Germany accepted the existing division in Germany and in Europe as the basis for relations in the region. West Germany accepted the Oder–Neisse line as the legitimate border of Poland toward the west and also recognized the division of Germany into two independent and sovereign states. By removing the obstacles to a more-stable and relaxed relationship with East Germany and the Soviet Union, the policy allowed trade relations with the East to expand considerably. Agreements signed in 1970 between the Federal Republic of Germany and the Soviet Union, and in 1971 between the Soviet Union and France, Britain, and the United States, on the status of Berlin gave formal sanction to the *Östpolitik*.

Outer Space Treaty   An agreement approved by the UN General Assembly in 1967 and signed by eighty-four nations. It prohibits the placing of nuclear or other weapons of mass destruction in space, on the moon, or on the planets; bans any claims of national sovereignty on any celestial bodies; provides that all exploration and use in outer space will be for the benefit of humanity; and calls for international cooperation in space exploration, in assisting astronauts in trouble in space, and in exchanging scientific information. Both superpowers have refrained so far from placing in orbit nuclear weapons or other weapons of mass destruction. They have not refrained, however, from developing other military uses of space vehicles. The difficulty of inspection and verification in space may contribute to mutual distrust and the further militarization of space.

Overkill   Term used by critics of the nuclear arms race to indicate that the two superpowers have the combined equivalent of approximately ten tons of TNT in destructive power for each human being on Earth. The corollary is that additions to their nuclear arsenals will not substantially improve the security or the ability of the superpowers to inflict cataclysmic devastation on one another and on the rest of the world.

Pacifism   A philosophical approach to the question of international conflict that holds that war is unacceptable as a method for settling disputes among civilized nations. Initially, Christianity advocated a total rejection of force. When the Christian religion became in effect an integral part of the state structure, theologians introduced a distinction between *just* and *unjust* wars, *just* usually being applied to the wars waged by the sovereign of the theologian. Theoretically, just wars were those of self-defense against aggression or against the infidels. In the twentieth century, pacifist thought held that war represented the greatest threat to the economic health of modern civilization. With the rise of Nazi Germany, European pacifism was discredited as a movement designed to appease the expansionist regimes. Today, pacifism holds with considerable justification that war (meaning a nuclear war under present conditions) will indeed destroy civilization and therefore any policy that tends to exacerbate conflict should be discarded in favor of peaceful forms of interaction. The slogan "better red than dead" represents an extreme and rather simplified version of pacifist thinking, meaning in effect that if the Europeans are confronted by the possibility of a Soviet takeover they should opt for surrender instead of military resistance.

Pacta Sunt Servanda   A customary rule of international law that holds that the provisions of treaties should be observed faithfully by the signatories because treaties are binding contracts. By extension, all international agreements should be honored by the parties. This contrasts to another customary rule that allows a signatory to free itself of its treaty obligations on the grounds that conditions have changed substantially *(rebus sic standibus)*.

Palestinian Liberation Organization (PLO)   A coalition of Palestinian groups united by their dedication to the goal of establishing a Palestinian state. The territorial extent of such a Palestinian state varies from the most extensive version, which would require the replacement of Israel with a new Arab and Jewish-inhabited entity on the territory of the *Palestine*—the League of Nations "mandate" administered by Britain from 1918 to 1947—to a more limited version, which refers to the West Bank of the Jordan river and to the Gaza strip.

Peaceful Coexistence   A revision of the Marxist–Leninist doctrine, which initially held that a final war between the capitalist and the socialist states is inevitable. Peaceful coexistence shifts the emphasis from the inevitability of war between the rival socioeconomic systems to the assertion that countries with opposing social systems may continue to exist side by side without going to war. However, during a prolonged period of peaceful coexistence, the Soviet Union would continue its support for people fighting for their "national liberation." In practical terms, this support for national liberation movements meant, in effect, Soviet support to such movements in the developing countries to bring to power pro-Soviet or pro-Marxist elites, thereby extending the area of Soviet influence. The rejection of a major war between the superpowers (under the doctrine of peaceful coexistence) reflects a realistic appreciation on the part of the Soviet leaders of the dangers inherent in a full-fledged nuclear war.

Per Capita Income (PCI)   The quotient obtained by dividing the annual gross national product (GNP) of a given country (that is the value of all goods and services produced during the year by the country's economy) by the total population of the country.

Petrodollars   Dollars received by the oil-exporting countries as payment for oil purchases by oil-importing countries; they are deposited primarily in Western banks in interest bearing accounts.

Population Explosion   The dramatic increase of world population in the last one-hundred years. Specifically, it took many thousands if not millions of years for the world population to reach the 1 billion mark (1830). It took one-hundred years to increase by another billion to 2 billion (1830–1930). It took thirty more years (1930–1960) to reach 3 billion, and only fifteen more years (1960–1975) to reach 4 billion. By the year 2000, the world population is expected to be over 6.5 billion. This population explosion is due primarily to improved health care for infants and longer life expectancy. Infant mortality has decreased dramatically with the result that more human beings survive and reach reproductive age.

Positivism   A school of thought that holds that the basis of international law is to be found only in specific agreements such as treaties and other internationally binding documents or in the common consent of nations expressed through generally observed customary rules. The positivist school rejects the views of the naturalists, who claim that international law is merely part of the law of nature. In a 1927 decision, the Permanent Court of International Justice formally accepted the positivist view that the rules of international law are created only by the free will and the voluntary acceptance of the sovereign states. Today, positivism is the dominant theory on the nature of international law.

Power   In politics, the ability of one actor to make another actor behave in ways it would not have behaved on its own. In international relations, an actor has power if it can obtain compliance on the part of another actor regardless of the latter's wishes or preferences.

Pragmatism   A philosophical theory recommending a practical assessment of situations and behaviors. (See Realism.)

Preemptive Strike   A nuclear attack launched by one side on the assumption that the other side is planning an imminent nuclear attack. The objective of a preemptive strike is to destroy as many offensive weapons of the side planning to attack as possible, thereby blunting its offensive capability. The possession by both sides of delivery systems that cannot be eliminated or seriously reduced in effectiveness by a preemptive strike makes such an option less attractive, especially when the remaining delivery systems are more than sufficient to inflict devastating losses on the side launching the preemptive strike.

Prescription   The acquisition of territory after a long period of continuous occupation of an area belonging to another state. Prescription requires that the "owner" not protest the occupation of the territory by the other state.   .

Prestige   In international relations, the favorable image other people and their governments have about a foreign state. Prestige is one of the intangible assets that strengthen a country's power or influence potential.

Producers' Cartel   An international agreement by states producing a certain key commodity to regulate its production, pricing, and marketing and thus reap maximum economic (or occasionally political) advantage for the participating states. The Organization of Petroleum Exporting Countries (OPEC) is such a producers' cartel.

Propaganda   The presentation of facts, arguments, half-truths, or even falsehoods with selective emphasis designed to implant in human minds impressions desired by the purveyor of propaganda. To be effective, propaganda must appear credible, convincing, and relevant in the judgment of the recipient. The techniques of propaganda include simplification of complex issues, appealing and memorable slogans, repetition, biased selection of facts, falsification of facts, manipulation of emotions, and the exploitation of errors committed by the other side.

Protectionism   The policies and practices employed by a sovereign government to restrict imports to protect domestic producers from foreign competition. Protectionist policies are employed by almost every country to a lesser or greater degree, even by countries favoring *free trade,* which is the opposite of protectionism. Protectionist measures include tariffs, quotas, and nontariff barriers.

Protracted Conflict   The perception that the Soviet Union is engaged in a long-term effort to promote Marxist-oriented and pro-Soviet revolutionary regimes throughout the world. According to the proponents of this doctrine, this protracted conflict is characterized by the ultimate objective of a worldwide victory of Marxism–Leninism, carefully controlled methods of interaction and conflict, selection of the most suitable battleground under specific conditions, maneuvers to confuse and demoralize the opponent, use of propagandist materials, and techniques to win over to the Soviet side prospective allies and to weaken and isolate the opponent, the whole process being expected to culminate in a "final annihilating blow delivered with every weapon available."

Rapid Deployment Force (RDF)   The Carter Administration, reacting in part to the Soviet invasion of Afghanistan and the perceived Soviet threat to the Persian Gulf region, initiated in 1979 the organization of a special force of approximately 100,000 troops equipped with transport facilities for rapid deployment in regions outside of the United States. The objective of this force is to prevent changes imposed by force and opposed by the United States in strategically important areas. The use of the RDF is handicapped more by political than technical or strictly military factors. Undesirable changes may come through coups, which are considered to be domestic affairs—making intervention by the RDF legally impossible. The entry of the RDF into the territory of another country is legally subject to the acceptance of its government. Even the passage of RDF planes over the airspace of another country or the use of facilities of other countries for refueling are subject to permission by the government of those countries.

Rationalization   In foreign policy, a spurious explanation, couched in rational terms, of a decision taken for reasons that are not easily justifiable.

Realism   In international relations, a major school of thought that holds that the ability of a country to protect and promote its national interests depends on its power. Without power, a country is unable to achieve its objectives regardless of the nobility of its aims or the justice and logic of its cause. The realist approach contrasts to the *idealist approach,* which holds that foreign policies based on moral principles are more effective because they achieve more durable benefits. Idealists favor policies designed to win the minds of people instead of relying on force and coercion (power politics).

Rebus Sic Standibus   The doctrine that a government may cease to abide by the terms of a treaty to which it is a party if the circumstances that made the signing of the treaty desirable on its part have radically changed. Indirectly, this doctrine holds by contrast that a government has an obligation to abide by the country's international agreements *(pacta sunt servanda).*

Recognition   An international law term referring to a formal declaration or acknowledgment by the government of a sovereign state that (1) another sovereign state has come into existence or (2) a ruling group constitutes the sovereign government of an existing state. The former refers to the recognition of a *state,* the latter to the recognition of a *government.* The recognition of a state as sovereign is given once and cannot be withdrawn as long as the recognized state exists and retains the attributes of sovereignty. The recognition of a new government may be withheld, delayed, or denied for political reasons. Normally, the replacement of one government by another under the usual constitutional processes of the state does not call for the *recognition* of the new government. The implication of recognition is that the recognizing government is willing to enter into relations with the recognized entity or government as sovereign equals. Recognition may be explicit (express), when a formal statement is issued, or implicit (tacit), when a government takes certain actions, such as concluding an agreement, voting for the admission of a new state to the UN, or participating with another government in an international conference. In such instances, however, there must be an intent to recognize. When one government establishes formal diplomatic relations with another by exchanging ambassadors, the recognition is *de jure.* Otherwise it considered to be *de facto.*

Regionalism   The doctrine that holds that peace will be promoted if countries situated in a given geographic area or sharing common interests agree to enter into formal cooperative structures to deal collectively with political, economic, military, or other problems of common concern. The underlying assumption is that many problems cannot be effectively resolved on either a global basis or unilaterally. The UN encourages regionalism as contributing to the organization's universalist functions and activities.

Reparation   Compensation demanded by one state from another for damages caused by the latter to the former mainly during war or military action. Usually a victorious country includes the payment of reparations in the agreements terminating the conflict.

Reprisal   A punitive action (short of war) taken by one government in retaliation for the actions of another. Reprisals are provoked by actions deemed detrimental to the interests of the retaliating country. Normally, reprisals are commensurate with the seriousness of the provocation. Under the rules of international law, a government claiming to have been wronged by the actions of another has an obligation to seek satisfaction by peaceful means.

Revolution   A drastic transformation of the political, economic, and social order in a given country, usually achieved through the removal of the previously powerful groups from their positions of control. Such fundamental changes seldom are accomplished without violence. The victorious revolutionary group establishes its own control over the political, economic, and social sources of power and proceeds to create a new constitution and power structure reflecting its ideological and political orientation.

Satellites Surveillance   Since the early 1960s, both the United States and the Soviet Union have been placing in orbit reconnaissance satellites to observe one another's military preparations, testing of new weapons (particularly nuclear weapons and delivery systems), compliance with arms control agreements, installation of missiles, and military maneuvers and movements. These "spy satellites" fly very high and therefore do not violate the airspace of other countries. As they go around the Earth approximately 16 times every 24 hours, they are likely to find clear weather over the target areas regularly, although the addition of infrared devices enables many of them to return data regardless of weather conditions. The technology of the reconnaissance satellites has already reached extremely high levels, especially in picture resolution and detail. Satellites are used for nonmilitary purposes as well: weather satellites, communication satellites, survey satellites, and the like.

Search-and-Destroy   A strategy followed by a government's armed forces in their effort to combat a guerrilla campaign. The tactics of this strategy consist mainly of sweeps through the countryside where the guerrillas are active, killing or capturing guerrillas or their sympathizers, and destroying any facilities, food supplies, and intelligence networks that can be useful to the guerrillas. (See also Seize-and-Hold).

Second Strike Capability   The capability of a superpower to retaliate after a first strike by its opponent has destroyed some of its nuclear missiles. In practical terms, it means that if, for instance, the Soviet Union were to destroy most of the land-based ICBMs of the United States, the American nuclear submarines and the aircraft of the Strategic Air Command would still have sufficient firepower to inflict on the Soviet Union destruction of cataclysmic proportions. The second strike capability is the very core of the strategy of mutual deterrence.

Second World   The Soviet Union and its allies, as distinguished from the Third and Fourth Worlds of the developing countries and the First World of the advanced market economies. The countries of the Second World have systems based on the doctrines of Marxism–Leninism.

Seize-and-Hold   A strategy used by the government forces in their effort to combat a guerrilla campaign. It centers on the following steps: (1) selection of one guerrilla-infested area and concentration of regular forces around the guerrilla stronghold; (2) sustained offensive operations against the guerrillas until they are severely reduced in number and firepower; (3) mop-up operations to clear remaining pockets of resistance; (4) measures to secure the cleared area against reinfestation; (5) organization of local defense units for static defense and for the pursuit and elimination of guerrillas attempting to reenter the area; (6) selection of another area and repetition of the process until the guerrilla forces are eliminated throughout the country. (See also Search-and-Destroy.)

Simulation   In international relations, the use of techniques and artificial situations to imitate the thinking processes, reactions, and actions of human beings under similar but actual circumstances of conflict, confrontation, or interaction. These techniques usually employ a small number of individuals under quasi-laboratory conditions to create replicas of complex organizations, systems, or social processes and have these individuals assume and play roles similar in content to those played by the officials actually representing such organizations or institutions and engaged in real conflict situations. Similar techniques may be employed in nonlaboratory but contrived natural settings. In some cases, the participants may use computers or other technical means to simulate mental and other processes to evaluate reactions and outcomes at a more rapid pace.

Sino—Soviet Rift   The gradual estrangement between the two largest Marxist–Leninist (communist) states, the Soviet Union and the People's Republic of China. The rift started in the late 1950s, became public in 1961, and reached high levels of tension in the late 1960s. One of the consequences of this rift was the rapprochement between the United States and the People's Republic of China. One of the several reasons for the rift is the Chinese claim that the Soviet Union occupies large areas taken over from China as a result of "unequal treaties" imposed on a weak China by the Czarist government.

Si Vis Pacem Para Bellum   A Roman dictum meaning that if you wish to preserve the peace you must be prepared for war. The assumption is that military weakness on one side tends to encourage the other side to resort to military action to achieve its objectives. Historically, many wars erupted despite the fact that both antagonists were well armed.

Socialism   Although several variations of socialism have appeared since the early nineteenth century, this ideology basically favors collectivist forms of economic organization with governmental or social ownership of the means of production. Socialism rejects the private ownership of the major or all production units, the pursuit of private profit, and the competition of private enterprises motivated by the pursuit of profit. Socialist doctrines range from those of democratic socialism, which tries to combine socialism with the principles of democratic pluralism, to those of Marxism–Leninism, which espouse total party control over the political, economic, and social structures. The socialist label is occasionally used to identify political parties espousing policies of "social justice" designed to bring about a more equitable distribution of the domestic product and provide social services to the lower-income groups.

Sovereignty   A legal concept which holds that the government of a sovereign state (1) has exclusive jurisdiction over the territory of the state and of its inhabitants; and (2) is not subject to any other superior authority.

Specialized Agencies   International entities that are part of the UN system. They include: Universal Postal Union (UPU), International Telecommunication Union (ITU), the International Labour Organization (ILO), Food and Agriculture Organization (FAO), UN Educational Scientific and Cultural Organization (UNESCO), World Health Organization (WHO), International Civil Aviation Organization (ICAO), World Meteorological Organization (WMO), International Maritime Consultative Organization (IMCO), International Bank for Reconstruction and Development (IBRD or World Bank), International Monetary Fund (IMF), International Development Association (IDA), and International Finance Corporation (IFC).

Two of them, the Universal Postal Union and the International Telecommunication Union, were formed in the nineteenth century. The International Labour Organization was established in 1919. All the others have been founded since 1945.

Some of them grew out of technical committees that have been set up by the League of Nations. All of them reflect the technological changes that have taken place in the last one-hundred years and the necessity for cooperation and coordination of activities in the common interest.

The Specialized Agencies owe their legal existence to multilateral treaties signed by the participating countries. Because their functions are not confined to a particular region, their membership is open to any country willing to join and to abide by the conditions of participation. Being in effect separate entities from the UN, they have signed special agreements with that organization. These agreements establish the parameters of cooperation but do not affect the legal independence of each agency. Their finances are not part of the UN budget. Each agency is financed primarily with contributions from its own members. Each has its own charter, rules of procedure, and bureaucratic organization to carry out the work of the agency. Although the specialized agencies cannot force any government to comply, most members cooperate routinely because the regulations and other rulings usually are adopted by concensus and because they are practical, technical arrangements that benefit all participants on the basis of reciprocity.

Spheres of Influence A tacit or formal agreement between major powers that the countries within a certain geographic region have special importance to power A and that therefore power B should not try to intrude or expand its own influence in that area with the aim of undercutting the influence of power A. For example, the Soviet Union considers Eastern Europe as being within its sphere of influence; the United States regards the Western hemisphere as being within its sphere of influence.

Stalemate A point reached during a confrontation or other interaction when both opposing sides are unwilling to make further concessions to accomodate the interests of the other side, or when both sides are unwilling or unable to commit further resources to overcome the resistance of their opponent.

Strategic Arms Limitation Treaties (SALT I and II) The treaties signed in 1972 (SALT I) and 1979 (SALT II) by the United States and the Soviet Union. The objective of these agreements was to limit the numbers of certain types of nuclear missiles on both sides. SALT I virtually stopped the deployment of antiballistic missiles. The agreement also set numerical limits on the number of ICBMs and SLBMs, but not on the number of warheads each could carry. SALT II set limits on MIRV missiles. SALT II was not ratified by the United States Senate, but the governments of both superpowers have stated that they will abide by its provisions as long as the other side does. Although SALT I and II did not stop the nuclear arms race, they were steps in the direction of at least slowing down the deployment of more nuclear-tipped ICBMs and SLBMs.

Submarine-Launched Ballistic Missiles (SLBMs) Long-range, nuclear-tipped missiles carried by submarines, which can be fired below the surface and reach targets several thousands of miles away in the territory of the opponent. Submarines equipped with SLBMs are now a crucial element in the arsenals of the superpowers.

Superpowers As currently used, the United States and the Soviet Union. Their continental size, military might, economic resources, and political influence set them apart from other major powers, such as Britain, France, or Japan, which in past decades were in effect the superpowers. The policies of the superpowers have a significant influence throughout the globe.

Supranational Actors International governmental organizations that have been assigned by the participating sovereign states the performance of certain functions normally carried out by each sovereign state independently. The European Economic Community (EEC) is one such supranational actor.

Tangible Assets In international relations, assets that can be used by a government to enhance its power and influence and that can be *measured*. Tangible assets include a country's material resources, industrial production, population, geographic area, and military forces.

Terrorism Violent activities by small groups trying to publicize, pursue, or realize their political objectives by causing or threatening serious harm to targets (human or inanimate) the fate of which is likely to attract wide publicity and force compliance with the wishes of the terrorists. Terrorists may be private individuals espousing a certain ideology or cause, or they may be directed by a government wishing to create problems to an adversary without its own direct and visible involvement. The tactics of terrorists include assassination, kidnapping, skyjacking, seizure of buildings and hostages, bombing, and dynamiting of public utilities.

Third World The countries, located mostly in the southern part of the globe (Africa, Southern Asia, Latin America, the Caribbean), whose economies are underdeveloped and that have extensive poverty, high levels of illiteracy, subsistance agriculture, and low productivity. They also are identified as less-developed countries (LDCs). Most of the Third World countries have followed a policy of nonalignment.

Totalitarianism A political system in which a single political party or other group uses the state authority to bring under its exclusive control all sources of power (political, economic, social). In a totalitarian system, citizens are left with few if any alternatives to arrange and lead their lives at their own discretion without following the dictates of the ruling elite.

Transnationals Private entities active in more than one country. Known also as nongovernmental organizations (NGOs), these entities include private enterprises, such as multinational corporations, religious groups, professional associations, and service organizations such as the Red Cross, as well as social, ideological, and political groups.

Truman Doctrine The policy enunciated by President Harry S. Truman on May 12, 1947, in which the United States promised to come to the aid of countries that requested its help to resist Soviet expansionism and subversion. This commitment to offer economic and military aid in peacetime represented a major departure in U.S. foreign policy tradition. The policy was prompted by communist efforts to seize power in Greece and by Soviet pressures on Turkey to alter to the advantage of the Soviet Union the status of the straits of Bosporus and the Dardanelles. The Truman Doctrine was the first major policy decision reflecting the policy of containment.

Uniting for Peace Resolution Under this ruling passed by the UN General Assembly in 1950, that body can now meet in an emergency session within twenty-four hours at the request of a majority of its members or a majority of *any* members of the Security Council. The Council still remains the organ with the primary responsibility for the maintenance of peace and security, as the Charter stipulates. However, if the Council fails to carry out its responsibilities because of the negative vote of one of its permanent members, the General Assembly may take up the issue and recommend to the members "collective measures, including in the case of a breach of the peace or act of aggression the use of armed force, when necessary, to maintain or restore international peace and security." No action involving the use of armed forces has ever been taken under the provisions of the Uniting for Peace resolution, although emergency sessions to deal with serious crises have not been uncommon.

Vienna Convention The 1961 treaty produced by the Vienna Conference on Diplomatic Privileges and Immunities. The articles of the Vienna Convention deal with the rules of international law that regulate the status, protection, and practices of diplomats. Most of these rules were already established and widely observed in the form of customary rules.

War The use of substantial military forces by opposing countries or groups of countries to resolve a dispute on the battlefield. War differs from military intervention, in which a stronger country uses superior military force to impose its will on a weaker country that does not have sufficient means to resist. In war, the antagonists must have comparable forces to engage in hostilities. International law now has rules—developed in part through custom but mostly through multilateral treaties—that prescribe the conduct of belligerents, primarily with regard to the humane treatment of prisoners and sick and wounded soldiers, the protection of civilian populations, and the rights of neutrals. War as a means of resolving international disputes was outlawed under the terms of the Kellogg–Briand Pact of 1928 and by the UN Charter.

War Powers Resolution   A resolution, passed by the U.S. Congress in 1973, that requires U.S. presidents to report to and consult with Congress whenever American troops are sent overseas, except for routine training or as replacements at existing U.S. bases. The War Powers Resolution contemplates three general situations under which troops might be sent overseas. One is a routine training mission or replacement of soldiers already stationed on foreign soil (as in the case of the U.S. troops in West Germany). The second involves troops "equipped for combat" sent to a foreign area where hostilities are not likely. In such a case, the president is required to inform Congress when the troops are dispatched and periodically thereafter. There is no time limit on such deployment. The third situation covers the dispatch of troops "into hostilities or into situations where imminent involvement in hostilities is clearly indicated by the circumstances." In this case, the troops must be brought back home within sixty days—or ninety days in special circumstances—unless Congress declares war or gives specific authorization for longer deployment. The War Powers Act, as it is popularly known, reflects the experience gained from the U.S. involvement in Vietnam, in which hostilities continued for eight years without a declaration of war.

World Government   The concept of a global political authority that would replace the current system of independent and sovereign states. Such a global government would have the authority and the means to keep the peace and to regulate developments (political, economic, social) to the benefit of all humanity. Most advocates of a world government envisage a worldwide federation in which today's sovereign states would be the constituent components in somewhat the same way the fifty states are the components of the United States. Presumably, the central authority would be representative of the component parts and would possess the necessary legislative, administrative, and coercive means to govern. The tremendous diversity of political, ideological, and economic orientations of people in the world makes the creation of such a global authority through the voluntary agreement of the existing sovereign states improbable in the foreseeable future.

......................Useful Books
on Major Topics

Theory and Concepts

Aron, Raymond. *Peace and War*. Garden City, N.J.: Doubleday, 1966.

Beard, Charles Austin. *The Idea of National Interest*. Westport, Conn.: Greenwood Press, 1977.

Breuilly, John. *Nationalism and the State*. New York: St. Martin's Press, 1982.

Buckley, Walter, ed. *Modern Systems Research for the Behavioral Scientists*. Chicago: Aldine, 1968.

Bull, Hadley. *The Anarchical Society: A Study of Order in World Politics*. New York: Columbia University Press, 1977.

Cantori, Louis J., and Steven L. Spiegel. *The International Politics of Regions*. Englewood Cliffs, N.J.: Prentice-Hall, 1970.

Carr, Edward Hallett. *The Twenty-Year's Crisis: 1919–1939: An Introduction to the Study of International Relations*. London: Macmillan, 1939.

Claude, Inis L. Jr. *Power and International Relations*. New York: Random House, 1962.

Dahl, Robert A. *Readings in Modern Political Analysis*. Englewood Cliffs, N.J.: Prentice-Hall, 1963.

Dougherty, James E., and Robert L. Pfaltzgraff, Jr. *Contending Theories of International Relations*. Philadelphia: Lippincott, 1971.

Frankel, Joseph. *National Interest*. New York: Praeger, 1970.

Graham, Allison T. *Essence of Decision: Explaining the Cuban Missile Crisis*. Boston: Little, Brown, 1971.

Haas, Ernst B. *Beyond the Nation-State*. Stanford: Stanford University Press, 1964.

Harrison, Horace V., ed. *The Role of Theory in International Relations*. Princeton: Van Nostrand, 1964.

Hartmann, Frederick H. *The Conservation of Enemies: A Study in Enmity*. Westport, Conn.: Greenwood Press, 1982.

Hoffman, Stanley. *Duties beyond Borders: On the Limits and Possibilities of Ethical International Politics*. Syracuse, N.Y.: Syracuse University Press, 1981.

Holsti, Ole R. *Change in the International System*. Boulder, Colo.: Westview Press, 1980.

Janowitz, Morris. *The Reconstruction of Patriotism*. Chicago: The University of Chicago Press, 1983.

Kohn, Hans. *The Idea of Nationalism*. New York: Macmillan, 1944.

Kolko, Joyce. *The Limits of Power*. New York: Harper and Row, 1972.

Kousoulas, D. G. *On Government and Politics*. 5th ed. Monterey, Calif.: Brooks-Cole, 1983.

Krejci, Jaroslav, and Vitezslav Velimsky. *Ethnic and Political Nations in Europe*. New York: St. Martin's Press, 1981.

Mayne, Richard. *The Community of Europe*. New York: W. W. Norton, 1963.

McClelland, Charles A. *Theory and the International System*. New York: Macmillan, 1966.

Mitrany, David. *A Working Peace System*. Chicago: Quadrangle Books, 1966.

Morgenthau, Hans. *Politics Among Nations*. 5th ed. New York: Knopf, 1978.

Osgood, Robert. *Ideals and Self-Interest in America's Foreign Relations*. Chicago: The University of Chicago Press, 1953.

Paterson, Thomas G. et al. *American Foreign Policy: A History*. Lexington, Mass.: Heath, 1977.

Rosenau, James N. *International Politics and Foreign Policy*. New York: Free Press of Glencoe, 1961.

———et al., eds. *The Analysis of International Politics*. New York: Free Press, 1972.

Russell, Bertrand. *Power*. New York: Barnes and Noble, 1962. Reissue.

Sabine, George H. *A History of Political Theory*. 3rd ed. New York: Holt, Rinehart and Winston, 1961.

Said, Abdul, ed. *Theory of International Relations: The Crisis of Relevance*. Englewood Cliffs, N.J.: Prentice-Hall, 1968.

Schwarzenberger, Georg. *Power Politics: A Study of World Society*. 3rd ed. New York: Praeger, 1964.

Sonderman, Fred A. et al. *The Theory and Practice of International Relations*. 6th ed. Englewood Cliffs, N.J.: Prentice-Hall, 1983.

Spanier, John. *Games Nations Play*. 4th ed. New York: Holt, Rinehart and Winston, 1981.

Spiegel, Steven L. *Dominance and Diversity*. Boston: Little, Brown, 1972.

Waltz, Kenneth N. *Theory of International Politics*. Reading, Mass.: Addison-Wesley, 1979.

Wright, Martin. *Power Politics*. New York: Holmes and Meier, 1978.

Wolfers, Arnold. *Discord and Collaboration*. Baltimore: Johns Hopkins Press, 1962.

War and Power Politics

Burt, Richard, ed. *Arms Control and Defense Postures in the 1980s*. Boulder, Colo.: Westview Press, 1982.

Carlton, David, and Carlo Schaerf, ed. *The Arms Race in the 1980s*. New York: St. Martin's Press, 1982.

Chaliand, Gerard, ed. *Guerrilla Strategies: An Historical Anthology from Long March to Afghanistan*. Berkeley: University of California, 1982.

Farrell, William Regis. *The U.S. Government Response to Terrorism: In Search of an Effective Strategy*. Boulder, Colo.: Westview Press, 1982.

George, Alexander L., and Richard Smoke. *Deterrence in American Foreign Policy*. New York: Columbia University Press, 1974.

Hartmann, Frederick. *The Conservation of Enemies: A Study in Enmity*. Westport, Conn.: Greenwood Press, 1982.

Howard, Michael. *The Causes of Wars*. Cambridge, Mass.: Harvard University Press, 1983.

Kousoulas, D. G. *Revolution and Defeat: The Story of the Greek Communist Party*. London: Oxford University Press, 1965.

Mitrakos, Alexandre S. *France in Greece during World War I: A Study in the Politics of Power*. New York: Columbia University Press, 1982.

Nicholson, Michael. *Conflict Analysis*. New York: Barnes and Noble, 1970.

Nincic, Miroslav. *The Arms Race: The Political Economy of Military Growth*. New York: Praeger, 1982.

Roberts, Adam, and Richard Guelff, eds. *Documents on the Laws of War*. New York: Oxford University Press, 1982.

Rostow, W. W. *The Division of Europe after World War II: 1946*. Austin: University of Texas Press, 1982.

Scott, Harriet Fast, and William F. Scott. *The Soviet Art of War: Doctrine, Strategy and Tactics*. Boulder, Colo.: Westview Press, 1982.

Yarmolinsky, Adam, and Gregory D. Foster. *Paradoxes of Power: The Military Establishment in the Eighties*. Bloomington, Indiana: Indiana University Press, 1983.

Ziegler, David W. *War, Peace and International Politics*. Boston: Little, Brown, 1984.

Nuclear Armaments

Bertram, Christoph, ed. *Strategic Deterrence in a Changing Environment*. Montclair, N.J.: Allenheld, Osmun, 1981.

Bracken, Paul. *The Command and Control of Nuclear Forces*. New Haven: Yale University Press, 1983.

Burt, Richard, ed. *Arms Control and Defense Postures in the 1980s*. Boulder, Colo.: Westview Press, 1982.

Frei, Daniel. *The Risks of Unintentional Nuclear War*. Totowa, N.J.: Littlefield, Adams, 1982.

Garfinkle, Adam M., ed. *Global Perspectives on Arms Control*. New York: Praeger, 1983.

Goldblat, Josef. *Arms Control Agreements: A Handbook*. New York: Praeger, 1983.

Hogg, Ian, and Christopher Chant. *Nuclear War in the 1980s?* New York: Harper and Row, 1983.

Katz, Arthur M. *Life after Nuclear War: The Economic and Social Impacts of Nuclear Attacks on the United States*. Cambridge, Mass.: Ballinger, 1982.

Park, Jae Kuy, ed. *Nuclear Proliferation in Developing Countries*. Boulder, Colo.: Westview Press, 1979.

Perry, Ronald W. *The Social Psychology of Civil Defense*. Lexington, Mass.: Heath, 1982.

Foreign Policy and Diplomacy

Brown, Archie and Michael Kaser. *Soviet Policy for the 1980s*. Bloomington, Indiana: Indiana University Press, 1983.

Brown, Peter G., and Henry Shue, eds. *Boundaries: National Autonomy and Its Limits*. Totowa, N.J.: Rowman and Littlefield, 1981.

Cassese, Antonio, ed. *Control of Foreign Policy in Western Democracies: A Comparative Study of Parliamentary Foreign Affairs Committees*. 3 vols. Dobbs Ferry, N.Y.: Oceana Publications, 1983.

Crabb, Cecil V. Jr. *American Foreign Policy in the Nuclear Age*. 4th ed. New York: Harper and Row, 1982.

Frank, Isaiah. *Foreign Enterprise in Developing Countries*. Baltimore: Johns Hopkins Press, 1980.

French, Peter A. *Ethics in Government*. Englewood Cliffs, N.J.: Prentice-Hall, 1983.

George, Alexander L. et al., eds. *The Limits of Coercive Diplomacy*. Boston: Little, Brown, 1971.

George, Alexander L., and Gordon A. Craig. *Force and Statecraft; Diplomatic Problems of Our Time*. New York: Oxford University Press, 1983.

Graham, Allison T. *Essence of Decision: Explaining the Cuban Missile Crisis*. Boston: Little, Brown, 1971.

Halperin, Morton H. *Bureaucratic Politics and Foreign Policy*. Washington D.C.: The Brookings Institution, 1974.

Halperin, Morton H., and Arnold Kanter, eds. *Readings in American Foreign Policy: A Bureaucratic Perspective*. Boston: Little, Brown, 1973.

Hilsman, Roger. *To Move a Nation: The Politics of Foreign Policy in the Administration of John F. Kennedy*. Garden City, N.Y.: Doubleday, 1967.

Janis, Irving L. *Victims of Groupthink*. Boston: Houghton Mifflin, 1972.

——— *Groupthink*. 2nd ed. Boston: Houghton Mifflin, 1982.

Johnson, Lyndon B. *The Vantage Point*. New York: Holt, Rinehart and Winston, 1971.

Keohane, Robert O., and Joseph S. Nye. *Power and Independence*. Boston: Little, Brown, 1977.

Keylor, William R. *The Twentieth-Century World: An International History*. New York: Oxford University Press, 1984.

Kissinger, Henry. *White House Years*. Boston: Little, Brown, 1979.

——— *Years of Upheaval*. Boston: Little, Brown, 1982.

Lebow, Richard N. *Between Peace and War: The Nature of International Crisis*. Baltimore: Johns Hopkins University Press, 1981.

Lockhart, Charles. *Bargaining in International Conflicts*. New York: Columbia University Press, 1979.

Löwenhardt, John. *The Soviet Politburo*. New York: St. Martin's Press, 1982.

Macomber, William. *The Angels Game: A Handbook of Modern Diplomacy*. New York: Stein and Day, 1975.

Neustadt, Richard. *Alliance Politics*. New York: Columbia University Press, 1970.

Nye, Joseph S. Jr., ed. *International Regionalism*. Boston: Little, Brown, 1968.

O'Neal, John R. *Foreign Policy Making in Times of Crisis*. Columbus: Ohio State University Press, 1982.

Osgood, Charles E. *An Alternative to War or Surrender*. Urbana: University of Illinois Press, 1962.

Schulzinger, Robert D. *American Diplomacy in the Twentieth Century*. New York: Oxford University Press, 1984.

Singer, David J., ed. *Quantitative International Politics*. New York: Free Press, 1968.

Snyder, Richard C. et al. *Foreign Policy Decision Making: An Approach to the Study of International Politics*. New York: Free Press, 1962.

Walker, R. B. J. *Culture, Ideology, and World Order*. Boulder, Colo.: Westview Press, 1984.

Wallace, William, and W. E. Paterson, eds. *Foreign Policy Making in Western Europe; A Comparative Approach*. New York: Praeger, 1978.

Economics and International Relations

Alexandersson, Gunnar, and Bjorn-Ivar Klevebring. *World Resources: Energy, Metals, Minerals*. New York: Walter de Gruyter, 1978.

Alpert, Paul. *Partnership or Confrontation? Poor Lands and Rich*. New York: Free Press, 1973.

Alting von Geusau, A. M. ed. *Allies in a Turbulent World*. Lexington, Mass.: Heath, 1981.

Cassen, Robert et al., eds. *Rich Country Interests and Third World Development*. New York: St. Martin's Press, 1982.

Chilcote, Ronald H., ed. *Dependency and Marxism: Toward a Resolution of the Debate*. Boulder, Colo.: Westview Press, 1982.

Connor, John. *The Market Power of Multinationals: A Quantitative Analysis of U.S. Corporations in Brazil and Mexico*. New York: Praeger, 1977.

Cross, John G. *The Economics of Bargaining*. New York: Basic Books, 1969.

Hinckley, Alden D. *Renewable Resources in Our Future*. New York: Pergamon, 1980.

Hosmer, Steven T., and Thomas W. Wolfe. *Soviet Policy and Practice Toward Third-World Conflicts.* Lexington, Mass.: Heath, 1982.

Jacobson, Harold K., and Dusan Sidjanski, eds. *The Emerging International Economic Order: Dynamic Processes, Constraints and Opportunities.* Beverly Hills, Calif.: Sage Publications, 1982.

Jensen, Robert G. et al., eds. *Soviet Natural Resources in the World Economy.* Chicago: The University of Chicago Press, 1983.

Knorr, Klaus. *The Power of Nations: The Political Economy of International Relations.* New York: Basic Books, 1975.

Knorr, Klaus, and Frank N. Trager, eds. *Economic Issues and National Security.* Lawrence, Kans.: University Press of Kansas, 1983.

Lee, Chae-jin, and Hideo Sato. *U.S. Policy Toward Japan and Korea: A Changing Influence Relationship.* New York: Praeger, 1982.

Leontief, Wassily et al. *The Future of World Economy.* New York: Oxford University Press, 1979.

Meadows, Donella H. et al. *The Limits of Growth: A Report for the Club of Rome's Project on the Predicament of Mankind.* New York: Universe, 1972

McMains, Harvey J. and Lyle Wilcox, eds. *Alternatives for Growth: The Engineering and Economics of Natural Resources Development.* Cambridge, Mass.: Ballinger, 1978.

Odell, John S. *U.S. International Monetary Policy: Markets, Power and Ideas as Sources of Change.* Princeton, N.J.: Princeton University Press, 1982.

Ophuls, William. *Ecology and the Politics of Scarcity.* San Francisco: W. H. Freeman, 1977.

Pierre, Andrew J. *The Global Politics of Arms Sales.* Princeton, N.J.: Princeton University Press, 1982.

Pinder, John, ed. *National Industrial Strategies and the World Economy.* London: Allanheld, Osmun, Croons Helm, 1982.

Pinelo, Adalberto J. *The Multinational Corporation as a Force in Latin American Politics: A Case Study of the International Petroleum in Peru.* New York: Praeger, 1973.

Sneider, William. *Food, Foreign Policy and Raw Materials Cartels.* New York: Crane, Russak, 1976.

Steward, Frances. *Technology and Underdevelopment.* Boulder, Colo.: Westview Press, 1977.

Tinbergen, Jan. *Reshaping the International Order.* New York: Dutton, 1976.

Tucker, Robert W. *The Inequality of Nations.* New York: Basic Books, 1977.

Weaver, James H., and Kenneth P. Jameson. *Economic Development: Competing Paradigms—Cometing Parables.* Washington D.C.: Agency for International Development, 1978.

Wilbur, Charles K., ed. *The Political Economy of Development and Underdevelopment.* New York: Random House, 1973.

Wu, Yuan-li. *Raw Materials in a Multipolar World.* 2nd ed. New York: Crane, Russak, 1979.

International Law and International Organization

Akehurst, Michael. *A Modern Introduction to International Law.* 4th ed. London: Allen and Unwin, 1982.

Anand, R. P. *New States and International Law.* Delhi, Kansas: University of Kansas, 1972.

Archer, Clive. *International Organizations.* Winchester, Mass.: Allen and Unwin, 1983.

Bennett, LeRoy. *International Organizations.* 2nd ed. Englewood Cliffs, N.J.: Prentice-Hall, 1980.

Bozeman, Adda B. *The Future of Law in a Multicultural World.* Princeton, N.J.: Princeton University Press, 1971.

Brierly, J. L. *The Law of Nations*. 6th ed. New York: Oxford University Press, 1963.

Cantori, Louis J., and Steven L. Spiegel, eds. *The International Politics of Regions*. Englewood Cliffs, N.J.: Prentice-Hall, 1970.

Christol, Carl Q. *The Modern International Law of Outer Space*. Elmsford, N.Y.: Pergamon Press, 1982.

Chiang Pei-heng. *Non-Governmental Organizations at the United Nations: Identity, Role, and Function*. New York: Praeger, 1981.

Cox, Robert W., and Harold Jacobson. *The Anatomy of Influence: Decision Making in International Organization*. New Haven: Yale University Press, 1973.

Deutsch, Karl W., and Stanley Hoffmann, eds. *The Relevance of International Law*. Garden City, N.Y.: Doubleday, 1971.

Finnegan, Richard B. et al. *Law and Politics in the International System: Case Studies in Conflict Resolution*. Washington D.C.: University Press of America, 1979.

Forsythe, David. *Humanitarian Politics*. Baltimore: Johns Hopkins University Press, 1977.

Gilpin, Robert. *U.S. Power and the Multinational Corporation: The Political Economy of Foreign Direct Investment*. New York: Basic Books, 1975.

Glahn, Gerhard von. *Law Among Nations*. 4th ed. New York: Macmillan, 1981.

Goodrich, Leland M. *The United Nations in a Changing World*. New York: Columbia University Press, 1974.

Goodspeed, Stephen S. *The Nature and Function of International Organization*. 2nd ed. New York: Oxford University Press, 1967.

Gordenker, Leon, ed. *The United Nations in International Politics*. Princeton, N.J.: Princeton University Press, 1971.

Halderman, John W. *The Political Role of the United Nations: Advancing the World Community*. New York: Praeger, 1981.

Hill, Christopher, ed. *National Foreign Policies and European Political Integration*. Winchester, Mass.: Allen and Unwin, 1983.

Jacobson, Harold K. *Networks of Interdependence*. New York: Knopf, 1979.

Kim, Samuel S. *The Quest for a Just World Order*. Boulder, Colo.: Westview Press, 1983.

Kindleberger, Charles P. *The International Corporation: A Symposium*. Cambridge, Mass.: M.I.T. Press, 1970.

Levi, Werner. *Law and Politics in the International Society*. Beverly Hills, Calif.: Sage Publications, 1976.

Lissitzyn, Oliver J. *International Law Today and Tomorrow*. Dobbs Ferry, N.Y.: Oceana Publications, 1965.

Lodge, Juliet. *Institutions and Policies of the European Community*. New York: St. Martin's Press, 1983.

Mitchell, C. R. *Peacemaking and the Consultant's Role*. New York: Nichols Publishing, 1981.

Murphy, John P. *The United Nations and the Control of International Violence*. Totowa, N.J.: Littlefield, Adams, 1982.

Pryce, Roy. *The Politics of the European Community*. Totowa, N.J.: Rowman and Littlefield, 1973.

Robertson, A. H. *Human Rights in the World*. 2nd ed. New York: St. Martin's Press, 1982.

Sheikh, A. *International Law and National Behavior*. New York: John Wiley, 1974.

Stoessinger, John G. *The United Nations and the Superpowers: China, Russia and America*. 4th ed. New York: Random House, 1977.

Taylor, Phillip. *Nonstate Actors in International Relations*. Boulder, Colo.: Westview Press, 1984.

Triska, Jan F., and R. M. Slussar. *The Theory, Law and Policy of Soviet Treaties*. Stanford, Calif.: Stanford University Press, 1962.

Wiseman, Henry, ed. *Peacekeeping: Appraisals and Proposals*. Elmsford, N.Y.: Pergamon Press, 1983.

The East–West Rivalry

Bornstein, Morris et al., eds. *East–West Relations and the Future of Eastern Europe: Politics and Economics*. Boston: Allen and Unwin, 1981.

Brown, Archie, and Michael Kaser, eds. *Soviet Policy for the 1980s*. New York: Columbia University Press, 1982.

Brown, Harold. *Thinking About National Security*. Boulder, Colo.: Westview Press, 1983.

Brown, Seyom. *Issues in U.S. Foreign Policy*. Boston: Little, Brown, 1984.

Frei, Daniel. *The Risks of Unintentional Nuclear War*. Totowa, N.J.: Littlefield, Adams, 1982.

George, Alexander L., and Richard Smoke. *Deterrence in American Foreign Policy*. New York: Columbia University Press, 1974.

Hogg, Ian, and Christopher Chant. *Nuclear War in the 1980s?* New York: Harper and Row, 1983.

Hosmer, Steven T., and Thomas W. Wolfe. *Soviet Policy and Practice Toward Third-World Conflicts*. Lexington, Mass.: Heath, 1982.

Kanet, Roger, ed. *Soviet Foreign Policy and East–West Relations*. Elmsford, N.Y.: Pergamon Press, 1982.

Kaplan, Stephen S. *Diplomacy of Power: Soviet Armed Forces as a Political Instrument*. Washington D.C.: Brookings, 1981.

Kegley, Charles Jr., and Pat McGowan, eds. *Foreign Policy: USA/USSR*. Beverly Hills, Calif.: Sage Publications, 1982.

Kennedy, Robert, and John M. Weinstein, eds. *The Defense of the West*. Boulder, Colo.: Westview Press, 1984.

Kennedy, William V. *The Balance of Military Power*. New York: St. Martin's Press, 1982.

Kolkowicz, Roman, and Neil Joeck. *Arms Control and International Security*. Boulder, Colo.: Westview Press, 1984.

Moreton, Edwina, and Gerald Segal, eds. *Soviet Strategy Toward Western Europe*. Winchester, Mass.: Allen and Unwin, 1984.

Morgan, Patrick M. *Deterrence: A Conceptual Analysis*. Beverly Hills, Calif.: Sage Publications, 1977.

Wallace, William, and W. E. Paterson, eds. *Foreign Policy Making in Western Europe: A Comparative Approach*. New York: Praeger, 1978.

Zagoria, Donald S., ed. *Soviet Policy in East Asia*. New Haven: Yale University Press, 1981.

East–West Economic Relations

Atlantic Council. *East–West Trade: Managing Encounter and Accomodation*. Boulder, Colo.: Westview, 1977.

Friesen, Connie. *The Political Economy of East–West Trade*. New York: Praeger, 1976.

Garland, John S. *Financing Foreign Trade in Eastern Europe*. New York: Praeger, 1977.

Goldman, Marshall I. *Détente and Dollars: Doing Business with the Soviets*. New York: Basic Books, 1975.

Holzman, Franklyn D. *International Trade Under Communism—Politics and Economics*. New York: Basic Books, 1976.

Kostecki, M. M. *East–West Trade and the GATT System*. New York: St. Martin's Press, 1978.

Nagorski, Zygmunt. *The Psychology of East–West Trade: Illusions and Opportunities*. New York: Mason and Lipscomb, 1974.

Nove, Alec. *East–West Trade: Problems, Prospects, Issues*. Beverly Hills, Calif.: Sage Publications, 1978.

Sternheimer, Stephen. *East–West Technology Transfer: Japan and the Communist Bloc*. Beverly Hills, Calif.: Sage Publications, 1980.

Sutton, Anthony C. *Western Technology and Soviet Economic Development, 1945–1965*. Stanford, Calif.: Hoover Institution on War, Revolution and Peace, 1973.

Wasowski, Stanislaw, ed. *East–West Trade and the Technology Gap: A Political and Economic Appraisal*. New York: Praeger, 1970.

Watts, Nita G. M., ed. *Economic Relations Between East and West*. London: Macmillan, 1978.

Yergin, Angela Stent. *East–West Technology Transfer: European Perspectives*. Beverly Hills, Calif.: Sage Publications, 1980.

The North–South Relationship

Alting von Geusau, A. M., ed. *The Lome Convention and a New International Economic Order*. Leiden, Netherlands: A. W. Sijthoff, 1977.

Amin, Samir. *Unequal Development: An Essay on the Social Formations of Peripheral Capitalism*. New York: Monthly Review, 1976.

———. *Accumulation on a World Scale*. New York: Monthly Review, 1974.

Baldwin, David A. *Economic Development in American Foreign Policy, 1943–1962*. Chicago: University of Chicago Press, 1966.

Ball, Nicole. *World Hunger: A Guide to the Economic and Political Dimensions*. Santa Barbara, Calif.: Clio Press, 1981.

Barratt-Brown, Michael. The *Economics of Imperialism*. Harmondsworth, England: Penguin, 1974.

Behrman, Jere R. *International Commodity Agreements*. Washington, D.C.: Overseas Development Council, 1977.

Bhagwati, Jagdish, ed. *The International Economic Order: The North–South Debate*. Cambridge, Mass.: M.I.T. Press, 1977.

Cassen, Robert et al., eds. *Rich Country Interests and Third World Development*. New York: St. Martin's Press, 1982.

Chase, James. *Solvency: The Price of Survival. An Essay on American Foreign Policy*. New York: Random House, 1981.

Chilcote, Ronald H., ed. *Dependency and Marxism: Toward a Resolution of the Debate*. Boulder, Colo.: Westview Press, 1982.

Clapham, Christopher. *Foreign Policy Making in Developing States: A Comparative Approach*. Westmead, England: Saxon House, 1977.

Cline, William R. *International Monetary Reform and the Developing Countries*. Washington, D.C.: The Brookings Institution, 1976.

Emmanuel, Arghiri. *Unequal Exchange: A Study of the Imperialism of Trade*. New York: Monthly Review, 1972.

Evans, Peter. *Dependent Development: The Alliance of Multinational, State, and Local Capital in Brazil*. Princeton, N.J.: Princeton University Press, 1979.

Faundey, Julio, and Sol Picciotto, eds. *The Nationalization of Multinationals in Peripheral Economies*. London: Macmillan, 1978.

Frank, Isaiah. *Foreign Enterprise in Developing Countries*. Baltimore, Md.: Johns Hopkins Press, 1980.

Gupta, K. R. *GATT and Underdeveloped Countries*. Delhi, India: Atma Ram, 1976.

Helleiner, Gerald, ed. *A World Divided: The Less Developed Countries in the International Economy*. New York: Cambridge University Press, 1975.

Hudson, Michael. *Global Fracture: The New International Economic Order*. New York: Harper and Row, 1977.

Hughes, Helen, ed. *Prospects of Partnership: Industrialization and Trade Policies in the 1970s*. Baltimore: Johns Hopkins Press, 1973.

Lall, Sanjaya, and Paul Streeten. *Foreign Investment, Transnationals and Developing Countries*. London: Macmillan, 1977.

LaPalombara, Joseph, and Stephen Blank. *Multinational Corporations and Developing Countries*. New York: The Conference Board, 1979.

Law, Alton D. *International Commodity Agreements*. Lexington, Mass.: Lexington Books, 1975.

Magdoff, Harry. *Imperialism: From the Colonial Age to the Present*. New York: Monthly Review, 1978.

McNicol, David L. *Commodity Agreements and Price Stabilization*. Lexington, Mass.: Lexington Books, 1978.

Mortimer, Robert A. *The Third World Coalition in International Politics*. 2nd ed. Boulder, Colo.: Westview Press, 1984.

Murray, Tracy. *Trade Preferences for Developing Countries*. New York: Wiley, 1977.

Nelson, Joan M. *Aid, Influence and Foreign Policy*. New York: Macmillan, 1968.

Payer, Cheryl. *The Debt Trap: The International Monetary Fund and the Third World*. New York: Monthly Review, 1974.

Raichur, Satish, and Craig Liske. *The Politics of Aid, Trade, Investment*. New York: Wiley, 1976.

Reuber, Grant L. *Private Foreign Investment in Development*. Oxford: Clarendon, 1973.

Reynolds, Paul D. *International Commodity Agreements and the Common Fund*. Lexington, Mass.: Lexington Books, 1978.

Rothstein, Robert L. *The Weak in the World of the Strong: The Developing Countries in the International System*. New York: Columbia University Press, 1977.

——— *Global Bargaining: UNCTAD and the Quest for a New International Economic Order*. Princeton, N.J.: Princeton University Press, 1979.

Rustow, Dankwart A. *Oil and Turmoil: America Faces OPEC and the Middle East*. New York: W. W. Norton, 1982.

Sauvant, Karl P., and Hajo Hasenpflug. *The New International Economic Order: Confrontation or Cooperation Between North and South?* Boulder, Colo.: Westview, 1977.

Seers, Dudley, and Leonard Joy, eds. *Development in a Divided World*. Harmondsworth, England: Penguin, 1971.

Stewart, Michael. *The Age of Interdependence; Economic Policy in a Shrinking World*. Cambridge, Mass.: M.I.T. Press, 1983.

Turner, Louis. *Multinational Companies and the Third World*. New York: Hill and Wang, 1973.

Uri, Pierre. *Development Without Dependence*. New York: Praeger, 1976.

Walters, Robert S. *American and Soviet Aid: A Comparative Analysis*. Pittsburgh, Pa.: University of Pittsburgh Press, 1970.

White, John A. *The Politics of Foreign Aid*. New York: St. Martin's Press, 1974.

Windstrand, Carl, ed. *Multinational Firms in Africa*. Uppsala, Sweden: Scandinavian Institute of African Studies, 1975.

Wriggins, W. Howard, and Gunnar Adler-Karlsson. *Reducing Global Inequalities*. New York: McGraw-Hill, 1978.

Young, Crawford. *Ideology and Development in Africa*. New Haven: Yale University Press, 1982.

Index

Page numbers appearing in boldface refer to entries in the "International Relations Digest."